BEECHAMS, 1848–2000
FROM PILLS TO PHARMACEUTICALS

D1419674

To the memory of Thomas Corley I (1802/3–1879),
'Preparer of patent medicines', author of *Emigration
Considered and its Baneful Influence Exposed* (Chelsea,
London: Jacques & Robinson, 1852), price *2d.* (1p),
and for Thomas Corley VII (b. 1996), who helped with
this book.

BEECHAMS, 1848–2000
From pills to pharmaceuticals

T. A. B. CORLEY

'The minutiae of commerce never fail to be
tedious in narrative, and it is no part of my
intention to bore the reader willingly.'

Sir Thomas Beecham, Bt.
(writing of the family pill firm), *A Mingled Chime* (1944), p. 185.

Crucible Books

Also available from Crucible Books

Roy Church and E.M. Tansey, *Burroughs Wellcome & Co.: Knowledge, trust, profit and the transformation of the British pharmaceutical industry, 1880–1940*
hardback ISBN 978-1-905472-04-8   softback ISBN 978-1-905472-07-9

Kenneth D. Brown, *'Factory of Dreams': A history of Meccano Ltd*
ISBN 978-1-905472-08-6

David J. Bricknell, *Float: Pilkington's Glass Revolution*
ISBN 978-1-905472-11-6

For a full list of titles and secure online ordering
see www.carnegiepublishing.com

Beechams, 1848–2000: From pills to pharmaceuticals

Copyright © T.A.B. Corley, 2011

First published in 2011 by
Crucible Books

Crucible Books is an imprint of
Carnegie Publishing Ltd,
Carnegie House,
Chatsworth Road,
Lancaster LA1 4SL
www.cruciblebooks.com

British Library Cataloguing-in-Publication data
A catalogue record for this book is available from the British Library

ISBN 978-1-905472-14-7

Designed, typeset and originated by Carnegie Book Production, Lancaster
Printed and bound in the UK by Short Run Press, Exeter

Contents

List of tables

Acknowledgements

I N JULY 1971 Professor John Dunning, my head of department at Reading University and a world renowned international business scholar, invited Frank Lomax (see Chapter 13), chairman of Beecham European Division, to address a graduate seminar on 'Planning in international business'. Lomax's account of his company's record of global innovation so captivated me that John Dunning agreed to approach Sir Ronald Edwards, then Beecham's chairman, with a suggestion that I should write a history of the company. Edwards' reply (Edwards to Dunning, 20 October 1971) stated that here was something he planned to do one day. He subsequently assigned the task to his predecessor, Leslie Lazell, whose book *From Pills to Penicillin: The Beecham Story* (1975) is a primary source for Lazell's period as chairman. Sadly, John Dunning died in 2009.

In between the day-to-day preoccupations of academic life, I have worked hard to secure information on Beecham's past from many quarters, almost always most readily supplied; the kindness and generosity of so many were exemplary. Anne Francis (Mrs Julian Wintle), great-granddaughter of the original Thomas Beecham, gave me a copy of her out-of-print life of the founder, *A Guinea A Box* (1968), and later filled in the gaps with much additional matter. Her son, Justin Wintle, has given me permission to quote from the book, which contains family and other reminiscences that would otherwise have been lost.

I. M. F. Balfour, secretary of the Beecham Group, granted me access to the Board Minutes from 1928 to 1951, much assistance being provided to me by R. S. Petrie. Sarah Darbin made available the Annual Reports and dealt with later queries. At St Helens, David Howarth of Beecham Proprietaries opened up the early archives then held in the factory, and Monica Coxhead did much valuable photocopying. Denis Pratt of MEPC plc (formerly Metropolitan Property Co. Ltd) unearthed for me the Board Minutes of Beecham Estates and Pills Ltd from 1924 to 1928, through the good offices of Max Keyworth, who supplied unpublished information, from his broad personal knowledge, about that company and its Covent Garden Properties successor. His privately printed *Cabbages and Things* (1990), of which he sent me a copy, was especially helpful because of the original research he had carried out into Philip Hill's origins and career. W. J. Ambrose hospitably shared with me much information about the Beecham companies he had served since 1926, latterly as a senior executive.

Lord Keith of Castleacre, Sir Graham Wilkins and Sir Ronald Halstead found time to inform me about Leslie Lazell, while I was preparing my entry on him for the *Dictionary of Business Biography* (1985); Paul Lazell, who earlier supplied a fine photograph of his father, has more recently helped with some valuable family reminiscences. Margaret Ackrill, author of entries on Sir Ronald Edwards for the *Dictionary of Business Biography* (1984 volume) and the *Oxford Dictionary of National Biography* (2004) has generously allowed me to quote from her unpublished typescript of her life of Sir Ronald, now in the Archives of the London School of Economics (see Chapter 14). Keith Moss lent me some evocative photographs and papers of William Moss, one of Beecham's first employees and later Works Manager at St Helens; Dora Moss was highly informative about the career of her late husband, Frank Moss, who had succeeded his father in that post. I thank Denis Allport, then a group director, for a fruitful discussion of events in the Halstead era.

Earlier company archives, some formerly with Beecham Proprietaries, have been deposited at St Helens Local History and Archives Library. Mrs V. L. Hainsworth, Mrs V. M. Tipping and their colleagues have been tireless in answering requests by correspondence and in photocopying documents during my successive visits there. Professor Theo Barker passed on to me some helpful notes he had made for his and J. R. Harris's publication of 1954, *A Merseyside Town in the Industrial Revolution: St Helens, 1750–1900*. Francis Sheppard, editor of the 36th volume of the *Survey of London* (1970), at some inconvenience to himself loaned to me the working papers for the chapter he wrote on the Duke of Bedford's sale of the Covent Garden estate in 1914 to Sir Joseph Beecham; the original documents recording the sale are now in London Metropolitan Archives.

Christine Watts, Heritage Services Manager at Wigan, sent me maps and other information about Thomas Beecham's period of residence in the town. Records held at the General Register Office in Edinburgh showed up the porkies – to be charitable, half-truths – which Helen Mackie Taylor, Joseph Beecham's long-standing mistress, had told about her age and place of birth. Her death certificate came by courtesy of the Registrar General of New Zealand, while Miss K. Israelson, Reference Librarian at Napier, New Zealand, provided press cuttings about her death and funeral.

Some even bigger porkies, spread by the family about the origins of

Josephine, the first Lady Beecham, were exposed through a scrutiny of Census and other returns in the – now greatly mourned – Family Records Centre in London, and by some on-line genealogical findings by Liz Longhurst. My son Felix Corley, helped by Thomas Corley VII, with terrier-like tenacity pieced together the story of Josephine's redoubtable parent, Martha Bowen; he discovered the latter's final years in Australia through the assistance of Elaine Kranjc and her fellow members of Geelong Family History Group; the photograph they took of Martha's imposing grave was especially welcome. Her very detailed death certificate came by courtesy of the Registry of Births, Deaths and Marriages, Department of Justice, Victoria.

Lucy Johnston, of the Fashion Department in the Victoria and Albert Museum, expertly analysed Jane Beecham's dress of the 1850s. Professor J. Mordaunt Crook of Royal Holloway, who wrote *The Dilemma of Style* (1987), clarified the role of progressive eclecticism in Joseph Beecham's choice of architectural style for his 1880s factory building. Dr J. H. Cumming, of the Dunn Nutritional Centre, Cambridge, sent me enlightening scientific articles about women's costiveness. Margaret Rose and her team at the History of Advertising Trust in Norfolk welcomed me to a fruitful day's search through the Trust's holdings of Beecham's publicity material. Alison Derrett, Assistant Registrar of the Royal Archives at Windsor, readily answered my query – in the negative – about whether Queen Victoria ever consumed Beecham's pills, as her one-line quip suggested (Chapter 4). Mrs B. J. Peters, archivist at Coutts & Co. in London, twice took me to a depository which held the ledgers of Thomas Holloway's bank account there.

Professor Mira Wilkins, of Florida International University, gave me invaluable comments on my Chapter 5, about Beecham's US operations. Dr Philip Waller, of Merton College, Oxford, advised me about Sir Hall Caine's reported testimonial for Beecham's pills. Professor Howard Cox, of the University of Worcester Business School, volunteered to pass on to me crucial information from The National Archives at Kew and other sources on Philip Hill's bid in 1933 to acquire the shares of Boots the Chemists. Thanks are due to The National Archives for permission to quote from Crown Copyright documents; the staff there have readily dealt with even out-of-the way queries, as have the librarians at the Wellcome Library in London.

Dr Tilli Tansey, at the Wellcome Trust Centre for the History of Medicine, has been a sage adviser on pharmaceutical matters and a long-term friend. Reading University Library has maintained its high reputation for tracking down abstruse data and securing difficult-to-find inter-library loans; there Kathy Paterson magically turned up facts on subjects ranging from Spirella corsets to Colton pill machines. At Reading, Jill Turner (who expertly typed all the tables), Carol Wright, Pat Wylie and Natalie Anderson have skilfully provided secretarial help and overcome computer-related problems.

My colleague in Reading University Business School, Professor Andrew Godley, perceptively commented on early draft chapters of this book, while Drs András and Moira Tárnoky have helpfully read through papers and articles of mine and advised me on all kinds of medical questions. Bernardo Bátiz-Lazo, Mark Billings and Eleanor Morgan sent me copies of important articles, and Sally Horrocks alerted me to some unpublished data. Judy Slinn and Viviane Quirke have shared with me some of their pharmaceutical researches. Even casual encounters at academic conferences have yielded bonuses. Theo Aronson drew my attention to Queen Victoria's one-liner on the pills, and Peter Martland to Sir Thomas Beecham's alleged exploits as a First World War spook; Professor Christopher Andrew of Cambridge and Sir Thomas's biographer Alan Jefferson both promptly replied – again in the negative – to an enquiry about that allegation. Philip Ziegler also took trouble to quash by letter a bizarre Beecham rumour (see Chapter 7).

I thank Sir Thomas Beecham for an unforgettable concert at the Albert Hall which my wife and I attended in the 1950s; he acknowledged the final applause with a quotation from Shakespeare's *Love's Labour's Lost*, 'The words of Mercury are harsh after the songs of Apollo'. If some of my words about him appear harsh, I wholeheartedly salute Sir Thomas's musical genius. My apologies are to those whom I have omitted to thank for help so freely given.

My final thanks are to my family. My daughter, Mrs Hilary Curtis, has cheerfully kept my morale high over the many years since her mother died, while my elder son, Fr Jeremy Corley, has guided me on computer work, expertly cut and pasted the Bibliography, and scrutinized a number of chapters with the rigour of a professional biblical scholar. Felix Corley's help was noted earlier. Margaret Corley and our youngest son, Peter, are forever in our prayers.

Abbreviations and chronologies

AHP	American Home Products (New York)
BA	Beecham Archives (St Helens)
BAT	British American Tobacco
BBC	British Broadcasting Corporation
BL	British Library
BMA	British Medical Association
BMJ	British Medical Journal
BOC	British Oxygen Company
BP	Beecham's Pills
BRL	Beecham Research Laboratories Ltd
CD	*Chemist & Druggist*
DBB	*Dictionary of Business Biography*
DNB	*Dictionary of National Biography*
DPS	Diversified Pharmaceutical Services Inc.
EEC	European Economic Community (now EU)
EMC	Executive Management Committee
EMI	Electrical and Musical Industries
FBI	Federation of British Industries (now CBI)
FTC	Federal Trade Commission
GLC	Greater London Council
GSK	GlaxoSmithKline (from 2000)
HGS	Human Genome Science Inc.
IBM	International Business Machines
ICI	Imperial Chemical Industries
ICL	International Computers Ltd
ILN	*Illustrated London News*
MBA	Master of Business Administration
MIG	Midland Industrial and General (Trust)
MIT	Massachusetts Institute of Technology
MMC	Merger Management Committee

NEDC	National Economic Development Council
NHS	National Health Service
ODNB	*Oxford Dictionary of National Biography*
OTC	Over-the-counter (proprietary) medicines
PATA	Proprietary Articles Trade Association
PJ	*Pharmaceutical Journal*
PP	Parliamentary Papers
PROV	Public Record Office, Victoria (Australia)
R&D	Research and Development
SB	SmithKline Beecham
SCAPA	Society for the Checking of Abuses in Public Advertising
STC	Standard Telephones and Cables
TNA	The National Archives (Kew)
TST	Tobacco Securities Trust
VCH	*Victoria History of the Counties of England*
WSO	Worldwide Supply Operations

Chronology of company management

Firm of Thomas Beecham, 1848–1924

Thomas Beecham (1820–1907)	1848–88
(Thomas Beecham and	1888–95
(Joseph Beecham (1848–1916)	
(Sir) Joseph Beecham (Bt. 1914)	1895–1916
Executors	1916–24
Under Court of Chancery	1917–24

Beecham Estates and Pills Ltd, 1924–28

Sir Arthur Wheeler, Bt. (1860–1943)	1924–28

Beechams Pills Ltd, 1928–45

Philip Hill (1873–1944)	1928–44
Sir Stanley Holmes (1878–1961)	1944–45

Beecham Group Ltd, 1945–89

Sir Stanley Holmes (Lord Dovercourt)	1945–58
Leslie Lazell (1903–82) chief executive	1951–58
chairman	1958–68
Sir Ronald Edwards (1910–76)	1968–75
Sir Graham Wilkins (1924–2003)	1975–84
Sir Ronald Halstead (b. 1927)	1984–85
Kenneth (Lord) Keith (1916–2004)	1985–86
Robert Bauman (b. 1931)	1986–89

SmithKline Beecham Ltd, 1989–2000

Henry Wendt (b. 1933, chairman)	1989–94
Robert Bauman (chief executive)	1989–94
Sir Peter Walters (b. 1931, chairman)	1994–2000
Jan Leschly (b. 1940, chief executive)	1994–99
Jean-Pierre Garnier (b. 1947, chief executive)	1999–2000

GlaxoSmithKline plc., 2000-

Sir Richard Sykes (b. 1942, chairman)	2000–2
Jean-Pierre Garnier (chief executive)	2000–8

Company history: important dates

1820	Thomas Beecham born in Oxfordshire.
1828	Becomes shepherd.
1847	Leaves Oxfordshire for Liverpool. Marries Jane Evans (4 children, dies 1872).

Firm of Thomas Beecham, 1848–1924

1848	Move to Wigan. Joseph Beecham born.
1856	Establishes chemist's shop in Wigan; closed 1858.
1859	Moves to St Helens.
1863	Begins workshop production; Joseph joins father.
1868	Installs first machinery.
1873	Marries Sarah Pemberton (no children, dies 1877); Joseph marries Josephine Burnett (10 children, dies 1934).
1877	First factory.
1879	Joseph's son Thomas (Sir Thomas Beecham) born.
1881	Thomas marries Mary Sawell (no children, separates 1884, dies 1937).
1882	Thomas and Mary move to Buckinghamshire (Mursley Hall). Joseph in charge of factory. Meets Helen Mackie Taylor (no children, dies 1920).
1887	New factory completed.
1888	Thomas takes Joseph into partnership. Charles Rowed general manager.
1895	Thomas retires; daughter with Jane Roberts (Violet) born (no children, dies 1988).
1900	Thomas junior quarrels with Joseph over treatment of his mother.
1906	Henry Beecham (second son) joins firm.
1907	Thomas the founder dies, aged 86; estate worth £87,000.
1901	Thomas junior reconciled with Joseph, who subsidizes operatic and ballet ventures in London and elsewhere, 1910–1914.
1912	Joseph knighted.
1914	Joseph baronet; awarded Russian order of St Stanislaus. Buys Covent Garden estate. Outbreak of World War I.
1916	Joseph dies; estate worth £1.5 million (final figure).
1917	Joseph's estate placed under jurisdiction of Chancery Court.

1918	Covent Garden Properties Ltd registered. First World War ends.
1921	Henry Beecham jailed for manslaughter; leaves firm.
1924	Joseph's estate released from Chancery.

Beecham Estates and Pills Ltd (registered 1924)

1924	Philip Hill and Louis Nicholas directors.
1925	Purchase Veno Drug Company (1925) Ltd of Manchester (cough syrup).
1926	Introduce Beecham's powders.
1928	Hill buys out operations at St Helens.

Beechams Pills Ltd (registered 1928)

1929	Hill chairman; begins acquisition programme, to create medicinal-cum-household product company.
1930	Acquires Yeast-Vite Ltd; (Sir) Stanley Holmes joins company.
1938	Acquires Macleans Ltd (toothpaste) and Eno Proprietaries Ltd (fruit salt).
1939	Acquires County Perfumery Co. Ltd (Brylcreem). Outbreak of World War II.
1942	Hill plans Central Research Laboratories.
1944	Hill dies; estate worth £3 million. Holmes chairman.

Beecham Group Ltd (name changed 1945)

1945	Plan introduced to acquire wholesale groceries. World War II ends.
1949	John Buckley managing director.
1951	Boardroom coup by Kenneth Keith (director since 1949). Leslie Lazell managing director, vice Buckley (removed).
1954	Lazell begins research project to make semi-synthetic penicillins.
1958	Holmes (Lord Dovercourt) retires. Lazell chairman and chief executive.
1959	Broxil, first penicillin, launched.
1968	Lazell retires. Sir Ronald Edwards chairman.
1971	Edwards' hostile bid for Glaxo.
1972	Bid rejected by Monopolies Commission.
1975	Edwards retires. (Sir) Graham Wilkins chairman.
1984	Wilkins retires. (Sir) Ronald Halstead chairman.
1985	Boardroom coup by Lord Keith, who becomes chairman vice Halstead (removed).
1986	Robert Bauman (US citizen) chairman.

SmithKline Beecham plc (merger of equals between Beecham and SmithKline Beckman, 1989)

1989	Henry Wendt chairman, Bauman chief executive.
1990	Jan Leschly director.
1991	J. P. Garnier joins company.
1994	Wendt and Bauman retire. Sir Peter Walters chairman, Leschly chief executive. Production at St Helens ends.
1995	Glaxo Wellcome formed by Sir Richard Sykes.

1996   Leschly seeks merger with American Home Products.

1998   Attempted merger with Glaxo Wellcome fails. Beecham's pills
            discontinued after 150 years.

1999   Leschly to retire, Garnier chief executive. Talks restored with Glaxo
            Wellcome.

2000   Merger of equals with Glaxo Wellcome. Sir Richard Sykes chairman,
            Garnier chief executive.

GlaxoSmithKline (Glaxo Wellcome and SmithKline Beecham, 2000).

Introduction

THE BEECHAM ENTERPRISE was the only major British healthcare company to transform itself from a patent medicine business into one of the world's major pharmaceutical enterprises.[1] Established during 1848 in Wigan, Lancashire, to make pills, it kept the title of Beecham until in 1989 a merger renamed it SmithKline Beecham. In 2000, again through a merger of equals, the company became part of GlaxoSmithKline, and the Beecham name – but by no means all its brands – disappeared.

Beecham's eventful century and a half of independent existence deserves recalling, not as an act of nostalgia, but to discover why it survived so long and prospered when so many rivals went under. It had its share of good luck, but – more importantly – a succession of able and innovative entrepreneurs, whose well-made products and persuasive advertising kept the Beecham name constantly in the public eye.

The entrepreneurs are listed in the foregoing 'Chronology of Company Management'. Here seven of the most prominent names appear in turn. The founder, **Thomas Beecham**, from 1848 onwards built up his business from scratch. Thomas was born with no advantage except a strikingly original mind, from an early age being drawn to innovate, or earn a livelihood by offering to others something entirely new. As a young shepherd from a desperately poor agricultural labouring family in Oxfordshire, he made himself known locally through his herbal cures of animals and humans alike. He then moved on to pills, using as his main ingredients aloes and ginger, the conventional stock-in-trade of earlier manufacturers for two centuries, but compounding them with greater care than ever before. In 1847 he migrated from southern England to Lancashire, where average wages were higher, and where medicines of all kinds were in constant demand.

Moving in 1859 from Wigan to the neighbouring town of St Helens, he progressed from domestic or cottage production to a workshop; being short of funds, he did not have even a frugally ordered factory until 1877. Yet the machinery he had largely invented gave him a competitive advantage over longer-established rivals, such as James Morison and Thomas Holloway in London, who paid little attention to the quality of their pills, inadequately mixed and of variable sizes as they were.

Thomas was joined in 1862 by his son, **(Sir) Joseph Beecham**, who combined his father's original thinking with his own broader strategic vision, and made the firm internationally famous. Assisted by a general manager of unusual talent, the Anglo-American Charles Rowed, Joseph pursued a dynamic course of action. He erected an imposing architect-designed headquarters in St Helens, completed in 1887 and equipped with the most up-to-date machinery, which was to be powered – almost uniquely in Britain at that time – by electricity. His firm became one of the country's largest spenders on advertising, making Beecham into a household word through seductive and often amusing publicity. He resolutely opened up markets overseas, mainly in territories of the British Empire and also in the United States. By 1914, Beecham was exporting nearly one-third of its output from home; a further one-fifth came from its New York branch, set up in 1890 after the introduction of high American tariffs. By then, the Beecham firm had overtaken all rivals and established itself as the leader of Britain's patent medicine industry.

As demand soared at home and overseas, father and son did not scruple to exploit the credulity of an ever-growing number of people who yearned for good health but kept clear of doctors. Most consumers were willing to pay high prices out of their steadily increasing wages, because they rejected cheaper pills as worthless. The Beechams' misleading assertions about cures for the gravest of illnesses such as Bright's disease, and hints about treating 'maladies of indiscretion' and how to end pregnancies rebounded on Joseph when in 1913 he had to justify himself before the Select Committee on Patent Medicines.

Although in 1910 he did furnish the New York factory with up-to-date machinery, by then Joseph had lost his drive to undertake innovation at home. Instead, he lavished much of his fortune on subsidizing the career of his son Thomas, shortly to become one of Britain's most eminent and colourful musical conductors of the twentieth century. Sir Thomas Beecham, and his rumbustious character, weave in and out of this book's earlier chapters; an Appendix discusses some bizarre aspects of his ancestry. In 1914, Joseph acquired the Covent Garden market in London for £2 million, but when he died two years later, most of the purchase price was still unpaid. His estate had to be placed under the Court of Chancery, where it remained until 1924.

The Beecham family then pocketed the residue of his fortune, but took no further part in the business. That year its purchasers, an investment trust, established a joint-stock company, Beecham Estates and Pills Ltd. The dominant director was **Philip Hill**, already experienced in property matters, who in 1926 introduced the first non-pill article, Beecham's powders. Yet the company scarcely prospered, as the low-earning real estate interests and the highly profitable patent medicine side, having little synergy or mutually reinforcing powers, could do nothing to assist one another's growth. In 1928, Hill therefore took the bold step of buying out the St Helens assets and forming them into Beechams Pills Ltd.

As its chairman, Hill planned to build up the Beecham company, through acquisitions, into Britain's leading enterprise that marketed medicines together with household products. In 1938–39 he made his four most significant purchases, comprising Macleans (of toothpaste fame), Eno's fruit salts (with its extensive overseas connections), the top-selling hair preparation Brylcreem, and the glucose drink Lucozade. Intent on promoting technical innovation, he authorized the company's first central laboratory for original research shortly before his death in 1944.

Hill's successors in the renamed Beecham Group Ltd wrongly forecast that the establishment of Britain's National Health Service (NHS) in 1948 would halt demand for proprietary (soon to be called over-the-counter or OTC) medicines. They therefore diversified into wholesale grocery businesses and gave little finance to its fledgling research and development (R&D) function. The poor earnings from the groceries so weakened the group's financial performance that in 1951 its institutional investors organized a boardroom coup. Instead **Leslie Lazell**, who had joined the company from Macleans in 1938, took over as general manager and at once began to carry out a series of radical reforms. He became chairman in 1958.

For the next half-century, Beecham and its successor company owed much of its progress to taking advantage of American technology and management skills. Lazell, even more than his predecessor, Joseph Beecham, confessed himself 'besotted' with the vibrant economic system of the United States. He followed a growing trend among American corporate giants in changing their structure from a unitary to a multi-divisional form. He thereby tackled the problem neglected by Hill – who had left 100 or more subsidiaries largely unco-ordinated – and grouped them into two divisions, namely Pharmaceuticals and Consumer Products: an intricate operation, not completed to his satisfaction until the mid-1960s. He also adopted American marketing techniques, and made senior managers directly responsible for all publicity, turning Beecham into the second largest advertiser in Britain, after Unilever.

The most innovative and risky decision of Lazell's career was to aspire to join the pharmaceutical industry by developing antibiotic drugs. His initial step was to approach a leading penicillin pioneer, (Sir) Ernst Chain, then based in Rome. With Chain's encouragement his scientists went on to uncover the penicillin nucleus, 6-APA, which after chemical modification yielded the group a run of increasingly efficacious and lucrative antibiotics from 1959 onwards. The organization for marketing the drugs was set up by a future chairman lately based in the US, (Sir) Graham Wilkins.

Although British scientific expertise provided the necessary groundwork, Lazell had to rely on an American corporation for know-how to organize full-scale production and to design the first antibiotic factory in Britain. Lazell soon perceived that, in order to keep abreast of the latest developments in the United States, he needed to set up a research subsidiary there, and whenever appropriate to utilize American management consultants. Before his retirement in 1968, Lazell had increased Beecham's return on capital to the highest of any UK quoted company.

Lazell was succeeded by the academic-cum-businessman, Sir Ronald Edwards, who resolved to merge Britain's highly fragmented pharmaceutical industry into a group powerful enough to compete against larger American and European rivals. In 1971 he therefore made a hostile bid for Glaxo, a research-based UK company further advanced along the antibiotic route. The bid failed thanks to Glaxo's tenacious resistance and a negative ruling by the Monopolies Commission.

After that setback Edwards and later chairmen seemed to lose their way. Beecham, then a middle-ranking company in global terms, pursued a less ambitious acquisition programme, in the process buying more consumer product than pharmaceutical companies, often as far removed from its core competences as perfumery and home improvements. Top management's failure to adopt a unified corporate strategy had the result of stirring up discord between the two divisions, which adversely affected profits. In 1985 a second boardroom coup removed the current chairman, Sir Ronald Halstead, with the aim of installing a more dynamic regime.

The man behind the coup, the Beecham director and merchant banker Kenneth (Lord) Keith – responsible also for the 1951 putsch – had no regrets when he was unable to find a suitable British successor as chairman. Keenly aware of the superior quality of entrepreneurship in the USA, he chose the American businessman, **Robert Bauman**, who from 1986 onwards energetically modernized the group according to Harvard Business School principles.

Once Bauman accepted that Beecham could never attain world pharmaceutical leadership on its own, in 1989 he negotiated a merger with an American competitor, SmithKline of Philadelphia. While the head office of the new SmithKline Beecham (SB) was in London, the operational headquarters would be in the United States. Bauman, appointed as SB's chief executive, insisted on overhauling every single function, so as to eradicate all memories of the two former units.

In 1990 the American influence gained strength when Bauman recruited two top executives from leading US pharmaceutical corporations, **Jan Leschly** and **Jean-Pierre (JP) Garnier**. Three years later, they astutely sought to change SB from a diversified to a unified group by changing the name of the Consumer Brands division (as it had become) to Consumer Healthcare, and selling off articles for personal adornment such as Brylcreem and Silvikrin. Leschly, who succeeded Bauman as chief executive in 1994, and Garnier together faced the decade's three subsequent events that had a direct impact on the group: the genetic revolution, cost-cutting moves by the drug purchasing authorities which set off the so-called management care revolution, and the hostile bid for Wellcome in 1995 by Glaxo's chairman, (Sir) Richard Sykes.

First, work recently begun elsewhere on the human gene was hailed as the forerunner to discovering drugs that were more focused on patients' needs. In order to secure the latest information about this pioneering process, SB was the first company in the industry to buy a share in a top American genome company, one which possessed the world's most extensive genetic database. Second, the pressure for managed care was a by-product of governments' and other authorities' initiatives around the world to curb drug costs. American wholesaling companies were therefore formed to economize on selling expenses; SB acquired a large wholesaler, retaining it until 1999.

Third, the formation of Glaxo Wellcome created Britain's most powerful pharmaceutical company; hence its enhanced market power might well pose a threat to the smaller SB. Rival corporations throughout the world were at that time undertaking their own mergers, as a result downgrading SB from second to eighth in the global pharmaceutical league. In 1996 Leschly therefore accepted that his group could survive as a major industry player only by seeking a new corporate partner. After some unproductive talks with Sykes at Glaxo Wellcome, he opened negotiations with American Home Products (AHP) of New York.

Outsiders found that choice to be an illogical one, because AHP differed so markedly from SB in lacking the group's go-ahead spirit. Moreover, many influential figures in Britain were concerned that any future agreement would create a wholly American-owned giant. The prospect of his country having to forfeit SB's valuable R&D and marketing resources to United States control reportedly moved the UK prime minister, Tony Blair, to ask Sykes to find some way of saving the group for Britain.

Sykes responded to that request with an initiative to create an all-British combine. He at once disrupted SB's negotiations with AHP by inviting Leschly to open merger negotiations with himself. Those rapidly yielded an outline agreement in January 1998 to establish GlaxoSmithKline (GSK), Glaxo Wellcome's shareholding stake being 59.5 per cent to SB's 40.5 per cent. Leschly was offered the post he desired, that of GSK's chief executive, while Sykes would be executive chairman. Within a month the hastily concluded agreement fell apart, causing panic on the London Stock Exchange.

Between that débâcle in 1998 and the merger's successful consummation two years later, the sequence of events cannot yet be interpreted with any certainty. Yet deeper issues than personality differences apparently caused that breakdown. A basic hurdle to overcome was the divergence, along national lines, in the two companies' styles of doing business.

Sykes's strategy was to build up a 'critical mass' in R&D, so as to gain economies of scale as well as enhanced opportunities to discover new and profitable drugs. Yet he failed to reduce Glaxo Wellcome's unduly high overheads, allowing the workforce to continue to grow. Consequently, between 1995 and 1999 his company's turnover increased by only 11 per cent, and trading profits by less than 2 per cent.

Using already well-tried American corporate strategies, Leschly for his part streamlined SB's research operations by creating smaller teams of scientists and allowing them greater freedom to experiment. He bought in promising compounds from small biotechnology firms and also marketable drugs from rivals. So as to concentrate on pharmaceuticals and healthcare, he sold off two substantial non-core businesses. He also reduced the total number of employees by 3,000, principally in manufacturing. Thanks to his reforms, in the same period SB's turnover improved by 20 per cent and its trading profits by almost 40 per cent.

It is not known what induced Leschly and Sykes late in 1999 to reach a self-denying compact, so as to facilitate the almost universally expected merger. They were by then on cordial terms, working hard to align two currently diverse production systems and supply chains. Their adoption of each other's best practices, it was later made clear, had transformed both companies. That December, Leschly announced that he was taking early retirement, to be succeeded by Garnier. Sykes at once asked a team from SB to meet him at a secret location abroad. There the two sides reached a definitive agreement, which in 2000 created GSK, Garnier becoming chief executive. Sykes, shortly to become rector of Imperial College in London, was content to be non-executive chairman.

They appointed an SB top manager as head of R&D, thereby passing over both Glaxo's chief executive and its research director in favour of SB people, even though Glaxo Wellcome held nearly three-fifths of GSK's total shareholding stake. Thanks to know-how gained from the United States, therefore, SB secured more effective control than it might have expected over the kind of national champion which Sir Ronald Edwards, by his abortive hostile bid for Glaxo, had in 1971 dreamt of creating. The chapters that follow will seek to explain in greater detail how the Beecham enterprise over a century and a half had grown from modest beginnings to securing a seat at the world's pharmaceutical top table.

I

Not quite a Smilesian hero, 1820–1865

Thomas Beecham was by no stretch of the imagination a good or clever man; yet through his Beecham's pill firm he made himself into a household name, throughout Britain and over much of the world.[1] That signal achievement should surely have gratified the Victorian publicist, Samuel Smiles, who in his best-known work, *Self-Help* (1859), praised those who, like Thomas – who got no mention – had risen from humble beginnings through sheer application and persistence. However, Smiles also regarded truthfulness, integrity and goodness as 'the essence of manly character';[2] by those criteria, Thomas had some distinctly unSmilesian traits.

A man of deep faith who steeped himself in the Bible, he had no time for the seventh commandment, against adultery. While being honest and a man of his word in business, when advertising his pills he could spread untruths and half-truths about the cures they could bring to the sufferer. Perhaps those failings, and others that will become clear during the present narrative, make him all the more interesting to later generations.

Thomas was born in 1820 into one of the poorest strata of English rural society.[3] His father had been an agricultural labourer, and then a shepherd, in the hamlet of Curbridge, ten miles west of Oxford; at that time agricultural wages in Oxfordshire were among the lowest in England.[4] Joseph Beecham, only twenty-one at his eldest son's birth – two months after an evidently forced marriage – was a depressive and lacked the strong constitution needed to withstand the rigours of farming life in all weathers. As so often with successful men, the dominant force in Thomas's early life was his mother, Sarah. Robust and quick-tempered, she passed on to him her small stature, blue eyes and fair hair, as well as narrow hands with long fingers, later useful for rolling pills. The parents were incompatible in temperament and separated before Joseph's premature death at fifty, setting off a sequence of marital discord that persisted into the fourth Beecham generation.

Ailing as an infant, Thomas was not expected to live; yet he survived to undergo a year's schooling at the age of seven. He needed to walk just over a mile into the nearest town, Witney, which had a National School (set up by the Church of England-based National Society) in the Town Hall. Although remembered as a not very bright or attentive pupil, he was given a useful grounding in the three Rs, of reading, (w)riting and (a) rithmetic. A year later, when only eight – as he later recalled in a fragment of autobiography – 'in the year 1828 I was sent out to work; that work consisted of minding sheep in the open fields, and my wages were 1s. 6d. [7½p] per week of seven days.'[5]

He did not record the stages of his self-improvement, but he would have commended Sir Walter Scott's saying that 'all men who have turnd [sic] out worth anything have had the chief hand in their own education'.[6] Had he been employed in a mill for twelve hours a day, winter and summer, he could well have become too fatigued to learn much in his slender leisure hours, besides lacking the fresh air that was to make him so hardy. He owed his excellent teeth and cast-iron digestion to the raw root vegetables that had eased his hunger in youth.[7]

Normally he slept in a shepherd's hut on Curbridge Down, but when out in the fields, he had the opportunity to read and ponder on his own. Those solitary hours, with all the time to think, turned him into a unique individual. There could never be a replica of Thomas Beecham, one who made little effort to adapt himself to the world about him or to mould his character upon those of others, as most mortals feel obliged to do.

'Very early in my teens,' he continued, 'I took charge of the entire flock,' thus showing a precocious sense of responsibility, 'and stuck to it until I was twenty years of age.' In about 1833 he began working for a progressive farmer, William Chamberlin, at Cropredy, near Banbury, and 26 miles from his native Curbridge. While once again occupying a shepherd's cottage on the 400-acre (160-hectare) farm, he was brought into more regular contact with other people. Like many loners, he proved ready to talk when given half a chance, being self-opinionated and at times obsessive on his own favourite subjects. He could also fly into a temper when crossed in any way.[8]

According to a local tradition, his observant eye noticed which herbs kept his flocks healthy, and might therefore be useful as medicines. 'In searching among herbs in the field for sources of food,' it has been suggested, 'primeval men must have discovered, in course of time, that some plant products alleviated physical ills.'[9] Thomas could also have learnt from local 'wise women', who gathered herbs and plants from hedgerows, ditches and fields and made them up into potions and pills. When treating the sick, those women often linked herbalism and the occult, prescribing simple remedies and performing rituals that humoured the superstitions of the day. Thomas was forever casting horoscopes; as will be shown later in this chapter, at one period of his life he became much sought after as a fortune teller.

Within a few years of arriving at Cropredy, he acquired a reputation there for curing illnesses by herbal means. His treatment of a sick horse, which recovered under his care, became the talk of the neighbourhood; in his own words, he then set about 'making decoctions [liquid medicines] of a human kind'.[10] To advance from easily processed herbs to vegetable compounds, he had to learn how to use a pestle, a club-like implement for pounding hard materials such as aloes and ginger, in a bowl-shaped mortar. Having from an early age been fascinated with mechanical devices, he soon invented a grinder or kibbler, subsequently discovered in his former cottage. He fed those hard substances from above into a small drum, containing knives that were rotated by a wheel rescued from an old agricultural machine. Once pulverized, the pill mass may have been sifted to remove any lumps; it was then carried through a pipe down to the floor below.

He added water, to give it the pliable consistency of dough. A pill board, which also turned up in the cottage, had two sets of grooves. The pill mass was spread out over the lower set, and then flattened by a roller. The top grooved cutter, fixed to a frame, ran to and fro over the mass until long strips of pill material emerged. Those were sliced by hand and the pieces rolled into spherical pills.[11] As Chamberlin employed him to buy and sell sheep in the local markets, Thomas became used to walking to market long distances in a swinging step typical of a shepherd. There he took the opportunity to sell some of his pills, thus picking up the ways of commerce.

In 1837 he acquired a pocket Bible, from which he rapidly learned whole passages by heart. He was moved to inscribe in the Bible some passable verses:

> Within this awful volume lies
> The mystery of mysteries;
> Happiest they of human race
> To whom their God has given grace
>
> To read, to fear, to hope, to pray,
> To lift the latch, to force the way;
> And better had they ne'er been born
> Who read to doubt or read to scorn.

The resonance of the King James version later moved him to pen pithy sentiments such as 'Hope leads us on' and 'Truth conquers all assailants'. To that biblical source he also owed the vigorous prose he used in his handbills and subsequent printed advertisements.[12]

Shortly before his twentieth birthday, he felt confident enough about his pill-making prospects to move on. According to his reminiscences,

> A slight turn in the tide of events caused me to give it [regular work] up. I may say here that for some years before the above age, a thirst for a little knowledge of humanity had sprung up within me; a slight wave of opportunity presented itself; and I launched my tiny barque into the ever-shifting sea of commercial uncertainty.[13]

Off he went from Cropredy in 1840, without ever revealing what the slight turn in events had been, nor what wave of opportunity came his way. Two years earlier, Chamberlin had moved to another house and hence relaxed his day-to-day control of the farm; that might have encouraged Thomas to think about his own departure. Perhaps the generous farmer gave him some cash as a leaving present, which Thomas could have added to the savings he had made by frugal living.

His uncle William, Joseph's elder brother, gave him lodgings in his cottage at the Oxfordshire town of Kidlington, about ten miles from Curbridge and six miles from Oxford. Although the cottage had only three rooms, Thomas was allowed to use one of them for pill rolling, and the money he could spare added to William's and his elder son's meagre pay as shepherds. Thomas also worked as the village postman or letter carrier.

Although the penny post had been introduced in January 1840, rural locations at first had no post offices. He therefore collected mail from Gosford, about a mile to the south, delivered it to households, and later in the day blew his horn at various locations in Kidlington for people to bring out their letters, which he took back to Gosford for onward despatch. Not until the 1850s did the author, Anthony Trollope, a senior civil servant in the General Post Office, establish Oxfordshire's network of post offices, well after Thomas's time there.[14]

Thomas did not remain a postman for more than a few months; he then became a jobbing gardener, clad in bright blue overalls, at a Kidlington mansion, Hampden House. Once again, he chose a considerate employer, John Sydenham, who allowed him time off during the winter months or when there was little gardening work to do; Thomas was then away peddling his pills in the markets. About this time he began to enjoy female companionship. He had strong sexual appetites and a personal magnetism, but women also relished his willingness to converse about matters that interested them rather than boring them with men's talk. He would give them small keepsakes such as bobbins and knitting sheaths; much later he enchanted his grandson's sophisticated American fiancée by presenting her with a golden sovereign and a pink and two yellow roses.[15]

However, while capable of showing genuine affection towards women, he found it fatally easy to exploit them for his own gratification: an unSmilesian foible that led him into scrapes from which he could rescue himself only by lies, evasions and at times threats. He was to be married three times, and drove his first wife to drink. The second wife was said (unjustly) to have been poisoned when she died in her twenties, and the third openly accused him of trying to poison her; people believed such accusations because he looked like that sort of man. He once admitted that he had only one love in his life, but did not wed her:[16] perhaps one of the unmarried women who are known to have borne him children.

In 1843 he bought a pocket edition of Edward Young's *Night Thoughts on Life, Death and Immortality* and echoed its melancholy tone in some further verses:

> Leaves grow green to fall,
> Flowers grow fair to fade,
> Fruits grow ripe to rot,
> All but for passing made.
>
> So do our hopes decline,
> So joys pass away,
> So do feelings turn
> To darkness and decay.

Of greater interest to posterity were the words Thomas wrote on the flyleaf, as they reflected another side of his life; whether they were copied from elsewhere or his own unaided work is not known:

> Be honest and just in all your dealings, for if the shadow follows the body in the splendour of the finest sunlight, so will the wrong done to another pursue the soul in the hours of prosperity.[17]

At Hampden House Thomas combined gardening and pill-making for nearly seven years; then in 1847 he determined to be once again on his way. This time he moved nearly 200 miles to the north-west of England: a momentous step that had been in his mind for some time.

He might have headed for London, where some of the most celebrated patent medicine firms were situated. However, in the capital he would have met heavy competition from rivals who already spent lavishly on advertising and had their own established networks of distributors. The provinces therefore offered a better opportunity to build up a market from scratch. His choice was Lancashire, where – in contrast with Oxfordshire – average wages for many occupations were among the highest in Britain,[18] while Lancastrians displayed a mighty appetite for nostrums. In the mid-1880s a survey found that the country's main outlets for patent medicines were in towns extensively populated by miners and industrial workers, such as Wigan, Bolton, Bury (Lancashire), Rochdale and Stockport, where occupational diseases were most rife.[19]

As Lancashire must have been unknown to him, he went first of all to its largest city, Liverpool. To earn ready money, he worked as a labourer in the farms then adjacent to Liverpool's city boundaries or for builders, fashioning pills in the evenings or at week-ends and selling them in the open markets. In May 1847 he married Jane, daughter of William Evans, a labourer from Bangor, and believed to have worked as a maid in a chemist's house; she was eight years older than himself. He clearly lost no time in choosing a bride. As with his own parents, he and Jane had few interests in common; both merely wanted to settle down.

However, throughout the decade less well-off residents were finding Liverpool an exceptionally unhealthy place to live. A work about the future publisher David Allen, who also migrated there – from Belfast – in 1847, portrays the conditions that both he and Thomas Beecham endured:

> Houses were built with little regard for drainage or ventilation. About a quarter of the population [out of a total of over 300,000] lived in stinking courts and alleys, which the municipal scavengers ignored. The only lavatories were privies – one to about eight houses. The few sewers that existed were never cleaned except by rain.[20]

As over half the town's children died before reaching the age of ten, the newlyweds would have been anxious to escape for the well-being of their future family. Later that summer, they therefore moved to Wigan, fifteen miles to the north-east.

At this turning-point in Thomas Beecham's life, it is worth asking how someone of such lowly origins managed to take the rare step of becoming an entrepreneur. Samuel Smiles, while conceding that the subjects in his book were from many varied backgrounds, did – as shown above – commend the few who had by pertinacity and inventiveness elevated themselves from the lowest ranks of society.[21] The economist Alfred Marshall later echoed Sir Walter Scott by declaring that 'the man, who proves to be endowed with business genius, has seldom owed very much to formal education', but instead learns with an independent cast of mind the art of rapidly identifying the key elements in a firm that were ripe for 'moulding and combining anew'. Hence, Marshall declared, most of the leaders in Britain's industrial revolution were rugged men with 'self-reliant, self-centred characters ..., much occupied with careful attention to detail and the teachings of long experience'.[22]

More sceptical scholars in the twentieth century enquired who precisely Marshall's unpolished and self-reliant businessmen were. François Crouzet, for example, having traced 'the myth of the self-made man' back to Dick Whittington (d. 1423), a poor apprentice who became Lord Mayor of London, compiled data on the founders of sizeable firms in Britain between 1750 and 1850. Judging by their fathers' occupations, only 7 per cent of those in his sample of 226 men had working-class origins, while 3 per cent came from the families of unskilled workmen. Beecham himself did not appear in the sample, which clearly under-represented those with impoverished backgrounds because Crouzet omitted small firms.[23]

To be sure, ambitious men in the poorest circumstances, lacking both resources and business connections alike, stood little chance of becoming entrepreneurs on any scale. Unless, exceptionally, they married well – as Whittington did – such men had to choose an industry needing little start-up capital, where they could painfully assemble enough funds for growth. Whether or not Thomas Beecham received a lump sum before he left Cropredy in 1840, he subsequently had to scrape that capital together pound by pound. Not until 1863, when he was in his early forties, was he able to advance even from household to workshop production. Two-thirds of his long life passed before in 1877 he could set up his first, still very basic, factory.

Wigan was a town of some 30,000 inhabitants, strategically placed on the cross-roads between Preston and Warrington from north to south and horizontally between south-east and south-west Lancashire. In Thomas's time it had two railways, the North Union and the Lancashire & Yorkshire lines, connecting with Liverpool, Manchester and other important centres. To be sure, at first he could not have afforded the train fares; instead, he had to walk or rely on horse-drawn transport between neighbouring towns.

Industry in Wigan comprised coal mines and ironworks as well as textile factories. As shown above, even in the 1880s its townspeople went after patent medicines in large quantities for their occupational or other ills. He supplemented his initially meagre income from pill-making by consultations, usually with young women, on foretelling their future, and is said to have met on a regular basis a white witch in the Midlands.

On 1 September 1847, once settled in the town, for the first time Thomas acquired from the local Office of Stamps and Taxes a licence to sell patent medicines. He invariably regarded his business as having been established a year later, reporting in a statutory declaration of 1906 about the pills, 'I first commenced to manufacture and sell the said medicinal preparation in or about 1848 and at or about the same period I applied as a trade description the words Beecham's Patent Pills.'[24] They were in fact proprietary products, not patented as such but having their trade names protected by law. Shortly afterwards, he adopted a distinctive label for the wooden boxes which replaced earlier wrappings of paper twisted into spills.

Mistakenly, the prospectuses of the successive Beecham joint-stock companies of 1924 and 1928 gave the firm's starting date as 1842, when pill-making in Kidlington had still been a part-time occupation for him. At Wigan he spent one day a week in making up the pills, while on the other weekdays he travelled round the markets of nearby towns. His sales technique was designed to attract the maximum amount of attention. Never bothering to hire a stall, he set up his pitch with a bamboo table, a large umbrella, and a basket of his wares, including an admonitory bottle of intestinal worms. His self-confessed 'little knowledge of humanity' had taught him how to excite people's curiosity; hence he paid youngsters several pence a time to distribute his vividly coloured handbills. He had to fit in any clerical work at nights or on Sundays.

For some reason he never sent for his pill-making apparatus from Oxfordshire. Manufacturing by hand, with perhaps a pill-board to help him, he must have gone back to mortar and pestle for grinding down the aloes and other raw materials. Unusually for the time, he did not involve his wife Jane in any of these tasks. She was illiterate,[25] but he made no effort to give her lessons. He lacked the patience to be a good teacher; she may have been either too diffident to learn or fearful of being drawn into helping him full-time.

Thomas did not feel the need to keep written records at home, but whitewashed his parlour walls and scrawled on them particulars of incomings and outgoings: the same method as he had earlier used for maintaining tallies of sheep acquired and sold. Nor was he troubled by income tax, introduced in 1842, as it was levied only on incomes over the net exemption level of £150; few small firms kept proper books, so that the Inland Revenue accepted rough estimates of earnings. He then had four different products: Beecham's 'celebrated herbal' pills, costing 1s. 6d. (7½p), including patent medicine duty (see Chapter 2), a 'female's friend'; a 'royal toothpowder' at 4d. (2p) and a 'golden tooth tincture'.[26]

Some time in the early 1850s he opened an order book for pills, headed by James Kershaw (1821–86), chemist of Southport and a member of Britain's Pharmaceutical Society since 1847.[27] He also started a mail order business. Since pills resembled seeds in weighing little in relation to their value, they could be sent by the penny post of 1840 that had given him employment in Kidlington. He now offered to send a 6d. (2½p) box of pills for 8 penny stamps, post free.

The routine of weekly production kept him fully stretched, as it involved selling in markets or from home, canvassing retail outlets and posting off orders. A few pages torn from a pocket book for 1856–57 indicate the current size of his business.[28] He sold only £3 worth over 28 of those weeks to wholesale customers he called on, mainly in rural districts south of Wigan, but £64 worth from regular visits to the town of St Helens, some eight miles away, between May 1856 and April 1857. His turnover can therefore have been hardly more than £250 a year, with profits of perhaps £100–120. His elder son, Joseph, had been born in June 1848,[29] and by 1855 there were four children to support, the younger ones being Sarah, Jane and William. Their mother had to manage with a 12-year-old locally born servant, Alice Tickle.

Seeking a more substantial return from his efforts, as well as an opportunity to undertake straightforward experiments, later in 1857 Thomas set up as a retail chemist. His rented shop in Wallgate, Wigan, also sold groceries and tea, but he took the pharmacy side very seriously, at a time when chemists treated many customers for their ailments by giving advice and selling remedies over the counter. In the previous autumn, a man had come over to Wigan from Haydock, six miles away, 'with Breackings out and Blotches on the body', and Thomas had prescribed a dilution of sulphuric acid and lavender water as a lotion and the purgative medicinal rhubarb, as well as his pills, to clear the unfortunate's blood.[30]

From an early age, he had collected books on pharmacy, including *The Unlearned Alchymist* of 1662 by the widow of the quack doctor Richard Mathew(s), which discussed at length the properties and merits of Mathew's diaphoretic (sweat-inducing) and diuretic pill. Thomas must also have been familiar with the bible of his trade, Francis Mohr's and Theophilus Redwood's *Practical Pharmacy: The Arrangements, Apparatus, and Manipulations of the Pharmaceutical Shop and Laboratory*, first published in 1849.[31] Its comprehensive section on the 'properties of pills' furnished the kind of detailed technical information that would have enabled him to ensure the quality of his pills.

According to Mohr and Redwood, a pill mass should be formed into a 'consistent, firm and adherent paste', plastic enough to be moulded easily but stiff enough to prevent the manufactured pills from losing their shape. The mass comprised two separate parts: the active ingredient, such as aloes, and the 'excipient' (passive or receiving matter) which gave it the required degree of 'consistence and tenacity' or adhesiveness, for instance chemists' soap and essential oils. 'The principal art in pill-making consists in selecting the proper substances as excipients to suit the peculiar nature of the other ingredients of the pills': something that Thomas at last possessed some leisure to achieve.

While his wife Jane was now serving in the shop, making routine sales, he remained behind the scenes, having the time and basic apparatus to manufacture pills and to experiment with the essential oils, of rosemary, juniper and aniseed, plus a mucilage or binding material of gum arabic. Joseph, then nine years old and a diligent scholar at a local free school, was also roped in to help. He was good at lessons, excelling at both English and arithmetic; he is said to have trained himself to add four columns of figures at the same time. However, his teacher regularly complained that he was being made to work too hard at home out of school hours.

Thomas's latest career change had thus been quite as dramatic as had been his previous moves, from Cropredy in 1840 and to Lancashire seven years later. He looked forward to a more certain future in a locality he had come to know well. For the first time in his life he was somebody, running a well-stocked shop in the centre of Wigan and earning an entry in both the town directory and the voting register.[32]

Not previously noted for taking much trouble over his personal appearance, he spruced himself up so as to impress the more influential among his clientele; family reminiscences perhaps exaggerated in portraying him then as a bit of a dandy. Likewise, he seems to have encouraged his wife Jane, who in the past had been allowed little enough housekeeping money for her own adornment, to buy a new gown, in which she was photographed about this time. Made of a checkered fabric, possibly wool, it had bishop sleeves and full skirts typical of the period. The length of the exposure may have responsible for the uncomfortable and even vinegary expression she wore; yet however discontented with her lot, she must have appreciated the new status and less cramped living space she now enjoyed. Thomas himself had reached the most fulfilling period of his career to date, and the shop prospered until, within a year, disaster struck.

Early in August 1858, a young woman bought some laudanum, an opiate drug, for her sick father. As it was a Saturday, Thomas was probably absent on his weekly visit to St Helens; Jane poured the medicine into a bottle but failed to remove the old label of a harmless preparation, to mark the bottle 'Poison' or to enquire why it was being bought. A small boy in the purchaser's family was later given the medicine; an emetic failed to save him, and he died of laudanum poisoning. At the subsequent inquest, the coroner returned a verdict of accidental death, but censured Jane Beecham's negligence which, although not the direct cause of the tragedy, emphasized the urgent need for all druggists to label poisons.

The coroner's remarks were extensively reported in the local press, as well as in the *Pharmaceutical Journal*, currently campaigning for controls over the unrestricted sale of poisons, and at a stroke damaged the shop's goodwill so painstakingly built up over the past year.[33] Another type of individual might have determined to ride out the gossip and strive to recover the inevitable loss of trade. However, Thomas's notoriously eccentric ways, quarrelsome nature and poor reputation as a womanizer prompted him to sell up. In November 1858 he sent all his stock-in-trade for auction.

There were so many items that the auction took two days. The grocery side included 'very superior teas', about 600 lbs of currants and raisins and 120 bottles of the best pickles, as well as 150 lbs of starch. The druggist's side of the business was quite as generously stocked, with 125 bottles of top-grade castor oil, 56 lbs of fine ginger and 200 lbs of chemists' soap, not including the scented variety. The ginger could have made 1¼ million pills; if half the soap had been used for the same purpose, it would have been enough for 4½ million pills. No aloes went under the hammer, unless they were hidden away in the 'assortment of drysaltery', a term which covered dyestuffs and oils as well as drugs. Having put most of his savings into these items, he found it painful to see them go, doubtless at knock-down prices. Equally distressing was the need to sell sixty books, some on medicine and surgery, and much-read volumes of *The Lancet* and other journals.[34] No record has survived of the amount raised.

He then had to resume his former life in a small terrace house, manufacturing pills in the parlour and going back to the routine of touring outdoor markets. A contemporary remembered him as driven as never before: 'No one worked harder, or stuck to it more than he did. And what he had not sold by the end of the evening he gave away.' He refused even to contemplate the possibility of failure. His great-granddaughter, Anne Francis, who wrote the only full-length biography of him to date, *A Guinea A Box* (1968), stated that, 'Thomas was a past master at believing what he wanted to, however much evidence might contradict it'. Although born in distant Oxfordshire, he possessed a northerner's 'brusqueness, wry tongue, zeal and commonsense attitude'.[35]

Being still on the electoral roll, he voted in the general election of April 1859, casting one vote each for the Conservative candidate and for the Liberal, a local cotton master and colliery owner respectively, both being returned; in 1857 his votes had gone exclusively to Conservatives. In politics, as in many other aspects of life, he was pragmatic and free of ideology. Having performed his last civic act there, he departed with his family from Wigan, after eleven years of unremitting toil and dashed expectations.

He knew that it was none too soon to move on. During 1861, when asked in a magistrate's court (see below) his reason for having left Wigan, he hesitantly replied that he wanted to better himself. Elsewhere he claimed to have been hounded out by the medical profession; apparently doctors had discovered that women were taking the 'female's friend' in the hope of ending pregnancies. Perhaps understandably, its formula has not survived.

Thomas's destination in mid-1859 was St Helens. He is said to have considered settling there in 1847, and the sales figures for 1856/57, quoted above, indicate a ready market for his medicines there. An authoritative account, in the *Victoria County History of Lancashire* (1907), offers some reasons for that demand for nostrums:

The aspect of the town is uninviting. The factories rear a forest of tall chimneys, [mine] shafts, kilns and other erections on every hand, and the fumes of acids and the smoke of furnaces render the atmosphere almost unbearable to a stranger.

In addition to the coal mines, copper working and glass-making took place, as well as a thriving alkali trade to supply local soap manufacturers. The industrial odours were reinforced by those emanating from cesspits and uncleared rubbish: even so, doubtless an improvement on Liverpool.[36]

As a base for his activities, Thomas felt the town to be in many ways inferior to Wigan. Because its population was smaller, at about 25,000, the opportunities for building up trade were that much more limited. However, it did have a vibrant market, its importance enhanced by the lack of other commercial outlets for locally grown farm and garden produce. He still had to resume his tours of neighbouring localities, finding the rail (which he could now afford) and other means of transport less convenient.

His ambitions thus seemed no nearer fulfilment than they had been on his arrival in Wigan, and he resolved to concentrate on his digestive and cough pills. The cottage he rented was in Milk Street, an out-of-the-way side road, but in the open market he made himself even more conspicuous by standing on a fish barrel, and using a door panel as a tray for his wares. Although his normal speaking voice was on the light side, he could bawl loudly enough against the hubbub of the market. His patter was said to be 'a mixture of hard fact and Biblical allusion', and he developed an effective line in repartee.

On the brink of his fortieth birthday, he was thus compelled to reconsider his entire mission in life. Over the next few years, he took the first of a series of steps that would soon disengage him from outdoor market trading for ever. From then on, the firm's progress depended on his undoubted skill in marketing high-quality pills through wider outlets.

Most significantly, he started inserting advertisements in the press, so as to reach a far wider audience than his earlier posters and handbills had provided. During August 1859 his first advertisement appeared in the *St Helens Intelligencer*, being repeated each week until the end of the year. That featured both a testimonial from a customer in Golborne, six miles distant, and at its head the slogan to be linked with the pills from then on. James Brockbank, in his *History of St Helens, with Local Landmarks*, published in 1896, related how Mrs Ellen Butler, 'a lady of good family and business attitude, vigorously declared they were worth "A Guinea A Box"'. However, when her declaration was picked up by *Answers* nearly two years later, Thomas straightaway informed that popular weekly magazine, with a typically attention-grabbing metaphor, that 'he himself, and no other, struck out from that mental anvil that spark of wit which has made the pills a household word in every quarter of the globe'.[37] A guinea was supposed to be the fee charged by fashionable doctors.

Further, less welcome, publicity was soon to dog him. While he was constantly immersed in business matters, a year or two after their arrival in St Helens his wife Jane began to take to the bottle, having all too few alternative diversions in her life. She had even lost the company of a teenaged slavey, as Alice Tickle had had to leave, presumably after the family vacated the shop at the end of 1858; three years later, Alice was working as housekeeper to a widowed textile dealer at Hindley, two miles from Wigan.[38]

In 1861 the outcome of a domestic row led to Thomas's appearance before the local magistrates. On the first of September he returned home at 11 p.m., ostensibly from his market stall, but in fact after carousing elsewhere in Milk Street with a Mrs Lowe. At the front door Jane noisily accused him of 'drinking with whores all night', whereupon he threw her into the street; being herself drunk, she struck her head on the pavement. A neighbour then began to threaten Thomas, who later in the month took him to the local court of petty sessions.

Both men were bound over to keep the peace; blaming Jane for the fracas, Thomas took his revenge on her in a mean and callous way. As their marital relations were now beyond repair, for consolation he took up with a spinster, not Mrs Lowe. In August 1862 his illegitimate daughter, Maggie, was born, and he wilfully pencilled her name in the family Bible.[39] When he persisted in regularly visiting mother and child and giving them money that could hardly be spared, he and Jane could no longer bear to live under the same roof, and they separated. Joseph moved with her to a different part of town.

That rift only strengthened Thomas's mounting resolve to throw all his energies into the pill business. The annual sums he was able to spend on advertising (see Table 4.2) chart his progress. The 1860 figure, of £69, fell slightly to £66 in 1861, but increased by more than a half to £100 in 1862, when he started to keep written records, none of which have survived before 1865. Significantly, in mid-1863 Joseph left school at fifteen and began to work with him full-time. Thomas's increasing turnover allowed him to raise advertising expenditure that year by a further half to £162, while the testimonials quoted in his press notices show that he was gaining satisfied customers in a number of Lancashire towns. Moreover, his success with customers as far afield as Cambridge encouraged him to advertise in the *Cambridge Independent Press.*

In the autumn of 1863, probably soon after his separation from Jane, Thomas left the Milk Street cottage he had rented since 1859 for a more prominent and accessible house in Westfield Street, nearer the town centre. He took the opportunity to announce with a flourish in the *St Helens Newspaper* that 'Mr. Beecham, the Proprietor of the World Renowned Pills' had moved to his new address, under the eye-catching headline, 'FLITTED'. The new dwelling, although no roomier inside, had a basement and also a shed in the back yard, doubtless more solidly built than a mere outhouse; as it abutted on to the road, he inserted a glass panel, through which he made cash sales.

Vigorous marketing caused demand for Beecham's pills to rise in a gratifying way. By 1864 he had nearly doubled to £306 his advertising expenditure, which reached £328 in 1865. The steadily mounting sales forced him to speed up production, still entirely by hand. He bought a pill cutter, with a giant wheel for turning two grooved rollers, which made long strips of the pill mass more quickly than the old pill board had done. Other machines must have cut these strips into pieces for rolling.[40]

In May 1864 Thomas, describing himself as a manufacturing chemist, joined the United Society of Chemists and Druggists. That was a rival organization to the Pharmaceutical Society, still persisting in its efforts to have noxious drugs controlled but scarcely to his taste after its publication, the *Pharmaceutical Journal*, had reported the inquest of 1858.

For the past seven years or so he had been calling himself 'Dr. Beecham'. Then in 1858 parliament passed the Medical Act, which regulated the qualifications of doctors, and imposed a £20 fine on those falsely pretending to be a registered practitioner of medicine, thereby blowing away Thomas's borrowed plumes.[41] A year later, he harmonized his selling prices with those of rival firms, charging 9½d. (4p) for 36 pills, 1s. 1½d. (6p) for 56 and 2s. 9d. (14p) for 168 pills, including patent medicine duty of 1½d. (1p) on the smaller sizes and 3d. (1p) on the largest one. He thus effectively joined the ranks of Britain's patent medicine industry.

Thomas owed his growing sales and goodwill to the successive innovations he made, which ensured that his pills were of a good and consistent standard. It will be shown in Chapter 2 how rival patent medicine firms then – and for many subsequent decades – hid behind the secrecy of their formulae to offer badly mixed pills and other remedies of poor quality. Most competitors were at that time spending far more on publicity than he was doing, but he knew that demand for an inferior product would not last indefinitely, no matter the size of the advertising outlay.

Thus during 1902 Thomas asserted, in his usual forthright manner, that a 'plausible advertisement, set forth in an attractive style' could 'temporarily arrest the attention of a certain number of readers and induce them to purchase a certain article'. However,

It is a more difficult matter to ensure their continued patronage.
Unless the advertised article proves to be all that is claimed for
it, not only do the purchasers discontinue its use, but warn others

against it as a thing to be avoided. Should it be, however, of genuine value, those who make a trial of it naturally become habitual users and advocates, their advocacy being the most effective and absolutely reliable advertisement possible.[42]

Notwithstanding that confident declaration, Thomas in his advertisements did cynically stretch the truth. The first publicity effort of 1859 lauded his pills as 'the best in the world for bilious and nervous disorders, wind and pain in the stomach, headache, giddiness, shortness of breath, etc., etc.' By the early twentieth century – just when he was uttering his lofty principles – he had the nerve to add, in capital letters, claims about curing 'Scurvy and Scorbutic [scurvy-like] Affections, Pimples and Blotches on the Skin, Bad Legs, Ulcers, Wounds, Maladies of Indiscretion, Kidney and Urinary Disorders and Menstrual Derangements'. For a time he even added Bright's disease, in actual fact caused by the degeneration of the kidneys.[43] Samuel Smiles, who survived until 1904, would have scarcely admired his publicizing of those deceitful claims.

Thomas had thus progressed through his own efforts from shepherd boy to a moderately well-known maker of pills. The early Beecham's business now needs to be placed in the context of the patent medicine industry of the mid-Victorian period. That forms the subject of Chapter 2.

Britain's patent medicine industry in the nineteenth century

B Y THE MID-1860S, Thomas Beecham would have made it his business to learn all he could about the industry he now belonged to.[1] It had first been officially recognized as such in 1783 when the government introduced a patent medicine duty. An Act of Parliament in 1804 listed not the firms themselves but the 462 brands of medicine liable to duty; that number increased to 552 in a further Act of 1812.[2] All medicinal retailers were required to have a licence of 5s. (25p).

The home turnover of all patent medicine firms can be roughly estimated from government data of annual receipts from the duty, through multiplying the figures by 6; according to that method, in 1865 factory sales to British outlets came to about £370,000. To estimate UK consumers' expenditure that year, a multiplier of 9 is used here, suggesting that they must have spent in all about £555,000 on remedies, of which some were imported.[3] As exports were not subject to tax, those figures do not reveal total turnover, but Thomas made no direct exports at that time.

In fact, the patent medicine industry remained an insignificant part of Britain's burgeoning mid-Victorian economy. Its sales at home accounted for well under one-tenth of one per cent of national consumption expenditure, £865 million that year of 1865, while the number employed in the industry in the 1880s was estimated at 19,000, representing less than one-eighth of one per cent of the country's working population.[4] Even so, the mass of ordinary people were habitually drawn to those remedies, catering as they did to one of the most basic human drives, to enjoy good health and find a cure when sick.

The trade journal, the *Chemist and Druggist*, in 1886 sought to explain 'the unquenchable demand of the public for put-up medicines', as follows:

> The majority of people get to feel very bad before they go through the processes of being prescribed for and dispensed for in the orthodox

fashion [by registered doctors]. But something definite, tested by experience, something they can purchase at a fixed price and by just naming the article, without being catechised as to all their physical miseries, will always be popular.[5]

Medical consultations cost money, although apothecaries, dispensaries and poor-law medical centres treated patients at little or no charge. Besides, most people had a deep-seated distrust of the health profession which – before the era of advanced drugs – could do little to cure infectious diseases outright and possessed only a sketchy knowledge of pharmacology. Sufferers, especially bread-winners on low incomes, were reluctant to risk being condemned by doctors to long periods off work, or even to the surgeon's knife or a sentence of death.

Of the scores of out-patients at the large urban hospitals such as St Bartholomew's in London, most were seen by inadequately trained medical students. The sick therefore looked for medicines of one kind or another, which the hospitals doled out in massive quantities. During 1869, St Bartholomew's dispensed 900 gallons of cod-liver oil, 1,200 ounces of quinine and three hundredweight of ammonium salts as a restorative after faints. In the words of a medical historian, the patients 'wanted their dose of medicine, and no undue fuss'.[6]

Commercial remedies were likewise popular as being easy to choose and to consume, and thus regarded as a more agreeable route to health than undergoing the disciplines of medical treatment or dieting. Even though the Victorian era has been dubbed 'the age of self-conscious hypochondria',[7] public demand for such remedies was not entirely due to the power of suggestion. In the 1840s the statistician, J. R. McCulloch, estimated that no fewer than 1.25 million, nearly 4.5 per cent of Britain's population, were 'constantly disabled by illness'. Three decades later Dr William Farr, a medical statistician, calculated a figure of those suffering from 'severe illness' at 1.4 million, or 4.3 per cent of the population, with 600,000 additional sufferers in need of medical relief.[8] At a time when foodstuffs were very widely adulterated, diet could well be either unwholesome or inadequate for health. All too many people owed their illnesses to poor living conditions; yet many of the rich harmed their systems through over-eating and excessive drinking.

The remedies on offer were largely vegetable-based compounds, often purgatives which could do little more than relieve symptoms without being able to act selectively on the many causes of disease, such as bacteria in the bloodstream. As Chapter 1 showed, herbal remedies had been very widely available to those living in rural areas. However, the government Statute of Monopolies in 1624 granted venturers the right by Letters Patent to manufacture new substances or articles for 14 years. A succession of nostrum-mongers began to take advantage of that measure, beginning with Patrick Anderson (*c*.1580–1660), who first advertised his Scots Pills in 1635. Men thereafter hijacked the personal treatment by 'wise women' through regarding the body – in Roy Porter's words – as a 'secular [soulless] property and health as a purchasable commodity'.[9]

Those male providers of drugs fell into two distinct categories. Apothecaries and pharmacists made their own preparations from roots, barks and leaves, occasionally using chemical substances such as arsenic and antimony; their formulae were taken from pharmacopoeias dating back to the seventeenth century. Patent medicines manufacturers, on the other hand, devised new compounds through trial and error rather than by scientific experiments, being therefore known as 'empirics'. Their pills or liquid decoctions, as patent or proprietary medicines, had legally protected brand names. Keeping their formulae secret, those manufacturers relied on heavy advertising which played on the subjective fears of the unwell and thereby built up consumer reliance on their nostrums, a pejorative name for quack remedies.

Nostrum makers therefore found it more profitable to concern themselves with marketing techniques than with good standards of manufacture. Once having discovered a winning formula, they lost any incentive to improve that formula or overhaul their methods of production. By contrast, apothecaries and wholesale pharmacists set up laboratories to carry out basic research as they gradually transformed themselves into manufacturing chemists; for examples of this one might look to the future pharmaceutical firms, Allen & Hanburys of London and Evans Sons & Co. of Liverpool (later Evans Medical).[10]

The patent medicine industry differed in kind not only from other health care enterprises, but also from all other industries in Britain. Since the medicine duty was levied, at 1½*d*. (1p) on the 8*d*. (3p) and 1*s*. (5p) sizes, and at 3*d*. (1p) on the 2*s*. 6*d*. (14p) sizes of commercial remedies, a price framework emerged into which most firms slotted their products. They could charge high prices because consumers were hoodwinked into believing that the efficacy of compounds was directly related to their cost. The half-price Poor Man's Pill, 'carefully prepared by a member of the Royal College of Surgeons and highly recommended by Dr. John Abernethy' – the eminent authority on the digestive system who invented the hard Abernethy biscuit – was widely advertised in the 1830s. It failed because the name and cheapness put off customers. In his later affluent days, Thomas Beecham's son Joseph remarked,

> I would certainly have sold my pills for a penny a box, and still have made a profit of more than a halfpenny on each one. But nobody would have bought them at that price. They would have regarded

them as too cheap to be of any use. So I sold them at 2s. 9d. and made a fortune.[11]

Competition throughout the industry was therefore of the non-price kind, so that the number of pills in a 1s. 1½d. (6p) box varied between 16 and 56, largely dependent on their weight. However, the main rivalry was in advertising, to gratify the vagaries of consumer demand, as illustrated by Thomas Beecham's claims for his pills quoted in Chapter 1. Given their high retail prices and the cheapness of basic ingredients such as aloes and ginger, firms had plentiful funds to spend on advertising. The industry's profit margin on sales, often as high as 50 per cent, must have been the highest among non-luxury products.

At any one time Britain's patent medicine industry tended to have a single leading firm, which broadly maintained its supremacy until the entrepreneur (usually the founder) died. A new leader would then emerge, perhaps hoping to avoid that predecessor's mistakes and to offer the public some novel attractions. In the nineteenth century, the first entrepreneur of note was the Scotsman, James Morison (1770–1840), also the first to enter the factory era.[12] During Morison's lifetime, Thomas Beecham was not yet in the industry, but Thomas knew from close inspection of their pills that Morison's successors had in place no proper system of quality control.

The youngest son of an Aberdeenshire laird, Morison was the only known member of the landed gentry to become involved in patent medicine manufacture. As a general merchant, he had gained a broad knowledge of European markets before moving to the Caribbean. However, from the age of sixteen he had suffered from chronic ill-health, brought on by constipation at boarding-school in Aberdeen.

Desperate to find a cure, he consulted over fifty doctors. As none of them brought him any relief, he went into a decline, so that his life was despaired of, or so he later claimed. Then in 1820 – the year of Thomas Beecham's birth – after half a century of what he called a life of disease, physical misery, and woe, Morison made a striking discovery: his whole system was being poisoned by bad humours originating in the digestive tract. Thereafter he loathed the medical profession, denouncing their enthusiasm for chemical-based and (to him) repellent medicines such as calomel and the mercurial blue pill.

In the early 1820s, therefore, having gained a formula from a Dr Hamilton of Edinburgh, as a lodger in the Aberdeen premises of a druggist, George Reid, he allegedly learned to make a wholly vegetable pill that would ensure himself and the wider world regular bowel motions. Using Reid's pill machine, he converted some ingredients at hand, namely aloes and oatmeal, into enough pills to fill two large meal casks, which he took off to London. However, once Morison had spread this unlikely tale, some doctors in Aberdeen fruitlessly urged Reid to deny it.[13]

two bottles of his Aetherial Essence of Ginger to King William IV. Having received from the Keeper of the Privy Purse £10 and a flowery letter, he boldly called himself 'operative chemist extraordinary to his Majesty'.[18] As the tonic was recommended to those with nervous dispositions, it may have done the unpredictable monarch some good. A Dr Scott, who dispensed his Bilious and Liver Pills in Britain and India from 1795 to 1835, advertised these as special favourites of the Duke of Wellington (who in fact never dosed himself), two other dukes, three marquesses, three earls and three bishops.

Not to be outdone, a London physician favoured by the élite, Dr James Cockle of New Ormond Street (1782–1854), by 1838 was boasting that five out of the thirteen ministers in the cabinet of the day, including Lord Melbourne, the prime minister, and Lord Palmerston, the foreign secretary, regularly used his Antibilious pills. He listed by name six dukes, six marquesses, eight viscounts, fifteen barons, one archbishop, fourteen bishops and 'other distinguished personages'. Charles Dickens in middle age used Cockle's pills not only as an aperient but also to relieve tension, recommending them to at least one close friend.[19]

An article on 'The advertising system' in the *Edinburgh Review* of 1843, when drawing attention to Cockle's roll-call, teasingly aired some 'curious speculations' about the 'comparative biliousness of the higher classes'. As if to corroborate these musings, a testimonial for the pills by Dr John Abernethy – who had even-handedly praised the Poor Man's Pill – cited the 'considerable derangement of the functions' of the stomach and the 'torpid state of the liver and bowels' they were aimed to remedy.[20]

Cockle pointedly differentiated himself from Morison, by insisting that his pills contained 'a careful and peculiar admixture of the best and mildest vegetable aperients, [together] with the pure extract of the flowers of camomile', then highly prized for its tonic properties. As the pills had 'been resorted to under all systems of diet, changes of climate or atmospheric alternations', he must have had a large following among those travelling or residing overseas.[21] His firm never gave away any information about its performance, but when he died in 1854, he left only £8,250, later resworn at £6,000.[22] His descendants showed no particular entrepreneurial skills, placing small-sized and discreet advertisements in *The Times* and better-class magazines. Somehow the firm survived until 1960.

Morison's successor as industry leader was Thomas Holloway (1800–83), also based in London.[23] His misjudgments in a long career as manufacturer and advertiser may help to explain why the Beecham firm in due course took over Holloway's enterprise, rather than Holloway being successful in snuffing out that late-comer while it was still insignificant and vulnerable.

The two men almost certainly never met, as the metropolitan-based

Holloway and the provincial Beecham moved in entirely different circles. They were quite dissimilar in appearance, one being tall, handsome as a young man and then impressively full-bodied, while the other was short, squat and far from personable. Apart from being the eldest sons of an inadequate father and resourceful mother, they had little in common. Whereas Beecham came from an impoverished Oxfordshire family of agricultural labourers, Holloway's mother was a moderately well-off shopkeeper in the West Country; her husband, who owned a pub, counted for so little that most people wrongly assumed that he had died early. After a commercial education, latterly in Penzance where he learned the violin with a Danish teacher named Lawrance, Holloway worked in his mother's grocery store for the next twelve years.

A story that he had been apprenticed to a Penzance chemist, named Joseph Harvey, dates only from 1943 and cannot be corroborated. In reality, he had no background knowledge of pharmacy. Under cross-examination in 1862 he admitted that he was incapable of analysing his own ointment, being no 'chymist'.[24] When at last he departed from Cornwall in 1828 he set up as a general merchant at Roubaix, near Lille in France, and later moved to Dunkirk. Apart from becoming a Freemason – as Thomas Beecham never did – learning several European languages and making a number of friends, he seems to have had little to show for his years abroad.

As a free-lance commercial agent in the city of London from 1834 onwards, finally in Broad Street Buildings, Holloway had scant success. A near-contemporary, if hostile, account rated him as no more than 'a dealer in "all sorts", here there and everywhere', for instance 'selling a bundle of cigars, or a few yards of printed calico, or anything else in the small way'. He is said to have bickered day after day with his younger brother and assistant, Henry (1807–74), for lack of serious business, in a dingy office scarcely larger than a cupboard.[25]

In 1837 a quite unexpected encounter transformed Holloway's life. Moonlighting as a part-time interpreter at Bacon's hotel in St Paul's Chain, he met the 52-year-old Felix Albinolo of Turin (1785–1872), newly arrived in the capital to market his invention of the St Cosmas and St Damian medicinal ointment. He soon made himself Albinolo's agent, energetically soliciting for the ointment as many as 540 testimonials from London's medical establishment. He then asked to be taken into partnership.

Despite being a man of 'searing simplicity', Albinolo grew suspicious of this extraordinary zeal and refused to divulge the formula of his ointment. Clearly with some outside help, Holloway devised a version of his own, made up of olive oil (44 per cent), lanolin (30 per cent), resin (15 per cent) and yellow and white beeswax (each 5½ per cent). He initially mixed them in his mother's saucepan, then in a long fish kettle and later in her small wash bowl or copper. Five months after Queen Victoria's accession, on 15 October

1837 he inserted the first advertisements, carrying some testimonials, of 'Holloway's Universal Family Ointment' in three London papers, including the *Sunday Times*. For some years thereafter, he invited his cronies to a 'singing' – accompanying them on the violin – and supper each anniversary of the 'glorious 15th October'.[26]

Holloway thus gained a foothold in the patent medicine industry by converting to his own use another man's intellectual property. Furious at such betrayal, Albinolo responded with press notices about his rival's 'garbled extracts' from the testimonials; yet he stood little chance against Holloway's unstoppable drive. The latter is credited with having spent £1,000 in 1838 on 'scenes and tricks', getting his name mentioned in the capital's pantomimes. No doubt that sum included outgoings on advertisements, under such eye-catching headlines as 'Winning by a Nose': the ointment supposedly cured a foreign diplomat's nasal swelling in a single night, thereby allowing him to attend a royal levee. That April, Holloway daringly linked baseless rumours of the teen-aged queen's anticipated wedding with an invitation to all young ladies to remove pimples and freckles, by means of his ointment, before reaching the altar.

Topical references now poured from his pen, for instance to the exploits of London's notorious villain, 'spring-heeled Jack', a slayer of young women who was believed to have springs in his shoes to evade capture. Holloway's boldness in making copy out of such arcane incidents as Don Carlos, the Spanish pretender, being bitten by a monkey soon caught the editorial attention of the press, and thus served to imprint his name and ointment in people's minds. After *The Town*, a seedy London paper, ran a series of articles on 'The Puffing System' which ironically exposed the effrontery and 'humbug' of his announcements, he grasped that there was no such thing as bad publicity and began to advertise in its columns; on one occasion, Albinolo's and his advertisements bizarrely appeared on the same page of the equally disreputable *Satirist*.[27]

The two opponents slugged it out in the press until well into 1839. That August, Holloway started advertising in *The Times*; shortly afterwards both men ran out of money. In October, Albinolo was jailed for debt; he became a pauper and lived for many years at the workhouse in Poland Street, Westminster, where he died of senility, aged 87, in December 1872.[28] Holloway ended up in Whitecross Street debtors' prison, for non-payment of sums owed to *The Times*: a paper he took several decades to forgive. He was bailed out with £600 of his mother's savings, enough to clear all outstanding debts; ever afterwards he strove to settle accounts, from wages to tradesmen's and professional bills, on the same day as they became due.

Early in 1839 he had begun the manufacture of pills, by means of a small hand-operated machine which he and his old clerk, Hibbert, used 'turn and turn about'. He must have secured his release from gaol before the year's end, as on the second Sunday in January 1840 – without sacrificing a day's business – he married the 25-year-old Jane Driver of Rotherhithe, a shipwright's daughter fourteen years his junior. No beauty, she was good-natured and robust, capable of enduring an over-long working day that often stretched from 4 a.m. to 10 p.m.[29] Unlike Beecham, who found no lasting companionship in his three marriages and kept all his wives well clear of pill-making, the Holloway couple remained devoted to each other for life.

In defiance of his initially meagre sales, that spring or summer Holloway moved to four-storey premises at 244 Strand, just outside the city of London boundary at Temple Bar, convenient for visiting both the city and the docks. A separate part of the building was No. 243½, which he later took over. Every penny the couple could spare went on advertising, and in the week their only relaxation was an evening stroll down Fleet Street or west to Charing Cross. On fine Sundays, they drove up to Hampstead Heath or occasionally into rural villages by horse-drawn buggy to sell their remedies. According to the *Medical Times*, he was a genuine hypochondriac, often consulting Dr Edward Digby who lived eight doors away in Fleet Street and preferring the doctor's medicines to his own.[30]

To distribute the pills, early on he approached the wholesale agents, Barclay & Sons of Farringdon Street, only to be told, 'Look here, young man, I have 350 articles on my list, and not fifty of them pay their way. Don't throw away your money.'[31] Barclay had earlier sold Albinolo's ointment and therefore had no time for this interloper, who went instead to the smaller and less prestigious Edwards & Co. in St Paul's Churchyard. We do not know when he took on his first employees.

Holloway's incessant quoting of testimonials soon began to rile the doctors. Thomas Wakley (1795–1862), editor of the leading medical journal, *The Lancet*, in October 1840 angrily contested his boast that the remedies were 'patronized by the greatest medical men of the age', nearly two dozen having been listed in one notice alone. Wakley demanded of those named a vigorous rebuttal of the claim, but only two were bold enough to reply. One asserted that he had been 'unwittingly trapped' when Holloway, 'whose outward appearance and demeanour caused me then to mistake him for a gentleman', doorstepped him at his private residence; having tested the ointment and found it wanting, he was 'pestered with repeated letters'. The other practitioner also condemned the ointment as rubbish, and in his reply to the journal deplored 'cunning and worthless adoptions' of extracts from doctors' letters by Holloway and other empirics.[32]

Holloway took all these onslaughts in his stride. By then able to spend £5,000 on advertising a year, in 1842 he induced Dr Richard Bright and the

Earl of Aldborough to swear affidavits commending his remedies before the Lord Mayor of London at the Mansion House. The first-named was widely assumed to be the queen's physician, who discovered Bright's disease, but the actual swearer had been an obscure and inebriated doctor of the same name. The peer, disdained by *The Lancet* as 'a poor, broken-down Irish earl, who in a fit of fantasizing, seems to have taken Holloway as his household god',[33] enthusiastically testified that the pills had corrected a liver and stomach disorder which the mineral waters of Carlsbad and Marienbad had failed to do.

That November the new humorous magazine, *Punch*, which quite as relentlessly pursued nostrum-mongers, joined the fray with a mock lecture, sarcastically observing

> Mr. Holloway, with the modesty which is the invariable attendant on real merit, declares that his 'Universal Ointment' will mend the legs of men and tables equally well, and be found an excellent article for frying fish in.

A few months later the *Edinburgh Review*, in the article on 'The advertising system' that had noted Cockle's lists of patrons, ridiculed Holloway's pretentious linking of his ointment with a passage from Dante's *Inferno*, 'And Time shall see thee cured of every ill'. Moreover, he had 'brought home to the meanest apprehensions' the remedy's 'wonder-working powers' with a representation of Aesculapius, the Roman god of healing, about to distribute pots to a crowd of clearly afflicted souls. Two finely dressed ladies were also shown, one wearing a blue Garter sash inscribed 'Cancer, Burns and Scalds' and the other a red sash of the Order of the Bath, inscribed 'Lumbago, Bunions and Soft Corns'.[34]

By 1845 Holloway could dismiss out of hand such carping, as there was every sign that his firm had turned the corner. In May, he opened an account with Coutts' Bank, exclusive enough to demand good references; his initial deposit was £409 10s., and over the next three years he left balances rising from £443 to £3,192 on transactions which more than trebled in value. Also that year he raised his advertising expenditure to £10,000, and in 1846 he took over 243½ Strand as he needed the extra space. For callers who sought free advice on the spot, he filled in printed forms with recommended quantities of pills to be taken. Later on, he employed a doctor, paying him 8s. (40p) a day for attendance from 11 to 4.

In 1848 he felt that the firm was progressing smoothly enough for him to be away for five months, travelling through Western Europe. His was partly a sightseeing tour, in Jane's company for some of the time, but he also established a number of agencies in the countries he visited, and placed advertisements in sundry newspapers. In charge at home was his brother Henry, who in 1850 walked out and set up a rival pill business further down the Strand. Thomas straightway obtained a court injunction against him; they soon made it up, and Henry stayed as manager until he died of bronchitis in 1874.[35]

For his main clientele Holloway looked to the affluent classes, who could afford 1*s*. 1½*d*. (6p) for 49 pills or ¾ oz. (21 gm.) of ointment; the pills do not appear to have been sold in pennyworths to poorer customers, as Beecham's were to be later on. Thus the former Effie Gray, in the throes of her dispiriting marriage to John Ruskin, was in 1849 taking Holloway's pills as a kind of placebo. Not that Holloway always hit it off with the intelligentsia. When at a subsequent literary and social gathering he asked the journalist, George Augustus Sala, to introduce him to William Makepeace Thackeray, the novelist responded with a very low and stiff bow, and quipped before turning away, 'I hope, Sir, that you will live longer than your patients'. Holloway privately observed to Sala with admirable forbearance, 'That Mr. Thackeray may think himself a very clever man, but I fancy that I could buy him up, ten times over'.[36]

According to the firm's purchases of patent medicine duty stamps, recorded in his Coutts' bank account, in 1851 British sales totalled £18,000. They then rose without interruption to £57,000 in 1856/57, so that its share of total UK demand went up from 10 to 25 per cent. After a slight decline to £49,000 in 1858/59, growth resumed from £58,000 in 1861/62 to £62,000 in 1865/66, when its national share was down to 18 per cent. The meagre amount of information that can be gleaned on exports is given below.[37]

As the pills and ointment were not well made or composed of novel ingredients (see Chapter 6), public demand for Holloway's remedies sprang from his impressive advertising expenditure, which in 1855 reached £30,000: according to that year's *Quarterly Review* a sum 'equal to the entire revenue of many a German principality' and to the combined amounts spent by Alexander Rowland on his Macassar Oil, Elias Moses on his garments and Dr de Jongh on his Cod Liver Oil. Ten years later that figure had reached £40,000. He was thus, according to the *Chemist and Druggist* of 1886, 'the pioneer of the great patent medicine advertising [phenomenon] of the present day', who created 'perhaps *the* characteristic of the century', namely a mass advertising era, and 'the indirect author of the power of the modern press', heavily subsidized as it was by advertisements.[38] Britain's national and local newspapers had proliferated since the advertisement tax was abolished in 1853 and the newspaper stamp duty and one on paper in 1861.

Holloway could not have met such massive sums for publicity without having alternative sources of income. As early as 1853 he had been noted for possessing 'both cash and energy for every speculation that promises large profits'. Later he did very nicely out of buying and selling wines that were

Mr Holloway's handbills, advertisements and placards, were as bald as correct English could be. They stated dogmatically that a certain alphabetical list of diseases could be cured by his medicines, without any carefully compiled semi-scientific treatise on physiology or diagnosis. People who felt out of sorts fitted their complaints to one of the items in the list, and then went and bought the medicine.

His feeble response to the Beecham slogan, 'Worth a Guinea a Box' was that Holloway's remedies were 'of equal value with the coin of the realm'.[45] Sales never grew in proportion to his advertising expenditure because many affluent people already knew who he was, but were not all that keen to purchase the remedies as lacking high or consistent quality.

The statesman, William E. Gladstone, for example, regularly dosed himself, although never with Holloway's pills. As prime minister, in June 1873 he met Holloway for a briefing on the latter's Sanatorium project, but did not scruple to make fun of him just over three years later during a Tory-bashing speech in South Durham. By then in opposition, he launched an attack on ministers for failing to 'serve the national interest and justice', offering them 'a perfect recipe – I may say – which … is as infallible and as sure to answer its purposes as Holloway's pills'.[46] In 1884 Lord Randolph Churchill, then a Conservative MP, got his own back by ridiculing Gladstone as 'the greatest living master of the art of personal political advertisement', so that 'Holloway, Colman [of mustard fame] and Horniman [seller of "pure tea"] are nothing compared to him'.[47]

Holloway died in December 1883, surviving his wife by eight years. People remembered him as a more than life-sized figure. According to a close acquaintance, he 'could not have been said to be the imitation of any man'. Admittedly, many industrial magnates of the day – not least Thomas Beecham – developed their idiosyncratic traits, but Holloway must have been in a category of his own; as the friend continued,

In character he stood alone. Apart from his commanding stature (he stood well over six feet), in conversation he invariably impressed his hearers with the accuracy of his judgment, to the extent that people were not only ready to follow his lead but were anxious to acquire information from him.

Another friend concurred. 'He was a man of very keen perception, and his ability to grasp a subject was a constant source of admiration to his subordinates.' Capable of keeping a number of different issues in his head simultaneously, he would often 'have three or four and occasionally half a dozen people [all male clerks] writing letters at his dictation at the same time'.[48] By contrast, the slower-thinking Thomas Beecham chose to deal with correspondence as a solitary chore.

Although rightly celebrated for his two philanthropic schemes of a Sanatorium and a Women's College, Holloway cannot be ranked among the great Victorian entrepreneurs. The firm he had set up so laboriously bore little chance of long-term survival. His remedies were not made professionally enough to attract the general public well into the future, so that his successor was incapable of reinvigorating a firm that was running down. After his death the former sea-dog, Henry Driver – now Driver-Holloway – took over, cut back on advertising and presided over a steady decline; home sales were only £23,000 in 1903/04, or 1.2 per cent of the national total. In 1930 (see Chapter 11) it was acquired by Beechams Pills Ltd.

A column-length leading article in *The Times*, an unprecedented editorial obituary of a business man, probed with deadly accuracy Holloway's besetting weakness: an obsession with making money.[49] He owed his 'gigantic fortune' mainly to an almost unerring adroitness as a financial speculator 'who well knew what was going on in the world, and who lost no opportunity of turning every incident [whether a great war, a fire or someone's death] to advantage'. Indeed, the leader-writer continued, 'money-making is an art by itself. It demands for success the devotion of the whole man. Sleeping or waking his thoughts must be absolutely surrendered to it.' For Holloway, 'it was the life work of a man who let no chance pass him, and who had a keen eye for the best possible use to which each choice could be put'.

If the author, Lytton Strachey, had known anything about business –which he did not – he could well have chosen Holloway to join Cardinal Manning, Dr Arnold, Florence Nightingale and General Gordon in his *Eminent Victorians* of 1918.[50] Strachey would have relished mocking Holloway's pretentious ways, such as taking pains to conceal his modest origins, and also his eye to the main chance, both as an industrialist and as a financier. There was the irony that his flagrant theft of someone else's recipe for the ointment did him no good in the long run. Having resolutely striven to build up a firm, he so neglected to innovate that in 1883, that firm was valued for probate at no more than £53,000 out of an estate of £720,000.

The source of the remaining Holloway fortune, and his acquisitive single-mindedness were exposed in *The Times* leader quoted above, one written with the kind of brutal candour meted out only to a subject who had left behind neither a widow nor children to threaten to cancel their subscriptions. The ultimate irony was that he had astutely earmarked that wealth for two areas neglected by Victorian philanthropy: a sanatorium for middle-income psychiatric patients, and a college for the further education of women. He impressed people of influence with his good sense, but spurned the openings thus offered him to make a splash in society. The way he conducted his lengthy and hyperactive life possesses a human interest that would have fascinated Strachey.

Whereas Holloway had spent an excessive amount of his time on amassing and then disbursing his wealth, Thomas Beecham concentrated on the making of pills. In the course of regular business travels, he clearly detected the gradual increase in the living standards of many ordinary people. Since the early 1860s, average real wages in Britain had been progressively rising above earlier near-subsistence levels. For the first time, therefore, consumers had money to spare for goods other than the bare necessities of life. Patent medicines were among their foremost demands, to gratify an innate drive for good or improved health.

Table 2.1 *Patent medicine industry-consumers' expenditure*

	UK total consumers' expenditure (£ million)	Consumers' expenditure on patent medicines (£000s)	% of total spent on patent medicines
1803	–	300	–
1813	–	376	–
1823	–	349	–
1833	419	345	0.08
1843	441	260	0.06
1853	605	379	0.06
1863	792	469	0.06
1873	1,123	898	0.08
1883	1,190	1,433	0.12
1893	1,310	1,919	0.15
1903	1,699	2,911	0.17
1913	2,070	3,243	0.16

UK total expenditure. B. R. Mitchell, *British Historical Statistics* (Cambridge: Cambridge University Press, 1988), pp. 831–3.

Patent medicine expenditure. PP, *First Report of Commissioners of Inland Revenue*, 1857 IV, p. 215 and subsequent reports. Patent medicine tax receipts multiplied by 9 (see Chapter 2, note 3).

In 1860–64, spending in Britain on these remedies was on average no higher, in relation to consumers' expenditure nationally, than it had been in 1835, at 0.06 per cent. Half a century later, that proportion had more than doubled. As Table 2.1 shows, in 1913 the money value of patent medicines sold in Britain was over eight and a half times that of 1853. Massive financial rewards awaited the manufacturer who could tap into that emerging market by offering remedies that were made with care and imaginatively advertised. At a time when Holloway was allowing his attention to be diverted elsewhere, Thomas Beecham single-mindedly strove to gain the industry's leadership. It remained to be seen whether his Smilesian application and innovative gifts were powerful enough to carry off that risky and toilsome feat.

3

From workshop to factory,
1865–1882

I N 1865 Britain's patent medicine industry, of which Thomas Beecham was now a member, had – according to the multiplied estimates from the medicine duty returns – a home turnover of just under £370,000. That year, his own sales of £2,223 contributed less than half of one per cent to the nation's total. As Table 3.1 shows, by 1881 he had increased sales to £28,374, an average annual rise of about a fifth to nearly 2 per cent of the total; figures for 1882 have not survived. Between 1865 and 1881 (see Chapter 2). Thomas Holloway's share of the country's domestic output, meanwhile, declined from 18 to 8 per cent. Over those years, the Morison firm's sales also fell; because its pills had lost much of their popularity, it diversified into an ointment and also into a lemonade powder. Its 'College of Health' later squandered resources on a costly and futile campaign against compulsory vaccination.[1]

Thomas Beecham was thus making headway against his rivals, at a time when regular increases in ordinary people's wages were creating a new surge in demand for patent medicines (see Chapter 2). To assist him in their labours, he had his son Joseph, reliable enough to allow him some freedom to roam. They manufactured the pills in batches, so that after perhaps a number of makes, Thomas could go on his travels round the kingdom by the rapidly expanding railway network, to visit wholesale agents. Earlier on, retail outlets could order directly from him; now he instructed any of those submitting orders to go through a local wholesaler. Kershaw of Southport's name does not appear in the firm's subsequent sales records.

From the beginning of 1865, Thomas introduced a new system of order books, kept together with the cash books.[2] They noted the wholesale value of each order received, the date when payment was made, the discount allowed, and special features such as bad debts. The corresponding workshop ledger recorded the number of boxes of each size required. The neat and rather mannered handwriting in the order book was that of Joseph, while Thomas wrote up the ledger himself.

At the outset, their clerical work was not heavy. In 1865 they received a little over 400 wholesale orders, from a total of 98 agents in 50 localities. As shown in Table 3.2, just over half of those orders came from the north of England, mainly the towns in Lancashire and Cheshire within easy reach of

Table 3.1   *Beecham's turnover, 1865–81*

	Gross turnover (£)	% increase (on previous year)	Discount given (%)	Net turnover (£)	% increase (on previous year)
1865	2,533	–	12.2	2,223	–
1866	3,511	38.6	12.5	3,072	38.1
1867	4,556	29.8	12.8	3,973	29.3
1868	5,818	27.7	13.1	5,056	27.3
1869	8,200	40.9	13.4	7,101	40.4
1870	9,402	14.7	13.7	8,114	14.3
1871	11,089	17.9	14.0	9,537	17.5
1872	12,956	16.8	14.3	11,103	16.4
1873	14,630	12.9	14.6	12,494	12.5
1874	16,339	11.7	14.9	13,888	11.2
1875	18,593	13.8	15.2	15,767	13.5
1876	19,913	7.1	15.5	16,826	6.7
1877	23,023	15.6	15.8	19,385	15.2
1878	24,544	6.6	16.1	20,592	6.2
1879	25,132	2.4	16.4	21,010	2.0
1880	28,640	14.0	16.6	23,886	13.7
1881	34,162	19.2	16.9	28,374	18.8

BA, Ledger, 'Pills sent out' 1865–73, BP 3/1/1, 1873–81, BP 3/1/2. Discounts assumed to have risen in a linear way between 1865 and 1881.

Table 3.2   *Destinations of Beecham's turnover, 1865 and 1881*

	1865 (%)	1881 (%)
London	38	47
North of England (excluding Liverpool)	31	17
Liverpool	21	15
Midlands	5	5
South of England (excluding London)	4	3
Scotland	1	12
Northern Ireland	-	1
	100	100

St Helens; very small quantities sold in two towns, Dalbeattie and Dumfries, just over the Scottish border. Of the northern sales one fifth were through Liverpool firms, such as Raines & Co. and the earlier mentioned wholesale druggists, Evans, Sons & Co.

The remaining country-wide half went to agents in the Midlands and southern England. London accounted for 38 per cent; the most prominent wholesalers in the capital were Barclay & Sons of Farringdon Street – who had rejected Holloway (see Chapter 2) – and William Sutton & Co. of Bow Churchyard. For his own reasons he chose certain Midland towns such as Coventry and Dudley, but not Birmingham, and some in the south, including Cambridge, Cinderford, Exeter and St Ives, while by-passing Oxford. He supported some of these wholesalers with advertising out of the meagre £328 he could afford that year.

As long as Thomas could spare so little for publicity, the only sure way he had of reaching out to markets far and wide was to offer very sizeable discounts. Those amounted to 32 per cent on the 9½d. (4p) boxes, nearly 30 per cent on the standard 1s. 1½d. (6p) size and 24 per cent on the 2s. 9d. (14p) size. He allowed a further discount to the largest wholesalers, on whose efforts he relied for future considerable growth. They would scarcely have given Beecham's pills a second thought when he had started up in Wigan; now his agents in London accepted an extra 20 per cent and those elsewhere 15 or 10 per cent, making a national average of 12 per cent. Some of them therefore enjoyed discounts totalling more than a half off the retail price; all had to meet the cost of carriage. Thomas rigidly enforced resale price maintenance.

Such lavish inducements did not encourage wholesalers to settle their accounts at all quickly. Many producers of ordinary consumption goods then had to spend a great deal of time on the road to collect debts or else issue face-to-face warnings; Thomas undoubtedly found that to be an essential task during his visits round the country. Early in 1865 he often had to wait six months for payment, occasionally accepting in lieu the free placing of advertisements in newspapers or almanacs. By the end of the year, his persistent battles with offenders had reduced the delay to an average of one to three months: doubtless a signal to all concerned that he was someone to be reckoned with.

Sales through the hatch of the workshop shed or by mail order began to dwindle in importance as soon as wholesalers' demand began to take off. He must have produced 3–3½ million pills in 1865; say an average of 58,000 a week or nearly 1,000 hourly in a ten-hour day, but even more at times owing to his batch production system. The amount of handle-turning and box filling was clearly formidable. For the teenager Joseph that remorseless pressure, on top of keeping the order books, drove him almost to the edge. 'I used to work until midnight and rise each morning at 5 to be at my desk at 5.30', perhaps an hour before beginning production, he later confessed. As a placebo, he used to take five or six pills regularly; in the later, more ordered, periods of his life he made do with one pill from time to time.[3]

Also in 1865 Thomas began a series of correspondence books, now lost; he copied all letters or memos by hand as he refused all secretarial help. These must have averaged about 500 a year; in 1884 (see Chapter 4) he had reached No. 9924. When Joseph was 18, in June 1866, Thomas for the first time disclosed the formulae of the pills to him.

The annual production figures for this period and the main destinations of pills in 1865 and 1881, in Tables 3.1 and 3.2, are from the order books that have survived only for that run of years. Advertising expenditure rose seventeen-fold, from £328 in 1865 to nearly £5,700 in 1881, but yielded only a twelvefold increase in turnover. The Beecham name still meant little to the general public, and wholesalers – who often sold rival brands as well – did not find it easy to cajole retailers into taking up their pill orders. As an spur to greater effort, Thomas was later compelled to increase the already generous discounts, which ate into his own profits. As shown below, in 1881 the average discount on wholesale terms was therefore raised to nearly 17 per cent. Still determined to keep clerical work to a minimum, he insisted on holding as few wholesale accounts as possible, which in 1881 were no higher than 111, compared with the 98 of 1865. In the later year they submitted 786 – almost double the previous 400 – orders, but Thomas was encouraged that the average size of orders had risen sevenfold from £6.25 to £43.50.

In 1866–69 sales grew by as much as one-third a year on average, so that by 1869 as many as 10 million pills were being turned out, or nearly 7,000 per hour. To speed up production, in 1868 he installed power machinery, perhaps in the next-door cottage he had recently acquired; that year he engaged his first employee, the 24-year-old Walter Robert Andrews, born in Bath and later to become works manager. As a rising businessman, in 1870 for the first time he made use of a St Helens solicitor, the 22-year-old Henry Oppenheim, perhaps to assist with the time-consuming task of collecting debts.

Two years later, in a letter to an acquaintance in Australia, Thomas Giles who had formerly been a fellow labourer in Cropredy, he boasted, 'I have the best machinery of anyone known (all works by steam power): the most effective part of it is my own construction' (see Chapter 6). He cheerily informed his acquaintance, 'If you could just step into my workshop at the end of a day when we are making [pills], you would wonder who in the world was going to take them all. I often make over a hundredweight in one day.'[4] That would have totalled 450,000 pills, and was a pardonable fib.

When he needed more juvenile hands, Thomas put up a notice outside the workshop, saying: 'WANTED, Two Sharp, Active, Trustworthy LADS, about 14 years of age', who would be expected to show precisely the kinds of quality he himself had displayed in his youth. The next known employee, the 12-year-old William Moss, joined the firm in 1872, when there were seven lads in all. Moss was engaged after submitting a manuscript version of the Lord's Prayer, written in Gothic script at the local Sunday school, which earned him a job as a packer.[5] Thomas Oldham came at the age of 11 in 1874, initially being employed on odd jobs. Nine years later he was appointed Joseph's coachman.

A St Helens directory of 1876 grandly named Joseph as the firm's 'assistant chemist', but the additional employees must have gone some way towards reducing his more routine labours. In 1869 he had joined the St Helens Cricket Club,[6] and in the musical season he travelled whenever he could to Liverpool, where he occupied a shilling balcony seat at the opera. He inherited a life-long enthusiasm for music from his Welsh-born mother, who had a good singing voice and somehow found the money for his piano lessons out of the tight household budget. He played the harmonium at a local school, and later became organist at two churches. Thomas, unlike his Holloway rival, never showed any interest whatever in musical matters.

It was through this involvement in music that, after several romantic disappointments, Joseph was able to woo Josephine Burnett, whom he had met in the home of mutual friends. Whereas Joseph had reddish hair and grey eyes, hers were both dark; she resembled both him and Thomas in being small-sized. No doubt through deception, Josephine sought to conceal her origins, claiming to have been born in Lille, into the French Bohan family that was of Spanish stock. Her marriage certificate gave her father as William Burnett, a silk dealer; according to family tradition he combined that job with a barber's business in St Helens. Yet Census records and the absence of his name in the town's directory for this period make it clear that he never existed, and the certificate of her birth, in Everton, Liverpool, left her father's name blank (See Appendix 1, on Sir Thomas Beecham's ancestry).

Josephine's mother, Martha Dickens (1819–95), had been born in St John, New Brunswick, Canada, the daughter of a sergeant in the 40th Regiment of Foot.[7] Henry (not William) Burnett was apparently the father of two sons as well as Josephine, all born between 1845 and 1850 and registered – also baptized in Manchester Cathedral – with no father named. Whatever may have happened to Henry Burnett, in 1851 Charles Bowen – not Bohan – a warehouseman, appeared on the scene, fathering three sons and two daughters with Martha. In the 1861 Census, when she and her children were living in Liscard, near Birkenhead in Cheshire, she described herself as a widow and milliner.

Martha as an adult seems to have resembled Geoffrey Chaucer's Wife of Bath, in *The Canterbury Tales*, for her unconventional sexual behaviour, as well as her interest in dress and dressmaking. Although the Bathonian lady owned to having had five husbands, no marriage of Martha's with either a Burnett or a Bowen has been recorded. Her modest social status can be seen from her sons' later occupations, of bookkeeper, upholsterer, joiner and cabinet maker.

Josephine was trained as a dressmaker, and learned to play the piano and to sing well; by 1871 the (still) widowed Martha and five of her children were living in Croppers Hill, which joined Westfield Street with the Prescot Road on the south-west side of St Helens. Thomas Beecham, who later moved to the same thoroughfare, did not care for Josephine, whom he found to be stuck-up, and he disapproved of the marriage, which nevertheless took place in April 1873, without his being present. The couple took up residence in a modest house – remembered as 'poky' – in Westfield Street, all too near the pill workshop.

The tangled web of truth and misrepresentation presented here and in the Appendix, of a kind that occasionally plagues family historians, would be of limited public interest had Josephine not been the future mother of twentieth-century Britain's most eminent performing musician. How much Joseph knew of her chequered past is not known; yet when much later he openly humiliated her, for being of low birth, in London's Probate and Divorce Court (see Chapter 7), he said nothing about her family background.[8]

Thomas's personal life was also transformed that same year. Since the household break-up he had managed contentedly with a 28-year-old live-in housekeeper, the widowed Mary Price from Stafford, and a maid in her teens. Then his estranged wife Jane died suddenly in August 1872, aged not quite 60, of 'habitual intemperance' according to the inquest verdict. He had never forgiven her for having brought about their enforced departure from Wigan, although since then that ill wind had blown him any amount of good. In point of fact, he owed Jane more than he ever admitted. As his biographer, Anne Francis, has written, she 'had provided Thomas with the sheet anchor of a home at a period in his life when it was most vital to have one';[9] otherwise he might have continued to combine peddling his wares with casual labour.

Thomas, who did not marry his housekeeper, remained a widower for less than six months. On one of his regular visits to the wholesale houses in London, he encountered Sarah Pemberton, a milliner residing in the capital's Blackfriars Road. They married in January 1873. She was 29 to his 52; perhaps significantly, he never bothered to inform his Oxfordshire relatives of his new wife. She bore him no children, and latterly – as Jane also seems to have done – suffered from hallucinations and screaming fits at night. After little more than four years of marriage, in May 1877 she died, the cause of death being recorded as uraemia. His insistence on behaving as he pleased, and disdain for the opinions of others, inevitably provoked local gossip that he had poisoned her.

While the poison charge is completely unfounded, Sarah's decline and death took place at a critical juncture for him, just when he had little time to spare for her. He later revealed that it was in the mid-1870s that the firm began to prosper and he earned enough to advertise more freely; yet (he added) he had to feel his way as publicity was such an 'expensive matter'.[10]

Indeed, although turnover rose without a break from £9,500 in 1871 to nearly £24,000 in 1880, Thomas cut back on advertising expenditure between 1872 and 1875, down to £1,250 a year on average as against £1,350 in 1871. He was busy purchasing houses adjoining his workshop in Westfield Street, as they became available or he could induce the owners to sell. He may also have skimped on the housekeeping in his own home, which doubtless saw little of him.

By 1877 – when Sarah was dying of her kidney disease – he owned enough land to plan a purpose-built factory, completed that year. Of necessity he made it utilitarian and without 'frills'. Entered through a high arched gateway, it was a long single-storey building, with large windows high up to yield adequate light. No views have survived to show how bare the interior was, but the time-keeper had to put up with a lodge that was scarcely more than a lean-to shed. The counting-house and office could well have been equally spartan. His only luxury was a square tower, crowned with a witch's cap shaped spire; from its gallery he could look down on the packing sheds at the rear.[11]

In that year of 1877 production was up by over a seventh compared with 1876. The increases in output over the next few years were more modest; then heavy advertising, of £4,600 in 1880 and £5,700 in 1881, rising to £7,000 in 1882, helped to boost the firm's turnover in 1881 to the £28,000 quoted above. Although some extra hands were taken on, they numbered only 18 in 1882. Andrews was appointed the first works manager, with William Moss as his deputy. Thomas insisted on the utmost cleanliness in the factory. He must have found ways of excluding the fume-laden atmosphere in that low-lying and congested central area of St Helens, described in Chapter 1. Perhaps the prevailing wind carried the vapours clear of the factory.

That was not his only preoccupation at the time. He was also having a new residence, Hill House, built in its own grounds at Croppers Hill, and moved in just a month or two after his wife's death. Only fifteen minutes' brisk walk from the factory, its situation was clear of the town's air pollution, but it set him that distance apart from the business. He was following the example of many industrial pioneers who in that decade were separating themselves from the vicinity of their works. Joseph benefited also, as before the end of 1877 he, his wife and two daughters – another had died – took possession of a larger house, complete with stables and an extensive dining-room, in Westfield Street next door to the factory.

All these changes created a new and more structured regime in Joseph's life, granting him additional leisure, so that in 1876 he was co-founder of the St Helens Cycling Club, its 80 members making it into the largest in England outside London. When on the road, they maintained an almost martial discipline, something that must have suited the routine-loving Joseph.[12] Whether or not he often went out for a spin, his still demanding business and family commitments limited the time he could devote to the sport. However, four years later the 25-year-old Charles Rowed joined the club and he and Joseph became close friends.

Of Anglo-American descent, Rowed had been born at Lymington, Hampshire, in 1855, the son of a surveyor and valuer. As he disclosed in a book on antiques he wrote much later, he had spent seven years as a choir-boy in Winchester Cathedral, being boarded at the bishop's palace there; he sang at the enthronement in 1869 of Bishop Samuel Wilberforce. He did not explain how he had come to St Helens, or where he was initially employed in the town. At any rate, his knowledge of both music and publicity methods impressed Joseph, who soon took him on as his private secretary. Rowed had enough confidence in the firm and its prospects to spend the rest of his working life there.[13]

How Joseph and Josephine as a newish married couple got on with her mother is not known. However, if Martha Bowen was still living in Croppers Hill, within easy walking distance of Westfield Street, she may have irritated them, or at least him, by frequent dropping in to see her grandchildren. In April 1879, when Josephine's first son Thomas – who became Sir Thomas Beecham – was born, she already had three living daughters. Then in July Martha, her two sons George Burnett and Eugene Bowen, plus a one-year-old unnamed Bowen infant, sailed as emigrants from Liverpool to Melbourne in Australia.

Their vessel, the 1,190-ton Liverpool-registered *Greta*, a three-masted sailing ship with figurehead and square sails, carried 39 passengers in all. Having taken 14 weeks, it docked in Melbourne at the end of October.[14] As their passages were not assisted by public funds, it is tempting to assume that Joseph paid their fares in order to remove his in-laws from the neighbourhood. He could easily have afforded the expense, as sales had doubled since the early 1870s, about half representing profit.

In 1881, with a net turnover of £28,000, the firm must have manufactured about 46 million pills, compared with some 3–3½ million in 1865. The altered destinations of its output by then, set out in Table 3.2, show how Thomas's policy of attracting the large wholesalers with heavy discounts had paid off. London's share had risen from 38 to 47 per cent since 1865: in cash terms from £950 to almost £16,000, no doubt at the expense of longer-established competitors' sales.

In the capital there were no fewer than 20 Beecham outlets; Edwards and Newbery (celebrated for marketing Dr James's Fever Powder), both of St Paul's Churchyard, had now joined the well-known houses of Barclay and of Sutton. The contribution of Liverpool had declined from 21 to 15 per cent, and that of the rest of northern England from 31 to 17 per cent. The Midlands and the south of England outside London together accounted for less than a tenth of sales. As to Scotland, Beecham by then had accounts in Edinburgh and Glasgow, which raised that country's share from 1 to 12 per cent.

Among the more noteworthy wholesalers in 1881 was Goodall Backhouse & Co. of Leeds, maker of the Yorkshire Relish. That year its orders to St Helens, valued at £3,200, made it the largest single customer apart from Barclay in London. Lewis's of Liverpool ordered £850 worth of pills for its Bon Marché-type department store and £250 worth for its emporium in Manchester. However, it insisted on selling to customers at below the fixed price. When taken to court by a local retail chemist, Lewis's asserted that its profit mark-up was only 10 per cent on the £20,000 or more drug sales it made annually. Thomas did not act against these stores' breach of his rule about resale price maintenance, nor against Jesse Boot of Nottingham, the founder of Boots the Chemists, who also defiantly cut its prices; Boot's orders in 1881 came only to £110.[15]

In 1881–82 the private lives of Beecham father and son changed dramatically, and those changes, although unrelated in origin, were between them to have a momentous effect on the firm's future progress. Mary Sawell, Thomas's third and last wife, and Helen Mackie Taylor, Joseph's mistress who remained loyal to him after his death, both have significant indirect roles in the Beecham annals.

It was in 1879 that Thomas, this time a widower for two years, married again. He had encountered Mary by chance that August on Banbury station, while returning from his half-brother's funeral in Oxfordshire; she also had relatives close by, having been born in that county. Normally taking little note of other people, Thomas made an exception in the case of nubile women who appeared worth the effort of chatting up. He seems to have got to know all three wives by accosting them as strangers, and in the 1870s it was by no means common for a lone woman of unsullied reputation – and Mary was nothing if not respectable – to be successfully engaged in conversation with a strange man on a country railway platform. Smitten with ardour for 'the prettiest woman he ever saw', he missed his rail connection; so did she, and they ended that fateful day chastely occupying separate rooms in a Banbury hotel.

Their subsequent courtship, boosted by fervent promises of gifts, can be truthfully described as a whirlwind one. Within a month, in September 1879 they were married in Christ Church, on the Croppers Hill side of St Helens, by Anglican rites although he had been a Congregationalist since moving to the town, until then regularly attending chapel in Ormskirk Street. He was just short of his sixtieth birthday and she was almost 28.

Mary's father had been a shoemaker who became a road-building contractor, and the aunt who reared her was apparently at one time housekeeper to the Archbishop of Canterbury. Since the age of 17, she had been married and then widowed no fewer than three times, remaining childless, and there was also a broken engagement. That rarely equalled *curriculum vitae* gave her a knowledge of men which the unambitious Jane and the colourless Sarah had conspicuously lacked. What the smartly dressed Mary saw in this diminutive man with hairy face, untidy rustic clothes – including paper collars – and perpetually damp lips could only be his money and gift of the gab. Thomas, in his turn, should have heeded the signs of her all too obvious independence of mind.

Despite finding St Helens, even viewed from Croppers Hill, an extremely poor substitute for her accustomed southern environs, Mary stuck it out for over a year and a half. Joseph got on surprisingly well with the stepmother who was three years his junior, but Josephine and she could scarcely have had anything in common. In April 1881 Mary had her younger brother to stay, but she could not have relished having to share her home with Jennie Murray, an unmarried lass of 22 from Scotland, described in that year's Census as a 'pill-maker's assistant'.

Whether or not because of Jennie, soon afterwards Mary began to voice her displeasure with St Helens. No doubt it was Joseph who persuaded the doctors to advise Thomas that, if his health and their marriage were to survive, he must take a prolonged rest-cure in the more salubrious atmosphere of England's southern counties. Within a few months the pair left St Helens, which Mary never saw again. They took temporary lodgings in the south while they house-hunted.

Thomas then bought 120 acres (nearly 50 hectares) of land in the Buckinghamshire village of Mursley, almost equidistant from Bletchley and Winslow, and built a mansion costing £10,000. They moved in during the autumn. Thomas's final act, before departing in December 1880, had been to raise the firm's wholesale prices. That fixed the discount on pills at 15 per cent, but granted an extra 5 per cent to many larger agents. Although the average worked out at nearly 17 per cent, turnover in 1881 rose by almost a fifth compared with 1880.[16]

Over the past three decades, Thomas had never relaxed his control over the firm for long, spending only short periods away on business tours or visits to Oxfordshire relatives. Although between visits he expected to be consulted by correspondence over all questions, it was Joseph who held the reins as the one on the spot. While still no more than a salaried manager, at last he had the chance of running the business on his own.

Yet Joseph then seemed unlikely ever to shine as an entrepreneur, or be more than a dogged follower of established routines. Observers of the day were fond of stressing that in British family firms the second generation seldom matched up to the first. As Alfred Marshall wrote in his *Principles of Economics*, published in 1890, businessmen's sons started off with significant advantages, both in receiving 'almost the only perfect apprenticeship of the day' and in being surrounded by a 'well-chosen staff of subordinates with a generous interest in the business'. Yet, Marshall continued, the son and to a greater extent the grandsons would have had a pampered upbringing and be distracted by a hankering for social or other kinds of advancement.[17] This generalization was to have some relevance to the history of the Beecham firm, but not yet.

Joseph had never been at all pampered in his formative years. Instead, his father's overbearing manner had left him with a crippling self-doubt and an incapacity to disclose his inner thoughts. A joyless and at times violent childhood had been marked by parental wrangling, his mother's intemperance and family breakdown. Music, cycling and possibly cricket yielded him some, but not much, escape from the stifling atmosphere of blinkered provincial life.

His own marriage in 1873, some months after his mother's death, had promised to be a liberating experience. Indeed, he and his wife may have shared genuine happiness for a while. But Josephine, for all her good qualities – and no bad woman could have put up for long with a Beecham of those generations – was pretentious and apt to put on airs despite her narrow horizons. Coming from a prolific family – her mother had at least eight children – she bore him a child every eighteen months on average; by 1881 she had had four daughters – two deceased – as well as Thomas. Whether or not Joseph acknowledged his responsibility for her pregnancies, the mounting burden of children and demand for pills alike locked him into a stultifying and ever more onerous routine, enjoying all too little proper solace at home.

Then in 1882 there occurred the second dramatic event, which in conjunction with Thomas's recent marriage and move to the south would propel the firm in a new direction. Joseph, like his father, was obsessively drawn towards women; at the age of 34, some time that year he chanced to entertain in his house the Scottish-born Helen Taylor.[18] Like Thomas, Helen had had to make her way in the world with no advantages whatever. Named after an illiterate grandmother, she was born in an impoverished district of Montrose, a shipmaster's daughter, being brought up by an aunt in New York until the age of thirteen. Her subsequent life remains a mystery until that enchanted evening. At twenty-two, she passed herself off as eighteen, and to avoid awkward questions falsely claimed to have been born at sea, changing her middle name from Mackie to the more distinctive McKey.

A victim of the nine-year matrimonial itch, the infatuated Joseph soon found himself embroiled in an affair with her. Besides impacting on the domestic arrangements of his own family, her arrival on the scene would soon transform his character. Her cosmopolitan and unconventional view of life was for him refreshingly different from the one he encountered at home, and went far towards releasing his creative energies. To be sure, she never turned him into an extrovert, and he continued to find it difficult to communicate with all but a few select people, ones who did not further reduce his already low self-esteem. Yet from 1882 onwards he became a decisive entrepreneur. As he later observed, 'My father thought he had reached the acme [or zenith of commercial success], but I knew very well that he hadn't'.[19] Later in the decade, he was to make the most of this newly acquired self-confidence.

4

New factory and bold marketing, 1882–1895

FOR A YEAR OR MORE after taking possession of Mursley Hall in the autumn of 1881, Thomas Beecham and his third wife Mary lived there in tolerable harmony. Thomas had originally intended to travel up to the factory once a month, via the rail connection with the London and North-Western line at Bletchley, five miles away. However, he soon threw himself with characteristic energy into the regulation of his new kingdom, even down to purchasing shrubs and selling off timber. He created a home farm in part of the estate and also took up country pursuits such as horse-riding and hunting, although not so enthusiastically as Mary, with the Buckinghamshire Stag Hounds.

The initial procession of friends and relatives to the hall soon dried up, put off either by Thomas's unwelcoming attitude to outsiders, or by his dreadful table manners, which involved shovelling in food whenever he felt hungry as a labourer might, frequently without even sitting down. The resulting absence of company only made their relationship that much more difficult. Apparently indulged by earlier husbands, Mary had a restless and capricious nature, and Thomas was the last person to put himself out to organize diversions for her. Instead, once the estate was running smoothly and rural life began to pall, he started wandering off for days and weeks at a time, sometimes to St Helens but often elsewhere, much to Mary's irritation as he seldom troubled to tell her where he was going.

Without him their large mansion, cut off from the rest of the world by a long drive, was a lonely place; yet life became even less bearable for her when he was at home and finding little enough to do. Unlike Thomas Holloway, he loathed domestic pets, and revolted Mary, an animal lover, by kicking her dogs. Once, when thrown by one of his horses, he rode and rode it until it collapsed and died. Frequent quarrels also broke out over her extravagance with money, and about his infidelities, all too predictable as she apparently refused to have sex with him.[1] A local vicar is said to have rebuked him about this time when he collected from the station a pram for his illegitimate child. Thomas silenced him by bellowing that the divine command was to be fruitful and multiply.[2]

Then Mary accused him of having tried to poison her by giving her two pills when she complained of feeling off-colour; she had to bring herself round with a diet of chicken and champagne. That incident proved to be the breaking-point, and in 1884 she left Mursley for good, being paid off with a lump sum – which she insisted on taking from the plentiful cash she knew he kept in his roll-top desk – and a yearly allowance. Joseph, all too aware of his father's failings as a husband, remained on friendly terms with her, making her alimony a charge on the firm after Thomas died in 1907. She then married her one-time fiancé, Colonel Hector, and they lived not far from Thomas's native village of Curbridge. Having clocked up no fewer than five husbands, she died childless in 1937, aged 85, and left nearly £4,700.

Thomas was back at St Helens by December 1884, when he wrote memo No. 9924 awarding the printers, McCorquodale & Co. Ltd of nearby Newton-le-Willows, a two-year contract for handbills, clearly the printed directions inserted in every box.[3] Without specifying the total print run, he requested the first million no later than Christmas, three weeks ahead: enough for four or six months' supplies as 2–3 million boxes were being sold each year.

By that date, Beecham was poised to become the industry leader. Thomas Holloway had died just a year before, when his annual patent medicine sales were probably about £94,000, those of Beecham being a little short of £79,000. Because Holloway's products were poorly fashioned, in an effort to maintain its market share his firm had relied on ever more extravagant levels of advertising, which its new managers were soon afterwards compelled to scale down drastically. In 1889 the value of Beecham's total output would be as high as £162,000, or an estimated two and a half times that of Holloway.

Joseph, now effectively in charge at St Helens, was responsible for more than doubling turnover in the intervening six years of 1884–89. The firm's prospects for the future encouraged him to plan Beecham's three major innovations of the decade: the construction of a new and far more impressive factory, the launching of publicity on an unprecedented scale, and the promotion of direct exports. The last-named overseas ventures are related in Chapter 5.

To keep up with the ever mounting demand, future extensions of the St Helens factory were sorely needed; that realization must have set off Thomas's recent buying spree of adjacent property. However, Joseph – by then artful enough to plant ideas in his obstinate father's head, in such a way that Thomas came to believe them as his own – secured his agreement not to enlarge the existing works but to start afresh. Thomas held out for rebuilding on the spot rather than moving to a new site; because production had to be transferred to temporary premises in nearby Lowe Street, building work took its time, and the factory was not completed until late in 1887. A rearing, or topping-out, dinner took place that November to reward the whole construction team; the 44-year-old Andrews as works manager headed the usual crop of congratulatory speech-makings.[4]

As sections of the factory became ready for occupation, the numbers of employees rose from 18 in 1882 to 26 in January 1885, 56 in August 1886, and 75 by end–1887. Turnover, £28,000 in 1881, was up to £79,200 in 1885 and to nearly £178,600 net of tax in 1890, when a total of 250 million pills were made for sale at home and overseas: almost wholly the digestive kind, as only 7 million were to treat coughs.[5]

In every detail, the new building reflected Joseph's innovatory ideas. Whereas the earlier factory had been frankly utilitarian, its replacement was architect-designed on a grandiose scale, covering 1,600 square yards (just under 1,350 square metres) on three frontages. Hugh V. Krolow, of Krolow & May, Liverpool and St Helens, has no other claim whatever to celebrity, and the style he chose, while pleasing to the eye, was totally predictable. For a couple of decades, fashion in British architecture generally had been dominated by what was known as progressive eclecticism. Architects offered their clients a style from the past, and then modified basic designs so as to incorporate the latest construction technology. In their commercial buildings at least, the Victorians did not strive to be too artistically purist.[6]

Krolow's design turned out to be a quite respectable pastiche of the Queen Anne style, which Thomas admired, having married his second wife Sarah in the genuinely Queen Anne-period – actually dating from 1740 – Christ Church, Southwark. Costing £30,000, it was in red brick and stone. Joseph from his own money splashed out nearly £1,000 on the factory's most prominent feature, a 150 ft high tower, with four clock faces and Cambridge chimes sounding every quarter of an hour. Perhaps at Thomas's prompting, the witch's-hat tower was retained, despite barely harmonizing with the rest of the structure.

Full particulars about the factory and its workings come mainly from a 36-page pamphlet, 'A familiar name', issued by the firm in 1891. Ostensibly the work of a (fictitious) MP, escorted round by an unusually articulate Joseph Beecham, it featured a number of interior and exterior photographic views as well as some of the more noteworthy advertisements. We learn about the flamboyance that Joseph permitted himself in the lavishly designed entrance hall, made to look larger by containing only a few pieces of walnut furniture and some sculptures. The decorated mosaic on the floor, the patterned ceiling hung with electric light pendants and dado were intended to impress, as were the elaborate staircase of polished mahogany, fitted with blue Persian carpeting, and the upper walls lined with coloured marble.

A commissionaire, usually an ex-army sergeant, required all visitors to fill in forms. While waiting to see Joseph or Charles Rowed – who dealt with all commercial matters – they were given the daily papers to read or magazines portraying celebrities to glance at, and were invited to step on to an automatic weighing machine, almost certainly of American make, and often lent out to charity bazaars. The emerging tickets recorded their weight and the current date: a useful face-saver for casual callers at the factory who were denied admission to the building itself.[7]

Those fortunate enough to be granted an interview were escorted up the staircase to the main offices, where both Joseph and Rowed had their own spacious rooms with roll-top desks. Joseph's office was adorned with a walnut wood cornice and sculptured reliefs; he sensibly preferred a solid-fuel stove in the centre of his office to an open coal fire. Whereas he hung only one picture on the otherwise bare wall, Rowed decorated his room with framed copies of favourite advertisements. Next door was an anteroom with a stained glass window, displaying landscape and marine views, and a visitors' book on the window ledge.

Behind these conventionally eye-catching features, Joseph had some highly innovative notions. He took an active interest in developing the use of electricity. As chairman of the St Helens Electricity Committee he was the first to bring to the town from America knowledge about that form of energy, so that tariffs there were among the country's lowest; the factory was claimed to be the earliest in Britain to have electricity. Its technical aspects are discussed in Chapter 6.

To make the firm as self-contained as possible, he set up a fully equipped printing office, while a carpenter's shop made the crates for large overseas shipments and constructed the hoardings for outdoor displays. Both of these activities took place away from the factory proper, and sections of the old premises were retained to hold stocks of ingredients, in case the factory or warehouse should be burnt down, although only one, swiftly extinguished, fire is known to have occurred.

The pill boxes had originally been made by Robinson & Sons of Chesterfield, but proved to be unsatisfactory because the lids would not fit tightly enough. As no British maker had sufficiently advanced machinery, Joseph imported boxes, made of white birch, from an unnamed New England supplier in the United States, 80 gross at a time arriving in pinewood containers.[8] By the early 1890s, annual requirements of boxes had more than doubled over the previous decade to 5–6 million.

Thomas Beecham did not have a large office of his own but instead found a hideaway, from which he emerged in a yellowing frock coat to take his turn with mixing the pill masses and to potter about the factory as he saw fit. The press magnate, (Sir) Albert Stephenson, once happened to meet Thomas in Liverpool, and returned with him to St Helens, where

Stephenson owned the local newspaper. Thomas invited him to lunch in the factory, which had no canteen. When Stephenson began to wonder where the lunch was coming from, Thomas sent out for a bottle of champagne, a luxury of his now that he could afford it, and produced a couple of buns from his coat pocket.[9]

By then, Joseph must have been earning a good salary; together with the other senior managers he received a share of the profits. In the summer of 1885, just before his house in Westfield Street was due to be demolished, in company with Josephine and four children he moved by landau to the village of Huyton, six miles away. Set in 13 acres (5 hectares) of mostly cultivated land, their new residence, named Ewanville, was square and cream-painted. Having its own generator, it was supposed to be the earliest private house in England to be lit by electricity, and boasted a central heating system.

He added a west wing as a nursery, separated by a gate beyond which the younger children were not allowed to go. He thus effectively shut himself off from them. His daily routine was to take the morning train from Huyton to St Helens, so as to converse with business acquaintances along the way, usually accompanied by an old sheepdog which had its own kennel at the factory. In the evenings, he was driven home by Oldham, his coachman.

Josephine for the first time had a bedroom and suite to herself, and acted as her own housekeeper. She treated the reception rooms, and over-ornamented dining room, as her territory now that she could entertain in style. Joseph was most at home in the billiard room, where he installed a Swiss-made orchestrion, or electrically operated super-organ, with gilded pipes and brazen glass-enclosed trumpets. To reproduce Beethoven and Mozart symphonies and selections from his favourite operas, it used perforated player-piano rolls. His son Thomas, already precocious in a sophisticated grasp of music, spent much of his youth in absorbing those pieces.[10]

Joseph's lubricious interest in Helen Taylor, by now thoroughly aroused, did not deter him from fathering three more lawful children between 1884 and 1889, including the second son, Henry, born in 1888. To quote Helen's later coy expression, 'afterwards we became on terms of intimacy'. In 1889 he bought and furnished a house for her in Craven Park, Willesden, west London, 'where we passed as Mr. and Mrs. J. Bennett', an alias cruelly close to his wife's maiden name of Burnett.

Joseph's choice of Willesden, thereby saving him the need to travel into the centre of London, illustrates how some Victorian entrepreneurs gave as much deep thought to their private pleasures as to complex business deals. He was able to leave St Helens station at 11.15 a.m., change at Warrington and be at Willesden Junction at 4.08 p.m., reaching the house (anonymously) on foot – he hated using cabs – well by half-past four. An earlier departure at 9 a.m., via Crewe, allowed him to arrive at the Junction at 2.42 p.m. and be with her soon after three.[11]

Helen clearly had no say about where she should live. Willesden was unforgettably described as having 'a high street and a slightly dreary reputation'. In this dispiriting locality Helen – who had seen the world – must have suffered exquisite loneliness in his absence, with no family anywhere near and having to rely on wholly discreet friends. Yet she was resilient enough to make a new life for herself, fortified by occasional gifts of grapes from the heated vines at Ewanville and an allowance which Joseph augmented by periodical increments from £300 to £1,000 a year, as if she were a civil servant. By whatever means, she spared him the burden of further children; the presence of a Steinway piano suggests that she participated in his musical tastes.[12]

Josephine could not have avoided learning about the new mistress in her husband's life. As early as 1889, the 10-year-old Thomas became aware that his mother was suffering from an 'intermittent nervous malady'.[13] She was therefore conveniently bundled off to find a cure in south coast resorts; as a biographer of her son later put it, 'Love and affection and quiet nursing were all that Josephine needed from her husband, but none was forthcoming'.[14]

Instead, when not abroad Joseph spent the working week in Lancashire, and escaped to Willesden from Saturday to Monday. He could scarcely have taken Helen to his favourite recreational haunts of the National Sporting Club in London or to League football or boxing matches. The Huyton residence was capacious enough to allow different sections of his family to live more or less independently of the others, so that his comings and goings were hardly noticed. A bizarre episode illustrates this compartmentalized life. In February 1894 one of the housemaids, with the appropriate upstairs-downstairs name of Eleanor Bellamy, entered the nursery, carrying a newly born sister, Amy Christine. The other children had no inkling that a baby was on the way, and were conscious that their mother was almost 44 years old and in declining health; the older ones therefore suspected that Christine could have been Eleanor's and Joseph's child.[15] The only certain facts are that Eleanor never married, and looked after Christine for some years, being granted an annuity of £1 a week in Joseph's will.

Joseph Beecham's second innovation in the firm was to stir up late-Victorian Britain with an imaginative marketing campaign. Thomas subsequently revealed their joint strategy in a newspaper interview for publicity-conscious American readers during a trip to New York in 1893, described later in this chapter. The Beechams reckoned to advertise in a range of British and overseas newspapers, in nearly all weekly and monthly magazines at home, throughout the colonies and in the United States. They ran those advertisements usually for three years, long enough to estimate whether they were earning a target return of 20 per cent. As most of the pills were believed to be bought by lower middle class and working class people, fewer notices went into papers costing more than 2*d.* (1p) a copy; even so, Thomas assured his Yankee interviewers, 'my pills are taken by dukes and lords, who conceal the fact from their family doctors ... Medical men take them on the quiet too.'[16]

As shown in Table 4.2, Beecham's advertising expenditure had in the 1870s averaged no more than 10–14 per cent of net turnover. That proportion rose to nearly 20 per cent in 1880–81. Then between 1885 and 1890, under Joseph's new innovative regime, between 40 and 50 per cent of turnover, net of duty, went on advertising. The total of £110,000 in 1890 – claimed to be a record among British firms at that time – was made up of £57,000 in Britain, £33,000 in the United States, and £20,000 elsewhere in the world.

According to Joseph's obituary notice in the *Chemist and Druggist*, Thomas had been 'terrified', in common with advertisers generally, when Joseph took a whole page in the *Daily Telegraph*, just after British newspapers for the first time permitted display advertisements. Once that gamble had paid off, Thomas is said at last to have trusted his son and thereafter fully backed him.[17] By 1890 about nine-tenths of the firm's publicity expenditure went on press advertising, in 12–14,000 papers, or ten times the number of titles covered in 1884. Poster advertising took up the remaining 10 per cent.

The other form of sales promotion, offering distributors attractive inducements, was still felt to be essential. The sales representatives, whom Joseph began to recruit for the firm, were not directly concerned with drumming up business – still a task performed by Joseph – but regularly monitored agents and pursued counterfeiters and those passing off rival makes as Beecham's pills. On average the firm brought several dozen well-publicized cases each year against offenders; more were warned off without being taken to court.

Once the new factory reached completion in 1887, the firm was by far the largest patent medicine maker in Britain; its rapidly growing reputation abroad is the subject of Chapter 5. While Thomas had pertinaciously nurtured the firm to reasonable success, it was to be Joseph who carried it to fame and fortune. He now possessed the breadth of vision to take the kinds of risk that yielded the winners substantial rewards. Thomas, having applied for trade mark protection in August 1887, did not formally recognize those attainments until on 17 May 1888 he gave Joseph, a few weeks short of his fortieth birthday, a half-share in the business.[18] The firm's name remained that of 'Thomas Beecham', not to be changed until it became a limited company in 1924.

They were ably assisted by Charles Rowed, who in 1886 at the age of 31 – nearly seven years younger than Joseph – had been promoted to the post of general manager. In 1894 the *Chemist and Druggist* described him as 'a very wideawake gentleman indeed, who combines Lancashire "grit" with more than Yankee "cuteness".[19] The word 'cute', in a later age applied with admiration to pert young women and precocious children, was then used in Britain pejoratively to disparage over-sharp American people and business practices. Perhaps at his suggestion, the firm did not go out of its way to make its advertisements particularly artistic, as did the manufacturers of, say, Pears or Vinolia soaps. If the visual matter was often technically crude, what mattered was the impact it made on the public through eye-catching and often humorous copy.

People in their hundreds, from all manner of trades and professions, regularly sent in ideas or designs for advertisements, being rewarded with a modest fee when accepted; one clergyman was said to do very nicely out of his contributions.[20] Such a practice of using outsiders' ideas was wonderfully cheap, but the firm also employed commercial artists. Instead of going through an agent, as most other large businesses did, Rowed and his staff placed advertisements directly in the press at home, so that the firm came to hold an impressive collection of British and overseas papers, each being checked on receipt to ensure that instructions had been correctly followed. Only publicity outside Britain was handled by an advertising agent. That seems to have been James W. Courtenay & Co. of the Strand, London, which then specialized in transport publicity and was later acquired by the firm as a subsidiary.

Despite the Beechams' declared concentration on cheaper outlets for their publicity, the weekly *Illustrated London News*, as the favourite reading of the moneyed classes, for many years carried the firm's advertisements on average once a month. Its insertions began in 1884, soon after that periodical followed the practice of newspapers in allowing display advertisements of half a page or more.[21] The earliest ones merely extolled in hackneyed phrases the very minor product of Beecham's cough pills as a 'Wonderful Medicine'; then two years later the firm started to focus on the events of the day. In April 1886 Mr Gladstone as prime minister and currently embroiled in the critical Home Rule bill, was represented as a magician, watched by Joseph Chamberlain, Lord Hartington and other political heavyweights, solving the Irish problem by conjuring a box of Beecham's pills out of the air.

A month later, a far more controversial advertisement appeared. The central panel, of a nun watching over a sleeping child, was surrounded by four vignettes, 'In the Cottage', 'At Sea', 'In the Study', and 'In the Palace'. The last-named showed Queen Victoria, in widow's veil and overlooked by a bust of the Prince Consort, working at her desk.[22] Perhaps that portrayal irritated her as much as had the poster two years earlier, where she was shown as being seated in a railway carriage accompanied by a daughter and imbibing Cadbury's cocoa; at any rate, it now provoked a characteristically outspoken private royal riposte. Over many years the queen had become adept at fielding pompous or over-familiar questions with one-liners. When asked by an obsequious courtier, Lord Clarendon, 'Ma'am, can you tell me the secret of your eternal youth?', she instantly replied, 'Beecham's pills!' In fact, the royal archives and medical sources contain no evidence that she ever took proprietary medicines, despite being known to gobble her food.[23]

Unlike the mature Holloway, Beecham appreciated the value of light-hearted advertisements, skilfully exploiting the infinite variety of situations where references to the pills could be worked in. One of the most famous, dating from 1887 and the work of the prolific commercial artist, T. Walker, used the popular song – inspired by Paul Dombey's dying words in Charles Dickens' *Dombey and Son* – 'What are the wild waves saying?' to portray two bare-legged girls on the shore, one listening to the supposed marine noises in a seashell; the message heard was 'Try Beecham's pills'. A plaster cast of a statue by the London sculptor, John A. Raemaker (d. 1894), of a child engaging her younger brother's attention with the same message, adorned the entrance hall of the new factory. Six years later the music-hall artiste Marie Lloyd's celebrated ditty, 'Oh, Mr. Porter', inspired the far less memorable Beecham advertisement of a distraught young woman who, having brought a box of pills away from Birmingham, had left it in a train that went on to Crewe.[24]

For the literary-minded, Mr Pickwick's 'immortal discovery' of Bill Stumps's stone was illustrated as revealing the words 'BEECHAM'S PILLS', while the firm had two stabs at *Hamlet*. The first, for the Christmas issue of 1888, was of an actor, clearly (Sir) Henry Irving, declaiming 'To Beecham, or not to Beecham, that is the question. Methinks I have heard they [*sic*] are WORTH A GUINEA A BOX.' The second, in 1894, reproduced a page of a fictitious academic lecture, attributing the uncertain temper of the 'Moody Dane' to Shakespeare's indigestion, which – the lecturer said – clearly afflicted Hamlet. 'Look at the whole plot of "Hamlet" – murder, madness, treachery and every imaginable misery – is that not something like what [*sic*] a bilious and dyspeptic mortal might weave into his fancies?'[25]

Occasionally the advertisements were scarcely worth the cost of a full page in the *Illustrated London News*, as when a piece of doggerel, in 'New Chimes for the Old Year' of 1888, announced that

> During Eighteen Eighty-Eight
> The sale of Beecham's pills
> Has grown at most tremendous rate,
> By reason of their virtues great
> To cure a hundred ills! …
>
> 'Tis blessed in India's sunny strand,
> And hailed with joy in Yankee-land,

Where, in the 'cutest spot on earth,
The 'cutest people know 'tis worth
A Guinea A Box!

In 1889, Beecham hazarded a rather tame parody of a song in W. S. Gilbert's and Arthur Sullivan's *The Mikado*, about 'the pimples that bloom in the spring, tra la, and make such a mess of your face', which the pills were guaranteed to clear.[26]

However, in the following decade, the firm adroitly moved back towards almost instant topicality. One month after Sherlock Holmes's death was reported in the *Strand Magazine* for December 1893, a passable imitation of the detective's style conveyed his so-called last letter. That requested that a large box of Beecham's pills should be sent to him by the earliest post – doubtless to Lhasa, Tibet.

Concurrently, the public outcry over that interesting play, 'The Second Mrs. Tanqueray', prompted a spoof letter to Mr T., which read, 'Had you insisted upon a judicious use of Beecham's pills by the first Mrs. Tanqueray, her sphere of life might have been extended to the present time, and you would have been saved from many complications.'[27] The Beechams would surely have concurred with the observation of the later American dramatist, Arthur Miller, that 'the structure of a play is always the story of how the birds [chickens] came home to roost'; the essence of their own message was that Beecham's pills could successfully chase away the roosters.

In 1891 there appeared a drawing of the Russian Tsar Alexander III, taking a pill. '"It is said that Beecham's pills had great favour with the Czar, inasmuch as he frequently carries a box in his pocket, and may be seen swallowing a couple before he sits down to meat" – Extract from foreign correspondence.' Too vague to fool anyone, that notice seems to have ruffled no royal feathers. However, Joseph was to be grilled in 1913 by a humourless member of the parliamentary Select Committee on Patent Medicines (see Chapter 7) about an advertisement which reported the exchange between an insurance agent and a housewife. 'Can I insure you and your family?' 'No need, we take Beecham's pills.' 'Very good, we can take you at a lower premium.' The shamefaced Joseph had to admit to the committee that he had never actually heard of an insurance company or agent offering better terms to regular consumers of his pills.[28]

To supplement these written and pictorial efforts, from the late 1880s onwards various 'novelties' took the firm's publicity up several notches. The first of these were the *Music Portfolios*, dear to Joseph's heart and imitating the sheet music dispensed by Holloway (see Chapter 2). Between 1887 and 1902 the Beechams issued, for twopence a go in paperback and sixpence in limp cloth, no fewer than 20 volumes, containing about 600 songs in all. Standard parlour pieces included 'Cherry Ripe' and 'Come into the Garden,

Maud', but others were blatantly puffing songs: 'Good Luck to Beecham's Pills' and 'The B. P. Polka'. A million copies of the first portfolio were soon snapped up, with the printers working night and day to meet the demand; nine million went within two and a half years.

A *Christmas Annual*, printed by London firm, came out in time for Christmas 1888; the second, and last, followed a year later with a circulation of 375,000 copies. Described as a shilling book for one penny, in its 70 pages it contained tales by such popular authors as Ouida (Marie Louise de la Ramée, who had written *Under Two Flags*) and R. M. Ballantyne, famous for adventure stories such as *The Coral Island*. A 48-page fiction omnibus, also sold at a penny each, included a contribution by the American writer, Washington Irving, and some minor short stories by Charles Dickens.

Even more sought after were *Beecham's Helps to Scholars*, first appearing in July 1889 and printed by McCorquodales, currently responsible also for the firm's handbills. Beecham distributed free copies to school teachers and others who wrote in for them. A pamphlet of 12 pages with bright red covers, small enough to fit in a boy's pocket together with conkers, marbles, pieces of string and scraps of food, it was similar to many such handy manuals, containing arithmetical tables, weights and measures and other useful information.

Eleven million copies had been given away by the end of 1897, and no fewer than 55 million by 1936; in the inter-war years of strict government economy, the Air Ministry requested copies for RAF personnel under instruction. The firm also gave away kazoos, namely cigar-shaped metal toys which, when sung into, vibrated the inner membrane: a joyous plaything for children, but home wreckers for grown-ups expecting their juniors to be seen and not heard.[29]

Among other novelties were Beecham's Oracles, small pieces of tissue paper with an apparently blank space in the centre, surrounded by advertising material. When touched with a red-hot needle or wire, it yielded a message such as 'The key to health is Beecham's pills'. Those were sent free to school pupils and to retailers for distribution to customers. More long-lasting were 20 volumes of photographic views, printed in Holland, comprising scenes in England, Wales and the Channel Islands, five million being ordered.

To handle the London end of all this publicity, as well as overseas advertising, Beecham needed an office in the capital, apparently from 1887 onwards. The manager there was George Quelch, appointed that year and related to Henry C. Quelch of Ludgate Square, a wholesale agent for perfumery and druggists' sundries. By 1916 he was officially the firm's London representative.

The Beecham firm announced in 1894 that – unlike almost all rivals – 'the proprietor does not buy, or publish testimonials', claiming that the pills 'recommend themselves' by their quality. Two years later it almost gleefully broke the rule over a story it ran as 'The Struggle for the North Pole'. An expedition – for which Beecham happened to be the sole toothpaste supplier – ran into the most atrocious weather and was given up for lost. After fourteen months, early in 1896 its members returned to Britain, not having achieved its quest. A survivor, the ship's carpenter, then wrote to St Helens, asserting, 'I did not have one day's illness, and I took no medicine but "Beecham's pills"'.

That tribute, accompanied by a graphic picture of the iced-in vessel, the *Windward*, took up a full page in the *Illustrated London News*; so had an earlier puff in July 1889. The 'favourite composer', May Osteler, having written the 'Beecham Waltz' for the third *Music Portfolio*, was featured wearing a quite remarkable hat some 8 inches (20cm) high made up of netting and wide ribbon. She did not explicitly recommend the pills; instead, nineteen surrounding messages proclaimed how they 'Saved the Lives of Thousands', warded off 'Disturbed Sleep and Frightful Dreams', and so on, while 'The First Dose Gives Relief in 20 Minutes'. Less reliably documented, the hugely popular – but nowadays entirely forgotten – Manx author, Sir Hall Caine, was so disliked by the press in the Isle of Man that one article noted ironically, 'He has now reached the top of the ladder of fame – he has appeared in an advertisement for Beecham's pills'.[30]

No less valuable than the paid-for advertisements and novelties were the free mentions in the editorial column that kept the Beecham name before the public.[31] Moreover, as the majority of Britons became better off and more literate, demand for newspapers and magazines of all kinds had soared. These had space for brief 'fillers' which gave journalists scope to display their often juvenile humour, preferably in the form of overworked catch-phrases. They related few anecdotes about Huntley & Palmers of Reading without slipping in the comment 'Take the biscuit'. Likewise, almost any good or discreditable incident affecting the Beechams or their firm earned the negative or positive description of a 'bitter pill'.

Thomas, having begun his career by treating what he biblically called 'cattle', must have been gratified to learn from the rabbit-fanciers' periodical *Fur and Feather* (*c*.1890), about a novel use of his products. One breeder discovered that while most competing rabbits died soon after shows, he kept his charges in good shape by feeding them with bread and milk, rounded off an hour later with a Beecham's pill.

Unlike the elderly Holloway, who compelled some newspaper editors, accepting his advertisements, to give him free plugs on the news pages (see Chapter 2), Thomas, or Joseph or Rowed writing in his name, developed an uncanny knack of encouraging unprompted editorial references by stirring up issues, and keeping them on the boil, sometimes for weeks on end. No topic in the firm's whole history caused such pother over such a lengthy period as the notorious 'hymn books' episode, the subject of Appendix 2.

However, an even more intense, if shorter lived, burst of gratuitous publicity arose from a back-handed puff by no less a personage than the recently appointed prime minister, Lord Rosebery. By that time the advertising stunts of patent medicine and other consumer goods firms had got seriously out of hand; as E. S. Turner, in his *Shocking History of Advertising !* (1952), has put it, 'in the last years of the nineteenth century outdoor advertisers sowed their wildest oats'.

Although not the first to do so, from 1884 onwards the Beechams began to put up hoardings in fields alongside main railway lines, and adorned St Helens station with a massive poster, 80 by 30 feet (24 by 9 metres) in size.[32] During the early nineties, they inflicted their most audacious disfigurements on the British landscape, such as large metal signs at Bowness and Lake Windermere, and in some foreign countries. In 1897 Lord Nelson's former naval flagship, the *Foudroyant*, on its final journey to be broken up, was driven ashore off Blackpool during a storm. Whether or not with head office's knowledge, an agent plastered the hull with Beecham advertisements. Both agent and firm were taken to court and made to pay £50 in damages: a small price for the publicity gained.[33]

To combat such excesses the journalist, Richardson Evans (1846–1928), established the Society for the Checking of Abuses in Public Advertising (SCAPA), in 1893, the year he published *The Age of Disfigurement* to promote his cause.[34] Almost on cue, at the Royal Academy banquet early in May 1894, Rosebery spoke of how, on returning by rail from Manchester, he was

> deeply and hideously impressed with the fact that all along that line of railway which we traversed, the whole of a pleasing landscape was entirely ruined by appeals to the public to save their constitution, but ruin their aesthetic sense by a constant application of a particular form of pill.

Rosebery was aiming his shafts at Beecham, as he quoted the free offer by the 'same enterprising firm' of mainsails bearing a 'hideous legend' – no more horrendous than 'Wonderful Medicines, Beecham's Pills' – to owners of leisure or fishing craft. He mused on what the 'illustrious' artist J. M. W. Turner would have said on seeing the luggers – small boats with several masts – and coasting vessels, which he had immortalized in his paintings, 'converted into a simple vehicle for the advertisement of a quack medicine'; he at once withdrew the word 'quack' as being actionable.

The Times at once ran a leading article which picked up Rosebery's strictures and deplored – as some of its magisterial leaders were to do from time to time over the next century – 'the growing hideousness of our daily surroundings', and the evidence in literature and in other media of 'contentment with the ugly, the trivial and the vulgar'.[35] The Thunderer left it to the more down-market papers to convey the reactions of the pill manufacturers themselves. The American agent in London, John Morgan Richards (see Chapter 5), who had after all been the first to place boards for Carter's Little Liver Pills along railway lines, hastily declared that he would be phasing them out.

For once the Beecham management was caught on the hop. When no response came out of St Helens, an enterprising reporter on the *Westminster Gazette* went to the town and interviewed Rowed, who confessed that he had been 'puzzling hard ever since how best to work it [the prime minister's speech] up for advertising purposes'. Joseph was on one of his regular trips to the United States, and Thomas had lately moved to Southport, visiting the factory only irregularly, as explained below. Not until 26 May, three weeks after the speech, did Thomas publish a letter in the *Chemist and Druggist*, craftily aware as he was that other periodicals would pick it up.

Thomas strove to turn the tables on his critics with a disingenuous claim that there was very little public interest in the matter, and that the few who wished to preserve a 'beautiful world' might do better to 'worry their minds more about the ugliness and squalor of the streets where people have to dwell' than to insist on 'depriving farmers, fishermen and others from getting a little [financial] help'. A week later, in the obscure *Public Opinion*, he promised not to erect any more boards in fields or offer more sails to boat-owners. Moreover, he had no wish to go in for sky signs – an emotive issue at that time – but was staying his hand in order to look out for 'pastures new', whatever those might have been.[36]

To sum up on the Royal Academy episode, rarely had the biter been so well and truly bitten. Queen Victoria – doubtless recalling with distaste the Beecham 'In the Palace' advertisement – was unamused enough to give her First Lord of the Treasury a rare wigging. As a 'sincere well-wisher', she informed the luckless Rosebery that she could not 'help grieving at speeches which she thinks are uncalled for'.

When Rosebery injudiciously sent a tongue-in-cheek reply, the queen advised him that 'in his speeches *out* of Parliament, he should take a more serious tone and be, if she may say so, less jocular, which is hardly befitting a Prime Minister'. Lord Rosebery, she continued, 'is so clever that he may be carried away by a sense of humour, which is a little dangerous'. Contrary to popular belief, Queen Victoria did have a sense of humour, but in the right place and time. She could merely have been warning her head of government not to go on making an ass of himself. An immensely gratified Thomas Beecham let readers of *Public Opinion* know that his earlier and widely copied letter was 'probably the most notable advertisement any firm has ever acquired'.[37]

All this to-do paid handsome dividends to pharmacists, as shown by the

Table 4.1 *Beecham's sales, 1865–1895 (£000)*

	Home sales	Overseas sales	Total sales
1865			2.2
1866			3.1
1867			4.0
1868			5.1
1869			7.1
1870			8.1
1871			9.5
1872			11.1
1873			12.5
1874			13.9
1875			15.8
1876			16.8
1877			19.4
1878			20.6
1879			21.0
1880			23.9
1881			28.4
1882			34.0
–			–
1885			79.2
–			–
1889			162.0
1890	154.0	24.6	178.6
1891	154.6	28.9	183.5
1892	153.7	23.2	176.9
1893	156.0	24.5	180.5
1894	157.1	26.6	183.7
1895	154.8	31.4	186.2

Sales 1865–81, see Table 3.1; 1882–89, estimates by author; 1890–95, BA, 'Report by L. Nicholas on St Helens business', November 1922, Schedule 7, BP 2/2/10, p. 31.

Table 4.2   *Beecham's advertising, 1860–1895 (£)*

	Home	Overseas (excl. USA)	USA	Total
1860	69			
1861	66			
1862	100			
1863	162			
1864	306			
1865	328			
1866	472			
1867	677			
1868	936			
1869	928			
1870	972			
1871	1,343			
1872	1,288			
1873	1,095			
1874	1,320			
1875	1,216			
1876	1,846			
1877	2,017			
1878	2,297			
1879	3,113			
1880	4,570			
1881	5,684			
1882	7,112			
1883	12,810			
1884	22,069			
1885	36,817	824		
1886	46,762	916		
1887	53,142	2,911		
1888	49,475	4,093		
1889	56,637	10,063	31,454	98,154
1890	57,169	19,957	33,669	110,795
1891	59,457	10,127	11,220	80,804
1892	63,094	5,322	26,042	94,458
1893	67,920	6,379	27,815	102,114
1894	65,003	5,687	22,883	93,573
1895	57,742	5,916	17,193	80,851

BA, 'Home advertising totals from 1860', 'Overseas advertising (excluding USA) from 1885', 'USA advertising from 1889', BP 3/3/4.

5

Beecham and the world of patent medicines

UNTIL THE EARLY 1880S, Thomas Beecham was not a direct exporter, but concentrated on developing a market at home.[1] In a letter of 1872 to his friend then living in Australia (see Chapter 3), he stated that while some of his pills went to parts of the Australian continent and 'many' to Africa, 'the wholesale houses whom I supply send them there.[2] To minimize office work, he referred anyone submitting orders from abroad to his UK wholesaling agents, at that time Barclay & Sons of Farringdon Street, William Edwards of St Paul's Churchyard and William Sutton & Co. in Bow Churchyard, London, and in Liverpool Raines and also Evans Sons & Co., much later to be renamed Evans Medical. Goodall Backhouse & Co. of Leeds, mentioned in Chapter 3, already had an export organization for its Yorkshire Relish, and doubtless sold Beecham's pills at the same time. Having extensive business networks overseas, those mercantile houses consigned goods from the nearest English ports to much of the world.

An export drive from St Helens was another of Joseph Beecham's radical reforms, which he launched after Thomas and his third wife Mary had departed from St Helens. Joseph's outlook was broadened in that direction as well after he first met Helen Taylor in 1882. Being herself well-travelled, she must have stimulated his latent interest in foreign lands; early in the next century he was to boast, 'I'm a true cosmopolitan. My tie I bought in Cairo, my coat in Australia, my boots in San Francisco.'[3] He certainly went over sixty times to the United States, twice to Egypt and once – in 1907 – to South Africa, but he would not have had time to make the lengthy voyage to Australia and back.

By 1883 Joseph had begun to open up the Australasian market, but from afar. Among the overseas agents he listed that year were Elliot Bros & Co., of Sydney and Brisbane, and Felton Grimwade & Co., of Wellington, New Zealand. Evans, Sons & Co. of Liverpool had become sole agents for Canada and South America. He first advertised directly to overseas countries in 1885, spending that year only £824 or 2 per cent of the firm's total budget of £37,600 (see Table 4.2, page 69). In 1886, when appointing an agent in Cape Colony, he claimed his sales to be the largest of any patent medicine ever introduced into the South African provinces, not formed into the Union until 1910. He also had an agency in Sierra Leone.

The Beechams, like Morison, built up their overseas trade through agencies. Holloway had preferred a more personal approach, establishing connections abroad by offering liberal discounts to shipping agents, making regular canvassing and information-gathering visits to vessels about to sail from the London docks, and writing thousands of letters to missionaries and other expatriates to secure the names of papers abroad in which to advertise.[4] The range of those informal contacts allowed him to create a substantial market among peoples of non-British stock, which the Beechams never did, as they relied on more secularly minded agencies.

Holloway's export strategy earned him some noteworthy successes. In 1857 ambassadors from Siam, now Thailand, on an official visit to London presented Holloway with a gold enamelled ornament and an autograph letter from King Maha Mongkut, and requested £5 worth of pills and ointment to be delivered to them at Claridge's hotel.[5] That visit occurred four years before the British Anna Harriette Crawford Leonowens became governess to the royal household there. Regrettably, her later reminiscences never refer to Anna and the king of Siam dosing his numerous progeny with Holloway's pills or treating their contusions with his ointment.

Holloway had in 1860 engaged Dr Sillen, a Swedish physician, to negotiate with the authorities in Paris to have his remedies admitted into France. Sillen submitted a bogus formula for the ointment, and was in consequence given permission for it to be sold as 'Pommade dite [named] Holloway'; pomades, unlike the ointment itself, were scented. The irate Holloway charged Sillen with gross incompetence for this fiasco and refused to pay up; Sillen sued him and won, but never got his money.[6]

By 1866, Holloway was able to announce that he had 'most ample directions [for the use of his remedies] translated into almost every known tongue', including Chinese, Turkish, Armenian, Arabic, Sanskrit and most Indian dialects. 'Among my correspondents I number Kings and Princes, equally with other distinguished foreigners of all nations.' More ordinary people were shown in a triple-folding card he circulated to the world in 1876–77, picturing both himself and consumers of many nationalities, including – from the east – Indians in turbans, veiled Turkish women and Chinese with pigtails. He revealed that two French priests had lately been touring China on his behalf.[7]

In 1886, by way of riposte to that circular, Joseph inserted an advertisement in the *Graphic* – the rival periodical to the *Illustrated London News* – of a rotund John Bull, flanked by a determined-looking Britannia complete with shield, trident and fearsome helmet, displaying a box of Beecham's pills to some thirty men and women, all stereotypes of their countries. Five women were seated in the foreground, being French (with cockade), Belgian, Asiatic and African, while the men – all standing – included Uncle Sam, a Red Indian with tomahawk, a Russian, Chinese and so on, wearing their national headgear. Under the globalizing slogan 'BEECHAM'S PILLS – THE WORLD'S MEDICINE', it asserted that these pills had 'the largest sale of any patent medicine in the world'.[8]

To turn that highly dubious claim into reality, Joseph used every effort to push overseas trade. Late in 1887, he was said to be contemplating a business tour to India and China; partly to deflect him from such a time-consuming jaunt, in May 1888 Thomas handed over to him a half share in the firm (see Chapter 4).[9] When two months later, Thomas in London dropped by to see the editor of *Chemist and Druggist*, instead of announcing that Joseph was now a partner, he boasted that his son was then in the United States (see below), 'to give the American public a taste of the advertising which has been such a phenomenal success in this country and Australasia'.[10]

No figure has survived for advertising expenditure that year in the United States, but for other overseas countries Joseph increased that outlay to more than £4,000, or 8 per cent of the £53,000 total. Through the firm's sole agent in the subcontinent, Naylor Son Grimes & Co. of Bombay, he was reported in the trade press to be 'attacking India on an extensive scale'.

In September 1888, about a ton of printed matter in English, Gujarati, Bengali and Hindustani was announced as ready for despatch from St Helens, together with enamelled signs in those three local languages for display on the platforms of the very extensively used Indian railways. The firm's own newspaper room included 'Indian papers galore', all featuring its advertisements. No wonder that Joseph, or Charles Rowed, felt moved to inform readers of the *Illustrated London News* at this time, in the verse offering quoted in Chapter 4, about Beecham's pills being 'blessed in India's sunny strand'.[11] A parallel campaign in the United States, commemorated in the same poetic effort, will be described shortly.

From 1890 to 1921/22, annual country-by-country data on the firm's exports and overseas advertising have survived. Table 5.1 summarizes the figures by continent, showing Beecham's involvement abroad – including results from the American branch – in 1890, 1914 and 1921/22.

Table 5.1 *Beecham's involvement overseas, 1890, 1914 and 1921/22*

	1890 Pill deliveries £	%	1890 Advertising £	%	1914 Pill deliveries £	%	1914 Advertising £	%	1921/22 Pill deliveries £	%	1921/22 Advertising £	%
Exports												
Australasia	17,057	44	4,114	8	43,275	35	4,661	9	55,991	39	7,375	14
America (except US)	1,017	3	1,229	2	13,565	11	3,189	6	10,454	7	5,555	11
Africa	901	2	190	–	6,786	6	1,108	2	8,516	6	2,050	4
Asia	4,788	13	7,223	14	3,813	3	1,161	2	2,483	2	852	2
Europe	847	2	7,201	13	1,342	1	474	1	1,315	1	3	–
	24,610		19,957		68,781		10,593		78,759	55	15,835	31
Production												
United States	(14,000)	36	33,669	63	53,548	44	40,849	80	63,589	45	34,711	69
Total overseas involvement	38,610	100	53,626	100	122,329	100	51,442	100	142,348	100	50,546	100
Total (home and overseas)	178,590		110,795		228,819		111,652		308,174		109,890	
Overseas % of total	22		48		49		46		46		46	

BA, 'Report by L. Nicholas on the St Helens business', November 1922, Schedule 8, BP 2/2/10.

The appetite for Beecham's pills turns out to have been overwhelmingly confined to English-speaking people, nearly 99 per cent of those years' exports going to the empire and the United States. Vast numbers of Britons had emigrated to the dominions and colonies: between 1880 and 1913 nearly two million to Canada, over one million to Australia and New Zealand and 600,000 to the provinces of South Africa.

Many of those expatriates sought remedies familiar to them from home, so that their nearest English-language newspapers gave plentiful information about local outlets. By 1890 Beecham's pills were said to 'reign supreme in Malta', benefiting from the regular flow of troops who passed through on their way to and from the east (mainly India), and of invalids on Mediterranean cruises to recover their health. Although the firm did not at that time export directly to East Africa, in 1893 the intrepid Anglo-French explorer, Lionel Decle, struck down by a bad dose of fever at Ujiji, a port on Lake Tanganyika (now in Tanzania), was convinced that he owed his life to Beecham's pills.[12]

From 1890 to 1921/22, Australia and New Zealand were easily the firm's largest export markets, averaging nearly 40 per cent of the total. India in 1890 came a poor second, even though that year 100,000 handbills were distributed among soldiers on that station. By 1914 exports to the subcontinent were lower both in money terms and as a proportion of the total, and the firm drastically curtailed publicity there. A dramatic improvement during the post-1918 boom did not last, and deliveries and advertising were by the early 1920s no higher than 2 per cent of the total.

To be sure, the marketing organization in India must have been poor. Twice early in 1902 the *Chemist and Druggist* reported a 'famine' of the firm's pills in Bombay and elsewhere in India, even though it had a representative also in Calcutta, the Viceregal capital until 1912. A *Punch* cartoon of 1903, about an Indian shopkeeper mistaking a memsahib's request for lemon and candied peel as about 'Cockle peel' and 'Beesham [*sic*] peel', suggests that most large towns there had 'Europe shops', supplying expatriates with luxury products imported from home.[13]

By contrast, two of the lesser markets in 1890, Canada and South Africa, had by 1914 overtaken India. Thanks to an advertising budget allocation second only to Australia's, that year Canada accounted for nearly one-fifth of all exports from St Helens, down to one-seventh in 1921/22. The market in South Africa grew steadily from 1895 onwards. After a slight dip in 1899, the first year of the South African war, deliveries there during 1900 more than doubled in value over those of 1898.

During that conflict Joseph, Mayor of St Helens in 1899/1900, founded the Mayor's (War) Relief Fund. After receiving complaints from the front about the difficulty of obtaining his pills there, he offered to send a box free of charge to any soldier in South Africa who wrote in for them. He also sent out 1,000 albums of photographs and an equal number of music portfolios to provide much-needed material for recreation.[14]

Exports to South Africa in 1901, of over 12 million pills, were nearly half as much again as in 1900, and then settled down to a yearly average of nearly 8 million. Measures under way to forge the provinces into a Union of South Africa, finally achieved in 1910, encouraged Joseph and his younger son, Henry – who had recently joined the firm – to spend two months there shortly after Thomas's death in 1907, touring round existing sales outlets and opening up new ones. Egypt and the Sudan, although British protectorates, remained very minor outlets for pills. Yet after the battle of Omdurman, Sudan, in 1898, a British medical orderly found a partly used box of Beecham's pills by the side of a wounded dervish.[15]

In non-British parts of the world, demand was low. Some extensive publicity campaigns of 1890–91 in Latin America yielded only moderate sales; thereafter the market struggled along with no assistance from advertising. Deliveries to China and Japan were equally meagre. The Continent of Europe, too, never accounted for more than 2 per cent of Beecham's exports. Tariffs there were high, and some governments erected further barriers by requiring pill formulae to be published, which Beecham refused to do. Unlike in Morison's day (see Chapter 2), no disclosure was by then needed in France, where since at least 1883 the Pharmacie Anglaise in Paris had imported and sold the pills. In 1890 an advertising campaign, planned to open up the French and Belgian markets, was a flop, and in 1896 the firm accepted that further advertising in those countries would be a waste of money.

Joseph Beecham seems to have used his periodical visits to Europe largely to gratify his passion for music; he heard Richard Wagner's opera *Lohengrin* over a hundred times in various countries, including France and Germany. He travelled to Venice in 1890 and was in the south of France in April 1907, being recalled at short notice to his father's deathbed.[16] He relied heavily on Edward Glover (1870–1918), tall and impressive, endowed with unusual gifts of persuasion. Having joined as a clerk in 1887, within seven years Glover was despatched to New Zealand to oversee an important prosecution case of local businesses for counterfeiting. He later travelled to India – after undertaking a crash course in Hindustani – as well as Australia, the United States and Canada. Having been appointed export manager, he went with Joseph and Henry Beecham to South Africa in 1907. His death from pneumonia in 1918 deprived the firm of a man whose professional expertise would have skilfully guided it through the post-war problems to do with overseas trade.[17]

In 1890 only 22 per cent of its total output, in St Helens and the United States (see below), had been directly exported, although some pills from the home market also went abroad via UK wholesalers. Joseph Beecham's recruitment drive for direct agents raised the proportion to 49 per cent by 1914, remaining as high as 46 per cent in 1921/22. Thereafter most recipient countries erected trade barriers as their economic difficulties mounted, crippling Beecham's efforts overseas. No subsequent data are available until 1940/41.

Beecham's pills were by no means the first patent medicines to be shipped to America from the UK. In fact, such British exports there went back to the early eighteenth century, Thomas Daffy's 'elixir salutis' being advertised in the *Boston News-Letter* of 1708. James Morison had an array of sub-agents in all the American states from 1830 onwards, under H. Shepherd Moat, general agent and son of his London partner, being assisted by J. Stanley in Broadway and William Beastall of 148 Fulton Street, New York. However, in a drive for autarky, since 1776 Americans had been energetically copying almost every known brand of British nostrums.[18] In 1834 Morison won a powerfully contested lawsuit in the New York State Superior Court, said to be a 'first' in American legal history, against two of the city's druggists. Although the figures of the firm's trade, given by his counsel in court, were wildly exaggerated (see Chapter 2), a lucrative market appeared to be under threat, and the judge advised the jury that proprietary products did not have to be patented so as to enjoy legal protection against imitators. Despite being awarded $400 damages, Morison's sales there never recovered, and collapsed after he died in 1840.[19]

Thomas Holloway, in his resolve not to be licked by the American counterfeiters, went in person to New York during 1853 and set up, at 80 Maiden Lane, off Broadway, a manufacturing branch for his pills and ointment. It was a propitious time to begin, as a rapidly growing American urban population had become accustomed to consume excessive quantities of rich and stodgy food at breakneck speed: according to a European observer, the national motto had become 'gobble, gulp and go'.[20] Since Americans had become so preoccupied with digestive troubles, Beecham's later publicity did not scruple to emphasize the perils of constipation in much earthier language – about that affliction leading to 'a kind of sewer-gas poisoning' from the noxious liquids and gases in the bowels – than would have been acceptable in Victorian Britain.

Holloway appointed as local manager his 23-year-old brother-in-law, Henry Driver, and entrusted the secret formulae to a trustworthy acquaintance, Mr Brown. His remedies took off so rapidly that in 1857 Driver had to warn all retail agents that William Leith, a New York drug broker, was imitating the pills, having had printed no fewer than 500,000 leaflets closely resembling the Holloway ones. Leith and a fellow counterfeiter in Philadelphia were both successfully taken to court.

Once Driver returned to London in 1863, Holloway's problems over the American market really began to mount. For the next two decades, from the British side of the Atlantic he strove to keep one step ahead of a succession of agents, Joseph Haydock (whom he branded an 'impostor'), Benjamin F. Stephens (not much better) and the honest but incompetent David Pringle.

Holloway's New York-made medicines sold briskly enough on the Union side in the Civil War of 1861–65, the pills being offered as ideal for coping with the unaccustomed diet and harsh life of men in the field, and the ointment a sure remedy for all external hurts, ranging from sores and scurvy blemishes to wounds in action. He took pains to educate enthusiastic but unprepared recruits about the realities of war, proclaiming:

TO ARMS! TO ARMS!! The CITIZEN Soldier will find a more
deadly foe in the brackish, muddy water and damp night air, than in
the most determined enemy.

Hence his pills would 'so purify the blood and strengthen the stomach and bowels' that the soldier could 'endure these hardships and still be strong and healthy'.

When peace returned in 1865 Haydock, after signing an unauthorized contract with Stephens for a $130,000 (£26,000) advertising campaign in Latin America and the West Indies, quitted and set up a rival agency. Pringle in his turn went ahead with introducing two novelties, Holloway's Worm Confections and Holloway's Expectorant for respiratory diseases ('consumption not incurable'); these not surprisingly failed, and he seemed powerless against that year's outbreak of counterfeiting.

By 1869, the market for genuine Holloway remedies in America was shrinking fast. In a bid to stop the rot, in 1872 Thomas Holloway despatched to New York a second brother-in-law, George Martin, to pursue a lengthy and in the end unsuccessful case against Haydock and Stephens. Martin, who remained there until 1876, did have Holloway's trade names registered in Washington; yet the protection of the law was not watertight, and administration officials delayed registration until 1879, by which time the firm's own trade was beyond recovery. In March 1883 Holloway finally resolved 'never again to make his medicine in any part of the United States'; by the end of the year he was dead.[21]

Joseph Beecham, undoubtedly aware of Holloway's travails in America, steered clear of that market for the time being, and pressed on elsewhere in the world. Then in 1883 the UK Trade Mark Act allowed its government to conclude agreements with foreign powers for the mutual safeguarding of inventions, designs and trade names. Four years later Britain and the United States signed a convention to that effect, and Joseph was more successful than George Martin in having his pills registered in Washington without delay.[22]

Once under that legal protection, in 1888 he appointed B. F. Allen & Co., of Canal Street, New York, as his sole export agent in the United States. Allen already represented the soap manufacturers, A. & F. Pears, as well as other British consumer goods firms. Joseph soon came to appreciate the brash and enterprising spirit of America, and immersed himself in the advanced techniques of electricity generation there, which were to benefit the factory, the town of St Helens and his Ewanville home alike (see Chapter 4). He welcomed the chance of making regular visits to supervise operations as well as to gain scientific knowledge in the United States.

On top of their current involvement in building up the Indian market, during August 1888 he and Rowed master-minded an equally vigorous drive in America. They posted no fewer than 10,000 circular letters to druggists throughout the Union, as well as 50,000 coloured show cards 'of artistic design'; they also despatched a hundred large cases of samples. To exploit the forthcoming presidential election in November, they sent out 250,000 cabinet photographs of the republican candidate, Benjamin Harrison, and the democratic president, Grover Cleveland – who was seeking re-election – as well as the vice-presidential hopefuls, for sale at a few cents apiece. After Harrison's victory, early in 1889 the new green-painted Beecham's horse-drawn van conveyed to St Helens station, for onward shipment in bulk, 27,263 reminder post cards to American druggists.[23]

A year later the McKinley tariff raised the duty on medicines imported into America from 20 to 50 per cent, and also made the pill boxes – even though of American origin – subject to duty. As the new tariff would have effectively priced Beecham's pills out of that market, Joseph at once arranged with B. F. Allen to have the digestive pills manufactured in a section of the Brooklyn premises, hitherto used for storing Pears' soaps. One ton of pill ingredients was to be sent out from St Helens every six weeks. To safeguard the secrecy of the pill formula, Joseph planned to travel for the mixing twice a year; as mentioned at the beginning of this chapter, by 1914 he had made a total of sixty round trips across the Atlantic. William Moss, also guardian of the formula as works manager, occasionally took his place, travelling ten times in all before retiring in 1929.[24]

In 1890 Joseph set off for New York to accompany the manufacturing plant, much being cast-offs from St Helens. He helped to assemble the gas engines, shafting and other parts.[25] James W. Atherton, appointed as production manager, remained there until his death in 1926; the assistants seconded with him were Walter Rigby and Atherton's eventual successor, James Grayson. That American venture was not a branch of the St Helens firm but part of

Joseph's private assets: a far from unique arrangement at that time. In a similar fashion, the grocer, (Sir) Thomas Lipton, set up businesses in America which remained his personal property and were not included in Lipton Ltd, registered in 1898, while William Lever's MacFisheries business, founded two years later, was a private one until he sold it to Lever Brothers in 1922.

The United States market and its opportunities so gripped Joseph's imagination that in 1890 he allocated nearly two-thirds of his firm's advertising budget to that country. Through druggists he gave away Beecham's *Music Portfolios*, printed by the Sackett-Wilhelms Litho Company of New York and offering an appropriate range of American and English ditties, from 'Coming thro' the Rye' to the 'Guinea a Box Polka'. These, he declared reassuringly, 'may be sung *everywhere* without permission'.

The front covers featured plump-cheeked girls, more eye-catching than those at home which unimaginatively showed a mature and formally dressed couple, the woman at the piano and the man in song. On the back page of each American portfolio was hard-hitting copy, listing the disorders curable by the pills, down to 'Cold Chills, Disturbed Sleep, Frightful Dreams, and all Nervous and Trembling Sensations, etc. The first dose will give relief in 20 minutes. This is no fiction.' The same invitation to suspend disbelief had already been tried out with the British public in the *Graphic* advertisement, portraying John Bull, in 1886.

The American version of *Beecham's Help to Scholars*, printed in England, contained suitably adapted arithmetical tables, weights and measures and geographical and drawing definitions. Between its first appearance in July 1889 and 1925 no fewer than 40 million copies of it had been given away throughout the United States. Its motto, prominently displayed, was the very Beechamite 'READER PERSEVERE'. As the users tended to be older than the schoolchildren in Britain – doubtless those seeking self-improvement – the cover portrayed an alluring young woman in a low-cut dress, above the slogan, 'The Way to Health. A Beautiful Complexion Comes from Within.'

One ingenious but later politically unacceptable advertisement was of a black minstrel, arrayed in a comic stove-pipe hat and horizontally striped trousers, holding an over-sized banjo and encouraging an amused crowd of whites to 'Just run your eye along dose strings'. When viewed sideways, the criss-cross read in one direction 'Beecham's Pills' and in the other 'A Wonderful Medicine'.[26]

Joseph Beecham admitted about the United States that he had to 'struggle and work to gain a foothold in that great country' and wage an 'uphill fight for many years'.[27] He even introduced from the US a new product in Britain, the first since Thomas had restricted his own output to the digestive and cough pills in 1861. That was a one shilling (5p) toothpaste, in a collapsible tube inside a cardboard carton. Never manufactured in England, it was bought in from the Sheffield Dentifrice Company, of New London, Connecticut. As Sheffield's sole agent, B. F. Allen must have introduced Joseph to the product.

The toothpaste's inventor, a New York dentist named Lucius T. Sheffield, claimed it to be the oldest preparation of its kind in the United States, although the American-based Colgate had been selling toothpaste in jars there since 1873. Analysts found Sheffield's secret formula to include chalk, powdered Castile soap, geranium and rose oil, carmine and glycerine. It was clearly a novelty in Britain, where those who bothered to brush their teeth normally used tooth powder. For some reason the Beechams tended to publicize the brand at the bottom of their advertisements, the part which is least likely to be read.

Beecham's toothpaste achieved its highest annual sale, of 41,500 tubes, in 1896, but that year Colgate launched the more enticing Ribbon Dental Cream in Britain, while in 1900 the US drug manufacturer, Parke Davis, introduced there the Euthymol toothpaste. The last-named was advertised to doctors and chemists, as well as the public, for its scientific contributions to oral hygiene, notably the germicidal agents which killed a range of bacteria in the mouth and kept teeth white. Such powerful competition reduced sales of Beecham's toothpaste by 1909 to less than 10,000 tubes a year, falling to a quarter of that figure in 1914. Joseph, conscious that his products sold on quality, should have accepted that a toothpaste without any advanced ingredients or special marketing points had no future in the new science-based century.[28]

The first surviving figures of Beecham's sales in the United States date only from 1906, when they came to $150,000 (£30,000) and yielded a net profit of $16,000 (£3,200). As that year's advertising in America cost over $100,000 (£20,000), Joseph accepted the need to offer heavy subsidies on his venture. The smaller Canadian market was at least paying for itself, profit for 1906 being £870 on sales of £1,876 and advertising no higher than £772. It is puzzling why the profit margins varied so dramatically between the two countries.

Joseph was forever on the look-out for profitable niche markets, and therefore launched a special advertising campaign in Yiddish, directed at Jewish districts in New York, then housing 600,000 Jews. By 1910 an agent reported that in these ethnic districts 'Beecham's pills are selling better than any other cathartic'.[29] However, the firm's increasingly visible profile in the city presented the counterfeiters with an irresistible temptation.

In 1904 four New York druggists conspired to drive the firm's pills out of the market, with imitations down to exact copies of the labels. Relying on the protection granted by the 1887 trade-mark convention, Joseph took them

1 Sarah, mother of Thomas Beecham, in her old ~~~e, *c.*1880. Thomas inherited her robustness and ~~~domitable nature.

Francis, *A Guinea a Box*

1.2 Kibbler, with manually operated wheel, for grinding hard substances such as aloes and ginger, late 1830s.

H.G. Lazell, *From Pills to Penicillin*

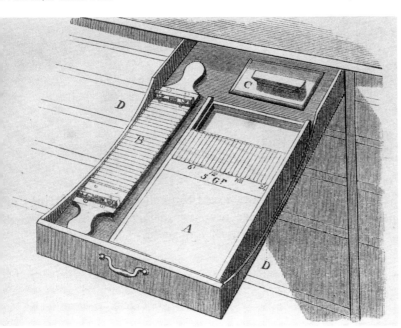

1.3 Pill board, to convert the pill mass into long strips, before cutting up and rolling, 1849.

G. Tweedale, *At the Sign of the Plough*

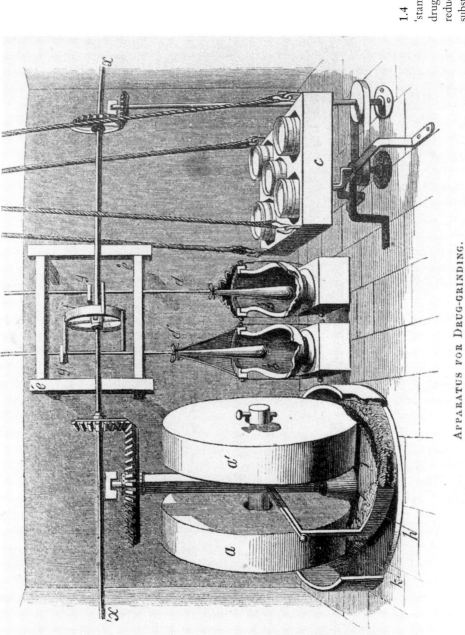

APPARATUS FOR DRUG-GRINDING.

a a'. Drug Mill.   h. The Plough.   b b. Stampers.
e e. The Guiding-frame for Stampers.   c. Sifting Apparatus.

1.4 Steam-driven 'stampers' and drug mills, which reduced hard substances to powder, 1849.

G. TWEEDALE, *AT THE*

1.5 The logo of the upward-mobile Thomas, having opened a chemist's shop at Wigan, 1857.

BEECHAM ARCHIVES, ST HELENS

2.1 James Morison, pill-maker in London and inventor of the Hygeian System for clearing the bloodstream, 1828.

W. HELFAND, 'JAMES MORISON AND HIS PILLS'

6 Jane Beecham, in a checkered woollen dress ith bishop sleeves, 1857.

JEFFERSON, SIR THOMAS BEECHAM: A CENTENARY TRIBUTE

BRITISH COLLEGE OF HEALTH,
EUSTON ROAD, LONDON.
WHERE ALONE MORISON'S VEGETABLE UNIVERSAL MEDICINES ARE COMPOUNDED.

2.2 Morison's grandiose 'British College of Health', in the future Euston Road; note the stone lion on the roof, 1828.

W. Helfand, 'James Morison and his Pills'

2.3 The elegant design for the labels of James Cockle's mildly acting Antibilious Pills, 1893.

Chemist & Druggist, 29 July 1893

2.4 Thomas Holloway in 1845, just when his pill and ointment firm was turning the corner to prosperity.

2.5 Jane Holloway, her husband's industrious helpmeet, said to have urged him to found a Women's College, now Royal Holloway, 1845.

2.6 Holloway's successive London premises, in the Strand until 1867 and in Oxford Street to 1909.

2.7 Holloway in the 1870s, concentrating more on his Sanatorium and Women's College than on his pill and ointment firm.

3.1 Thomas Beecham's 'Wanted' notice outside his workshop, seeking bright 14-year-olds, mid-1870s.

3.2 William Moss, one of the earliest 'sharp' lads and a future works manager, in his best suit, *c.*1874.

3.3 The Byronic Joseph Beecham and his dressed-to-the-nines wife, Josephine, holidaying in the Isle of Man, 1873.

3.4 Thomas Beecham's first basic one-storey factory at St Helens, 1877. Note the skylight and the witch's c[...] tower.

BEECHAM ARCHIVES

3.5 Factory courtyard, with senior managers, time-keeper and two workmen, 1877.

BEECHAM ARCHIVES

3.6 Thomas and Mary Beecham on horseback outside Mursley Hall, wit[h] his second son William, *c.*1881. Note the horses gazing at the camera.

A. FRANCIS, *A GUINEA A BOX*

to court, attended in person, and won his case. Two years later, he was up against an even more resolute opponent in the counterfeiter of his pills, Mark Jacobs of Brooklyn. Early in 1906 he took out an injunction against Jacobs, but the subsequent proceedings took their leisurely way through ever higher courts; not until April 1911 was the case finally settled in the United States Supreme Court.

There Jacobs entered a plea that the so-called patent pills had never been patented, and that Beecham's leaflets incorrectly spoke of manufacture taking place in England. The eminent Supreme Court judge, Oliver Wendell Holmes Jr., son of the celebrated author, had no time for petty point-scoring. In upholding the guilty verdict of earlier courts, he rejected the appellant's high-flown phrase about Joseph attempting to 'wash the stain of unconscionable conduct from his hands by a denial of misrepresentation' with the pithy phrase, '*corruptio optimi pessima*' (corruption of the best becomes the worst).[30]

Besides joining the New York Athletic Club, then the headquarters of all American sports, Joseph put to good use the time sacrificed to the law's delays by purchasing a factory in Brooklyn, close to his existing rented premises; the warehouse and offices remained in New York. Costing $110,000 (£22,000) and completed in May 1910, it had enough capacity to meet the expected levels of demand that – so long as the counterfeiters could be held at bay – were growing satisfactorily.

He installed the most up-to-date American labour-saving plant, with its own power and electric light, because skilled wages there were so high. He had no intention of replacing the current machinery at St Helens, where he could still rely on a cheap and partly juvenile workforce, as described in Chapter 6. He announced that the 80 million pills a year produced in the US were equal to nearly one-quarter – according to the statistics 23 per cent – of the annual output at home.[31] Results for 1914 were not greatly different from those for 1911, except that advertising now cost almost $200,000 (£40,000).

Demand in America for his pills had been boosted by the Pure Food and Drugs Act, passed by Congress in 1906, which outlawed harmful ingredients in those products and also misleading publicity statements about them. Beecham's pledges to American gobblers and gulpers, about the pills curing 'wind and pain in the stomach, sick headaches, giddiness, fullness and swelling after meals', among other related ills, therefore avoided any assertions, currently being made to British readers, that the pills had no equal for 'removing any obstruction or irregularity of the [female] system'. By 1911, the United States branch's sales there had increased by two-thirds since 1906. He claimed to be the second largest advertiser – perhaps of medicines – in the United States.

Partly to tap Joseph's extensive knowledge of the American market, in 1909 Thomas Barratt, the chairman of Pears (Chapter 7), appointed him a non-executive director of the soap company. They had shared the same New York agency from 1888 onwards and had been neighbours in the Hampstead district of London since 1903, with a common interest in advertising. As the very energetic Barratt was so overworked at home, Joseph gladly agreed to act as his representative in America, where Pears' soap was one of the two most popular toiletries.

Joseph soon found his expertise to be of value to Pears. In 1909 the Payne-Aldrich Tariff Act increased many customs duties, to an all-round 50 per cent for Pears' products, and Barratt at once planned to avoid that tariff by manufacturing there. A year later he travelled to New York with Joseph, who took him through the technicalities of securing land, buildings, appropriate grades of labour, materials and machinery, and ways of keeping the soap formula secret.

At Pears' Annual General Meeting in October 1911, Barratt announced his intention to begin production overseas; the ensuing furore led to a question being asked in the House of Commons about the potential threat to British jobs. The Liberal President of the Board of Trade, Sydney (later Earl) Buxton, brushed it aside by maintaining that he had no powers to prohibit investment abroad.[32] In the event, the United States authorities scaled down the tariff increases, and Barratt thankfully abandoned his scheme of investing overseas. He died in the spring of 1914, whereupon his company was absorbed by Lever Brothers, Joseph remaining a director of the Pears subsidiary until his death.

Joseph was happy to provide funds from his personal wealth, incorrectly estimated by the *New York Times* at $130 million (or £26 million), making him – as he clearly was not – the third richest man in England.[33] Indeed, his annual deficit in America, at £36,600, was only a little higher than the £30,000 loss he was then incurring from his son Thomas's musical activities (see Chapter 7). Between 1914 and 1921/22, sales showed a modest further increase, but advertising consumed between 55 and 75 per cent of receipts. Profits in the United States therefore only just exceeded pre-war levels.

After Beecham overtook Holloway as the leading British pill firm in the 1880s, its main threat at home was not so much from domestic rivals as from the competition of Americans in Britain itself. F. A. McKenzie, who warned readers in his book, *The American Invaders* about the penetration of many British industrial markets by US entrepreneurs, asserted that in 1902 Britons were spending £4,000 a week on American patent medicines imported into their country. That suggested a retail value of just over £200,000 a year. As the Customs and Excise in London did not collect data of those imports, the only alternative evidence is from the United States Customs, which stated that in 1911 about 15 million packages of medicines were exported from there to

Britain, with a total value of some £400,000.[34] To put those calculations in perspective, the British Census of Production showed national output of patent medicines in 1907 to be worth £1.5 million, with exports of some £600,000, while in 1932 about $30 million (£8 million) had been invested in some 32 companies manufacturing United States medicines in the UK.[35]

The earliest known importer of American pills into Britain had been Benjamin Brandreth (1807–80), son of a Liverpool doctor who had emigrated to New York in 1837. Two years later he was advertising his pills in England, distributed by a London agent, but their sales must have been on the small side. Then in 1867 one of the most eminent, if little known, advertising magnates of the Victorian era, John Morgan Richards (1841–1918), was sent by Demas Barnes & Co. of New York – the largest wholesalers of bitters, pills and concoctions in the world – to open a branch in London.

According to Richards' later evidence, that year the three most popular American remedies in Britain were Perry Davis's pain-killer, Brown's troches or lozenges for sore throats, and Mrs Winslow's Soothing Syrup.[36] The last-named concoction was hugely popular among desperate mothers and indolent nannies, being laced with morphia to stupefy fractious infants. (In 1879 the British composer, (Sir) Edward Elgar, appears to have been so struck by the syrup's mellifluous name that he bestowed it on a brief Wind Quintet, 3 minutes and 45 seconds long, marked *adagio cantabile*).[37] Four years earlier Richards had set up his own business; as agent of a major tobacco firm, he enjoyed the highly dubious distinction of being the first, in the late 1870s, to popularize cigarette smoking in Britain.

Richards posed no challenge to British pill-makers until 1886, when he began to import Carter's Little Liver Pills. Invented by Dr James Carter of Erie, Pennsylvania and currently made by an acquaintance, Brent Good (1837–1915), the pills were shipped over in bulk to be packaged in Richards' workshop there. Analysts could find nothing out of the ordinary in them, apart from the cathartic resin podophyllin, but Richards achieved a publicity coup by scaring the daylights out of British hypochondriacs with lurid portrayals of liver disorders. The narrator in Jerome K. Jerome's *Three Men in a Boat* (1889) describes himself as reading a patent liver-pill circular, 'in which were detailed various symptoms by which a man could tell whether his liver was out of order. I had them all.'

Two decades later the soap entrepreneur and leading advertiser, William Lever – the future Lord Leverhulme – noted approvingly how 'the pill and patent medicine man [Richards] in his pamphlet' had found 'a way of attracting attention and impressing the reader'. After quoting Jerome K. Jerome's remarks about patent liver pills, he declared, 'We want to have this hypnotic effect with soap … The whole object of advertising is to build a halo round the article.'[38]

Undoubtedly through such frightening publicity, by 1896 the Carter enterprise had become lucrative enough for the notorious company promoter, Ernest T. Hooley, to offer to float in London the Carter Medicine Co. Ltd, with £1 million capital. That proposal would have rewarded the vendors handsomely, and Richards opened talks on their behalf with Hooley's syndicate. Brent Good soon joined them from the United States for more detailed discussions, but these ended in breakdown. The Carter company was therefore spared the heavy over-capitalization which afflicted Hooley's next target, Schweppes Ltd, when registered in 1897: the year before Hooley went bankrupt.[39]

If Carter, like Cockle a generation earlier, stressed the dire effects of failing to invigorate a torpid liver with pills, those who lacked blood in their veins could turn to Dr Williams' Pink Pills for Pale People, bulk-imported from Schenectady, New York, and packed in London. Egg-shaped and coated with pink sugar, they were expensive at 2s. 9d. (14p) for 30 pills; containing iron sulphate and potassium carbonate, they were found by analysts to be a lazily prepared version of the generic Blaud's pills. The promoter, George T. Fulford (1852–1905) of New York (known as 'Napoleon' for his autocratic ways), spent over £250,000 a year on world-wide advertising of them and on his death left $4.1 million (£825,000).[40]

Neither the Carter nor the Dr Williams companies ever revealed their sales or profits in Britain, so that we cannot tell how far they eroded the sales of Beecham's, Holloway's and others' pills. Much is known, however, about the patent medicine tycoons from the United States who in the two decades from 1884 onwards came over and set up their own companies in Britain. Already owning other businesses in quite different industries, they had every confidence that American hard-hitting publicity methods could be as effective as at home, and did not bother to acquire any specialist knowledge of the UK market. Most took full advantage of Britain's lax corporate laws, by forming and re-registering companies with successively higher and more liberally watered capital, money not backed by real assets.

An early venturer was the New Yorker, Alfred J. White (1824–98), a maker of typewriters who having exported Mother Seigel's Syrup since 1877, seven years later began production in England. The Seigel lady, allegedly a pillar of the Shaker sect, never in fact existed; her potion to relieve dyspepsia was unforgettably described as a 'dark brown, emulsion-like turbid, watery extract, of fresh smell, bitter taste and acid reaction'.[41] White in 1897 re-formed his original £100,000 company of 1884 with £1 million capital, bearing a suspiciously high goodwill item of £929,000 and yielding him a £900,000 capital profit. It delivered the company's *Home Service Magazine* free to every household in Britain; so unimpressed were readers and consumers alike that annual profits sank from £89,000 in 1897/98 to £13,000 in 1904/05.

After White's bankruptcy and death, the company came into British hands in 1907 and its capital was written down to £300,000. The directors then took the extremely rare step of establishing a reputable subsidiary – although with a fictitious name – Menley & James Ltd, to produce an iodine-based ointment named Iodex, invented by Dr Frank Crossley-Holland. Iodex was soon being marketed in soap, powder, pessary and other forms. During the mid-1920s, Menley & James began to produce vitamins, including Vitaminose, made from the juice of raw spinach mixed with honey.

That unappetizing compound deservedly flopped, but in 1927 the chairman of the prestigious Smith Kline and French Laboratories of Philadelphia thought enough of the company's research capabilities to offer it the agency for making Neuro Phosphates in Britain. In 1956 A. J. White and its subsidiary became part of the Smith Kline empire and thus in due course a minor unit of SmithKline Beecham, and from 2000 of GlaxoSmithKline.[42]

Hulbert H. Warner (d. 1923), an American maker of fire- and burglar-proof safes at Rochester, New York, in 1885 began UK manufacture of Warner's Safe Cure, to treat liver and kidney ailments; his punning trademark was an iron safe. In 1889, having achieved a turnover of £63,000 a year in Britain alone, he sold out to a syndicate which at once registered H. H. Warner Ltd, with a £700,000 capital. On hearing that news, old Thomas Beecham dryly observed that he was not at present minded to offer *his* business to a limited company. Warner's profits declined from £105,000 in 1889/90 to £3,000 in 1907/08. He died, a forgotten man, at Minneapolis in 1923, and his UK company had long disappeared from view when in 1946 it was formally liquidated.[43]

One other company of some note was founded by one of the Brandreth family. In 1895 Henry D. Brandreth, manufacturer of Allcock's Porous Plasters at Birkenhead who also sold some Brandreth's pills, registered in London a £25,000 company, Homocea Ltd, two years later re-registered as a £250,000 company under the same name. He advertised his antiseptic ointment with the inspired slogan of 'Homocea Touches the Spot': the double meaning, that it achieved exactly what was needed, and also hit the precise infected area, was driven home by an index finger pointing towards the sore spot. Despite an encouraging initial response, it had to write down its capital several times before being wound up in the early 1930s.[44]

The headlong descent in the fortunes of Warner and A. J. White moved the *Chemist and Druggist* in 1899 to offer stern reflections on the tactics employed by American patent medicine promoters in Britain. These gentry, according to the trade journal, seemed to have the knack of choosing the highest point of their remedies' popularity to sell out to the public: a process encouraged by temptingly worded prospectuses. Few of such companies remained profitable for very long after registration, always plausibly explaining away their poor results as due to exceptional circumstances.[45]

Two entrepreneurs even strove to recreate in Britain the medicine show: a form of travelling entertainment that wended its way through American rural communities. Every night itinerant hucksters would warm up potential dupes with enticing music and other diversions before embarking on their hard sell of snake oil or similar compounds. Onlookers, according to sympathizers, 'like to pay a little for a tonic and an evening's entertainment rather than pay a lot to a doctor who gives you no fun at all'. In 1885 Charles A. Vogeler of Baltimore, having allegedly 'conquered the world' with his novel unguent, St Jacob's Oil, shipped to Britain a pair of horse-drawn advertising 'chariots'. Lavishly adorned with plate glass and gilt decorations, those were intended to progress slowly round the country from Liverpool onwards.

Five years later William H. Hartley, manufacturer of the Sequah Prairie Flower liniment for rheumatism, brought over his own vehicle, even more stunningly embellished; its fairground steam organ gave forth what was claimed to be 'really excellent music'. They reckoned to sell their nostrums at the conclusion of each show.

To the dismay of those entrepreneurs, Britain's Inland Revenue officials, not known for having much sense of fun, soon brought their diversions to an untimely end. The law prohibited patent medicine sales except in bona fide outlets such as chemists' shops. Even when the American promoters took on registered druggists as salesmen, their activities remained illegal. Both British companies were wound up in the new century, the one in 1913 and the other in 1909.[46]

The sole active survivor from these American direct investments of patent medicines in Britain was the Bile Beans (for Biliousness) Marketing Company in Leeds from 1899 onwards. In 1905 the promoter, Charles Fulford – related to the Napoleonic maker of Dr Williams' Pink Pills – was unwise enough to sue a Scotsman who had been counterfeiting the Bile Beans. Having perused the clearly fictitious account of the company's origins and its extensive publicity material, the Scottish judges threw out the case, condemning what they called 'a gigantic and too successful fraud'. Somehow the company overcame that severe dent to its reputation: in 1934/35 its home sales were no less than £380,000, not far short of the combined sales of Beecham's pills and powders, estimated at £420,000.[47]

Even so, most adventurers who crossed the Atlantic to produce low-technology patent medicines in Britain sooner or later came to grief. Their disregard for innovation and lavish but poorly planned marketing strategies gave no sure entry into the British market.

In nearly four decades, from 1883 to 1921/22, the Beecham enterprise had increased the value of its direct involvement overseas from nil to £142,000, of which £79,000 comprised exports and £63,000 the sterling equivalent of production in the United States (see Table 5.1). Such involvement represented 38 per cent of the combined output in St Helens and New York. From having virtually no international standing in the early 1880s, by the 1920s it enjoyed fame throughout much of the English-speaking world.

Data on global production of commercial remedies do not exist, but Beecham's main overseas rivals were American pill manufacturers, whose performance in this period is officially recorded. The United States Census of Manufactures shows that in 1919, that country produced $212 (£42) million worth of 'patent medicines and compounds', or double the $102 (£20) million worth in 1914.[48] During the five-year period of the First World War, Beecham's production – including that of its branch in the United States – fell from the equivalent of 1.3 per cent to 0.9 per cent of that census total.

The Beecham firm's operations thus met only a minuscule part of world-wide demand for patent medicines. As already explained, many countries were closed to its marketing, partly because the pills were expensive but also because they appealed mainly to those of British, or American, stock. However, it enjoyed a disproportionately high reputation by means of the advertisements it splashed on hoardings or elsewhere out of doors and inserted in very many foreign and colonial newspapers and magazines. By 1921/22 it was spending on publicity £35,000 in the United States and an additional £15,000 elsewhere outside Britain. Over the coming decades, then, much effort would be needed to keep the Beecham name alive in a rapidly changing and economically turbulent world.

6

Machines and manpower in the firm

ON ENTERING HIS CHOSEN INDUSTRY in the mid-1860s, Thomas Beecham would have noted that few if any other patent medicine producers were genuine innovators, as they lacked any incentive to make regular improvements to their technology. Hiding behind secret formulae, they relied for their sales on branding, through the adoption of easily remembered trade names, and on intensive marketing of those brands. Consumers, once having become dependent on their favourite remedies, hardly seem to have troubled themselves over the quality of what they were taking. What mattered to them was how much better they felt after each dose.

Manufacturing methods in earlier firms' workshops or factories are not known, but James Morison's College of Health, some time after 1828, had two steam engines, apparently for mixing the ingredients. Many food and consumer goods producers were at that time mechanizing their operations, to boost profits by achieving a faster throughput and a more standard quality of product. Yet Morison's steam-powered machines failed to deliver anything like an even consistency for his pills. Sizes could vary by as much as a third, while analysts found that their composition often differed from one mixing to the next.[1]

Thomas Holloway's pills were of no higher quality. Like Morison he was a one-time foreign merchant with no previous industrial experience, and installed no steam machinery at 244 Strand in London. Even when he subsequently bought two extra premises to the rear, the site remained too congested for steam power to be introduced. In 1851, when home turnover was £18,000, he had 29 employees, 12 being men operatives, 9 boys, 3 females and 5 clerks. Two years later, out of a total workforce said to number 50–60, thirty of them were to be seen behind the counters, boxing up pills, inserting the ointment in pots, labelling, and fixing revenue stamps on home deliveries.[2]

Once the Strand premises were compulsorily purchased in 1867 and the Holloway firm migrated to a more extensive five-storey building on a corner site in Oxford Street, Holloway did little to overhaul production methods. The ground floor, with its lofty marble pillars and carved-wood ceiling, housed the offices and the surgery of the doctor, who proffered medical advice – regarding the amount of Holloway's remedies to take – for the benefit of callers between 11 and 4.[3] On the middle floors, it was reported, 'young women [were] filling boxes from small hillocks of pills containing a sufficient dose for a whole city': a labour-intensive and unhygienic method of performing a straightforward and easily mechanized operation. Holloway had his private residence on the top floor.[4]

By 1867, he used wholly female labour for producing and packaging his remedies. To turn out almost £100,000 worth of pills and ointment for the home and overseas markets in 1877, there were 67 employees, 32 being women and girls, 9 porters, one boy, a forewoman, housekeeper and doctor, plus 22 clerks.[5] Their wage rates are given in Table 6.1. The widely quoted size of the workforce after Holloway's death in 1883, of nearly 100, is surely an exaggeration, as total turnover seems to have fallen slightly to around £94,000. The Inland Revenue inventory for probate, early in 1884, put the value of the firm's goodwill at only £45,000: a low figure if annual profits were in fact as high as £50,000.

Since no engineer was listed, there could not have been a steam engine in Oxford Street either. That inventory described the second floor as containing a hand bell room – perhaps for the forewoman as timekeeper – a drug room, a mixing room, with stone pestle and mortar, and a work room. The last-named held four Penders pill machines, a 'dressing piping machine' for extrusion of the pill mass, and a punching machine, all clearly hand-operated. There was also a Matthews diagonal cutting machine. The basement held a large copper for mixing the ointment, a far less popular remedy than the pills. The authorities valued the whole plant and the stock-in-trade at no more than £1,665.[6]

In the absence of steam-driven machinery, the pills were not fashioned in a scientific way, being described in 1853 as very irregular in size, the weight of each varying between 1½ and 2½ grains (0.1–0.2 gm). Even in 1876, nearly a decade after the move to Oxford Street, analysts found no improvement in the pills, which remained of unequal size, weight and diameter, while no two samples of the ointment were identical in composition. Holloway had thus learned nothing from the eclipse of Morison's firm.[7] Without any formal training in pharmacy, both men cared nothing for quality control.

By contrast, Thomas Beecham was resolved not to inflict carelessly made pills on the world. He may have been equally untrained as a pharmacist, but as Chapter 1 showed, his early experiments had given him a sure grasp of the complexity of proper pill-making; the firm's operations therefore resembled

Table 6.1   *Holloway and Beecham: employee numbers and wages*

Holloway		Beecham			
1877		*1890*		*1914*	
Status	*Numbers and wages in shillings*	*Status*	*Numbers and wages in shillings*	*Status*	*Numbers*
Forewoman	1 @ 21	Foremen	3 @ 34.40	Foremen	4
Females	2 @ 12	Men	2 @ 39.5, 6 @ 25–30	Drug grinder	1
	2 @ 11		11 @ 20–24	Pill makers	8
	4 @ 10		6 @ 15–19	Packers	18
	20 @ 9		4 @ 12	Shipping clerk	1
	4 @ 6	Boys	2 @ 10.5	Printer	1
Porters	9 @ 21–33		1 @ 10	Warehouseman	1
Boy	1 @ 6		4 @ 9	Advertisement checker	1
Housekeeper	1 @ 20		6 @ 8	Case makers	2
Doctor	1 @ 56		1 @ 7.5	Engineer	1
Senior clerks	2 @ 78		6 @ 7	Boiler men	1
Clerks	20 @ 28–60		9 @ 6	Joiners	5
			13 @ 5	Brick setters	6
		Housekeeper	1 @ 14	Boys under 16	49
		Senior Clerk	1 @ 32	Gardener	1
		Clerks	7 @ 15–26	Coachmen	2
		Boy clerks	2 @ 7–8	Senior clerk	1
				Clerks	6
				Boy clerks	3
				Secretary	1
				Inspectors	4
No of employees	67		85		117
Weekly wages (average)	23.5		15.25		21.5*

Sources: Holloway: Surrey Record Office, Holloway papers, 'Mr. Holloway's letter to Mr. Driver, 14 October 1877', THPP; Beecham: BA, Wages Book No. 1, 1886–90, BP 1/5/14; List of male employees before the [First World] war, 30 July 1914, BP 1/5/3.

* Operatives' wages only. See note to Table 6.2.

those of wholesale druggists, forever seeking technical improvements. In 1868 he fitted up his workshop with steam power, most equipment being of his 'own construction' (see Chapter 3), and nine years later he installed in his first factory more elaborate machinery, of which no particulars have survived.

In the early 1880s, having taken over from his father, Joseph Beecham meticulously planned the technical specifications of his new factory. In Chapter 4, the imposing front offices in the architect-designed factory were described. Its mechanical fittings, widely publicized soon after completion, were the fruit of lengthy consultations between Joseph with his managers and a range of experts. The St Helens firm, Turton & Allin, carried out the engineering work; that must have given complete satisfaction because Joseph poached one of the family, John C. Allin (born in 1848 and better known as Allen), to become the firm's engineer, at £2 a week, William Moss receiving the same salary as deputy to the works manager. Allen was remembered also for his powerful tenor voice, which he showed off *con brio* once a week when winding the clock on the 150-foot high tower, projecting the sound over much of the town.[8]

The extensive basement provided airy storage space for the ingredients, which the firm imported from many parts of the world. Thomas already had a reputation for ordering excessively large quantities of inputs; it was nothing out of the ordinary for him to buy 2,000 bottles of quinine in 1885 through the respected wholesale chemists, Howards & Sons, later of Ilford – founded by the celebrated pharmacist, Luke Howard – and up to 1,000 boxes at a time of the finest Curaçao aloes in 1894 through A. Moryoseph & Co., of Leadenhall House in London. Beecham father and son are said to have tested with care the quality of these ingredients. Thomas knew enough to make some simple experiments, but his and the managers' tests on finished products were in fact very rudimentary. They discovered whether or not a suspect pill was spurious by cutting it in half and observing how well it had been mixed: a reflection on the woeful production standards set by their rivals.

The engine rooms were on the ground floor. A 20 horsepower engine, with dynamos, generated electricity for the whole works, supplemented by a 4 horsepower auxiliary machine to illuminate the offices after production shut down. The machinery was run by a 12 horsepower Otto gas engine, which for some reason attracted Joseph's love of display, being nickel-plated, while the belting was of ornamental leather. Tiles made by the Stoke-on-Trent ceramic firm, Minton & Co., decorated the walls, and electric lamps inside porcelain globes hung from the mahogany ceiling.

Nearby was the mixing room, as a rule kept securely locked and dubbed 'masonic' because of the highly secret formulae known only to the Beechams, their works manager and his deputy. The works manager ordered the raw drugs through a Private Order Book (since destroyed), and personally passed the invoices, writing the cheques and posting them off himself.[9]

The cough pill recipes have survived for August 1859, the same month in which he first advertised in the *St Helens Intelligencer*, and for November 1862, perhaps when he began to keep proper sales records (see Chapter 1). However, the definitive version was that for February 1884; either Thomas had by then returned to Lancashire for good after his wife Mary's final departure, or production plans for the new factory at St Helens had reached a point where the precise formulae needed to be established.

The main ingredients of the cough pills were 10 lbs (4.5kg) of gum resin, an expectorant, 10 lbs of squill, a diuretic and expectorant, and 8 lbs (3.6 kg) of powdered aniseed, a 'carminative' or soothing substance. Over and above aniseed oil, there were added 7 fluid ounces of morphia, which was dropped in 1893 after the UK government had prosecuted the makers of the narcotic drug Chlorodyne owing to its morphia content, widely blamed for numerous deaths. The cough mixture was 'made up' with Solazzi or liquorice juice: clearly to relieve rather than to tackle the causes of coughs.[10]

As to the digestive pills, three quarters consisted of purgative substances, aloes (50 per cent) and ginger (25 per cent). One-eighth was hard soap, and there were smaller quantities of coriander powder, light magnesium carbonate, and rosemary, juniper, ginger, aniseed and capsicum oils. After the aloes had been broken into pieces some 2–3 inches long, a cracking machine reduced them to the size of marbles. Those were left for four weeks in a drying machine; then two heavy rollers pulverized them, inside a large hopper with a capacity of half a ton at a time. Joseph, constantly on the look-out for ways of improving operations, had in the United States come across and purchased a sifting machine, to remove impurities from the ingredients. The amount of trouble he took over those hard substances helps to explain why people appreciated the quality of his pills.

For each mixing, the machine was loaded with 20 lbs (9kg) of aloes and 12 lbs (5.5kg) of ginger, to which 20 ounces (0.6kg) of juniper, rosemary and aniseed oil and a bar of soap were added, plus a 'sufficiency' of gum arabic. Such quantities probably made 170,000 pills, about five mixings being needed each day. The ingredients were turned into a brownish pill mass, softened by injections of water to the consistency of dough. The mass then travelled in a hydraulically powered hoist to the second floor, where a mechanical press extruded it in twelve thin strips. Cut into lengths of about a foot each, they went to a shaping machine, with double cylinders which formed them into round pills.

In its advertising pamphlet of 1891, 'A familiar name' (see Chapter 4), the firm claimed a production rate of 15,000 a minute: equivalent to 7.2 million in a working day of eight hours. That must have been a tenfold exaggeration, as in 1890 pill output at home averaged 800,000 a day, or 250 million per annum.

Unlike Morison and Holloway, the Beechams imposed a series of thorough quality checks on their made pills. A perforated cylinder allowed underweight ones to fall out. Four rounding machines then reshaped any that were too large, before the rest went through a 'picker', said to be Rowed's or Moss's invention. The trade press of 1889 featured a hand-operated machine of a similar kind, made at Coventry by Herbert & Hubbard, later the celebrated machine tool makers, Alfred Herbert Ltd. Both models had a sloping tray; when the handle was turned, the cams on the wheel rocked the tray, causing any sub-standard pills to fall into a special box.[11]

The correctly sized pills were placed on trays and taken to the drying room on the second floor. The Beechams were well aware that once made, they could deteriorate if subjected to drastic changes in light and atmosphere. Hence that room was well ventilated and had skylights. Its racks lined the walls, and held over 2,000 sliding trays, on which the pills dried out. In 1890, there were said to be upwards of 77 million pills being prepared for despatch, equivalent to 16 weeks' supply.

Thomas Beecham had many years earlier devised his own method of counting and boxing the pills, using a form of butter-pat with enough grooves to fill each box. When thrust into a mound of pills, it took out the correct quantity, to be emptied through a funnel into the boxes which a young lad guided through by hand. However, Andrews as works manager had recently invented the Alpha machines, for which Thomas in 1884 gave him £100. Operated by water power, these machines filled six boxes at a time and were said to be able to deal with 3,000 dozen boxes a day: over 10 million a year. As the firm was then claiming to sell annually 6 million boxes, that left enough capacity for future growth.

A team of boys then placed lids on boxes, stacked them on trays and took them to the labelling room, where a government stamp, for the patent medicine duty, was put on those destined for the home market. These were originally wrapped up into large parcels, but later on packed in cardboard boxes. For overseas, every six pill boxes went into a container, labelled with the consignee's name. In common with foodstuffs such as biscuits, the containers were sealed in lead-lined wooden cases, to keep the contents fresh during their often lengthy journeys.

Those millions of pills need to be set in the perspective of Britain's patent medicine industry as a whole. In 1890, the value of the medicine stamps actually used by the Beecham firm was £25,325, somewhat less than the £32,000 of which Joseph boasted in 'A familiar name', mentioned above. That represented 10.7 per cent of the national market, according to Inland Revenue returns. Although the Holloway firm was then asserting that its pills and ointment had 'the largest sale of any medicine in the world', its own usage of stamps in 1890 revealed its share to be only 3.2 per cent of home sales. It was still making the same fictitious claim ten years later.

Total pill consumption throughout Britain in that decade can be calculated from two independent sources of 1890 and 1897 respectively. Observing how national sales of pills had soared since the early nineteenth century, the *Chemist and Druggist* in 1890 ran a post-card poll (see Chapter 4) to obtain an estimate of current demand. The consensus of responding chemists' opinions was that nationally no fewer than 5.6 million pills were being taken every day, giving a total consumption per year of about 2,060 million.

Nearly seven years later the London evening paper, the *Star*, estimated from firms' advertising expenditure that the output of proprietary pills totalled about 20 million a week. Roughly an equivalent number were being dispensed by chemists for doctors or being made by wholesale chemists; the weekly 40 million came to 2,080 million a year. Britain's population then totalled 37.7 million: thus every man, woman and child appeared to be swallowing on average just over one pill a week.[12] The 220 million home deliveries of Beecham's pills in 1890 accounted for 10.7 per cent of that estimated total pill consumption, or 21 per cent of the proprietary kind.

About half the pills produced in Britain were thus generic ones, manufactured according to formulae in the *British Pharmacopoeia* and thus differing from the patent or proprietary kind, where the formulae were kept secret. The Bethnal Green factory of a leading wholesale druggist, Allen & Hanburys, had a pill room, complete with rolling, cutting and shaping machinery: possibly not steam-driven, as that firm did not install its own design of high-speed automatic machines for compressed tablets until 1903. The Evans Sons & Co. firm was by 1890 using steam-powered machines for every stage of production in its 'pill-mill' at Liverpool.

It was Leicester which saw itself as the headquarters of the nineteenth-century generic pill-making industry in England. The leading firm, John Richardson & Co., established in 1793, claimed to be the most extensive manufacturers of coated pills in the world. A former long-service employee, T. Howard Lloyd, had helped to pioneer its mechanization; in the early 1890s he set up his own business, Howard Lloyd & Co. Ltd, using Werner & Pflederer's kneading and mixing machines, and a rounding machine designed by a Mr Niblett. As the retail end of the market was being progressively enlarged by the spread of multiple-branch chemists, often pushing for low prices and quick turnover (see Chapter 7), reputable proprietary and non-proprietary firms alike had by then every incentive to offer well turned-out varieties.[13]

Allen & Hanburys made gelatine-covered pills, and Richardson and Lloyd in Leicester pearl-covered ones, of bluish-grey hue; both those coverings possibly disguised the taste. American consumers expected their pills to be sugar-coated, and at St Helens that coating process took place in three revolving copper cylinders, driven by machinery with an eccentric action to cover them completely while being spun. For the rest of the world, Beecham's pills were merely dusted with powdered liquorice; they were so thoroughly mixed that they needed no coating to maintain their shape.

The firm's accounting system was simplicity itself. Until 1916 it operated on a cash basis, as if it were a corner shop replenishing and drawing out of the till. By law, Joseph did not need an auditor for his unincorporated business, and as late as 1913 he admitted to the Select Committee on Patent Medicines (see Chapter 7) that no balance sheet existed, so that the firm lacked any capital as such.[14] Visiting St Helens every year to calculate the annual profits – which as sole owner he pocketed – he had no trouble about persuading the Inland Revenue to accept the figures submitted. Only after his death did revenue officials begin to challenge his distinction between personal expenses and those incurred by the firm, even down to ground rents for property he himself owned. The accounts then had to be reconstructed from the cash books back to 1899, much to the gratification of later historians.

In the 1880s, the firm's main capital expenditure had been on erecting the factory, at a total cost of £30,000. Progress payments, as they became due to the contractors, must have come from the Beechams' private banking accounts, Joseph paying £1,000 for the clock tower. After 1899, the profit and loss accounts do not refer to any new plant until 1919–21. Shortly before 1907, Rowed is said to have devised some 'ingenious machinery for perfecting the manufacture of the pills'. Whatever the nature of that innovation, Joseph clearly dissuaded him from going ahead. Not until 1914 were some auxiliary machines ordered, in case of breakdowns. Delivery was halted by the war; eventually those cost £1,400 plus £1,100 for 'electric installations'.

The firm's only financial reserve was a special deposit account, set up in 1891 on Joseph's prompting to meet any unexpected outlays. That account grew to £21,000 by 1895, when Thomas took out £7,000 on his retirement. Joseph paid in no more money until he deposited £15,000 in 1910, perhaps in case it were needed for the New York factory (see Chapter 5). He did not then draw on it, but from 1914 onwards again added large sums to use the account as a nest-egg after his finances came under strain, as explained in Chapter 8.

These retrospective accounts give plentiful profit and loss details. In 1899, of the £153,000 total sales (net of medicine duty), costs totalled £76,600; the largest cost item was advertising expenditure of over £64,000. Purchases of new drugs and boxes came to less than £4,000, works wages to £3,700 and managers' and office employees' salaries to £2,400. Now that the firm itself paid for outward despatch of pill orders, £1,050 went on carriage and freight; the massive volume of letters and parcels – in the days of the penny post – set the firm back £475 in stamps and postage expenditure. Remaining costs, such as rates, insurance, gas and electricity, totalled less than £1,000. The net profit margin was therefore just under 50 per cent.[15]

That was not an unusual return in the patent medicine industry. For example, J. C. Eno Ltd manufactured its celebrated fruit salt, a saline preparation mixing tartaric and citric acid with sodium bicarbonate to make, when water was added, an effervescent drink that was a more palatable digestive remedy than any pill. Exempted from duty as not considered to be a patent medicine as such, in 1914 it made a 56 per cent profit on turnover (see Chapter 8); the founder, James C. Eno, died a year later worth £1.6 million.[16]

By 1914 Beecham's profit margin had risen slightly to 53 per cent. Financial problems caused by the First World War, from that August onwards, pushed up the cost of imported drugs and boxes by over a half; yet that increase was more than offset by a fall in advertising costs from £81,000 to £71,000. The accounts for 1921/22, when the distortions of the post-war boom were correcting themselves, show a 55 per cent margin. The cost of drugs and boxes had come down roughly to the pre-war level, as had carriage and freight. Rates, insurance and Schedule A tax (on buildings) had, by contrast, shot up. No detailed financial accounts are available for subsequent years.

Capital and finance may have underpinned the structure and progress of the Beecham firm, but the key contribution was made by labour. Table 6.2 sets out particulars of the number of employees between 1872 and 1960. Where known, operatives are noted separately from office staff, and their weekly wages given. A 'Wages Book No. 1' – the only one to survive – for 1886–90 reveals the pattern of wages and salaries in those years;[17] Table 6.1 above had made a comparison with Holloway's workforce and its remuneration in 1877 and 1890.

A striking difference between the two firms by the late nineteenth century is Holloway's employment of females wholly for production, packing and labelling. Perhaps the pressure of making, with hand-operated machinery, up to £100,000 worth of remedies a year, explains why the Holloway firm's production processes were so slapdash. The lower average wages in St Helens reflected the cost of living there compared with in London. In 1908, for example, St Helens' rents were on average 44 per cent below those in the capital, while prices of meat, groceries and coal were 9 per cent lower; the rents and prices charged in 1912 were 40 per cent and 5 per cent lower respectively.[18]

The one deduction by the Beechams from their operatives' wages – but not from office salaries – was for the firm's sick fund. Wage-earners of at least 12s. (60p) paid 2d. (1p) a week, and those earning less paid 1d. In Table 6.1 that division is taken as separating adults from boys. Sick pay seems to have been 2s. (10p) a week, for a maximum of seven weeks, jobs being kept open until a

Table 6.2   *Beecham: number of employees*

	Numbers	Operatives	Office staff	Annual turnover (£)	Total weekly wages
1872	7	–	–	11,100	–
1882	18	–	–	34,000	£14–4–6
1884	19	–	–	(66,500)	–
1885	26	–	–	79,200	–
1887	54	50	4	(120,600)	£41–12–4
1888	76	71	5	(141,300)	£56–17–3
1890	85	74	11	178,600	£65–15–0
1897	90	74	16	132,400	£76–11–4
1914	117	102	15	228,800	£109–14–2*
1917	120	104	16	278,150	£108–14–1*
1922	138	115	23	308,174	£215–3–0*
1944	3–4,000	–		8,700,000	–
1960	15,000	–	–	54,745,000	–

Sources: 1872, *St Helens Reporter*, 27 February 1942; 1882, 1885, 1897, A. Francis, *A Guinea a Box* (1968), pp. 93, 107, and 91 respectively; 1884, T. C. Barker and J. R. Harris, *A Merseyside Town in the Industrial Revolution. St Helens 1750–1900* (1954), p. 379; 1886–90, BA, Wages Book No. 1, BP 1/5/14; 1914, BA, 'List of male employees before the [First World] war, 30 July 1914 ('no females employed'), BP 1/5/3; 1917, TNA, J4 8854/285, 15 February 1917; 1922, BA, 'Report by Louis Nicholas on St Helens business, November 1922', Schedules 3 and 6, BP 2/2/10, pp. 27–30; 1944, Beecham Group Board Minutes, 27 September 1944 ('mostly women'); 1960, Beecham Group *Annual Report 1959/60*, p. 10.

* Operatives' wages only; office salaries distorted by those of Henry Beecham and Charles Rowed.

return to work. Doctors' visits were allowed, and Thomas made a practice of calling on the sick in their homes. Apparently in the 1880s the firm started medical inspections before prospective employees could join.

Between 1897 and 1914, when the number of pills made increased by 43 per cent, from 250 million to nearly 358 million, the number of operatives went up by nearly 38 per cent from 74 to 102. Between 1914 and 1921/22, there was a further increase of 38 per cent in pill production, but only of 13 per cent in numbers of operatives, some by then being women; the new electrically powered plant and machinery no doubt helped to improve labour productivity.

A list of Beecham employees in 1914, apparently drawn up to prepare for the conscription that was introduced two years later, gives their ages and positions within the firm.[19] All were men, as Joseph Beecham refused to employ females. When the so-called MP in the firm's publicity pamphlet, 'A familiar name' (see Chapter 4) suggested to him the uses – especially for packing – to which their 'deft and nimble fingers' could be put, Joseph argued that many St Helens women found employment in the town's glass, watchmaking and other industries, where demand for their labour outstripped supply. He did not add that those industries normally paid better wages than his.[20]

In any case, Joseph opposed mixing the sexes in business. Since he made a point of advancing employees who showed diligence and aptitude for higher positions, he would find it impossible to promote women to some of these posts, presumably over the heads of men. As late as 1914, therefore, males undertook jobs that were being done elsewhere by women. Operatives cleaned their own sections of the factory, while in 1891 the general office had four shorthand clerks (all men) and two typewriters in constant use.[21] Although Joseph was very taken with all aspects of American business, photographs in 'A familiar name' of his, Rowed's and the general offices reveal that no telephones had been installed by that year.

Jennie Murray, mentioned in Chapter 3 as a pill-maker's assistant at the time of the 1881 census, appears to be a unique case when the first factory was in operation. She had departed by the time the wages book of 1886–90 started. That book does list a handful of women, perhaps engaged to supervise the dining room or keep the offices tidy. Mrs Donlon earned 10s. (50p) a week in 1887, followed by Ellen Tagg at 12s. (60p) from late 1887 to 1889. In 1889–90, Michael Rohan's wife earned 14s. (70p) a week, husband and wife being included in the clerical staff. They probably occupied the commissionaire's house, where she assembled the packed lunch, covered by a linen cloth, which Joseph Beecham regularly ate at his desk.[22] The house disappeared when the factory was extended in the 1930s.

As the First World War dragged on, shortages of men affected manufacturing businesses in St Helens, as elsewhere in the country. Pilkington Brothers became a heavy recruiter of labour, both for its main activity of glass making and for the shell factory set up in part of its premises. Employees there enjoyed some of the highest wages in town, and that company had the added attraction of being unionized, as Beecham was not. Joseph's death in 1916 removed any bar to having women in his firm, and by August 1917 the first seventeen female operatives were being taken on.

Those women, kept segregated from the men, all worked on 'packing, wrapping, labelling, affixing revenue stamps etc.' They were required to have clean fingernails and, where possible, some experience of piano playing, believed to enhance the suppleness of their fingers. The first supervisor was Emily Oldham (1892–1977), daughter of Joseph's former coachman, Thomas Oldham. In 1922 she earned £2 10s. (£2.50) a week, and from 1932 to 1947 she served as welfare supervisor. To humour the men's susceptibilities, the foreman continued to be male, earning nearly double at £4 15s. (£4.75). Mrs Van Schaik was the residential welfare woman, at 15s. (75p) a week, plus rent. There were in 1922 sixty female employees. William Moss, the works manager, that year commended the packing department as 'very efficiently managed', so that the transfer of jobs from men and boys to 'girls' had been a resounding success.[23]

Little is recorded about any other arrangements the Beechams may have had for the well-being of labour, apart from the sick fund, the provision of liquid refreshment (see below) and recreational activities, such as a billiard table and a reading room in the basement. The boys used a playing area on a piece of ground near the printing office, which Joseph had earmarked to provide an outlet for juvenile energies.[24]

The post-1899 accounts include an item of 'compassionate allowances', introduced in 1916/17 after Joseph's death. That ranged from £378 to £212 a year until 1919/20, after which it averaged only £24 annually to 1921/22. Some men must have died on active service, but no record of them has survived. Thomas, who had a genuine interest in employees' welfare, may in his time have helped out with small payments to hands faced with troubles such as bereavement or family illness, but Joseph and Rowed were remote figures and less personally involved. William Moss, who was an active churchman, a Sunday school superintendent and vice-president of the local YMCA, may perhaps have dealt with any compassionate matters in the factory.

At least after he took over the firm, Joseph treated his senior staff generously. By 1916 he was paying Rowed and William Moss, as general manager and works manager respectively, 0.5 per cent each of the annual profits. Charles Scrymgeour, the home sales manager, and Edward Glover, the foreign and colonial manager, received 0.3 per cent, and Edward Bamford, the office manager, and Austin Scott, his private secretary 0.2 per cent. In 1922, Rowed was earning £3,000 and Moss £1,500 a year; they both lived rent-free in St Helens, their houses being provided by Joseph. Scrymgeour and Bamford earned £850 and £650 respectively, and Austin Scott £600, Glover having died in 1918.

The Beecham factory's working day, in the decade or so after 1877, was an excessively long one, from 6 a.m. to 6 p.m. on Mondays to Saturdays, with half an hour for breakfast from 8 to 8.30 and an hour for dinner from 1 to 2 p.m. There may also have been a mid-afternoon break, as cocoa or tea were provided in a special room. That made a 60-hour week, longer than the 55½ hours worked at the Pilkington factory, namely 6.00–5.30 on Monday to Friday and 6–12 noon on Saturdays. The hours of 6 to 6 were the longest permitted under the Factory Acts from 1874 onwards.[25]

To compare Beecham's hours of work with those of food manufacturing firms, the biscuit maker, Carr's of Carlisle, had originally worked from 5.15 a.m. to 6 p.m., or 63½ hours a week; to comply with the 1874 Act, it apparently adjusted the starting time to 6 a.m. The other major biscuit firms, Huntley & Palmers of Reading and Peek Frean of London, operated a 58½ hour week until in 1872 they both changed to 54 hours. Rowntree of York, making cocoa and chocolate, had a 56-hour working week, from 6 a.m. to 6 p.m. on Mondays to Fridays and from 6 a.m. to 2 p.m. on Saturdays.

At the Royal Porcelain Works in Worcester, work was from 6.30 a.m. to 6 p.m. in 1851, but manufacturing ceased at 4 p.m. on Saturdays. Thereafter employees had the task of 'cleaning rooms and benches, putting tools & c., in order throughout the works', before payment of wages took place at 5 p.m. Those paid could presumably then go home. In the St Helens factory, floors and other washable items such as benches were scrubbed on Saturday mornings.[26] It is not known when wages were paid.

However, the Factory Acts laid down that 14- to 18-year-olds could work on Saturdays only from 6 a.m. to 2 p.m.; in their absence many adult workers could thereafter have had little to do. In 1876 a government enquiry into the operation of those Acts found that Saturday half-holiday had become all but universal; perhaps after all the entire factory closed at 2 p.m. A rare but welcome interruption to the unvarying routine occurred in extremely hot weather. The ingredients, especially chemist's soap, became too sticky to be put through the machines; hands were instead found jobs sweeping, polishing, dusting and carrying out other cleaning.

In 1890 Joseph is said to have reduced the hours of work, apparently to 48 hours, with Saturday working from 9 to 4.[27] Such a drastic reduction sounds quite unusual at a time when many similar manufacturing firms were still on 54 hours. An employee who joined in the mid-1920s recalled the factory hours as then being from 8.30 to 5.30, the offices starting at 9 o'clock, and on Saturday from 9 to midday. By 1936 there were two breaks in addition to the midday dinner hour, reckoned to benefit employees' health. All firms in the Beecham Group went on to a five-day week as from 1 August 1939.

Before 1914, the firm did not normally grant holidays, although the Factory Act of 1878 allowed all young people the whole of Christmas Day and Good Friday (or equivalent days) and 8 half-holidays a year. In 1889 most employees earning 12s. (60p) a week and above had Christmas day – a Wednesday – off. The others worked only 4–4½ days that week. No hands were paid for the time lost. The Factory and Workshop Act of 1895 for the first time imposed on all firms bank holiday closing, which had been introduced for banking houses as long before as 1871. The Act specified Easter and Whit Mondays, the first Monday in August and Boxing Day, as well as the religious festivals of Christmas Day and Good Friday. Because there was no trade union activity in the factory, the changes elsewhere in Britain, said by the 1870s to have 'radically altered the country's conception of what constituted a day's work', must have bypassed Beecham for two decades.

Annual excursions for the workforce, normally held on a Saturday, were a prominent feature of paternalistic late-Victorian businesses. The first recorded Beecham excursion, another of Joseph's initiatives, was in 1885. Joseph and 112 employees and their families departed from St Helens station at 7.20 a.m. for Liverpool. They spent the morning at the New Ferry Pleasure Gardens, on the Birkenhead side of the river Mersey, and were given their midday dinner in a hotel. Five horse-drawn wagonettes took them to Chester, where some toured the city and others sailed on the river Dee. After a 'substantial tea', they returned to Liverpool in time for the 11.10 p.m. train home.

The 1887 excursion, departing for Liverpool at 6 a.m., provides a few extra details of the arrangements. Again visiting New Ferry, that year's group (number not known) had breakfast at 8 and dinner at 1 p.m. After a knife-and-fork tea at 6 p.m., there were sports and entertainments, which included the favourite pastime of dancing. They were back in St Helens at midnight, but had the Sunday in which to recover.

Between 1891 and 1896, the excursions were to Morecambe, Blackpool or Llandudno. In 1893, 16 married men and 12 of their wives, 24 single men and 49 boys, accompanied by Thomas Beecham, two friends and some of Joseph's domestic servants from Huyton, went to Blackpool. To commemorate Queen Victoria's diamond jubilee in 1897, employees and any wives were given a week's holiday, with expenses paid, at Douglas, Isle of Man. Because of the numbers involved and the need to keep production going, there were two shifts, in successive weeks. The furthest cross-country journey was in July 1900, to the Dukeries in Nottinghamshire; it is not known which of the county's ducal seats was actually visited.

The party returned to Blackpool for the 1901 outing. Then in 1902, the year of Edward VII's coronation, Joseph authorized a further week's holiday in the Isle of Man, once again in shifts. No more excursions were held, as he cancelled them, allegedly because one of the participants misbehaved while drunk. Joseph was by then taking progressively less interest in the firm and had his matrimonial problems, but he may possibly have made up this deprivation to the workforce in some other way.[28]

Beecham father and son paid for these excursions out of their own pockets, as there was no item in the profit and loss accounts to which the expense could have been allocated. While Thomas went at least once and must have relished every minute of the occasion, Joseph had little talent for hobnobbing with the hands, and after the first excursion he chose to send his household staff instead.

Although the working day before 1890 was undoubtedly a long one, and pay tended to be poorer than in other St Helens businesses, morale among employees appears to have been high. They took pride in the atmosphere of order and cleanliness, even at the expense of frequent scrubbing down. All welcomed the so-called healing vapours from the ingredients and their production methods, which pervaded much of the works, for keeping colds and other ailments at bay. Operatives in sauce-making factories, too, swore by the health-giving pungent odours around them.

Adult employees as a rule chose to spend their working lives in the firm, and encouraged younger relatives to seek jobs there, even though the boys, once they were sixteen, had to leave unless chosen for work at full pay. Any of those who survived until seventy had to retire, and were eligible for the government's non-contributory pension of 10s. (50p) a week, introduced in 1908. However, the nominal list of 1914 shows only two employees as old as 66, one being John C. Allen (or Allin) the engineer, the other a joiner.

Rowed, at 59, was the next oldest, Moss the works manager being 54. Only three operatives were in their fifties, the rest being younger. As late as 1922 the sole pensioner was Allen, then 74, whose £1 10s. (£1.50) pension appears among the works employees' wages. In 1924 the first Beecham limited company took over responsibility for its three pensioners, including Allen and Thomas Oldham, Joseph's 60-year-old former coachman, at £1 10s. (£1.50). Oldham had received a lump sum of £100 on his employer's death; the board, always on the look-out for saving a few pounds, sought but failed to reduce his pension from £2 10s. (£2.50). He died in 1929, aged 65. A pension scheme for the whole of the successor company, Beechams Pills Ltd, was introduced in 1937.

Most nineteenth-century manufacturing firms possessed a written schedule of rules and regulations. The Worcester porcelain works in 1851 required silence and order, sobriety, civility and punctuality, and forbade bad language, smoking and the introduction of intoxicating drink; 'useful reading at proper times approved' while all immoral publications and prints found were confiscated 'and their owners DISCHARGED'. The Beecham business must have had similar rules; if so, they no longer exist. Its first factory in 1877 had a time-keeper, and lateness would have been punished by fines.

Thomas himself, invariably present at the outset of each working day, enjoyed a reputation for constant 'watchfulness and care' over all operations. Unruly behaviour, which could lead to dismissal, was rare, but some Polish refugees, taken on as hands in the early days, constantly made trouble and were not tolerated for long.[29] Employees had to be respectably dressed, and to arrive with washed hands and faces. As all operatives wore white linen coats and flat white hats, those would have had to be laundered every week. So as to instil a sense of decorum throughout the firm and to minimize time-wasting, the management forbade casual conversations at work.

After his death, Thomas was remembered as a just and upright man in the factory, a hard worker, most methodical in business, and one respected by his subordinates.[30] That memory appears not to have been challenged; Anne Francis, his great-granddaughter, has referred to employees' keen awareness of the right and the wrong way of behaving and attitude to work in the factory, which they called 'Beecham' and 'not Beecham'. According to her, there was a '"Beecham mystique". The family had style, pace, a way of doing things that was somehow different' from elsewhere in industry and commerce, creating a genuine sense of comradeship among employees. They were interested enough to give Henry Beecham, Joseph's son who had recently joined the firm, a silver loving cup to commemorate his coming of age in 1909, doubtless because he was seen as representing the future of the business.[31]

However, there was clearly a downside to that seeming harmony between managers and workers in a non-unionized enterprise which turned out, month after month, only two products with little or no variation. From the late 1890s onwards, the drive to innovate that had dominated Thomas's and Joseph's lives for so many years lost its impetus. The new factory was, it seemed, already at the technological limit for that period, and further improvements would not be introduced at home for nearly four decades.

The future conductor, (Sir) Thomas Beecham, unwillingly recruited into the firm by his father, Joseph, as a trainee in 1898 at the age of nineteen, much later portrayed what he termed 'our smooth-running and highly organized business' in dismissive terms: 'I was expected to fit in with and settle down to a routine through which the course of life flowed lazily and insignificantly.' To him at least it lacked any true significance. That judgment was supported, in a back-handed kind of way, by George Statter, who had joined the firm in 1901 at 14. Having stayed on as a low-paid packer, in his old age he recalled, 'It was a convalescent home in a manner of speaking', and asserted that when he first entered, his workmates had said the same.[32] Perhaps the undeviating routine made employees old before their time.

As no slacking was allowed among employees, the torpor indicated by these witnesses must have been a mental one. However acceptable a place to work in, the organization – although not its output – was year by year running down. Sooner or later some entrepreneur, whether a Beecham or an outsider, would need to inject a new spirit of innovation into the firm. Otherwise, its long-term future looked bleak.

As more and more distributors took advantage of the £5 minimum order, the average factory gate prices of a box of 56 pills, selling retail for 1*s.* (5p) net of duty, fell from just under 4p to 3¼p in 1913. The firm was unable to calculate the impact on its home profits, having no means of separating out domestic and overseas earnings so long as its accounts were drawn up on a cash-only basis (see Chapter 6).

Rowed as general manager still ran the firm's publicity, but observers noted that the firm was not projecting itself as effectively as hitherto. After the voting successes of earlier decades (see Chapter 4), a post-card competition in the *Chemist and Druggist* of January 1902 found that chemists rated the most interesting advertisement to be one for Pears' soap, even though Beecham's pills remained the best-selling speciality product.

That August, the *Advertising World* noted a deterioration in the firm's most recent advertisements, which 'read very nicely' but failed to impress themselves on the public mind as powerfully as in the past. The *Chemist and Druggist's* post-card competition of January 1905, on advertisements calculated to yield most sales, put Beecham's pills behind those of Vinolia soap, Daisy Powders – a headache remedy – and products of the wholesale druggists Allen & Hanburys.[7]

The firm hazarded one or two – nowadays quite incomprehensible – catch-phrases, such as 'You see what I mean?', and there was some feeble copy about (Sir) James Barrie's play, *Little Mary*, exploiting its title that was a euphemism for the human stomach. That inspired a ditty which merits preservation:

> So let our morning greeting be
> As Mr Barrie wills –
> 'Is "Little Mary" well?' Why, yes,
> And thanks to Beecham's pills.[8]

In April 1908, a bright notion about 'The Promise of Spring', pointing to a Beecham's pill box as 'The Best Easter Egg', descended into a wordy effusion about the 'youth of Nature' and such high-flown observations as 'The scented earth answers to the joyous impulse, and laughs forth in buds, in flowers, in foliage'. Yet in 1904 the firm invented the slogan, 'that tired feeling', doubtless to be linked with the 'lowness of spirits and all nervous affections' which it already claimed the pills would cure. Beecham thus anticipated by sixteen years 'Bovril prevents that sinking feeling', which the makers of that beef extract drink launched in 1920.

More strikingly, the firm commissioned the poster artist, John Hassall (1868–1948), who later famously popularized the 'bracing' Lincolnshire resort of Skegness, to say it all in his copy, 'You've got the hump [feel out of sorts]. You want Beecham's pills.'[9] It also put out clever vignettes, of the incredulous vicar exclaiming, 'Why! Surely they must all take Beecham's pills', and the young girl in smock with upturned face, about to receive a pill from her mother: 'All good children take – Beecham's pills.'[10]

Scarcely by coincidence, less punchy Beecham advertisements came out in the years when Joseph was deep in his marital problems. Those were largely of his own making, as he refused to leave his hapless wife alone. On 21 January 1895 he signed a formal agreement with the widowed headmistress of a Huyton day school, Annette Amanda Davidson, for her to retire from that post and devote herself exclusively to the charge of the three middle daughters, Josephine, Edith and Jessie, 'to mother them, make her home their home and superintend their education'. Aged about fifty and of generous proportions, she was assumed to have been yet another of his harem; she later received a £100 annuity, enough to live on at that time.[11]

To be sure, Josephine suffered from epileptic fits that were usually brought round with stimulants and made her increasingly dependent on alcohol. Spending so much time well away from Ewanville, she also had to give up to Mrs Davidson the running of the household. At the best of times she was not an easy person to get on with, being moody as well as highly strung. Small and neat of figure, she 'had the mouth and intent eyes of a person easy to hurt'.[12]

Only two weeks later, on 7 February, Josephine's mother died of cancer at Geelong, 45 miles from Melbourne in Australia. How and why she had settled in that town is anyone's guess; an oversized gravestone, surrounded by railings, can be seen to this day in its Eastern Cemetery.[13] As she left no will, the names of any descendants who might have remained with her are not known. It seems unlikely that she had kept in touch with Josephine or received news of her numerous grandchildren. At least she was spared any knowledge of Joseph's next move to erode even further her eldest daughter's self-esteem.

On 13 April 1895 the *Illustrated London News* carried an appallingly provocative – for Josephine – advertisement, 'A Divorce Court Incident'. Counsel, with a more than passing resemblance to Joseph (who had shaved off his mutton chop whiskers; perhaps Helen did not care for them, but the drooping moustache is evident in the picture), is seen interrogating a young woman standing in the dock. Readers were invited to submit up to 100 words of 'the most appropriate dialogue' between them. For whatever reason – perhaps because few bothered to send in a suitable dialogue – apart from a further one a fortnight later, no Beecham advertisements appeared in that publication until 29 February 1896, when there was a full-page splash about 'The Struggle to the North Pole' (see Chapter 4). More of the divorce theme appeared somewhere else, in which the respondent and co-respondent are sharing a box of pills, while Counsel surmises, 'Then he was, after all, only her guide, pill-offerer, and friend': a dreadful word-play on Alexander Pope's 'guide, philosopher and friend'.[14]

Given Joseph's current state of high tension, Walter Adams as works manager in 1896 chose the worst possible moment to provoke him. One day Joseph instructed Moss, the deputy, to display a poster about evening classes at the St Helens technical institute. On seeing the poster and asking who had wanted it put up, Andrews told Moss, 'Then take it down and give it back to Mr. Beecham.' Whether or not there had been earlier conflicts, Joseph sacked Andrews on the spot, and appointed in his place the more amenable Moss.[15] Andrews thereafter set up his own mineral water business near Stafford, while Moss remained as a totally dependable works manager through successive regimes until 1929.

Meanwhile, Thomas the younger was often parked with friends or relatives during holidays from Rossall. In 1897, he went up to Wadham College, Oxford, to read Greats. Enjoying an unusual talent for and obsessive interest in music, plus a handsome allowance from his father, he hired a piano, which he had installed in his lodgings outside college. After the first term he paid scant attention to the classics. Twice he went off, on one occasion without the college's permission, to Dresden in Germany; there he sampled operas and other musical treats. Having enjoyed a season of cricket, he left Oxford for good at the end of Trinity Term 1898. According to a – doubtless much embellished – story he related to the composer, Ethel Smyth, his college Warden observed at the leave-taking interview, 'Your untimely departure has perhaps spared us the necessity of asking you to go.'[16]

Joseph had every expectation that his elder son, having sown his musical wild oats, would settle down, readily enter the firm, and undertake an apprenticeship to fit him to take over in due course. Thomas had totally different ideas. He at once requested permission to spend time on the continent, learning foreign languages – and incidentally revelling in music. Greeted with a blank refusal from his father, that autumn he was given an office job of looking after the firm's artistic side, namely pictorial illustrations and music: a slot traditionally reserved in paternalistic firms for the duffer of the family.

Thomas did make efforts to speed up the publication of the *Music Portfolios*, and he founded the short-lived St Helens Orchestral Society. Yet he made himself disliked in the firm by behaving in a 'not Beecham' way, treating fellow employees with disdain, letting his hair grow long, and not so surreptitiously keeping musical scores under his desk blotter. His musical opportunity arrived in 1899, when Joseph for the first time became mayor of the town, the 18-year-old daughter Josephine acting as mayoress because her mother was reported to be indisposed.

For the mayoral installation that December, Joseph invited down from Manchester the Hallé Orchestra, under the eminent conductor, Hans Richter. When Richter pulled out at the last minute, Thomas as a 20-year-old volunteered to conduct: his sheer verve and the players' familiarity with the repertoire carried him through with credit.[17]

Despite still residing at Ewanville, Thomas appeared to be unaware that in the previous March, his father had had Josephine committed to St Andrew's Lunatic Asylum in the sufficiently remote town of Northampton, where the poet John Clare was incarcerated from 1851 until his death in 1864. She had been diagnosed as suffering from hysteria and delusions, believing herself to be the Princess of Wales; a tame JP signed the committal order.

When Thomas at last woke up to her enforced departure, he called his eldest sister, Emily, back from the United States, where she had enrolled as a medical student, and then left most of the donkey work to her. Petite like her mother but resolute, Emily acted decisively. She went behind Joseph's back to confront Mrs Davidson, whose evidence had been crucial in having Josephine put away. Stressing her own medical knowledge, Emily declared that she would personally investigate Josephine's condition, with the aid of a psychiatric specialist and a lawyer. She then engaged a private detective to track down both Josephine's whereabouts and the haunt to which Joseph disappeared at the week-ends.[18]

By chance, both brother and sister could rely on an independent base in London. Thomas had lately struck up a friendship with Utica, the 18-year-old daughter of Dr Charles Stuart Welles, the American-born physician to the United States embassy in London.[19] She and her family visited Ewanville several times in 1899, Josephine's prolonged absences being somehow explained away. Early in the new year of 1900, Emily and Thomas confronted their father over Josephine's committal and his keeping of a mistress; he is said to have been so enraged as to order them out of the house, whereupon they decamped to the Welles' London residence. Dr Welles, although without a private income, backed Thomas in his musical studies and in preparatory work to mount a legal case before the Probate and Divorce Court. It took until December before the court even allowed relatives and a solicitor access to her.

In February 1901 Joseph returned from a holiday in Egypt and brought Josephine back from Northampton to Ewanville, having her minded by attendants. A court order secured her release, and she moved to the Welleses in London. That summer she was formally granted a judicial separation, on the evidence of her husband's adultery, and was awarded alimony of £2,500 a year. The detective hired by her children then visited St Helens and discovered that Joseph's annual income was no less than £85,000, of which £30,000 came from the pill firm. The latter was probably an under-estimate, as net annual profits then averaged £80,000, and no funds were currently being put to reserve.

Once the assiduous private eye had discovered Mr and Mrs Bennett's hideaway in Willesden, Joseph had it sold, and packed Helen off to her aunt in New York. As the Beecham court case had already made the headlines across the Atlantic, she received no welcome from her kinsfolk. 'My people heard of what had occurred and were very displeased' with her conduct, she admitted in a deposition of 1917 (see Chapter 9). To make plain a final split, 'they handed me certain securities to which I was entitled'; they 'have not since been in communication with me'.[20]

Joseph once again took himself off to Egypt for the Christmas of 1902 and the following months. He then brazened it out in St Helens by giving a lecture to employees about incidents that had taken place on his travels. In March 1903, the issue of the alimony payment once again came before the court. There he maintained that his total income was no higher than £30,000. In a bid to demolish his wife's case, he testified that when he married her, she was only a small-time dressmaker, 'without position or property', whereas he himself had been manager of an important firm, 'and just beginning to earn an income'.

Moreover, Joseph's counsel submitted that Emily and Thomas had brought the case 'in the hope of getting money from their father, as they feared they would not be left money in his will'. In fact, as Emily later revealed in a public statement, three days before the hearing Joseph had 'threatened them irrevocably with disinheritance if they proceeded with the suit on behalf of their mother': a charge he never attempted to deny.[21]

The president of the court, obsequiously asserting that Joseph had 'behaved with exemplary firmness and generosity' in the matter, ruled that Josephine was no lady but of mean origin, and could therefore manage comfortably on £1,000 a year, not even deserving a further £1,500. The Court of Appeal showed more backbone, and increased her alimony by an undisclosed sum: in fact, to £4,500 a year. Old Thomas Beecham, never known to have much consideration for womanly feelings, could scarcely contain his delight that Josephine's predicament was generating 'the best bit of free advertising I've ever had' – almost the same phrase as he had used after Rosebery's speech of 1894 at the Royal Academy (see Chapter 4) – with the journalistic cliché about a 'bitter pill' working overtime.

In 1903 Joseph acquired for himself a thirty-room London residence, West Brow in Hampstead, which he had refurbished and enlarged in *art nouveau* style. His study was hung with wall tapestries in silver, brown and gold; over the fireplace a carved panel bore his monogram and the year 1903. On the newel post at the foot of the main staircase, there was an alabaster globe, one foot in diameter, said to represent – even though in mottled green – a pill.

Observers, apparently ignorant of the definitive breach with his elder son, regarded his new acquisition as the splendid residence of a wealthy magnate who was laying it down, so to speak, for his descendants into the remote future.

To that end, Joseph began to collect works of art, specializing in the period between the death of Sir Joshua Reynolds in 1792 and the arrival of the pre-Raphaelites during the 1850s. His particular favourites were English landscapes, especially by John Constable and George Morland, and he also went in for water colours. At first purchasing through agents, in May 1905 for the first time he personally attended an auction, accompanied by his Hampstead neighbour, Thomas Barratt (see Chapter 5). As 'Joe' and 'Tom' to each other, they were seen as inseparable; Barratt even gave up purchasing on his own behalf so as to assist and advise Joseph.[22]

To display that collection, Joseph had a commodious picture gallery built, with an illuminated skylight showing a Highland scene. His son's biographer subsequently commented that its purple, green and other bright colours 'must have clashed regrettably with the Constables'. In both music and art, Joseph liked what he knew, and anything experimental or out of the ordinary was not for him. He would listen over and over again to well-loved musical works. Likewise, when at home he would go up to his picture gallery late at night, fill his pipe, turn off all but one lamp, and scrutinize a selected picture while enjoying a smoke.[23]

Barratt had taken over the Pears' soap company after marrying a daughter of the family. He then unceremoniously dumped her and lived openly in Hampstead with his mistress. Joseph preferred to keep the public and private sides of his life entirely separate. Only in 1904 did he feel it safe to purchase another home for the long-suffering Helen, this time in Holland Villas Road, near Shepherd's Bush, promising her an annual allowance of £1,000 for life.[24]

His pursuit of artistic masterpieces so possessed Joseph that for a time music lost its earlier attraction. Friends no longer saw him regularly play the three-manual organ – costing all of £3,200 – in his mahogany-panelled music room. Perhaps they were also spared his excruciating performances on the violin which meant more to him than any other possession in the world; in Barratt's words, 'When Joe plays it he imagines he hears something quite different from what you hear'.[25] Likewise, his art collecting further limited the amount of time he could give to the firm. To deal with routine matters at St Helens, in 1904 he appointed one of his office staff, Austin Scott, as his confidential secretary there.

In 1906 Joseph's younger son, Henry, joined the firm at the age of eighteen, to be trained by Rowed. Like Thomas, Henry was dark, with a swarthy complexion. His piercing black eyes are said to have 'possessed the same hypnotic power as his brother's', perhaps a throw-back to his assumed Spanish ancestry. Henry had a Habsburg lip; while attending the Madrid opera in 1909, he was mistaken for his near-contemporary, King Alfonso XIII, so that the audience stood up when he entered his box. Yet he had been educated at Liverpool Grammar School and a commercial college; his father did not permit him to acquire Thomas's grand ideas at a public school and Oxford.[26]

From the outset, Henry settled down to learn diligently, and conduct himself in a 'Beecham' manner. Although he later expressed his flamboyance well away from St Helens, he is not known to have indulged in any local escapades, and in 1914 married advantageously into a Leicestershire county family. At that stage of its history, with Joseph patently withdrawing himself from the firm, it could have done with someone of Thomas's brains and independence of spirit, raising pointed but constructive questions about its management.

Meanwhile, Thomas had married Utica Welles in July 1903, Josephine – but not her husband – being present and Emily the chief bridesmaid. As a wedding present, his grandfather Thomas gave him the freehold of Mursley Hall and £300 a year. With no other visible means of support, the 24-year-old bridegroom found himself and his family – a son Adrian being born in 1904 – taken over by the Welleses, as Josephine had already been. The whole party spent much of 1904 on the continent, not returning to London until the spring of 1905. Shortly afterwards the composer, Cyril Meir Scott, met Thomas and remembered him as a small figure in a frock coat, brown boots, pork-pie hat and dark woollen gloves (with pattern), who sat and talked away with clasped hands, unable to look anyone in the eye. According to the critic, Neville Cardus, he was then 'an uncertain Beecham, a Beecham afflicted with a feeling of inferiority, of some frustration in himself': frustration doubly galling for someone of Thomas's musical gifts and pent-up physical energy.[27]

Not knowing what else to do, in May 1905 Thomas wrote to Joseph's solicitor, Henry Oppenheim, stating that his greatest desire was to be reconciled with his father. In total disregard of Utica's wishes, he would be prepared to live close to St Helens and resume his career in the business. Joseph's reply imposed draconian conditions for that to happen: Thomas – by then 26 – must come back, he insisted, 'as a contrite son willing to acknowledge his disobedient conduct and asking for his father's forgiveness'. Moreover, Josephine must free herself from the household and influence of Dr Welles and set up her own establishment, Thomas likewise severing himself from his in-laws. Thomas was naturally in no position to detach his mother, let alone his wife, from the Welleses' clutches. In desperation, he attempted to touch Oppenheim for a loan of £500, secured on the Mursley Hall estate, to enable him 'to make headway with his musical business'.

Oppenheim would not oblige, and it was Josephine who financed Thomas's first public concert in London that December: a lack-lustre performance that forced him to spend the following year in an intensive study of orchestral techniques. Thomas was by then so irked by Dr Welles's use of Josephine's alimony to pursue private litigation and also his habit of reading all her correspondence, that he took his case to the Court of Appeal. As nothing ensued, he made a further plea to his father in May 1906; the parental response made it clear that Joseph's attitude had not softened in the slightest degree.[28]

In April 1907, Thomas Beecham the founder died of congestion of the lungs, aged 86. His death received a ten-line mention on the main news page of *The Times*, concluding, 'he took no part in public life'. Unlike Holloway, he was spared a leading article. A few years later he joined the worthies of his era with a distinctly unrevealing entry in the 1901–11 supplement of the (British) *Dictionary of National Biography*.[29] Despite his life-long penchant for publicity, he left word that as little notice as possible should be taken of his demise. By the standards of the day, his was a low-key funeral in the municipal cemetery at Denton Green, St Helens; there were no flowers by request, but six pall–bearers chosen from among his long-serving foremen.

Out of his decidedly modest £87,000 estate, by coincidence equivalent to the firm's net profit that year, Thomas left the family of his old age comfortably off. He had already made over £13,000 to Jane Roberts and their daughter Violet, 12 years old in 1907; he now bequeathed Jane a further £2,000, Violet inheriting a mortgage deed worth £10,000. The residue of Thomas's estate was shared equally between his two sons, Joseph and William the London physician; his one daughter surviving into adulthood, Sarah, had died in 1893. Violet Roberts later took the Beecham name, married but bore no children and lived until 1988; thus the two generations spanned no fewer than 168 years.[30]

Joseph might have been expected to reinvigorate the firm now that his father had died. In the event, so convinced was he that the pill formulae were entirely appropriate that he merely updated the leaflet enclosed with the pills. In June 1908 he passed his sixtieth birthday and is said to have contemplated retirement. However, Henry as his successor-designate was only just twenty and not yet showing much sign of an entrepreneurial spirit. Joseph therefore soldiered on, but made no major changes to the St Helens factory, instead concentrating his innovations on the American branch (see Chapter 5). For him personally, there were good times just around the corner, to arrive from an unexpected source: a mending of his shattered relations with Thomas.

On 25 May 1909, Thomas Beecham wrote to his reigning mistress, Maud Foster (see below), that he was due to meet Joseph on the following day, when he hoped to prove to the 'old boy' that his musical ventures were financially sound as well as '"high-falutin" art'. Thomas's later reminiscences suggested that Joseph had only to expostulate, 'You dam' well annoyed me', and Thomas to retort, 'And you annoyed me too', for them to patch things up. In reality, healing the nine-year-old breach involved various intermediaries and successive meetings over a number of weeks.

A gala performance of the composer Ethel Smyth's opera, *The Wreckers*, at His Majesty's Theatre, was due to be held on Thursday, 8 July; through a contact at court she arranged for King Edward VII and Queen Alexandra to be invited. Thomas as the conductor was presented, and Joseph must have been tipped off about the event. For some time he had been spotted at Thomas's performances, characteristically lurking behind a pillar; Ethel Smyth hoped that this token of royal approval would seal the reconciliation process, which in fact took place two days later. The cold-hearted Joseph had not at all forgiven his son's disobedience, but felt that Thomas was now worth cultivating as a rising star in the musical world.[31]

The shy Thomas of five years before had meantime grown in self-confidence, being appointed conductor of the New Symphony Orchestra and then founding his own Beecham Symphony Orchestra. That had some talented young players and a novel repertoire, including works by Frederick Delius, the composer whom Thomas had begun to place on the musical map. Joseph, well able to back up his dreams with almost unlimited cash, anonymously let it be known that he was willing to spend £300,000 to promote the cause of opera in Britain. Aware of Thomas's recklessness with money, he proposed to run these musical ventures himself, in a businesslike manner. As Thomas light-heartedly informed Delius, 'Well, I hope he does and smashes about a bit.'[32]

Joseph duly opened at his bank an 'opera' account, to be drawn on for expenses. He suggested one musical season in 1910 to Thomas, who countered that two would be better. In the event, three took place, two at Covent Garden and one at His Majesty's Theatre, lasting 28 weeks in all; Thomas conducted or directly involved himself in no fewer than 190 performances. The season ended in July to mixed reviews. While some nights had been memorable, such as the English première of Richard Strauss's *Elektra*, the general standard of performance was judged to have been low. Thomas, who confessed to have put on some – mainly British – operas just to hear what they sounded like, had attempted to do too much, and his venture ended up £40,000 in the red: a single year had eaten up nearly one-seventh of the fortune earmarked by Joseph.[33]

Such a hefty sum might have warned Joseph of the expenses ahead; yet in August 1910 he authorized Thomas to sign a contract with the impresario,

Sergei Diaghilev, to bring over to London the Imperial Russian Ballet in 1911 and again in 1912. Diaghilev was advanced the equivalent of £1,200, to be repaid in instalments out of future box-office takings. Joseph was resolved to make the 1911 season, spanning the coronation of King George V in June, an unforgettably splendid one, which he did.

That season, at Covent Garden, opened on the evening before the coronation, and ran until the end of July. Among the highlights were the Polovtsian dances from Borodin's *Prince Igor*, Rimsky-Korsakov's *Scheherazade*, and Fokine's *Le Spectre de la Rose*. Diaghilev's company returned for a further season, from October to December, playing Coralli's *Giselle*, and Tchaikovsky's two best-loved ballets, *Swan Lake* (starring Anna Pavlova), and excerpts from *The Sleeping Beauty*. Joseph was to pay dear for his resolve, because each performance by Diaghilev, a notorious spendthrift employing each night no fewer than 100 dancers and 200 supernumeraries, was reported to cost £1,000.[34]

After the first season of 1911 closed, in September Thomas accompanied Joseph and Thomas Barratt on the Cunard liner, the *Lusitania*, to New York. There, the *New York Times* reported, 'in an earnest, deliberate fashion, with carefully chosen words', the young conductor spoke of his plans – in the event coming to naught – for Mozart and Strauss festivals in the United States.[35] He had to return early, in order to appear as co-respondent that October in the divorce case involving the American-born Maud Foster. The jury found that they had committed adultery, and £3,000 costs were awarded against him.

While Joseph paid off the legal bills, Thomas was busy arranging some financial deals on the side, and some time during 1911 he resorted to moneylenders.[36] He was desperate to hide those transactions from his father, shortly to be knighted for services to music in the following New Year's honours. At the beginning of the 1912 season at Covent Garden, Thomas lent £950 to Diaghilev, who on his part would receive not the normal performance fee but a quarter of the takings, net of the costs of orchestras, lighting and publicity. That year was noteworthy for the performances of Stravinsky's *Firebird* and at a subsequent winter season the première of Richard Strauss's *Der Rosenkavalier*, Thomas conducting 17 of the 21 performances.

Joseph was further honoured by being made Mayor of St Helens in 1910/11 and again in 1911/12, while in January 1913 he was elected, appropriately enough, as a member of the Royal Society for the Encouragement of Arts, Manufactures and Commerce. These marks of public recognition did not save him from having to perform a professional task that could only be painful for one so buttoned up. As chairman of the Proprietary Articles Section of the London Chamber of Commerce, in 1913 he agreed to appear before a House of Commons Select Committee on Patent Medicines, set up the previous year.

Public anger had recently erupted on both sides of the Atlantic about the misleading claims made for proprietary medicines and about the harmful substances, such as the pain-killer Acetanilide, contained in some of them. From 1904 onwards the *British Medical Journal* (*BMJ*) ran a series of articles comprising scientific analyses of the main medicines sold in Britain, republished in 1909 as *Secret Remedies: What they Cost and What they Contain*. Analysts of Beecham's digestive pills had estimated their prime cost, in the 56-pill box sold at one shilling (5p) net of duty, at half a farthing, or one-sixteenth of a new penny; that year's accounts show the raw drugs and containers together costing the firm one farthing per box.

Publication of that independent analysis had stung the Beecham firm into an uncharacteristically tetchy piece of copy. In December 1909, when the two houses of the Westminster parliament were at loggerheads over David Lloyd George's tax-raising budget, its advertisement declared, 'The Lords and the Commons agree over Beecham's pills'. It explained that 'in spite of all opposition, and in the face of calumny prompted by jealousy caused by success [*sic*], the voice of the people is practically unanimous in favour of BEECHAM'S PILLS'.[37] In his written submission of 1912 to the Select Committee, which has not survived, Joseph had been at pains to distance his well-tried remedies, with a solid reputation built up over six decades, from quack nostrums that were at best discreditable and at worst both fraudulent and dangerous to use.

In January 1913 Joseph appeared before the committee, expecting deferential treatment as a respected industrialist and knight of the realm. Instead, he became both embarrassed and tongue-tied in the face of rigorous and persistent questions on such matters as the amount of morphia in his cough pills – 'trivial', he replied, but discontinued some time ago (see Chapter 6) – and the hints in leaflets that the digestive kind might help to terminate pregnancies and cure venereal diseases. He was unable to substantiate earlier claims that the pills had saved the lives of thousands of women or that they cured specific maladies, including Bright's disease. He refused to divulge the pill formulae, and said merely that some ingredients – clearly the essential oils – were not specified in the *BMJ* analysis.

He revealed that his firm, being a private one, published no balance sheet, but made a million pills each day of the year: a correct statement, as about 360 million were turned out at St Helens in 1913, plus about 73 million in the New York branch. Nor did he have any idea about the relative demand for his pills by men and women. However, with the experience behind him of an estranged wife, six surviving daughters and a plentiful assortment of mistresses, he maintained that 'women are more habitually constipated than men'.

Joseph's hunch about female costiveness was supported years later by medical research findings: that in women it took roughly twice as long for food to pass through the gut than in men. Women were in any case more prone to constipation through their habits of slimming, tight-lacing to create wasp waists, and following low carbohydrate diets. Joseph and Rowed made sure that the firm generously advertised in women's magazines, where from time to time they were rewarded with editorial commendations of Beecham's pills, along the lines of 'a certain cure for most of the ills of childhood'. As the vignette, noted above, of the mother giving a pill to her young daughter showed, a cycle of dependence on laxative pills often began early in the life of each new generation.[38]

During 1913, the Beechams put on three opera and ballet seasons. Those at Covent Garden, from January to March, and at His Majesty's Theatre from May to June, were curtain-raisers to the Diaghilev season in June and July at Drury Lane. There the main novelties were presentations of Russian opera, most notably Mussorgsky's *Boris Godunov*, sung by Fyodor Chaliapin at the unprecedented fee of £400 a night. The French impresario, Gabriel Astruc, had over-lavishly created for a Parisian theatre the scenery and costumes for that and another opera; after Astruc went bankrupt, the Beechams bought up these properties for the knock-down price of £1,600. Financial relations with Diaghilev were predictably rocky; by mid-July a friend, Misia Sert, told Stravinsky (whose *Rite of Spring* had also appeared in the repertoire) that Diaghilev was 'going through a dreadful period of money problems with [Sir Joseph] Beecham which will end, I fear, in a civil-war lawsuit between them'.[39]

Neither party actually went to court, but Joseph resolved to strengthen the venture's plainly inadequate financial supervision by appointing a general manager. The 30-year-old Donald Baylis had once been an office boy and clerk at St Helens and from 1908 onwards Rowed's private secretary, before being sent by Joseph to Italy for his voice to be trained. Having learnt about opera management, he was then appointed the Beechams' assistant stage manager, where his skill in disentangling back-stage problems at the last minute earned him high praise. Rumours abounded that he was Joseph's illegitimate son, said to be like Thomas. (In reality, he was buck-toothed, with thinning hair and a premature stoop, but at least he had the Beecham short stature and piercing eyes). Baylis's mother was Ann Perrott, possibly an indoor servant at Ewanville, who had him adopted as a small child. Yet Joseph might have pushed him ahead for his musical and problem-solving talents alone.[40]

From August to November 1913, Joseph was away on an extended business tour of the United States and Canada. At the National Sporting Club in London, he had of late met James White, a property speculator from Rochdale who was currently advising the Dunlop Rubber Company. Joseph had been much taken with his fellow-Lancastrian's open charm and resourcefulness over money matters, and dazzled by the wealth of inside information that White gleaned from affluent and humble sources alike. As Joseph yearned above all to be on the inside track, White could gratify that craving in a way that Barratt and others could not really do. Joseph then engaged him as paymaster of Thomas's outgoings.[41]

Before his departure for America, Joseph announced that Thomas had been formally taken into the pill business. As there was no question of his being made a partner or residing anywhere near St Helens, that move must have been a device for giving Thomas a regular income out of profits. The 25-year-old Henry, still doggedly at work as a salaried employee, may well have emulated the brother of the prodigal son in Luke's Gospel and caused a fuss about this act of generosity. At any rate, he was compensated with a gift of the American branch, which happened to be Joseph's personal property (see Chapter 5). In February 1915, Henry formally took ownership of it.[42]

The 1914 season was again to be held at Drury Lane. In March Joseph signed a contract with Diaghilev, loaning him the equivalent of £4,000, repayable in instalments within two days of each performance. Since Diaghilev was unlikely to stump up on time, a penalty clause required him to surrender his scenery and costumes to the Beechams in the event of default. Thomas later took those over and made use of them in his own productions.

Further honours came Joseph's way in 1914. Early that year he was the first British citizen to be appointed by the Tsar to the order of St Stanislaus, in recognition of having brought the Russian ballet to western Europe. On 22 June, in the royal birthday honours, he found himself advanced to the rank of baronet, for musical services and for a recent generous gift of £30,000 to Bedford College for Women in London, lately opened by Queen Mary. According to a family tradition, the authorities offered him a peerage, which he turned down: Thomas would eventually inherit the title, and given his controversial views, especially on the philistine nature of the English, it might be inappropriate to give him a platform in the House of Lords.

On 16 July 1914, Joseph was one of the many dignitaries invited to the state ball at Buckingham Palace. The 25th was the last night of that year's Drury Lane season, and during the final curtain calls he was summoned up on to the stage. The company presented him with a gilded laurel wreath, which he sensibly kept in his hand. He told the ecstatic audience that, many years before, he had paid his hard-won shillings 'to come into the gallery of this theatre and listen to opera'. Perhaps understandably in the excitement of the moment, he mixed up Liverpool's opera house with Drury Lane; he did, however, promise an even more splendid season in 1915.[43] That promise was not to be fulfilled: eleven days later Britain, in common with the other great European powers, was at war.

8

The Covent Garden estate, 1914–1916

F OR Sir Joseph Beecham, the seven months from January to July 1914 were probably the most exhilarating of his life, bringing him adulation in the opera house and honours from the sovereigns of both Britain and Russia. He must have been equally gratified that since he had taken sole charge of the pill enterprise in 1895, its total turnover, net of duty, had risen by no less than a fifth, from £186,000 to £229,000 in 1913. Profits had done even better, with a 40 per cent increase from nearly £77,000 in 1899 (the earliest available figure) to £107,000 in 1913 (see Table 8.1, page 130).

The Beecham firm had in those years consolidated its leadership in Britain's proprietary pill market. None of its major domestic rivals any longer posed much of a threat. Most notably, Holloway's sales of pills and ointment in Britain were down to a third or less of their 1880s level, despite slavishly copying the Beecham labels and boxes. When its lease on the Oxford Street premises in London expired during 1909, it had moved to the humbler Southwark Street, near Waterloo Station. The current proprietor, Henry Driver-Holloway, then wrote to Joseph, asking him to purchase the business. Joseph had declined.

How far, if at all, the sales in Britain of Carter's Little Liver Pills and Dr Williams' Pink Pills affected Beecham's market is unknown, as neither American firm disclosed any figures. The only patent medicine enterprise of overseas origin to enjoy good sales was the Bile Beans Company, which had somehow survived the devastating censure by Scottish judges in 1905 of its fraudulent activities (see Chapter 5).

Perhaps a greater threat to Beecham's trade came from those suffering with digestive ills and coughs who turned to liquid remedies, as being more palatable and also cheaper because exempt from the medicine duty. Thus Scott & Turner of Newcastle claimed in 1907 to be selling over 2 million tins a year of its Andrews Liver Salt, and Owbridge more than three times as many bottles of its lung tonic. Eno's, maker of the celebrated fruit salt (see Chapter

6), had a total turnover of £230,000 in 1914, slightly exceeding Beecham's that year; its net profit was £79,000, compared with the latter's £112,000. As the British sales of Beecham's cough pills declined from an average of 6.5 million in 1890–92 to below 1.1 million in 1913, Owbridge's and Veno's cough linctuses were clearly capturing much of that market. Veno's profit in 1918, admittedly after wartime inflation, was a little short of £300,000, as against Beecham's £186,000 that year.[1]

Despite its commanding lead in the domestic market for pills, Beecham managed to increase its sales in Britain only by 4 per cent, from £155,000 in 1895 to £161,000 in 1913. That had required an increase of a fifth in home advertising, from £58,000 to £71,000. Indeed, nine-tenths of the firm's advertising budget, excluding the United States which was still under Joseph's personal management, by 1913 had to be spent at home. As many British producers of consumption goods were discovering, the real growth area was overseas. Beecham's exports more than doubled from £31,000 in 1895 to nearly £69,000 in 1914; only since 1911 had non-US advertising overseas risen above the £10,000 level. The firm's cash-based accounting system (see Chapter 6) did not allocate profits between home and overseas transactions.

Beecham managers must have debated among themselves about the likely effect on their business of the National Health Insurance scheme, which Lloyd George as Chancellor of the Exchequer introduced in 1911, due to come into operation at the beginning of 1913. As the scheme provided for lower-paid employed workers to be given free medical treatment, including prescription drugs, demand for Beecham's pills might well be seriously affected. As will be shown later, any fears on that score were not realized.

Notwithstanding the current good things in Joseph's life, he still had his own troubles. On the personal side, Helen Taylor was nearing her mid-fifties – still knocking four years off her age – and therefore no longer so attractive to a sexagenarian with a roving eye. In 1913, for some unexplained reason he had made her leave the house in Holland Villas Road, which he put up for auction. The furniture went to a depository of Whiteley's, the department store, and the Steinway piano for safekeeping to Henry Beecham's residence at Hartford in Cheshire. Wherever she ended up, it would not have been with Joseph in Hampstead. Then the house failed to reach its reserve price, and he bought it back on her behalf for £4,000.

In January 1914, he took Helen to lunch at the Café Royal, and revealed a new financial settlement to benefit her. His will later included a sum of £19,000, placed in trust with his solicitor and banker; when added to dividends on the securities she owned, that would yield her an income of £1,500 a year for life. The beneficiary's name was not given there but appeared only in the

Inland Revenue's confidential schedule of the estate. As Claire Tomalin wrote of another 'invisible woman', Charles Dickens's mistress, Ellen Ternan (who happened to die in April 1914), 'This is the story of someone who – almost – wasn't there; who vanished into thin air. Her name, dates, family and experiences very nearly disappeared from the record for good.' Helen Taylor would likewise have been airbrushed out of the Beecham family portrait had she not, with spirit and admirable candour, claimed her rightful debts from the executors after Joseph's death.[2]

By contrast, Thomas was an all too visible presence, and likely to land in one scrape or other. He later made fun of his father, for example during his bogus account of the hymn books episode (see Appendix 2), in his memoirs portraying Joseph as 'a man of pathetic simplicity and uncertain judgment' who allegedly stood in awe of Thomas. In truth, Joseph had good reason to be wary about his son's extravagance. Early in 1914 Thomas appealed to him, being totally incapable of meeting financial liabilities of £50,000 as they fell due. Having owned up that he had been in moneylenders' hands since 1911, he solemnly promised his father to keep clear of loan-sharks in future. Joseph at once put £100,000 at Thomas's disposal, but prudently arranged for James White, his financial adviser, to pay out the money as needed. By June, that sum was already overdrawn, and Joseph had to guarantee a £75,000 loan to Thomas by the Standard Life Assurance Company.[3]

White was also managing Joseph's portfolio of stocks and shares, and between 1913 and 1916 made him a total profit of £40,000. That was not a difficult feat, in a period of generally rising market values. In 1903, at the height of the alimony rumpus (see Chapter 7), counsel acting for his estranged wife had declared that Joseph 'revelled in every luxury and had only to put his hand in his pocket for banknotes and spend them as freely as he liked';[4] indeed, Joseph kept £100,000 in his current account for whatever he fancied. By 1914, that agreeable dispensation was coming to an end, under the pressure of Thomas's relentless financial demands, but as well from an altogether new and unexpected drain on his fortune.

It was the pursuit of another relatively trifling sum that led Joseph into the biggest commercial blunder of his life: the purchase of Covent Garden – fruit and vegetable – market and estate, which included the Covent Garden and Drury Lane theatres.[5] He was not to know that, thanks to a profligate son, a not entirely straight Midlands business man, and a conflict brewing in a faraway Balkan country, he was signing his ultimate death warrant.

Since 1905, the landed estates of Britain's numerous aristocrats had been under constant attack from the reforming Liberal government, as it strove to implement its costly social legislation. Lloyd George, the Chancellor of the Exchequer, in his battle with the House of Lords (see Chapter 7), openly taunted aristocratic landowners, remarking in 1909 that 'A fully equipped duke costs as much to keep up as any two dreadnoughts [battleships], and dukes are just as great a terror, and they last longer.'[6] One of the wealthiest, alleged by Disraeli three decades earlier to enjoy an annual income of £300,000, was Herbrand Arthur Russell, eleventh Duke of Bedford, who in the early years of the twentieth century had sold half his agricultural estates, mainly to sitting tenants. As the nineteen-acre (nearly 8 hectare) Covent Garden estate brought him in more than £100,000 a year, his advisers suggested that, under the current political threat, it would be sensible to dispose of that property.

Such a large chunk of central London had never before been sold off in one lot, and by the autumn of 1913 the duke's agents were disappointed to find only one capitalist prepared to bid £2 million for the entire estate. That was (Sir) Henry Mallaby-Deeley MP, like James White a property tycoon already noted for his daring speculative deals in London. Vendors should have been on their guard against the immaculately attired prospective buyer, who never bothered with valuations or legal searches, but reckoned to close a deal on a half-sheet of writing paper. On 25 October 1913 he secured an option on the sale.

The duke did not find his terms all that attractive. Only 10 per cent would be paid on signature, and no more than one-third in cash by 1918, while the balance was to remain on mortgage. As Mallaby-Deeley was known not to be heading a consortium, many suspected that he lacked the private means to raise even the initial £200,000. Already resentful over being expected to forfeit his private boxes in Covent Garden and Drury Lane theatres, the duke was soon challenging the validity of the agreement, and the two parties seemed destined to end up in court.[7]

In June 1914, the well-informed James White revealed the impending collapse of those negotiations to Joseph, and also to Alexander L. Ormrod, a Manchester stockbroker. White dangled in front of Joseph the advantages of his becoming the front-man for the sale, by buying Mallaby-Deeley's purchase option for £250,000, and then contracting with the duke to acquire the Covent Garden estate outright for £2 million. Joseph would pay a £200,000 deposit when the contract was signed and a further £50,000 shortly afterwards. Ormrod was willing to repurchase Joseph's option for £550,000, leaving him a clear profit of £50,000.

That sum was to be Joseph's reward for giving his name to the transaction. On 6 July, he therefore signed a contract with the duke, paying over the full £250,000 on signature. Ormrod for his part submitted a letter to confirm his side of the deal. The duke, heartily relieved to be in business with such a wealthy purchaser, offered a discount of £70,000 if the remaining £1.75 million were paid in full by 11 November.

Ormrod's scheme was to float two companies, one to deal with the market itself and the other with the rest of the estate. The elegant draft prospectus for the former, the Covent Garden Market Ltd, forecast a share capital of £450,000 ordinary and 5 per cent preference shares and £700,000 4½ per cent debentures; bank rate was then 3 per cent. Ormrod would be a director, together with a merchant and a publisher, both Londoners. According to an official valuation, the gross site value of the market was £1,015,000, set to yield a net annual revenue of about £50,000, or a little under 5 per cent before tax. Drastic cost-cutting would, it was hoped, easily boost that revenue, the estate contributing a further £45,000.

A stylish historical survey of Covent Garden since 1670, by John Murray the publisher – not the proposed director – came before the small print at the end. That disclosed that the contracts between Joseph and Ormrod, and between Ormrod and the projected company, for the sale of the market properties and the underwriting of the debentures and preference shares, had yet to be signed. Matters were no further forward when war was declared on 4 August, and the dismayed Joseph found himself carrying the full burden of the transaction.[8]

On the outbreak of war, the government at once closed the London Stock Exchange and banned new company share issues. Joseph correctly guessed that those official actions would rule out the possibility of raising shareholders' funds to pay for the Covent Garden sale. He therefore instructed his secretary at St Helens, Austin Scott, to carry out a survey of his securities portfolio. Not until January 1915 did the Treasury sanction the reopening of the Stock Exchange, and then required government approval of all new issues. Property companies, which contributed nothing to the war effort, stood no chance of gaining such permission.

A slim hope was that Ormrod, who reportedly had a group of Manchester business men behind him, would honour his side of the deal. However, when asked to do so, he cravenly replied that his letter of 6 July was not a legal document, and in any case he was unable to lay his hands on that kind of money. Once the date of completion in November 1914 went by, the duke was not unsympathetic towards Joseph's plight in the current emergency, and accepted that the agreement would have to be renegotiated.

As some cheer for Joseph, the Beecham firm's results for 1914 showed that it had been performing tolerably well in the circumstances. The total number of pills despatched from the factory, nearly 358 million, was less than 1 per cent down on 1913. Exports were very slightly up; for some reason, the number of cough pills demanded overseas had increased by nearly a half over the previous year, to 2.4 million, or double the number sold at home. Total profits had risen from £107,000 to £112,000, or from 50 to more than 52½ per cent of an almost unchanged turnover of £229,000. The firm's bill for the imported raw drugs and pill boxes had risen by over a half; it was undoubtedly stocking up against future shortages now that everyone acknowledged that the war would no longer be over by Christmas. Advertising costs at home were reduced by over £10,000, roughly a 15 per cent drop, while the amount spent overseas was almost unchanged.

Indeed, as the war progressed, sales of pills remained buoyant, as they had done in the South African war of 1899–1902. For the second time, following John Hassall (see Chapter 7), the firm used a very well-known commercial artist: Bruce Bairnsfather, creator of 'Old Bill', whose drawing and caption, 'If you knows of a better 'ole, go to it', summed up the private soldier's ironic acceptance of the inhuman conditions in the trenches. This time, Bairnsfather lost his touch when he portrayed a buffoon of a German soldier being prodded by a British bayonet: 'A good point to remember. Take Beecham's pills.' Yet once again it was the artist's name that counted.

Many in stressful but well-paid civilian jobs were using the pills as placebos. Until shortages and rationing came in, they often consumed greater amounts and sometimes novel kinds of food than before the war. The millions in the services were being fed more meat than their digestions could properly manage. Although the firm's surviving archives contain no figures, government departments are known to have purchased Beecham's pills in substantial quantities for troops at home and abroad.[9] Demand was helped also by government restrictions on imports of foreign medicines. Yet the war was bound to cause far more pain to many as it dragged on.

A year into the Covent Garden estate imbroglio, Helen Taylor could see at first hand how Joseph was being weighed down by his financial troubles. There were three above all. First came the decline in the market prices of his many securities and property holdings since 1914, sharply reducing the value of his realizable assets. In May 1915, on government prompting he asked Helen to do her bit by handing over to him all the American and Dutch bonds he had given her, worth £15,000. Of the proceeds, he invested £9,000 in War Loan, to give her a life interest of £450 a year; the rest he would borrow himself.

Second, his son Thomas's enthusiasm for keeping music alive in wartime Britain, however commendable, was bound to intensify Joseph's difficulties over money. In October 1914, the incorrigible Thomas wrote light-heartedly to his composer friend, Frederick Delius, 'with the exception of my projected tours on the Continent, I am in no way altering my plans. Concerts are going on here as usual, and I look forward to another Opera Season next Summer.' As many orchestras were struggling to survive, in 1914–15 he conducted without fee both the Hallé Orchestra and the Royal Philharmonic Society's orchestra, and paid half the wages of the latter's players to reduce its deficit. He also became chief conductor of the London Symphony Orchestra.

As if orchestral ventures were not costly enough, Thomas went on to found the Beecham Opera Company, which from October 1915 onwards ran two series of concert performances at the Shaftesbury Theatre in London; Joseph gave a guarantee of £2,000 and later backed bills for a total of £25,000. The 76 performances of popular operas in English, with gallery seats costing no more than a shilling (5p), were sold out on most nights. Thomas's biographer, Charles Reid, noticed in the audience not only soldiers on leave but also 'groups of girl clerks from the vast Government offices of the neighbourhood, where some of them were putting in a twelve-hour day'.[10]

Yet the third of Joseph's problems remained the most intractable: how to pay off his massive liabilities to the Duke of Bedford. James White had sensibly advised him to build up a fund against future cash payments to the duke, and he regularly topped up the special deposit account (see Chapter 3); by April 1915 that stood at £104,000 and by September 1916 would be just short of £250,000. However impressive in its way, the latter sum represented only a fraction of the total outstanding debt. Joseph also hoped to raise more ready money from the financial institutions that had already done well out of his deposits, and Helen accompanied him when he visited his main banker, Parr's Bank, as well as the Alliance Bank, and sat in a waiting room while he interviewed the managers. Coming away empty-handed, in September he had no option but to conclude with the duke a supplementary agreement.

Joseph proposed a new completion date of 24 June 1917; that the duke accepted, offering a token discount of £8,750, well below the previous £70,000. However, as from the earlier date of November 1914, Joseph would be liable to 5 per cent interest on the outstanding £1.75 million. The interest did not have to be paid over until 1917, but it still ran at £87,500 a year, or £235 a day. Although the duke kept his legal title to the estate's assets, Joseph had the right to approve all future important transactions. James White and Joseph's London solicitor, Sir Henry Paget-Cooke, of Russell Cooke & Co., on his behalf therefore maintained daily contact with the Bedford Estate Office.

Meanwhile, the Great War pursued its terrible course. Joseph was spared the worst anxieties undergone by parents of young officers being mown down in their thousands on the Western Front. He secured a non-combatant posting in Britain for the 26-year-old Henry, as a lieutenant in the (later Royal) Army Service Corps. For his part, Thomas was seen as undertaking musical activities of national importance. However, Rowed had a beloved only son, with whom he had in pre-war days made motor cycle tours throughout England, enthusiastically searching for antiques. Charles Henry Rowed, commissioned on his twenty-first birthday in the South Lancashire Regiment, was killed in France during September 1915. Doubtless showing no outward sign of grief at the time, in his book, *Collecting as a Pastime* of 1920, Rowed revealed the depth of his feelings, as he mourned his 'lovable companion, who for nearly ten years had played such a sharing part' in his agreeable pastime of collecting antiques.

It was Helen Taylor who cracked under wartime stress, as she attempted to keep up Joseph's flagging spirits. During the autumn of 1915 her health broke down; he arranged for her to go on a prolonged sea voyage to Australia and New Zealand. Having pulled many strings with the shipping authorities, he got her away that November. Shortly before her departure, they visited together the National Safe Deposit Company's office where she stored her share certificates, jewellery and lace, to update the entries in the red contents book. Joseph appeared more than usually preoccupied, hardly aware of what he was doing, and they never finished that task. His youngest but one and favourite daughter, Elsie, had a few weeks earlier – entirely against his will – married in a register office William Senior Ellis, a St Helens accountant thirteen years older than herself. He was doubly hurt by that act of rebellion, as he had gone to extraordinary lengths to shield his daughters from fortune-hunters; and Ellis was no rich man. In reply to an angry protest, she had written a vitriolic letter detailing his infidelities, which he made Helen read. Elsie never saw Joseph again; but neither did Helen after their farewell at the dockside.[11]

That autumn Thomas had been sent, according to him at the government's suggestion, to Italy, a wartime ally since the previous May. His mission was both a musical one and to show the British flag, since many factions in the country openly sided with Germany and Austria. Apart from one or two minor contretemps of his own making, he enjoyed a successful trip. Returning to Britain early in January 1916, he found that in the New Year honours he had been knighted for services to music. Towards the end of his life, he disclosed to his third wife that he had been engaged in wartime intelligence work.[12]

One biographer has suggested that 'several incidents in Beecham's life up to the end of the First World War point to a close connection with the Foreign Office', as his persuasive ways often allowed him to obtain information abroad 'within the social and industry circles in which he was a welcome guest'. True or not, the Foreign Office archives of those years contain no references to his Italian trip. The department's comprehensive card-index of names cites only the award in 1918 of the Cross of Commander of the Order of the Crown of Italy, for having promoted that country's music in England through concerts to benefit the Italian Red Cross.

More probably, Thomas was honoured as the one individual in Britain with the energy, single-mindedness and financial backing to keep performing music alive in the country. In November 1916 an MP raised a parliamentary question: as he was of military age – being 37 – which tribunal had exempted him from military service? Amid laughter, the minister gave the stock reply that enquiries were being made.[13]

Meanwhile, demand for Beecham's pills showed no sign of slackening. Although the duty on patent medicines was doubled in October 1915, that year's pill deliveries at home were up to a record 286 million, ten million higher than the year before. Because the firm did not increase overseas publicity, exports fell slightly, while advertising in Britain was scaled down to £42,000, only three-fifths of the unprecedented £70,500 in 1913. Profits grew from £112,000 to £134,000 in 1915, even though the bill for drugs and boxes had increased from nearly £14,000 to £17,000. Costs of postage were also up; the government kept unchanged the penny post until 1918, but the weights that could be carried for a penny had been reduced.

In March 1916 the firm's operations were hampered by a government ban on certain imports, notably manufactured wooden articles. That prohibition cut off the supply of American beechwood pill boxes, at least 6 million of which were needed each year, so that the firm had to make do with cheap home-made boxes. However, Thomas claimed to have secured some relaxations by his personal efforts.[14] While raw drugs were unaffected, Beecham's toothpaste could no longer be imported from America. Its sales had declined further from 3,000 tubes in 1914 to just over 2,000, and the product should surely have been phased out earlier.

Thomas's opera season in Manchester ran from early May to mid-June 1916. Whatever his qualms about the expense, Joseph continued to take an active interest in this venture, and made a point of inviting business associates to one or other of the operas. His tolerance must have been strained when Thomas allowed the number of orchestral performers to grow to levels found in London. Even so, Joseph opened at the bank a new Beecham Opera account of up to £10,000, and in July added a further guarantee of over £1,150 to cover future performances. Thomas lost no time in planning the Beecham Opera Company's programme for 1916–17 on an ambitious scale, to include two London seasons, one in Manchester, and others in any English localities that boasted a large enough theatre.

The Covent Garden sale, and dealings with the Duke of Bedford as vendor, increasingly perplexed Joseph's mind. By mid-1916, he had to accept that the completion date of June 1917, requiring a cash payment of the full £1.75 million, was totally unrealistic, given the financial constraints of war. From July onwards, Sir Henry Paget-Cooke was striving to persuade the Bedford Estate officials to allow at least part of the debt to be placed on mortgage. The duke recalled his refusal in 1914 to accept mortgage terms from Mallaby-Deeley, and the task of winning him round was far from easy. In the end he agreed to renegotiate terms, as long as Joseph gave a personal guarantee over both principal and interest, to remain valid even if the Covent Garden estate were conveyed to other parties. That October, letters were exchanged, and both sides' solicitors drew up formal deeds.

On signature of the fresh agreement, the duke was to be paid £250,000, conveniently available in Joseph's special deposit account. The remaining £1.5 million would be left on mortgage, fully secured by his personal guarantee. However, £250,000 of the latter sum had to be paid within two years after the end of the war: an event still plainly some way into the future.[15]

All parties were now anxious for the agreement to be signed without delay, and the date of 23 October was chosen. On Thursday, the 19th, Joseph attended a Hallé Orchestra concert at Manchester, conducted by Thomas. As the concert ended sooner than expected, he chose to travel back to London, looking forward to a quiet week-end before the formal signing session there on Monday the 23rd. That Sunday, he travelled over to see Thomas's estranged wife, Utica, and her two sons in the north London home he had bought for them; they were all invited back to Hampstead, where he played them some pieces on the organ.

He had arranged to take Utica the next evening to hear Camille Saint-Saëns' opera, *Samson and Delilah*, at the Aldwych Theatre, to celebrate the signature of the agreement that would at last bring uncertainty to an end. During that night, he died in his sleep at the age of 68. A post-mortem had to be held, and the inquest verdict was one of death by heart failure, caused by disease of the arteries: a condition of which his doctors were entirely unaware. Indeed, for some time he had been a poor sleeper, apparently becoming over-reliant on barbiturates.[16]

As happened in other family firms, the plentiful press tributes to Sir Joseph Beecham, Bt., were posted with great care into a handsomely bound volume. Those obituaries covered almost every aspect of his life known to reporters. For example, he hated having his photograph taken in public; he preferred to ride in a bus than a cab, or even better, to walk. He never gave a penny for a halfpenny newspaper, and he enjoyed playing the card-game of nap for pence. Once, when a halfpenny fell off the table and rolled away, he hunted on his hands and knees until he found it. Yet as Mayor of St Helens, he had entertained the children of the town by bringing down from London the full company of the Aldwych Theatre.[17] One topic on which the newspapers exercised a judicious discretion, in the halcyon days before investigative journalists (or their editors) showed no mercy towards private citizens, was his family break-up. No one recycled the earlier press coverage of his wife's alimony suits.

To sum up his character, Joseph Beecham was not in the accepted sense an evil man, although he deliberately inflicted unhappiness on a number of people, not least his own wife.[18] His streak of cold cruelty, so different from his father's impulsive rages, doubtless sprang from a life-long sense of frustration. A millionaire and recipient of public honours, he lacked the genial ease of manner that would have opened all doors of the élite to him, being inhibited by an off-putting combination of small stature, shyness and a broad Lancashire accent. Passionate about music, he was only a moderate pianist and organist, and an even worse performer on his beloved violin. Terrified of being mocked, he could not freely express himself on any subject apart from business. Well endowed as he was with children and grandchildren, he never related to the young, apart from Thomas's two sons towards the end of his life.

On the positive side, he retained the enduring affection of Helen Taylor, possibly the only person who ever fully understood him. Moreover, his benefactions to music did help to promote a social revolution of sorts in England. Thanks to his unstinting generosity and Thomas's drive to exploit his own musical talents to the full, their seasons of 1910–14 and in wartime brought opera and ballet to ordinary people who were content to sit in the gallery. They refused to be put off by the Beechams' wealthy and influential friends, such as Emerald, Lady Cunard and the Marchioness of Ripon, whose guests in the top-priced seats kept up conversations during performances and disturbed others by arriving late and leaving early.

Joseph must finally be assessed in his role as a business innovator. Some economic historians, when challenging the widespread view that the quality of British entrepreneurship declined sharply in the pre-1914 era, have cited Beecham and Lever (the soap magnate) as 'progressive types' who showed positive entrepreneurial dynamism. Previous chapters of this book have amply illustrated Joseph's achievements in his field. Yet (see Chapter 6) by the time of his death the Beecham organization was gradually losing momentum, for which as sole proprietor he was ultimately responsible.

Modern thought on entrepreneurship would see Joseph as typical of the many business leaders of the age who made all the important decisions and left the routine but not their firms' development strategies to their managers.[19] In the Beecham business, Rowed as general manager, Moss in production and Glover in sales had neither the authority nor the training to push for innovations at St Helens as soon as Joseph became distracted by family quarrels and the excitement of his, and Thomas's, musical ventures. Thus when Rowed had not long before proposed acquiring some 'ingenious' production plant, Joseph had choked him off (see Chapter 6).

Even in the field of advertising, of which the firm was so proud, an obituary of Joseph in the *Advertisers Weekly* had touched on the all too plain 'weak spot in our world of advertising', namely the endless repetition of an identical theme by proprietary medicine manufacturers. Hence Beecham, the journal felt, could have made better use of its record advertising budget by regularly putting new messages into its displays.[20]

For all his earlier innovations, therefore, Joseph in 1916 left behind a host of long-term problems that sooner or later would have to be addressed. The massive debt of nearly £2 million, hovering over a firm linked by a contract to the Covent Garden estate that had no synergy with the pill business, only intensified the dilemma that there was no one remotely capable of replacing the dead man. With no entrepreneur poised to step into his shoes, the future of this too narrowly organized business remained in jeopardy.

Table 8.1   *Beecham's sales and profit, 1896–1916 (£000)*

	Home sales	*Overseas sales*	*Total sales*	*Profit*
1896	184.9	32.9	217.8	
1897	97.4	35.0	132.4	
1898	120.1	35.1	155.2	
1899	122.7	37.6	160.3	76.5
1900	121.5	42.4	163.9	80.6
1901	122.0	42.4	164.4	77.9
1902	128.7	46.9	175.6	82.8
1903	129.9	40.8	170.7	75.1
1904	129.0	44.6	173.6	77.5
1905	134.3	50.5	184.8	80.4
1906	139.8	43.7	183.5	89.1
1907	144.9	48.5	193.4	87.6
1908	166.7	46.9	213.6	89.6
1909	151.8	51.3	203.1	93.8
1910	154.0	59.6	213.6	97.9
1911	158.3	64.1	222.4	106.4
1912	157.0	67.1	224.1	102.5
1913	160.9	68.3	229.2.	107.3
1914	160.0	68.8	228.8	112.4
1915	171.8	67.9	239.7	133.5
1916	128.4	65.3	193.7	131.0

Sales 1896–1916, BA, 'Report by L. Nicholas on St Helens business', November 1922, Schedule 7, BP 2/2/10, p. 31.

Profit 1899–1916, *ibid*, Schedule 2, p. 21.

Note: 1916, 10 months to 31 October.

Table 8.2 *Beecham's advertising, 1896–1916 (£)*

	Home	Overseas (excl. USA)	USA	Total
1896	57,633	4,242	12,505	74,380
1897	58,146	5,072	9,123	72,341
1898	56,113	5,085	20,596	81,794
1899	53,259	4,766	14,829	72,854
1900	55,296	4,734	6,113	66,143
1901	60,220	4,277	1,013	65,510
1902	64,560	4,559	19,022	88,141
1903	64,802	5,280	13,679	83,761
1904	67,162	5,914	21,348	94,424
1905	63,105	5,272	20,252	88,629
1906	66,953	5,948	20,889	93,790
1907	68,337	6,881	22,306	97,524
1908	71,559	6,969	23,822	102,350
1909	69,802	8,330	29,387	107,519
1910	69,341	9,759	34,602	113,702
1911	70,358	10,041	38,932	119,331
1912	70,136	10,224	41,110	121,470
1913	70,880	10,670	43,634	125,184
1914	60,210	10,593	40,849	111,652
1915	42,328	9,795	36,228	88,351
1916	46,770	10,088	39,349	96,207

BA, 'Home advertising totals from 1860', 'Overseas advertising (excluding USA) from 1885', 'USA advertising from 1889', BP 3/3/4.

9

In Chancery, 1916–1924

S IR JOSEPH BEECHAM's totally unexpected demise, leaving behind any number of outstanding problems, caused consternation in many quarters, at St Helens and elsewhere. All interested people therefore awaited his will with some concern. He had in fact signed a new will less than a month earlier, on the assumption that a workable agreement on the Covent Garden estate had been concluded with the Duke of Bedford. As that agreement had provided for a mortgage, there would have been no need to seek large quantities of cash while wartime restrictions on borrowing remained. However, in the absence of such an agreement, the various parties could no longer plan ahead as intended.[1]

Joseph was found to have appointed four executors and managing trustees of his estate: Henry Beecham, Charles Rowed, and two sons-in-law, Charles Boston and Frederick Woolley. If the unimpressive Henry, still in his twenties, had set his hopes on succeeding his grandfather Thomas and Joseph as the third pill entrepreneur, there was a strong rival in Boston, who possessed many of the necessary qualifications. He owned a leather importing company in Liverpool and a tannery in Runcorn; highly lucrative government contracts had raised his company's annual turnover to £1.5 million, about six times that of the pill firm.

Boston's energy and business acumen were widely acknowledged, and Thomas in retrospect described him with admiration as 'a man of sound practical sense who gave us willing and regular support'.[2] Yet he possessed an authoritarian and ruthless streak; his thirteen-year marriage to Josephine, the second oldest Beecham daughter, broke up in 1918 under the strain of recurrent family tensions. Woolley, a London medical practitioner with no business background, went along with whatever Boston decreed.

The will required the executors to convert, as soon as possible, the St Helens firm into a private limited company, Thomas Beecham Ltd, with a modest capital of £50,000, the sum for which they would sell the firm's assets. Thomas and Henry would be the main shareholders, owning 46 per cent each. Thomas, conspicuously omitted from the trusteeship, could become a director if the trustees agreed, but his shares were to be held in trust so as to allow him only the dividends. Two per cent of the shares would go to senior managers in the same proportions as the percentages of profits they currently received (see Chapter 6): these were Rowed, Moss the works manager, Glover the foreign and colonial manager, Scrymgeour the home sales manager, Bamford the office manager, and Austin Scott his former private secretary. All other employees with at least ten years' service were granted an extra year's wages from his estate.

Joseph's will also made clear with cold precision how he rated his daughters. The eldest, Emily, was cut out altogether owing to her earlier intransigence; the executors later required Thomas to provide her with an annuity of £2,000 a year and to pay premiums of £450 a year on two life assurance policies. She never qualified as a doctor, but became a Roman Catholic and a teacher of dancing for ballet and opera as Madame Helene Dolli. She died unmarried in 1965.[3] Elsie, having thwarted Joseph by her marriage in 1915, received only an annuity of £250. Jessie, whose husband he plainly detested, was given no company shares. That left three 'favoured sisters', Josephine, Edith and Christine, who were allotted 2 per cent each of the future company shares. Jessie benefited together with them as a residual legatee, but her husband had no legal right to that residue. Josephine, their widowed mother, had to be content with an income reduced from £4,500 to £2,500 a year, in accordance with the final alimony terms of 1903.

Joseph clearly anticipated that the executors would keep the Beecham firm as it was, rather than spending time on introducing any new developments. Indeed, that firm as it stood was not a partnership, since they could not act as partners according to the normal rules, but a business-in-commission. They jointly agreed how it should be run when they met for the first time at St Helens on 31 October 1916, four days after Joseph's interment, amidst much pomp, in Denton Green cemetery, close to his father. Rowed was confirmed as general manager, with the power of attorney he had held for twenty years. They fixed his salary at £1,000 a year, later to be raised by steps to £3,000 in 1920. Austin Scott became the firm's confidential secretary. While it remained unincorporated, the firm did not need by law to have an auditor, but Joseph's will sensibly laid down that the estate's, and hence the firm's, accounts should be placed in professional hands. Boston therefore recommended a chartered accountant who had acted for his leather company only since September, but in that brief space of time had greatly impressed him.

The 51-year-old Louis Nicholas, head of a Liverpool practice, took on that accounting post, and thus became the executors' financial adviser, exercising key influence over all their operations.[4] Thomas was to commend his ability, technical knowledge and personal loyalty, as well as a 'talent for figures nearly akin to genius', supplemented by boundless energy. A junior colleague, who worked with him for years, never saw him smile, and Nicholas was overbearing with subordinates; yet all agreed that the estate's finances could not have been in more capable hands. He was to remain at the centre of Beecham's corporate affairs for the best part of the next three decades.[5]

As a start, Nicholas drew up the firm's accounts to 30 September, the nearest practicable date to Joseph's death. Subsequent financial years, until a limited company was finally registered in 1924, ran from October to September. He then prepared the first-ever balance sheet, as at 23 October. No capital was entered, and its land and buildings were valued at £22,500. Stocks of drugs and work in progress came to £8,000, perhaps reduced by wartime restrictions to 12 days' supplies at manufacturers' prices, compared with the 16 weeks' supply of 1890 (see Chapter 6). Pill boxes and printed items such as handbills were estimated to be worth under £2,250. A form of advertising material only occasionally mentioned elsewhere in the extant archives was toilet paper, stocks being held at two London sites and valued at almost £232 in Joseph's death duties accounts;[6] encouraging messages were no doubt printed on every sheet. Cash in hand and at the bank was relatively high at £19,500, and the firm's total assets came to £130,000. Allowing for sundry creditors, the net balance was just under £118,000.

However good the firm's new accounting procedures, they did nothing to solve the executors' difficulties over Joseph's estate. Most alarmingly, the Duke of Bedford refused to honour the draft agreement, intended for signature on 23 October; the parties' earlier letters of intent had no legal validity, and he refused to grant a mortgage now that Joseph's personal guarantee was no more. The agreement of 1915 therefore remained in force; somehow the executors would have to find the outstanding £1.75 million, while the interest bill accumulated at the rate of £235 a day.

Immediately after Joseph's death, Thomas and Henry Beecham engaged James White as their independent financial adviser. The ever-resourceful White speedily devised a scheme which he claimed would generate some cash. Early in December he persuaded the two brothers to offer to buy for £400,000 their four sisters' residuary rights under the will, and their shareholding interests in the St Helens business for a further £60,000.

Thomas and Henry must have fallen for this plan on the expectation that they would be allowed to draw on the 92 per cent of the firm's profits – then running at over £130,000 a year – due to them under their father's will. The canny White probably urged them to make a pre-emptive strike against any move by Boston to secure control of Joseph's entire estate.

Whatever their motives, Boston and Woolley at once turned down the scheme flat; as long as the financial prospects remained so murky, no pill earnings were to be released. In any case, Thomas and Henry stood very little chance of raising that kind of money from any alternative source. When the brothers submitted a revised offer, which included an undertaking to secure these sums on mortgage, Boston and Woolley declined to budge. Those rebuffs inevitably caused a rift between Thomas, Henry and White on the one side, and Boston, Woolley and Nicholas on the other. To cap the bad tidings of this ill-starred year, on 31 December Ormrod disclaimed his right to purchase the Covent Garden estate.

Two weeks later, on 15 January 1917 the Inland Revenue granted probate on Joseph's will. If fewer than three months seem a very short period in which to unravel all the complexities of this huge and massively indebted estate, the authorities were anxious not to impede the executors' efforts to wind it up. The provisional valuation came to £1 million; a final figure, of roughly half as much again, was not agreed until 1923.

At once a flurry of legal actions started up in the Chancery Division of Britain's High Court, which dealt with cases of contested wills.[7] On 16 January Woolley and Boston, together with Charles Rowed, brought an action against Thomas, Henry and the most favoured sisters, to have a receiver or manager appointed for executing the terms of the will. The plaintiffs were determined to ensure that all relevant assets should be applied to meet the estate's massive liabilities. In particular, any undisclosed loans and advances from Joseph to Thomas would have to be made public; Thomas must not be allowed to extract more money from the estate than was specified in the will.

Henry, caught unawares by the lawsuit, straightway put pressure on Rowed, who changed sides and joined the defendants. On 20 January, Thomas launched a counter-suit against all four executors, principally to establish whether he was entitled to draw his 46 per cent share in the firm's profits, or whether their release depended on securing a comprehensive solution to the problems over the Covent Garden estate.

Three days later Donald Baylis, as former manager of Joseph's musical ventures and still owed £3,200 arrears of salary, began an action to compel the executors to appoint a receiver. Baylis's was clearly a test case, put up by the other creditors who were fearful of the major litigants squeezing out their claims; his action revived talk that he was a son of the deceased. The Court imposed a stay on the two later suits. To allow the first to proceed, it formally placed Joseph's estate in Chancery, assuming to itself the power to vet all major decisions.[8]

Now that Rowed had defected to the Beechams, Boston and Woolley moved smartly to seize the initiative. They served notice to quit on White and Paget-Cooke, still maintaining regular liaison with the Bedford Estate Office over the sales and upkeep of properties at Covent Garden. Yet as the latter pair were the only ones in the Beecham ranks who understood the procedures, they rightly ignored such a high-handed act. The firm's solicitors at St Helens, Oppenheim & Co., were given notice as well, but calmly went on with routine tasks such as securing payment of a £70,000 insurance policy on Joseph's life. An even deeper gulf had now opened up between the two sides in the case; when the executors and their solicitors met at Nicholas's office towards the end of January, 'heated discussions' ensued.[9]

Meanwhile, Rowed was the caretaker boss at St Helens. In the first nine months of 1916, once adjusted to an annual basis, pill turnover had risen by just 1 per cent over the 1915 level. A slight fall in home deliveries had been offset by an increase of one-fifth in exports, with sales in the United States, at $281,000 (£56,000), being also at a record level. Joseph had been advertising heavily in America ever since his technically updated New York factory was completed in 1911; the cost approximated to two-thirds of turnover, a proportion that showed the intensity of competition there. For the British and rest-of-the-world markets, by contrast, advertising outlay accounted for no more than a quarter of sales. Interestingly, running costs of the American branch, now in Henry Beecham's hands, were only fractionally higher than in Britain, around 15 per cent of sales as against 13 per cent. Perhaps the recently installed machinery kept those costs low.

For the time being, no one considered following Joseph's instructions to float a joint-stock company. Incorporation would not have made the government any more willing to authorize new issues, nor would the banks have been prepared to lend the sums needed while the economic outlook remained so uncertain. The executors and their advisers had to spend much time in attempting to unravel problems caused by Joseph's former inability to explain to others the reasons for some vital business decisions.

Most puzzlingly, Joseph was found to have outstanding overdrafts at the London and St Helens branches of Parr's bank, totalling over £475,000: well above the £250,000 level he had regularly maintained since 1914. At the same time, there was the £250,000 special deposit account, entitled 'The firm of Thomas Beecham, Sir Joseph Beecham proprietor' and earmarked for the outstanding progress payment to the duke.[10] The executors would have gladly used that sum to pay off part of the overdraft, thereby reducing the interest charges. However, the lawyers judged that its title definitively linked the account to the firm, and thus prevented its being put to outside use as if it belonged to his personal fortune. So far from easing the debt to the duke, the account remained an inert part of the St Helens assets until the formation of a company in 1924.

During 1917, tension could only be expected to grow between the St Helens group of executors, namely Henry Beecham and Rowed (aided by Thomas) on one side, and the sons-in-law Boston and Woolley on the other. Thomas scarcely improved those brittle relations when he announced, after addressing a meeting – chaired by the Lord Mayor of Birmingham – to launch an ambitious plan to found an orchestra there. That project collapsed a year later, his out-of-pocket expenses amounting to £2,000.[11] A further source of irritation was that in February, Thomas and Henry agreed to become directors of a £100,000 company registered by White as the Beecham Trust Ltd. Joseph had earlier been talked into bestowing his surname on that company, and White was all too obviously using it to give a shine to his financial speculations. The two brothers did not long remain on the Trust board.[12]

Thomas was pursuing his operatic schemes with the same verve as if his father were still behind him, and in March he once again, as he had done in January, asked Boston and Woolley for the share of the firm's profits that were his under the will.[13] The latter pair not only refused, but informed the Court that they no longer had confidence in their co-executors' impartiality; hence a receiver or manager was needed at once to run Joseph's estate. Boston was plainly eager to gain full control of the St Helens firm as the generator of cash, expecting that even if he himself were not appointed, a future receiver would nominate him as manager.

Rowed had already condemned any outside imposition of a supremo at St Helens as 'disastrous'. Such a newcomer, he had argued, would lack 'a peculiar knowledge of management', namely expertise in the production and marketing of pills, which he himself – he modestly refrained from adding – possessed after three decades of effective stewardship.[14] After that further rejection, Thomas was so desperate that he broke the promise he had made to his father and once again resorted to moneylenders.[15] In April he raised extra funds by mortgaging his father's Hampstead home with the euphemistically named Clarebell Investment Company.

In May 1917 the London auctioneers, Christies, sold the collection of pictures which Joseph had so painstakingly assembled. The total proceeds were £97,000, or just over £100,000 counting some silver and other valuables. Then, as these things happen, relations between the two sides took an unexpected turn for the better. During that same May, Boston and Woolley withdrew all objections to Thomas's and Henry's plan to purchase their father's residuary estate; the agreed consideration was now £475,000. The Court gave approval to this step.

Nicholas had astutely won the day with a confidential memorandum to Boston and Woolley, listing all the assets and liabilities involved, and showing that the residuary estate was currently worth only £204,000, making the transaction 'an advantageous one, and in the best interests of all beneficially entitled'. Thomas in due course got wind of this remarkable piece of creative accounting, and never forgot how he and his brother had been taken in. Much later he recalled in his memoirs how he and Henry had mistakenly pledged themselves 'to pay for the residue about twice as much as it eventually proved to be worth'.[16]

Thomas did not use the proceeds from the Clarebell transaction for anything as mundane as part-payment for the residuary estate. Instead, he hired Drury Lane Theatre and promoted opera and ballet seasons for the summer of 1917 and then into 1918. His initiative did create a landmark in British operatic history, with a pioneering version of Mozart's *The Marriage of Figaro*. However, both seasons were poorly attended, in the main because of air raids on London, and his losses were estimated at £500–£1,000 a week.[17]

Helen Taylor now brought herself to the executors' attention. After reading of Joseph's death while in Sydney, Australia, she took the next boat home. She discovered that a total of £700 in bank drafts, sent her by Joseph, had been frozen when he died; she was also concerned about the many other gifts of cash and kind, as well as nearly £17,000 worth of securities, mainly American railroad bonds, that he had taken care of. Having never given a thought to ask him for receipts, she was incapable of proving her entitlement. Moreover, the safe deposit box which she had inspected just before her departure, in her case did not turn out to be a girl's best friend, since Joseph also held a key which was impounded when he died. The executors reduced her claim of £2,240 to a mere £360; fortunately, they could not touch her income from the settlement of 1914.[18]

Helen did not survive Joseph for all that long. In January 1920, she died suddenly of heart failure, aged 56, while visiting relatives in Napier, New Zealand. Her funeral was conducted by the local Anglican bishop, at Park Cemetery there, and she was interred as the widow of the late John Bennett, of London. This adherence to a fictitious husband was probably motivated not just by an understandable yearning for respectability, but also by affection for a man who had stood by her for thirty-four years as a helpmate in his fight against loneliness and rejection. Having no issue or other dependants, she bequeathed her assets of £2,500 to two Liverpool seamen's charities and to the Governesses' Benevolent Institution. The invisible woman almost, but not wholly, took her secrets to the grave.[19]

Meanwhile, the Duke of Bedford and his advisers were following the Chancery Court proceedings with manifest concern. In spite of having declined to recognize the unratified accord of 1916, they expected full repayment on the previously agreed completion date of June 1917. In July the executors wrote to the duke, making plain that the agreement could not be honoured in full until substantial funds were released from Joseph's estate, the bulk of which stayed inextricably tied up in one form or another.[20]

The executors therefore revived a project to turn the Covent Garden estate into a limited company, with power to make outside share and loan issues.

The Treasury, when approached, would not shift over granting permission. In September, the duke agreed to a new completion date of 11 November 1917; yet even that leeway was impossibly short, and the concluding months of that year saw sundry plans and counter-plans being hatched. The duke had to allow payment to stand over, in the hope that something might turn up.[21]

A measure of relief came in January 1918. Some of Thomas's supporters from the north of England registered a private company, The Sir Thomas Beecham's Estate Ltd, to take over the whole of his interests in Joseph's will and also his liabilities.[22] The £500,000 capital, and £150,000 worth of 6½ per cent debentures, was reckoned to provide enough funds to meet his share of the £475,000 and go some way towards fulfilling the purchase agreement with the duke. The company's promoters were bound by Treasury regulations to see that the capital and debentures came privately from investors, as no new issues could be floated through the market. Because the executors would thus benefit from some additional money, the duke consented to delay any fresh arrangement until March, on condition that he received £100,000 on account. That sum was handed over a month late. Thomas and Henry apparently did not object to £60,000 being taken from the ever growing undistributed profits in the pill firm.

Those moves foreshadowed progress in other directions as well. In June 1918 the Chancery Court at last sanctioned the establishment of a company to take over the Covent Garden assets, including the St Helens business. The Covent Garden Estate Company Ltd was registered a month later, on 18 July, its £100,000 authorized capital being held partly by the executors and partly by Thomas and Henry as individuals. The executors also received £1.17 million from the 6 per cent mortgage debentures, in return for the sale of the entire estate to the company for just over £2.5 million. To be sure, the Covent Garden market itself was acknowledged to be in a precarious financial condition through wartime restrictions and interruptions to normal business. The pill firm was valued at £500,000, a little under four times its annual profits, which totalled nearly £161,000 for the year ending September 1918.[23]

Some banks were now prepared to lend money to a registered company, especially one with such an extensive collateral, and Nicholas at once borrowed £400,000, which he paid over to the duke shortly after the new company's registration. Perhaps because he felt that the arrangement was financially sound, the duke allowed £1.25 million to be left on mortgage.

Boston predictably became the company chairman and managing director, with Thomas, Henry and Woolley as the other directors. The board was thus evenly balanced between two factions with few common aims. When Boston claimed a casting vote, the Beechams objected because they would have lost effective control over future decisions. They also sought the right to appoint successors in the event of any vacancy on their side. Those were no mere quibbles. Boston and Woolley were again insisting, without any legal right, that White and Paget-Cooke must accept their ejection from the duke's estate office. However, both agreed to withdraw, and Boston took over their task. Louis Nicholas was company secretary; in view of Boston's other business commitments, he became *de facto* managing director.[24]

The end of the war came at long last in November 1918, and was calculated to speed up the unravelling of the Chancery case in two respects. The market's tolls and charges could now be raised to more remunerative levels, and thus help to improve earnings. Moreover, restored business confidence would allow the company to sell off property in Covent Garden as and when practicable, while Joseph's personal mortgage holdings in dwellings and any remaining outside corporate shares could be liquidated more rapidly. By the early months of 1920, almost all of the latter assets had been sold, apart from ones still protected by rent controls and other wartime legislation.

During the post-war boom, demand for Beecham's pills soared to unprecedented levels; in 1918/19 the number of pills despatched was as high as 542 million, rising to 580 million in the following year. Meanwhile, the estate company rather neglected the duke's interests. In December 1919 his solicitors had to remind Nicholas that £250,000 should have been paid over within a year of the armistice. Nicholas responded by borrowing £100,000 against the proceeds of asset sales; he despatched that sum on account, promising the balance by November 1920 at the latest.

More than a year passed beyond that date without any movement, and in March 1922 the executors' solicitor had to plead with the Bedford estate people not to take the directors to court. The threat was now serious enough for Nicholas to borrow £150,000 from the bank and hand it over two months later. By that time, the bulk of the Covent Garden residential and commercial properties, apart from the market itself, had been sent to auction, yielding £290,000. Early in September 1922, the balance of £1 million was paid to the duke and his mortgage thereby redeemed. It is not known when or how the outstanding interest charges were settled.[25]

The Beecham firm continued to do well; even in 1921/22, when the post-war boom was nearing its end, the numbers of pills sent out were not far short of 500 million. Turnover (net of duty) was over £308,000, and the resulting profit of £162,000 exceeded that of every year before 1918/19. Advertising costs came to nearly £150,000 that year. With buoyant sales expected in 1922/23 – in due course they reached £345,000, its profit being a little down at £132,000 – the firm could look forward to a more settled future now that the Chancery case seemed only a whisker away from final settlement.

It was Thomas whose actions derailed that winding-up process. After the armistice, he had aspired to repeat the brilliant operatic and ballet ventures of the pre-war years. Returning to the Covent Garden Theatre for a season from May to August 1919, he gave 82 performances of no fewer than 20 operas. Yet that season, together with one from May to July in the following year, were described as 'pale, confused echoes of pre-1914', which even the fleeting return of Diaghilev and his company could not infuse with the earlier legendary glamour.

In between, Thomas gave a series of winter performances at Covent Garden between November 1919 and April 1920. As Donald Baylis was all too visibly sick of laryngeal tuberculosis, brought on by overwork, and died in May 1920, most productions were indifferently staged. Poor takings at the box office landed Thomas with a bill for £104,000, which included £40,000 interest on his outstanding debts. The interest total was at that level because in 1918–19 he had borrowed no less than £63,000 from moneylenders, one loan for £1,600 being at the usurious annual rate of 120 per cent. As it was not in his nature to repay debts, disaster was plainly just around the corner.[26]

The first, ignored, warning sign had loomed up in May 1919, when a moneylender took out a petition of bankruptcy against him for non-payment of a £900 debt. Thomas was already in trouble for not fulfilling certain obligations to his sister Emily; those were eventually paid. The two bulky files of official bankruptcy proceedings against him disclose a tale of evasion, procrastination and obfuscation on his part, either because he relished pitting his wits against a legal establishment he detested, or because to him money was just something to be spent.

The roll-call of moneylenders include those with imposing titles such as the City and County Private Finance Company Ltd; among the creditors, for £1,198, was Princess Serafina Astafieva, a former ballerina with the Diaghilev company and currently a highly esteemed ballet teacher in the King's Road, Chelsea, where a Blue Plaque marks her former home. In October 1919, Nicholas on his behalf drew up a statement of Thomas's financial affairs, revealing total debts of nearly £108,000, a figure which the Official Receiver suspected did not tell the complete truth.[27]

Unfazed by these legal proceedings, Thomas went ahead with organizing a six-month winter tour of English provincial cities for 1920–21, notwithstanding his Beecham Opera Company's collapse into bankruptcy the previous July, which set him back a further £104,000. The tour ended with a bump in Glasgow that December when funds ran out, abruptly terminating his musical ventures for several years to come. In March 1921 the Sir Thomas Beecham Estate Ltd was compulsorily wound up amid rancour on the part of debenture holders, whose interest payments Thomas had done nothing to meet.

The liquidators were dismayed to find that the company – effectively Thomas as managing director – had infringed the law by keeping no books of account.

The Beecham Opera Company likewise had no proper accounting system, but relied on weekly and monthly pay sheets; board meetings, planned only for once or twice a year, were often cancelled because the directors were away on tour or otherwise engaged.[28]

The bankruptcy court held a series of widely publicized hearings into Thomas's affairs, broken up by frequent adjournments. His gross liabilities were estimated at £2.1 million – including the £1.25 million then owed to the duke – and his assets at under £75,000. He avoided settling many debts because they could not be proved, while his father-in-law Dr Welles, who was owed nearly £50,000 under the marriage contract, gave in for his daughter's sake. Even so, the executors of Joseph's estate, who were sitting on £190,000 of undistributed profits belonging to Thomas, felt it only prudent to set about liquidating the debts he had acknowledged. They feared lest the Official Receiver might come nosing round their own account books, and raise awkward questions about whether earlier payments made to him had been fully taxed.

Now that their debt to the Duke of Bedford had been redeemed, very early in 1923 the executors calculated that Thomas would need about £260,000 to restore him to solvency. Nicholas, on the other hand, creatively and comfortingly estimated that £150,000 would cover the lot. The executors therefore borrowed £190,000 on the strength of the pill firm's earnings, and in March of that year Thomas received a discharge from his debts. Thanks to their prompt action, he was saved from being officially declared bankrupt.[29]

During the time from the end of 1920 to early in 1923, Thomas had withdrawn entirely from musical activities. He later explained his absence as follows:

> For over three years I sat daily in the newly built offices of the [Covent Garden Estate] company and completed satisfactorily the labour we had undertaken by selling over a million pounds [worth] of property and appreciably increasing the revenue of the balance.

In his memoirs Thomas waxed lyrical about that period as 'without doubt the most tranquil and orderly' that he had known since entering public life. He recalled it as a 'fortunate interlude in every way beneficial for me mentally and physically', which entailed negotiations in 'a highly complex organization with an individual routine of its own'.

On the basis of those statements, he has been hailed as a 'first-rate businessman, something not generally appreciated by those who saw him merely as a profligate spender of money for artistic purposes'. Rather, it was argued, he was able to use constructively for commercial ends his 'persuasive manner and rapid brain'.

To be sure, despite being hailed as 'the most gifted executive musician

England has ever produced', Thomas was indeed a master of persuasiveness and quick thinking. Yet the evidence shows that he had neither the aptitude nor the inclination for business, a quality which requires accepting the need to undertake as a matter of course all those routine duties to be found in commerce. The financial affairs of both the Sir Thomas Beecham Estate Company and his own opera company had been in a chronic mess. He boasted that his most used filing cabinet was the waste-paper basket; in 1920, when the receiving order was issued, the executors found an accumulation of 2,000 unopened letters addressed to him.[30]

The people in the Bedford Estate Office, who had every reason to know, deemed him 'absolutely stupid' over finance. In 1925 the lawyers acting for his sister Emily – after years of bombarding him with letters and taking out writs over the sums owed to her – in desperation turned to Henry, observing, 'Not only has Sir Thomas been unbusinesslike to a [marked] degree, but [he] has been foolishly evasive, causing trouble and inconvenience to himself as well as others.'

It defies logic that the abrasive Boston and the happy-go-lucky Thomas could have sat at adjoining desks for one whole day, let alone for upwards of two years. An authority who had worked with those in the estate office commented on Thomas's explanation as follows:

This is all rather a heroic account of his activities; independent contemporary evidence does not support the idea of arduous devotion to duty; rather was it an occasional visit to the offices, often accompanied by a nubile companion (referred to as 'my Australian cousin'), seeking a substantial advance from the petty cash.

The art historian, Sir Kenneth (later Lord) Clark, summed up Thomas elegantly and succinctly as 'so irresponsible in other respects, [he] was deadly serious about conducting'.[31]

Some historians of business have written about the Buddenbrooks syndrome. Thomas Mann's novel of that name chronicled successive generations of a German mercantile family, which expired with the death, at sixteen, of the last of the third generation, a somewhat mixed-up musical prodigy. According to the syndrome, entrepreneurial skills tend to erode over three lifetimes, leading to corporate decline and closure or an outside take-over. One scholar has starkly portrayed the sequence in British industry of 'shirtsleeves to hunting jacket' in three generations. According to him, the hard-working and thrifty founder might have been succeeded by a more ambitious son who raised the firm to 'undreamt-of heights'. Then the grandsons, 'children of affluence, tired of the tedium of trade and flushed with the bucolic aspirations of the country gentleman', either sold out or ran down the firm thanks to 'a combination of amateurism and complacency'.[32]

In the Beecham instance, after the parsimonious Thomas and the entrepreneurial Joseph, Sir Thomas had gone his own way, remaining a musical prodigy for five times the years of the last Buddenbrook. Joseph's younger son, though, remained in post. Unlike his grandfather, father and brother, Henry was an uxorious man; yet he had his own means of self-expression.

With James White's assistance, in about 1915 he purchased Lympne Castle in Kent; he gambled on the Stock Exchange and also relished driving fast cars. In an era when the general speed limit was 30 miles an hour, he predictably encountered some spectacular brushes with the law. Then in January 1921, during a tour of Hertfordshire, his car skidded at speed, mounted a bank and ploughed through a group of children, killing one and injuring two others. He was had up and found guilty of manslaughter, being sentenced to twelve months' imprisonment in the second division. On the ground that he had been tricked by prosecuting counsel into admitting earlier convictions, he took his case to appeal, and lost.[33]

Henry must have incurred heavy legal expenses, being defended in both cases by a prominent King's Counsel; he also had to meet some pressing financial claims on the American business. The executors advanced him a total of £23,000, and he then sold that business to them in July 1921 for £22,500, that year's profit being $30,500 (nearly £6,300) and the advertising bill nearly $190,000 (£39,000). He must have been released from prison in the spring of 1922; towards the end of July he composed a lengthy and not very lucid memorandum for his fellow executors. After criticizing various current business practices at St Helens, he complained about Rowed's failure any longer to share with him the affairs of the pill firm, ostensibly because of Henry's preoccupation with Covent Garden estate matters. He now urged the formation of a management committee, headed by Thomas or himself, and comprising also Rowed and William Moss.

Apparently for the first time since his release, Henry at once began to attend at St Helens. For the next two weeks he sat there each day, but no papers arrived on his desk; he was consulted only once, on a trivial matter. As his memorandum was ignored, early in August he wrote to Rowed, demanding that all managerial questions in the firm should be brought to his notice. The sale of the US assets had severed all direct connection of his with the firm, and the other executors must have taken the opportunity to make Beecham a Henry-free zone. Soon after writing that letter he and his wife entered the firm, together with a picnic lunch. Having cleared his office, he left for good.[34]

Meanwhile Thomas, in a more reflective frame of mind, was becoming alarmed lest Charles Boston might be tempted away from the Covent Garden

4.1 The founder, Thomas Beecham, in his mid-sixties, by then the leading patent medicine maker in Britain, *c.*1885.

BEECHAM ARCHIVES

4.2 Joseph Beecham's architect-designed and meticulously planned St Helens factory, 1887.

BUILDING NEWS, 9 APRIL 1886

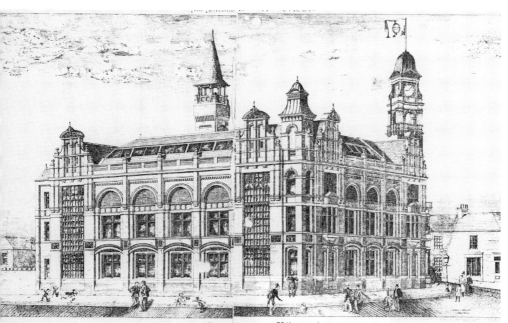

BEECHAM'S PILLS NEW MANUFACTORY ST HELENS LANCASHIRE.
H V KR?LOW ARCHITECT

THE GRAND OLD MAGICIAN'S IRISH POLICY.

4.3 Mr Gladstone, prime minister, magically resolves the 'great Irish problem', observed by (left to right) Joseph Chamberlain, Lord Hartington and Lord Randolph Churchill, 1886.

ILLUSTRATED LONDON NEWS, 24 APRIL 1886

4.4 Never having taken Beecham's pills, Queen Victoria was not amused to be represented 'in the Palace', together with her subjects 'in the Cottage', 'At Sea' and 'in the Study', 1887.

ILLUSTRATED LONDON NEWS, 25 JUNE 1887

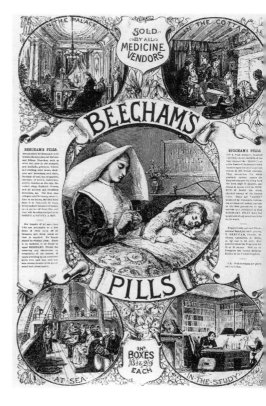

4.5 The actor (Sir) Henry Irving misquotes the celebrated soliloquy in Shakespeare's *Hamlet*, 1888. 'To Beecham, or not to Beecham' advertisement.

ILLUSTRATED LONDON NEWS, CHRISTMAS ISSUE, 1888

5.1 John Bull, accompanied by Britannia, displays 'the world's medicine' to thirty different nationalities, 1886.

GRAPHIC, 15 MAY 1886

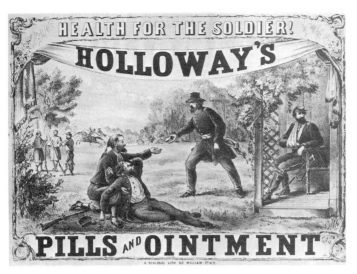

5.2 A Union officer in the American Civil War offers some Holloway's ointment to a wounded private soldier, 1863.

5.3 *Left*, a black entertainer, holding an outsize banjo, points to its strings, which read one way 'Beecham's Pills' and the other way 'A Wonderful Medicine'.

Right, the US version of *Beecham's Music Portfolio*, hosted by an American beauty, *c.*1900.

5.4 A memsahib at a 'European shop' in India, at odds with the shopkeeper over the difference between 'peel' and pills', 1903.

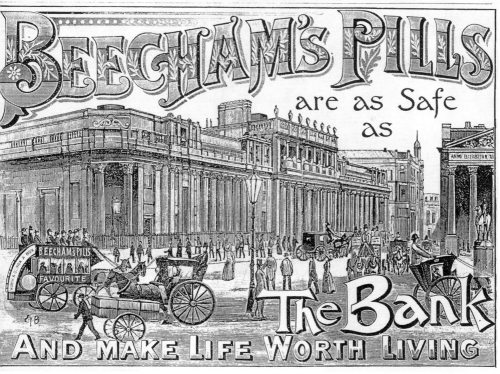

A DIVORCE COURT INCIDENT.

A PRIZE OF ONE GUINEA will be given to the reader who suggests the most appropriate dialogue for the above sketch, which illustrates the cross-examination of a lady in the divorce court. The words "Beecham's Pills" must be introduced, and the dialogue should not exceed 100 words.

A few Consolation Prizes will be given to those readers whose efforts may be considered very near the mark. **Address: The Proprietor of "BEECHAM'S PILLS," St. Helens, Lancashire.** Do not trouble to send this advertisement: better to keep it, and show it to your friends. It will be re-inserted in this paper shortly with the winning dialogue added.

"On the Move" and "A Friend in Need" Competitions. The result will shortly be given in the papers in which readers last saw the pictures appertaining to them.

7.1　Bank of England staff were doubtless as unamused as Queen Victoria had been at such a respected name being used in a Beecham advertisement, 1896.

St Paul's, 4 January 1896

7.2　An apparent bid by Joseph Beecham, portrayed here as Counsel, to humiliate his separated wife, Josephine. Nothing more was heard of this so-called 'competition', 1895.

Illustrated London News, 13 April 1895

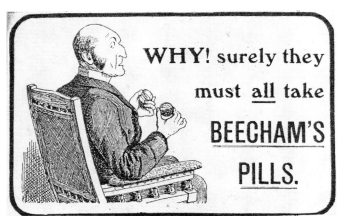

A very clever inferential advertisement puts " Beecham's Pills " amongst the best advertisements of the month.. The word-ing, " Surely they ALL take Beecham's Pills " is pregnant with meaning, and is worth a whole cartload of laboured argu-ment or alphabetical nonsense such as Beecham's have too often been guilty of loading on to the advertisement reader. The expression on the man's face also conveys a neat argument in a very effective manner. Altogether it is a very clever and very humorous advertisement.

7.6   A striking vignette, of an astonished clergyman, attracted the warm approval of *Advertising* in May 1905.

BEECHAM ARCHIVES

7.7   The conductor, (Sir) Thomas Beecham in 1910, about to inaugurate the first of the legendary opera and ballet seasons in London, ended by war in 1914.

MUSICAL TIMES, 1 OCTOBER 1910

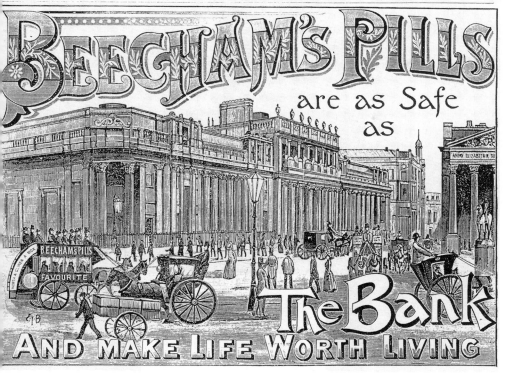

A DIVORCE COURT INCIDENT.

A PRIZE OF ONE GUINEA will be given to the reader who suggests the most appropriate dialogue for the above sketch, which illustrates the cross-examination of a lady in the divorce court. The words "Beecham's Pills" must be introduced, and the dialogue should not exceed 100 words.

A few CONSOLATION PRIZES will be given to those readers whose efforts may be considered near the mark. **Address: The Proprietor of "BEECHAM'S PILLS," St. Helens, Lancashire.** Do not trouble to send this advertisement; better to keep it, and show it to your friends. It will be re-inserted in this paper shortly with the winning dialogue added.

"On the Move" and "A Friend in Need" Competitions. The result will shortly be given in the papers in which readers last saw the pictures appertaining to them.

7.1 Bank of England staff were doubtless as unamused as Queen Victoria had been at such a respected name being used in a Beecham advertisement, 1896.

ST PAUL's, 4 JANUARY 1896

7.2 An apparent bid by Joseph Beecham, portrayed here as Counsel, to humiliate his separated wife, Josephine. Nothing more was heard of this so-called 'competition', 1895.

ILLUSTRATED LONDON NEWS, 13 APRIL 1895

7.3 William Moss, aged 36, when appointed works manager in 1896.

7.4 Thomas Beecham in his eighties, enjoying domestic bliss with the family of his old age at Southport, *c.*1900.

ALL GOOD CHILDREN TAKE—BEECHAM'S PILLS

7.5 This vignette illustrates how the cycle of dependence on laxatives was being transmitted by one generation to the next, 1901.

BEECHAM ARCHIVES

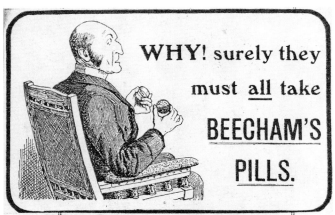

A very clever inferential advertisement puts " Beecham's Pills " amongst the best advertisements of the month. The wording, "Surely they ALL take Beecham's Pills " is pregnant with meaning, and is worth a whole cartload of laboured argument or alphabetical nonsense such as Beecham's have too often been guilty of loading on to the advertisement reader. The expression on the man's face also conveys a neat argument in a very effective manner. Altogether it is a very clever and very humorous advertisement.

7.6 A striking vignette, of an astonished clergyman, attracted the warm approval of *Advertising* in May 1905.

BEECHAM ARCHIVES

7.7 The conductor, (Sir) Thomas Beecham in 1910, about to inaugurate the first of the legendary opera and ballet seasons in London, ended by war in 1914.

MUSICAL TIMES, 1 OCTOBER 1910

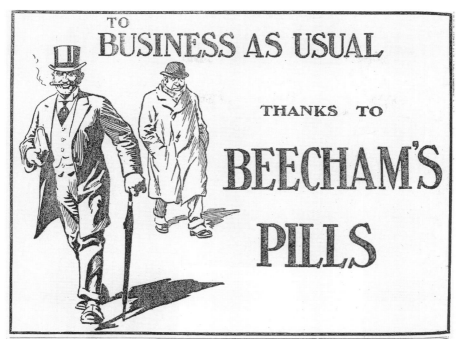

London: Published Weekly at the Office, 172, Strand, in the Parish of St. Clement Danes, in the County of London, by THE ILLUSTRATED LONDON NEWS AND SKETCH, LTD., 172, Strand, aforesaid; and Printed by THE ILLUSTRATED LONDON NEWS AND SKETCH, LTD., Milford Lane, W.C.—SATURDAY, OCTOBER 24, 1914. Entered as Second-Class Matter at the New York (N. Y.) Post Office, 1903.

8.1 A glum raincoat-clad man eyes the frock-coated gent, ready to face the problems of the recently declared war after his daily dose of Beecham's pills, 1914.

ILLUSTRATED LONDON NEWS, 24 OCTOBER 1914

8.2 Bruce Bairnsfather, creator of the fatalistic warrior, Old Bill, mocks a captured German buffoon, 1915.

CHEMIST & DRUGGIST, 10 OCTOBER 1942

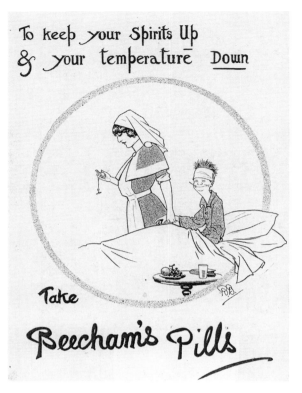

8.3 Bairnsfather, wounded in action, relishes having his wrist held by a curvaceous nurse, 1915.

ILLUSTRATED LONDON NEWS, 19 JUNE 1915

9.1 American child, with kiss-curl and in smock and shorts, repeats her mother's conviction that Beecham's pills are good for everyone, *c.*1919.

B. HOLME, *ADVERTISING, REFLECTIONS OF A CENTURY*

10.1 Philip Hill, influential director of Beecham Estates and Pills Ltd, while modernizing the pill operations at St Helens, *c.*1925.

Lazell, *From Pills to Penicillin*

10.2 William Moss, in his final years as works manager, *c.*1925.

Keith Moss

10.3 William Moss, at work in his home, *c.*1925.

10.4 Frank Moss, his father's deputy and works manager from 1929 until his death in 1955, *c.*1940s.

11.1 Pill-making machines in the first extension of the St Helens factory, 1937.

INDUSTRIAL CHEMIST, JUNE 1937

11.2 Philip Hill, chairman of Beechams Pills Ltd, having created the UK's largest medicinal-cum-household product company, *c.*1935.

PHOTOGRAPH BY ELLIOTT & FRY, M. KEYWORTH

11.3 An automatic machine in Macleans' London factory, used to feed the toothpaste into collapsible tubes.

INDUSTRIAL CHEMIST, PHARMACEUTICAL AND COSMETIC SUPPLEMENT, NOVEMBER 1935

I keep fit

and so can You!

A timely dose of BEECHAMS PILLS will ensure a regular, gentle natural bowel action and so ward off liverishness, stomach upsets, morning drowsiness and other signs of ill-health to which you may have become accustomed. Get some Beechams Pills now. They are wonderfully reliable. *Obtainable everywhere.*

Beechams Brand *Pills*

WORTH A GUINEA A BOX

Purely vegetable.

11.4　Broadcasts by the 'Radio Doctor' (Dr Charles Hill) made it acceptable to mention bowel movements in the media, 1941.

12.1 Strip cartoon, which Beecham introduced in the 1930s, claims in graphic form the rapid relief from headaches achieved by Beecham's Powders, 1951.

12.2 Beecham's Research Laboratory at Brockham Park, Surrey, opened in 1947, photographed in 1971.

13.1 Leslie Lazell, managing director and then chairman, who converted Beecham from a medicinal to a pharmaceutical company, *c.*1960.

estate – burdened with a host of outstanding property matters – by offers of directorships in some London companies. Suggesting that 'it would be to the greatest advantage of the St Helens business if the regular services of Mr Boston were at its disposal', Thomas proposed him as managing director of Thomas Beecham Ltd, by then at last on the horizon.[35] Boston refused to be drawn, and the days of family control were numbered.

In April 1923, Thomas celebrated his return to the musical platform by organizing a lively concert at the Albert Hall, with two combined orchestras and a majestic but decidedly off-key Dame Clara Butt as soloist. Two months later, Nicholas reached agreement with the Inland Revenue over the value of Joseph's fortune, namely £1.48 million, the estate duty amounting to £300,000. Meanwhile, the St Helens firm lost none of its financial buoyancy, despite the onset of harsher economic conditions, when unemployment nationally reached 15 per cent of the labour force. Over 500 million pills were sold in the year to September 1923, bringing in £345,000. Profits fell only slightly to £152,000.

Then some time in 1923, Thomas – as he recalled in his memoirs – 'made the acquaintance of a personality of resource, Philip Hill, who talked more sense about the position of our affairs than anyone I had yet met'. James White had already faded from the scene, but continued to use the Beecham name – without any family representation – in that Trust, which crashed in 1927 after a speculation in oil shares went catastrophically wrong and drove him to take his own life. Thomas summed up White as 'one of that group of financial wizards who appeared and vanished like comets in the sky of the business world during the period 1910–30'. Hill, on the other hand, was no transient wonder, and his arrival on the scene gave real hope for the Beecham firm's deliverance.[36]

Not tall, but heavily built, Hill was just fifty. As a young estate agent in Wales, while undertaking some London property transactions he had noted that metropolitan deals were far more lucrative than those made in the provinces; in 1912 he therefore moved to London's west end. During the First World War he had started up as a public works contractor. When that business ran down after 1918, he was left with a large overdraft, not finally repaid until 1922. Having some decades of involvement in property behind him, he perceived what could be made of the Covent Garden company, still owning most of the market. As he had no practical knowledge of manufacturing industry at that time, it is not clear how he sized up the pill firm, which brought in money but had no logical corporate links with property.

Hill's business partner was Sir Arthur Wheeler, Bt., an 'outside' share broker who, not being a member of any stock exchange, was allowed to advertise for and to clients. His spectacularly successful if unorthodox efforts to sell war savings had earned him a baronetcy in 1920. From his Leicestershire base, he made it easy for investors to put their money into reputable unquoted companies. Wheeler was also chairman of the Midland Industrial and General Trust Ltd, an investment trust which tapped funds in central and northern England to finance new issues and traded in unquoted company shares from its own portfolio. During November 1923, Hill and Wheeler secured a £2.5 million option on the Covent Garden market and the pill business, from Thomas and Henry as beneficial owners. In return, Thomas received a loan of £75,000 and Henry £5,000 in cash.[37]

The Covent Garden market was estimated by the London property valuers, Goddard and Smith, to be worth £1.47 million, and early in 1924 the executors commissioned a London consulting accountant, Arthur Collins, to value the St Helens firm. The land, buildings, machinery, plant and office furniture had already been assessed for estate duty purposes at £99,388; together with the special deposit account, by then standing at £258,421 and still judged by the lawyers to belong to the firm, the total came to about £357,800. To this Collins attached a goodwill item, defined as a sum over and above the firm's tangible assets, but representing value because of its earning capacity; in this case equivalent to six years' profit, namely £900,000. He added a rider that it was impossible to forecast the future earnings of a firm depending wholly on patent medicines. Having subtracted £150,000 for the estimated expenses of forming a limited company, he arrived at the sum of £1,117,000.

In mid-April 1924 Boston, Woolley and Rowed as plaintiffs, and no fewer than 24 other parties, comprising interested relatives and their lawyers, successfully petitioned the Court of Chancery for the Beecham case to be wound up.[38] The whole Chancery affair had taken seven and a half years to resolve, and the extent of the legal and other costs in time and effort could only be guessed at.

The Court sanctioned the establishment of a joint-stock company. For the first time Beecham was about to present itself to the world as a managerial and no longer as a family concern. It remained to be seen how the future top management could possibly address the problem of running in tandem two such diverse businesses as the Covent Garden estate and the pill-making operations.

Beecham Estates and Pills Ltd, 1924–1928

T HE NEW FIRM was at last incorporated in May 1924, not as Thomas
Beecham Ltd, but as Beecham Estates and Pills Ltd, the head office being
in the Central Avenue of Covent Garden market.[1] It was scarcely typical of
many British enterprises in having enjoyed a more than average run of luck.
Had Joseph Beecham died before the 1870s, his younger brother William,
who became an easy-going doctor and married well, would doubtless have
taken his place, fallen out with their father Thomas, and let the whole concern
go to waste.

If, on the other hand, Joseph had lived to 1928 at the age of eighty,
partnered by his unremarkable son, Henry, and done little to overhaul the
firm, it would have joined its Morison, Cockle and Holloway rivals in entering
imperceptibly into decline. If Charles Boston had forsaken his malodorous
tannery for the fragrance of the pill factory, his insensitiveness and push
might have shaken the organization to pieces. Finally, if the younger Thomas
had not been profligate over money, thereby delaying the ultimate settlement
of Joseph's affairs in Chancery, Philip Hill would not have been able to
free himself from his earlier business commitments and emerge as the right
entrepreneur at the right moment.

As it turned out, the promoters chose as good a year as any since 1918 to
form a joint-stock company. Financial markets in Britain had taken time to
adjust themselves after new issues were freed from controls late in 1919. A
speculative bubble gave way to a recession once the post-war boom collapsed
in 1921; however, three years later the new issue market was at last settling
down. Bank rate remained no higher than 4 per cent for nearly two years
after mid-1923. Notwithstanding the depression in its staple industries and
a million unemployed, demand for consumer goods throughout the country's
more prosperous areas remained buoyant. Likewise, international confidence
in general was mounting as the world economic system gradually recovered
from its wartime disruption.

As a first step in the transition to a managerial business, the company acquired its assets from the family vendors for £2.8 million. That valued the Covent Garden market at the previously agreed £1.47 million and the pill firm at £1.33 million; the latter's £900,000 goodwill figure had been further raised to cover 'formulae and trade marks'. Sir Thomas Beecham was responsible for disbursing £1.85 million in cash. In typically carefree style, he asked for just over £2 million to be paid to some thirty recipients. The board was having none of Sir Thomas's financial contrivances, and insisted on his repaying the £15,000 excess on the spot.

Of these beneficiaries, Joseph's executors received a total of £1,178,000 on behalf of the residuary clients. Henry was entitled to £533,000 and his three most favoured sisters to £113,000 between them, slightly above their entitlement to a 6 per cent share of the business. The six senior managers, from Rowed to Austin Scott, between them received their 2 per cent stake. Various solicitors at last got back a total of £14,750 out-of-pocket expenses: a fraction of the substantial legal fees incurred during the Chancery case. Other creditors, including the tenor Webster Millar, were repaid sums owed to them over all too many years.

Thomas also accepted the remaining £950,000 of the £2.8 million sale proceeds in the form of ordinary shares, which he sold to a narrow range of holders. £600,000 went to the Covent Garden Estate Company, in July 1924 renamed as the Wallbrook Trust, after a London street near the Mansion House. A nominee of Wheeler's took £250,000 worth; Thomas kept back the £1,000 worth he would be required to hold as a director.[2]

Meanwhile, the company's organization was taking shape. Sir Arthur Wheeler became chairman. One of his associates from the Midland Industrial and General Trust joined as company secretary; yet the most influential director was Hill, thanks to his lengthy experience in property matters. Goddard and Smith, the valuers, had in their report on Covent Garden stressed the 'considerable latent value' in reverting to 'rack rentals' – nearer to current rather than to the artificially low wartime levels – for the Opera House and other premises adjacent to the market. A non-executive director was Sir Arthur Marshall, KBE, a barrister and former Liberal MP enjoying many business contacts through a range of outside directorships. Sir Thomas Beecham gained his seat on the board as soon as shares had been allotted, and also the right to nominate a further director. He chose Louis Nicholas, who was at once appointed managing director.

The authorized capital was £1.85 million, of which the company issued £900,000 as 8 per cent preference shares. Although the interest offered was double the current bank rate, the shares had to be underwritten at an unusually high 4 per cent, and the *Economist* took the opportunity to stress the considerable risks investors would be running. The tangible assets at St Helens were worth only £104,000, principally buildings and plant valued at £59,000, the insurance value being a little higher at £96,000, plus the two warehouses at £42,000. Thus the pill operations had a low break-up value and depended wholly on their ability to produce and sell some 500 million pills a year and earn an annual income averaging £150,000.

The extra funds, required for future growth, came from £1 million worth of 6 per cent debentures, which the stockbrokers Myers & Co. underwrote for no more than a 2 per cent fee. The prospectus confidently forecast that, on the basis of recent earnings, after prior charges and interest on debentures had been paid there would be more than enough to meet preference share interest and a 10 per cent dividend on ordinary shares. In the end, the hoped-for 10 per cent was paid each year of the company's brief existence, but its profit margins were so narrow that it could spare only an average of £20,000 a year for allocating to general reserve.[3]

At the St Helens works, it was high time to resume the innovation process, all but halted there since the beginning of the twentieth century. Accordingly, the new company's prospectus looked forward to the directors having at last 'a free hand to develop the [pill and estate] businesses to their utmost advantage'. Although, it continued not untruthfully, those businesses 'have been successfully managed by the executors during the period of their control [since 1916], it will be appreciated that their scope of operations has been necessarily limited'. The board at once required Hill and Nicholas to investigate closely the pill operations.[4]

In his first direct experience of working in a large industrial company, Hill learned quickly under Nicholas's skilful guidance, and a noteworthy business partnership was born. Hill, as a former manager happily described him, was the accelerator, forever pursuing new schemes and financial opportunities, with Nicholas as the brake, advising caution when those ideas seemed premature or unrealistic. Since Hill's rare errors of judgment occurred when he struck deals on his own at the golf course or at sea in yachts, Nicholas's counsel was of inestimable value in the task of turning round such a diversified company.[5]

Nicholas already knew something about the organization at St Helens, having in 1922 written a lengthy report for the executors on each department's work. Without at that earlier stage proposing any radical changes, he had regrouped the offices into five functions, namely advertising, bookkeeping, cash, exports, and the American branch. Currently, resolute day-to-day management of the factory was absent, as both its senior men were near retirement age; Rowed the general manager and William Moss the works manager would be 70 and 65 respectively in 1925. Pill production, however satisfactory in terms of numbers, was undertaken almost wholly with outdated equipment. Sir Thomas Beecham's observation in the 1890s (see Chapter 6) of a 'routine through which the current of life flowed lazily and insignificantly' rang no less true in the 1920s.

The absence of a go-ahead spirit came as a shock to Hill on his first visit to St Helens. According to his wife, when he returned from an intensive tour of the works and offices he exclaimed in despair, 'What shall I do about it?'[6] His solution was for him and Nicholas to go painstakingly through every section of the business and note down possible improvements. Nicholas at once closed down the joiner's shop and placed carpentry requirements out to tender. That proved a useful cost-saver, and a year later he also sold off the printing works and plant.

The long overdue reforms there would be costly to undertake, and Hill judged that the key to boosting sales and hence profits was more effective publicity. Reporting to the board on the company's future global advertising strategy, he pointed out that the current method of handling this function, by Rowed in-house and by its subsidiary J. W. Courtenay, did not yield enough value from the £76,000 outlay at home and £40,000 overseas. Hill therefore proposed to seek expert advice from such high-ranking agencies as Barnards Press Ltd and Dorlands.

The board therefore appointed Hill and Nicholas to a special marketing sub-committee, tactfully but fruitlessly co-opting Thomas, then still a director. They commissioned Barnards to place material in the most advantageous newspapers and magazines.[7] Evelyn Waugh, in his novel *Brideshead Revisited*, happily captured how the company was wooing the affluent end of the market; a fictional character of the period observed about the heroine, Lady Julia Flyte, a recent debutante, 'Her photograph appears as regularly in the illustrated papers as the advertisements for Beecham's Pills.'[8]

For the British Empire exhibition of 1924–25 at Wembley, the company bought a painting (subject unknown) for £250, to be reproduced as a poster, and hired an aeroplane for sign-writing; the latter stunt would have gladdened the heart of old Thomas Beecham. It distributed a million free boxes of matches, suitably labelled, at the exhibition, handing out any left over at subsequent football fixtures. On the production side, the indestructible Victorian machinery was doubtless performing satisfactorily, as it was in many other long-established manufacturing companies of the period. Yet the far more efficient American machines, made by Arthur Colton Co. of Detroit, Michigan, remained beyond the directors' budget as long as the company's earnings were so inadequate. Its only new machinery was for manufacturing paper 'twists', at the rate of a million a year, ordered from William Sumner, a Liverpool blacksmith's firm. Adorned with the Beecham trademark, each twist contained a pennyworth of five pills, for sale to those in the depressed areas of the country who could not afford whole boxes.

In April 1924 Rowed, Moss and Scrymgeour, the export manager, carried out a survey of the current national patent medicine scene, to assess how it had changed over the previous four decades. Relying partly on inside information, they noted that most of the prominent names of the 1880s had all but faded into obscurity. Thomas Holloway's 'family squabbled and spent so much time in litigation that they had not enough money to continue advertising'. The Cockle descendants, 'old-fashioned in their ways', had sold out to a syndicate which set up a £1 million company in 1917 and 'spent thousands in making a flutter. The result was [a] fiasco'. Their report did not even mention the about-to-close Morison firm, whose ugly and decrepit British College of Health would shortly be torn down to widen the Euston Road.

According to that survey, the foreign companies operating in Britain had all overreached themselves. Even Carters with their liver pills and Dr Williams' pills (for pale people) were not selling as briskly as they had at one time; only Bile Beans seemed to be flourishing.[9] Such a chronicle of decline brought home to Hill and Nicholas that most patent medicine firms, hiding behind their secret remedies, had lost out by not reforming themselves. Beecham, formerly so keen to innovate, must begin again by diversifying into new products or eventually risk extinction.

A possible novelty was a replacement to the Beecham's toothpaste, previously made in the United States but discontinued during the war (see Chapter 8). Late in 1924, the board agreed that the company secretary should seek a formula for a 'first-rate [toothpaste] article'. Directors examined various specimens, none of which satisfied their requirements, and the proposal lapsed.[10] A few years later the manufacturing chemists, Macleans Ltd, began making a peroxide toothpaste; that was destined to become a leading product of the Beecham successor company when it acquired Macleans in 1938 (see Chapter 11).

The establishment of Beecham's first laboratory proved to be a significant innovation. In December 1924, the board accepted Nicholas's suggestion to engage an analytical chemist, E. E. Abrahams. The site of his laboratory, costing £500, is not known, but by the following May it was in operation, for testing the pill ingredients apart from the essential oils.[11] Meanwhile, Hill was about to purchase a remedy for headaches and neuralgia, Liqua Fruta. Closer inspection led to second thoughts: a fortunate outcome, as by 1929 that product had joined the Beecham managers' list, as a follow-up to their 1924 survey, of 'medicines that have risen and fallen'. Emprote, a milk extract drink considered next, was intended to rival the hugely popular Horlicks and Ovaltine. It passed the company's scientific tests, but dropped out as the costs of breaking into an already intensively advertised market proved to be too high.

Midol, another headache remedy, was looked at but rejected. Then Hill engaged his first outside consultant, (Sir) Jack Drummond, a London professor of biochemistry, to test the possibilities of the company's manufacturing vitamins, then all the rage among the public. Drummond found that the process would be too 'complicated' in view of Beecham's current rudimentary technical knowledge.[12]

An alternative strategy was to expand by means of a corporate take-over. At the end of 1924 Wheeler, Hill and Nicholas opened negotiations with the Veno Drug Company of Manchester. That business had since 1898 marketed Veno's Lightning Cough Cure, a linctus of the kind rapidly displacing the old cough pills that formed such an insignificant part of Beecham's output. Veno had recently added to its product range Dr Cassell's tablets for headaches and the antiseptic skin ointment Germolene. The *Chemist and Druggist* praised its factory's production methods for being more advanced than any other in Britain.

The founder, Sir William Henry Veno, had as a young man learned American business methods at first hand in the United States, and currently boasted that his Manchester factory was the only completely self-sufficient one on either side of the Atlantic, buying in raw materials alone from outside. It undertook its own printing and carton manufacture in-house, while the bottles for the cough medicine came from an adjacent subsidiary company, Automatic Bottle Makers Ltd. Its research and experimental laboratory was controlled by William Veno junior. Because the chief chemist, W. H. Cockton, had engineering expertise as well, he planned and personally supervised technical improvements to speed up operations. The Veno cough cure and Dr Cassell's tablets were made and packed entirely by machinery, the latter in a dust-free atmosphere, so that nothing was touched by hand.[13]

As Veno's current family-held capital, of £40,000, was well out of line with its 1924 profit of £125,000 on £670,000 net sales, the Parent Trust and Finance (formerly Parent Tyre) Company was overhauling the company's financial structure. Sir Arthur Du Cros, that trust's chairman, happened to be the former chairman of the Dunlop Tyre Company, which had unwisely hired James White as corporate adviser. After White's over-ambitious schemes had reduced Dunlop to near bankruptcy, Du Cros was sacked from the company and thereafter concentrated on his finance house. He had already sought to involve himself in Beecham's affairs, as early as 1920 offering £2.5 million for its assets while they were still in Chancery. Well aware of Dunlop's travails at that time, the Chancery court had rejected the offer. Now that the Parent Trust was more soundly based, it floated the Veno Drug Company (1925) Ltd, with a more realistic capitalization of £625,000.[14]

Beecham then bought, for nearly £67,000, half the new company's £50,000 worth of deferred ordinary shares, and a further tranche from Wheeler's private firm, Arthur Wheeler & Co., which had underwritten the issue.

The high purchase price reflected the future opportunities of developing this technologically superior company. Once he obtained shareholding control, Hill became chairman of the Veno company, with Nicholas as managing director jointly with the incumbent general manager, Henry Gregory. Sir William Veno retired at the age of 60, and was appointed the company's 'adviser'. Hill and Nicholas planned to co-ordinate improvements in both businesses; although Veno's turnover in 1923/24 was nearly double that of Beecham, its net profit was only £125,000 compared with Beecham's £141,000 over just nine months.[15]

In their reforming zeal, Hill and Nicholas drew up detailed plans to integrate without delay the workings of the two companies; their efforts were long remembered as how not to go about merging business activities on two sites 25 miles apart. Austin Scott accordingly moved to Manchester and took over both companies' sales and accounts departments; he did not even harmonize the financial years which ended on 30 June at Veno and 31 March at Beecham. Charles Scrymgeour joined him there to co-ordinate exports, and also marketing which would be undertaken by Veno's subsidiary, the advertising agent J. Varney & Co.

From the outset, employees of the two well-entrenched companies failed to hit it off with one another. Once in place, the Beecham managers scarcely relished finding themselves no more than Veno's agents on commission. Existing business routines were so engrained in the management of both companies that inter-firm rivalries inevitably sprang up. Not until 1928, under a new Beecham regime, was Abrahams, from the St Helens laboratory, despatched to Manchester, and then as assistant to Cockton, Veno's chief chemist. That ill-conceived attempt at integration lasted longer than it should have done, and was not reversed until 1931 (see Chapter 11).[16]

Beecham had no success in tracking down new products until January 1926. Nicholas then informed the board that he had obtained an 'excellent prescription' for a cold and headache powder; he did not specify the source. Hill and two colleagues, detailed to investigate the remedy and secure a medical opinion, enthusiastically backed that purchase, and the company offered a hundred-guinea prize for a really good name. Suggestions must have poured in, but the one chosen could not have been more apposite. That September, Beecham's powders were launched.

Their main ingredient was phenacetin, an antipyretic to combat fevers; they also contained quinine and caffeine, as well as the antacid magnesium carbonate and small quantities of cinnamon oil. The set-up costs were £18–20,000, while £15,000 of the company's total £100,000 advertising expenditure went on initial publicity. A year later, the company introduced a tablet version in amber bottles.[17] Beecham's powders turned out to be the only novelties introduced in the years 1924–28. They helped to boost company profits; yet a quarter of a century passed before their sales overtook those of the pills. A laxative chewing gum and that singular anomaly, laxative tonic pastilles, came before the board, only to be turned down.[18]

Beecham Estates and Pills remained under the control of what was now the MIG Trust until September 1925, when ownership abruptly changed hands. One of the trust's representatives resigned as director, whereupon Sir Arthur Du Cros and Edmund Spyer joined the board. Their organization, the Parent Trust – mentioned above as having previously acted on Veno's behalf – had thus acquired close knowledge of Beecham; by 1925 they had built up a 16 per cent stake in the company's ordinary shares, bought in from various Wheeler holdings. Their motive for this take-over soon became clear.

In 1922, James White had secured an option on the old Foundling Hospital estate, covering 56 acres (23 hectares), just off the Grays Inn Road in Bloomsbury, London. White sold on this option to the Parent Trust, which planned to transfer the Covent Garden market, covering 5 acres (2 hectares), to the 8½ acres (3.5 hectares) of the hospital site itself, and develop the other 47½ (19.5 hectares) acres for commercial use.[19] At the Beecham annual general meeting of 1925, Wheeler as chairman informed shareholders, 'The young man of the Foundling Hospital has been observed casting the glad eye on your daughter; he has even been observed peeping over the garden wall.' To pursue his coy metaphor, the suitor never scaled the wall to capture his quarry.[20] The Beecham company did not enjoy anything like unfettered rights over its market offspring, given the legal complexities of successive royal grants, which stretched back to the time of King John. Indeed, the royal charter governing the 'dedicated market' itself dated from Charles II's reign.

Nothing venture, in November 1926 the company had a private bill introduced before the House of Commons, at once arousing robust opposition. The Covent Garden tenants were already fearful that any removal elsewhere in London would seriously damage their trade, while the various local authorities in the capital, not yet able to present a united front through the London County Council on planning issues, all raised their several objections. Then once the bill was found to include the compulsory purchase of the neighbouring Mecklenburgh and Brunswick squares, opponents set up a Foundling Estate Protection Association. Public hostility became too widespread to save the bill. When in February 1927 the Beecham directors called shareholders to an extraordinary general meeting, originally planned to approve the terms of the bill, they had to announce that it was being withdrawn, and the option surrendered.[21]

That whole episode had turned out to be a huge and expensive irrelevance for everyone involved. The precise cost to the company was never divulged, but Beecham's overall earnings in 1926/27 fell by £18,000. It had wasted much top management time, and the need to raise £157,000 as liquid funds to steer through the scheme had compelled the board in June 1926 to dispose of Beecham's holdings in Veno. All the purchasers happened to be insiders, namely Wheeler, Hill, the MIG Trust and the Parent Trust. Because the sale would lead to a loss of shareholding control, each party had to sign a formal declaration not to manufacture or market products calculated to compete with Beecham's 'principal commodities'. Once the Foundling Hospital scheme collapsed, by mid-1927 Beecham had bought back all the Veno shares.[22]

Exports of pills, which as recently as 1921/22 had been running at a quarter of total turnover at St Helens, are not known in detail from that date until 1940/41. Yet barriers to trade, erected by countries around the world after 1918, were depressing sales in some of Beecham's most lucrative overseas markets. For many years Australia had been by far its largest customer, in 1921/22 accounting for 70 per cent of all Beecham's deliveries overseas. Then the Australian Commonwealth government in Canberra sharply raised tariffs and introduced import licences, so that in 1924 exports there from St Helens almost halved.

Joseph Nathan & Co. in London, a trading house from the antipodes celebrated for its powdered infant milk – which grew into the pharmaceutical giant, Glaxo – offered to market Beecham's products in Australia and New Zealand. That offer was overtaken by a Beecham board decision in July 1924 to establish an Australian factory without delay. The office manager, Edmund Bamford, was sent out to take charge. Having started up production in Melbourne by May 1925, he asked St Helens for managerial help so as to build up the appropriate marketing organization. In his first six months, sales were 10 per cent above the 1924 level, at £2,000.[23] The branch went on to earn a reasonable income until the slump of 1929, with consequences narrated in Chapter 11.

Canada, the second most important overseas market, seldom accounted for more than 15 per cent of Beecham's total exports. In 1919, the go-ahead Toronto mercantile firm of Harold F. Ritchie & Co. Ltd had been appointed as agent. Its founder was remembered as a dashing character whose enthusiasm for selling on a grand scale made him known as 'car-load Ritchie'. However, although sales shot up in the post-war boom, they soon fell back, so that the branch earned no more than a £136 profit in 1923. A year later Nicholas persuaded his board that local production was essential, and he asked directors whether manufacture there should be from scratch or by processing imported pill masses. The board chose the former method, and a factory opened in Montreal by mid-1925, the Ritchie firm continuing as the distribution agency.[24] In the first year of trading sales rose sharply, but a loss was made in 1925/26 and a profit of only £146 in the following year.

Meanwhile, the American branch in New York had been intermittently profitable. After especially good results in the 1917–20 period, sales briefly fell back to the pre-1914 level, before plummeting in 1923. During June 1924 Charles Boston, who characteristically held that resolute management was the answer to every problem, asked the Beecham board if he could purchase the branch; 'not to be considered' came the directors' reply. Nicholas also thought it time to overhaul the US organization on the spot, since 1888 in the hands of B. F. Allen & Co. Wheeler as chairman went out to New York, and set up a committee of management there, appointing staff from B. F. Allen and executives of the Morse Advertising Agency which took over the branch's publicity.

Such a mixed committee of that kind could not be expected to act decisively, and the consequent decline in sales caused a loss of over £3,000 in 1925/26. Given the equally disappointing outcome in Canada, the ever-resourceful Nicholas had the notion of transferring both branches to Niagara, where a road bridge separates the two countries; a common management of production and marketing was reckoned to save on overheads. As the New York manager, James W. Atherton, had just died, the board terminated the contracts of both the Allen and the Morse agencies, and placed the Canadian manager, James H. Howard, in charge of the joint operations. Early in 1927, Howard acquired leasehold premises on each side of the border, for manufacturing Veno's cough syrup as well as Beecham's pills.[25] In the event, by 1928 losses ensued in the United States and only meagre profits in Canada. A drastic reorganization was clearly overdue.

Now that Beecham had its headquarters in London's Covent Garden, strong local management was that much more essential at St Helens. However, in 1924 Rowed was in his 70th year; significantly, his £3,000 annual salary had not been further raised since 1920. He had an absorbing outside interest in antiques, and his book, *Collecting as a Pastime* (1920), with 68 half-tone illustrations, touchingly recalled his son who had been killed in the war (see Chapter 8). In a printed sheet, *The Rowed Name* (1921), he claimed descent from the Roet family, which had provided both John of Gaunt and Geoffrey Chaucer with spouses. Tantalisingly, he made no mention of the most recent generations, except that one branch had emigrated to the United States.

In May 1927 his wife Christine died; the board expressed its sympathy in the briefest of terms. A month later he informed the directors that he was unwell, and asked permission to cancel his contract in exchange for a year's salary. They beat him down to £2,000, and he retired at the end of July, after 40 years as general manager, Austin Scott taking over home sales and

Scrymgeour the foreign and colonial trade. Neither the board minutes nor the *Annual Report* contained one word of gratitude for his signal achievement in helping to create one of the most noteworthy marketing-based firms in the whole of Britain.[26] He died in 1933, aged 78 and left £28,000.

William Moss's contract as works manager was due to run until 1929, when he would be just short of 70, but his son Frank was already his deputy, authorized to mix the pill mass. That position had lately been regarded as of lower status than that of sales or office managers; when in 1925 the 26-year-old Frank asked for a salary increase from £286 to £364 a year, Hill granted it, but spread the rumour that Frank was plotting to divulge to some outsider the secret pill formulae: that could only have been a heavy-handed joke. Yet there was a further, and distinctly bizarre, source of friction between them. Several times in the 1920s Lady (Utica) Beecham, Thomas's estranged wife, travelled to St Helens, and Frank had to entertain her at the town's Fleece Hotel. She asked him to forward to London a request that her two sons, Adrian and Thomas, born in 1904 and 1909 respectively, should be allowed to join the business that bore their name. Although Frank was aware that the directors wanted nothing more to do with any of the Beecham clan, he may have expressed greater sympathy towards her plea than was wise in the circumstances. He stayed as deputy until his father retired in 1929.[27]

By June 1927, as it completed its third financial year, the Beecham Estates and Pills company appeared to be going nowhere. As shown in Table 10.1, its pre-tax revenue for 1926/27 had declined by nearly 7 per cent and its post-tax profit by 9 per cent over the previous year. Directors attributed those unwelcome results to the costs of introducing the Beecham's powders, even though earnings at St Helens had gone up, and of promoting the abortive

Table 10.1   *Beecham Estates and Pills Ltd, 1924–27 (net revenues, £000s)*

	1 Beecham Estates and Pills	2 Pill operations	3 Estates	4 Beecham Estates and Pills
(y/e 30 June) 1924–25	272.4	162.1	110.3	188.3
1925–26	271.1	131.9	139.2	165.0
1926–27	252.5	154.3	98.3	149.6
1927 (July–Dec.)	120.2	48.4		

Beecham Estates and Pills Ltd, *Annual Reports* (net revenue and net profit).
Pill operations: Table 12.1.
Estates: residual (col. 1 less col. 2).
Notes:
Net revenue = before tax and debenture interest payments.
Net profit = after tax and debenture interest payments.

Foundling Hospital scheme. As the total reserves were no higher than £63,000, little spare cash was left for carrying out much needed reforms. Pills continued to do well and the powders had been successfully launched; yet the estates side of the business, where capital values remained out of line with earnings, was not improving its performance.

Given all his experience of property matters, Hill must have spotted the flaws in the Foundling Hospital deal; yet he lacked the voting strength on the board to intervene in any way. Once that deal had to be abandoned, he moved swiftly to tackle the company's basic weaknesses. He and Nicholas talked frankly to their fellow directors, who showed no interest in change.

Sir Arthur Wheeler was very much a part-timer, constantly preoccupied with his outside dealings in stocks and shares, and with the two companies he had helped to found: the Charterhouse Investment Trust Ltd and the Gresham Trust Ltd, to manage larger and smaller industrial share issues respectively.[28] Likewise, the Parent Trust people, in control through their four seats on the board and holding of 360,000 of the 950,000 ordinary shares, after the recent Foundling Hospital débâcle had no fresh ideas on how to make the Covent Garden assets more profitable.

Hill and Nicholas thus felt they had a responsibility to work out how to implement the goal, expressed in the 1924 prospectus, of promoting the company's overall growth. Yet they came up against two difficulties. The patent medicine side could not be further developed while being tied to the low-earning Covent Garden market and estate. At the same time, it would be impossible to hive off the pill operations as the Beecham company's balance sheet then stood.

The Covent Garden properties, although valued at £1.6 million of the £2.8 million capital, had over the past three years earned only £115,000 on average annually, thus meeting no more than half the fixed prior charges. The 6 per cent debenture interest and the 8 per cent preference share interest left only two-fifths of the distributed profits for ordinary shareholders, who expected the 10 per cent dividends already promised to them. The still buoyant profits from St Helens thus played an essential part in keeping the company afloat.

It was Hill who found a neat solution to this conundrum, which he outlined to the board in November 1927. He had secured an option to purchase from the Earl of Derby residential properties in Liverpool, Bootle, Kirkdale and surrounding townships of the city for £1,717,500. On the basis of their gross rentals Beecham's valuers, Goddard and Smith, estimated those assets to be worth £2.2 million. Hill offered them to the Beecham company at cost, in exchange for the St Helens and Manchester businesses, worth £1.2 million, some related assets, and £515,000 in cash.

A major problem remained. The debenture holders stood to benefit, as their £1 million worth of holdings would be further backed by the Liverpool properties. However, chopping off the more lucrative part of the company's assets could only put existing shareholders' stakes at risk. The company therefore arranged to reduce the preference share interest from 8 to 7 per cent, again because the collateral of those easily marketable residential properties offered them greater security. As an incentive to acceptance, each assenting holder would be allotted one deferred share of 2s. (10p) for every two preferred shares held; however, those who wished could sell back to the company their deferred shares at a premium of 25 per cent. The £1 ordinary shares were subdivided into one 10s. (50p) share, carrying 8 per cent interest, and five deferred shares of 2s. (10p) each. Beecham thereby increased the issued share capital from £1.85 million to £2.025 million.

As half the board members, exercising nearly 40 per cent of shareholding control, represented Parent Trust interests, Hill confronted them with two possible outcomes. First, an extraordinary general meeting would have to be held, together with meetings of preference and ordinary shareholders, and eligible voters could well reject those proposals. Second, even if the proposals were accepted, Hill might be unable to raise the money for completing his contract to buy the pill assets. In the event, the Parent Trust people agreed – for a consideration – to indemnify both Hill and the company against either or both of these eventualities. Hill's proposals went through in late December and he secured the necessary funds.[29] He had won the first of the major cliff-hanging deals of his career. Not by coincidence, he had a reputation as a formidable poker player.

Hill and Nicholas rapidly planned the organization of the St Helens firm, now for the first time since 1916 free-standing and liberated from low-earning property assets. Appropriately enough, they called the new company Beechams Pills Ltd, registered on 23 January 1928. Although its productive activities took place in St Helens and Manchester, its head office was to be sited in London, at 55 Pall Mall, the headquarters of a number of Hill's companies.

A month later, on 22 February, the estates and pills company changed its name to Covent Garden Properties Ltd, likewise moving its head office to 55 Pall Mall.[30] Hill became its chairman as well and Nicholas remained as managing director. As Sir Arthur Wheeler and the other Parent Trust representatives had resigned from the board, they were replaced by managers expert in the estate business. On its side, Beechams Pills Ltd was now free to carry out an ambitious strategy to modernize and expand out of its local roots into a business of far greater consequence.

The Beechams Pills company, 1928–1944

THE ISSUED CAPITAL of Beechams Pills Ltd amounted to £1.25 million, of which £1 million comprised 8 per cent preferred shares, all sold to the public. Philip Hill placed on offer no more than £50,000 of the £250,000 deferred shares, giving priority to wholesale and retail chemists as the main outlets for home remedies. In 1928 he also floated Taylors (Cash Chemists) Trust Ltd, followed by Timothy Whites (1928) Ltd, financially independent of Beecham; six years later he merged those two companies as Timothy Whites & Taylors Ltd. That group was acquired in 1968 by the Nottingham-based Boots Pure Drug Company Ltd.

Fixing Beecham's authorized capital at £2.25 million, Hill announced in the prospectus that the unissued £1 million preferred shares would over time be used to acquire 'other businesses of a similar nature'.[1] Future corporate purchases would, he hoped, yield substantial economies by spreading production and administration costs, partly through the co-ordination of marketing and advertising policies.

The first acquisition was of Prichard & Constance (Manufacturing) Ltd, of London, which made Amami, the nation's market leader in shampoos. George Royds, the advertising agent who also handled Beecham's publicity, was responsible for the inspired slogan, 'Friday night is Amami night', which in consequence emptied places of entertainment such as cinemas of eligible young women who stayed in to adorn themselves for their Saturday evenings out; many doubtless nourished their week-end expectations on the *Amami Dream and Fortune Telling Book*. Hill also purchased the veterinary pharmacists, A. F. Sherley (1928) Ltd, another London company, which brought in a range of dog and cat remedies. That same year, he acquired Lintox, a Badminton maker's canine distemper cure, and also Lactopeptine from the firm, then in liquidation, of John Morgan Richards (see Chapter 5) for £7,500; never really popular, the latter indigestion remedy was scrapped in 1951.[2]

Having already set up Beecham's first laboratory, Hill made sure that all its products were of the highest quality. He had a further technological ambition, fuelled by his engaging as consultant to the company (Sir) Charles Dodds, a leading clinical biochemist in Britain. During September 1928, Hill offered to buy, on behalf of Taylors the chemists, a part or the whole of May & Baker Ltd of Dagenham, Essex, manufacturer of fine chemicals. Established in 1834, it was by then a subsidiary of the French pharmaceutical enterprise, Rhône-Poulenc, whose chairman took time to consider the offer before turning it down. Hill must have been prepared to finance in full May & Baker's costly research programme, which in 1938 developed the pioneering sulphonamide drug M & B 693, a remedy for the previously incurable bacterial pneumonia.[3]

Hill continued to seek businesses to be bought for cash or through share exchange, by 1935 using up the authorized capital. Beecham's net profit rose only from £134,000 in 1928/29 to £182,000 in 1932/33, years of economic depression; hence the market value of preferred shares – despite bearing interest of 10 per cent interest – fell below par. Likewise, paying dividends of 15–17½ per cent on deferred shares, and thereby leaving inadequate funds for placing in reserve, did not halt a decline in their market price.

The investing public's lack of enthusiasm for Beecham, manifested by sagging share prices, was wholeheartedly echoed by the financial press, which never shrank from driving home the message that the company's shares were basically speculative: much to the irritation of Hill, who in his chairman's speech of June 1933 was driven to maintain defiantly that 'there were very few old industrial businesses which had been in existence upwards of 100 years which could show the same consistent profit and sales' as Beecham achieved.[4] To be fair to the critics, the company did have a goodwill item in its balance sheet of nearly £940,000 and tangible assets of only £70,000; moreover, sales of pills might well tail off now that there were so many palatable liquid alternative remedies on the market.

As an equally serious difficulty, little noted at the time, Hill was not realizing his promised cost economies from integrating those newly acquired companies into the Beecham structure. Nor did he merge their separate financial accounts; hence they had the authority to retain their undistributed profits instead of transferring them to head office. A later chairman, Leslie Lazell, explained that in those years 'the headquarters of Beecham took no real interest in the way in which [subsidiary] businesses were run'.[5]

Bernard Hobrow, the company secretary, administered its head office. Having come from the prestigious accounting firm of Deloittes in India, he was reckoned by subordinates to have ideas above his station and to be unimaginative. So as to expose cases of subsidiaries' overspending, he made them fill up schedules of capital expenditure but carried out no budgeting for the future. When calculating Beecham's annual tax bill, he included in its profit and loss accounts only earnings remitted to headquarters as dividends.[6] Hill showed no interest in workaday matters such as improving the company's organization, while Nicholas – who might have been expected to do so – had heavy internal and external commitments.

Hill's first major purchase in 1930, paid for by a share exchange, was of Yeast-Vite Ltd, at Watford near London. Yeast-Vite, a much advertised tonic introduced in 1923, had become a rival to Beecham, having outstripped Veno's Dr Cassell's tablets in popularity; other Yeast-Vite products included Iron Jelloids. Through a subsidiary, Dinneford & Co. Ltd, manufacturer of some passable indigestion remedies, it had become the owner of Holloway's Pills Ltd, since the 1890s fallen on hard times. In addition to acquiring those medicines, Hill gladly recruited into Beecham's management the Yeast-Vite chairman, Joseph Stanley Holmes.

A 52-year-old chartered accountant, former MP and London county councillor, Holmes was among a number of professional men, having practical experience of industry, who since 1918 had become management consultants, helping to wake up somnolent British family firms. Many consultants of his kind, including Holmes, had submitted pungent reports and then been appointed as top executives of failing businesses in order to turn them round. His brothers-in-law were Lord Camrose and the future Lord Kemsley, who owned Allied Newspapers and soon featured Beecham advertisements in their flagship paper, the *Daily Telegraph*.[7]

Hill at once made Holmes a Beecham director, to oversee various subsidiaries, and a few months later group managing director, jointly with Nicholas. Unfortunately, Holmes had fallen out with Nicholas in 1929 when both were serving on the board of the Charterhouse Investment Trust (see Chapter 10).[8] As they still hated each other, they had to be given quite separate responsibilities. Nicholas concentrated on Beecham's sales and liaison with chemists, while Holmes took over production and general administration.

For a time, Holmes turned out to be the vigorous key executive whom Hill, averse to routine and exceptionally busy in all kinds of other directions, sorely needed. Holmes brought to an end the abortive effort to merge the Beecham and Veno managements by recalling Scott and Scrymgeour to St Helens and allowing each company to take back its own responsibilities.[9] Gregory, once again Veno's sole managing director, straightaway began to undertake a radical overhaul of the factory and offices at Manchester; Hill agreed to postpone the deferred share dividend payments accruing to Beecham as the main shareholder. That overhaul caused Veno's profits to rise steadily to a healthy £90,000 a year, and in 1936 Gregory repaid in full the £255,000 that it owed to Beecham. A year later Veno earnings exceeded £200,000, twice the total of the early 1920s.

The Veno factory, already highly regarded for its advanced technology (see Chapter 10), had become a model one, with hoods and air exhausts to ensure maximum cleanliness and a dust-free atmosphere, especially for the pulverizers which processed the ingredients of Dr Cassell's tablets. Its cough medicine was mixed in a huge emulsifier, and then poured through an enamelled earthenware pipe down to the vacuum fillers, capable of filling 2,000 bottles an hour.[10]

In 1933 Holmes approved the introduction of a new Veno product, Phensic; containing aspirin and phenacetin, it was a stronger brand of influenza and headache remedy than the mild Beecham's powders. After losing money for some years, by 1949 its sales of £250,000 a year equalled those of the powders. Holmes also replaced the virtually defunct cough pills with Beecham's lung syrup, in reality the Veno brand shipped in bulk to St Helens and bottled there.

Veno's thoroughgoing innovations provided a pattern for the extension of the St Helens factory, joined on to the 1880s building and completed in 1935. To maximize natural light, it was built round a central well, and the powders and lung syrup each had a floor to itself, as did the pills, manufactured by the most modern American Colton machines, which the company could at last afford. So as to avoid the accumulation of dust, the floors had a rubber surface, regularly cleaned by electric scrubbing machines. For the same reason, tables and work benches were covered with linoleum and edged with stainless steel. At the top of the building were recreation rooms, including one for a variety of games.[11]

Meanwhile Hill, assisted by Nicholas, was steadily expanding his business empire. In 1932 he established an investment trust, Philip Hill & Partners Ltd, which eventually became part of Hill Samuel, the merchant bank. Despite being a relative newcomer to the London new issue market, he scored his first major success when that trust, together with Rothschilds, floated the British shares of the American-owned Woolworths, a very popular retail multiple store. He further aspired to concentrate other fragmented industries, so as to enhance their efficiency and capacity to withstand overseas competition.

As chairman of the Staffordshire biscuit company Scribbans-Kemp, in 1931 Hill began to canvass rival biscuit-making giants, such as Huntley & Palmers of Reading, in order to create a combine on the scale of his household products business. None proved to be interested, and that failure allowed the Canadian entrepreneur, Garfield Weston, from 1934 onwards to set up the Weston Biscuit Company, erecting mammoth factories in Britain which undercut established firms with cheap biscuits.[12]

A second project involved an attempt to make a share issue on behalf of a company even more prominent than Woolworths, having 1,000 branches on almost every high street in Britain. Since 1920 Boots the Chemists had been owned by the (American) United Drug Company; then in 1932, at a low point in that country's economic depression, its president, Louis K. Liggett, was forced to sell Boots. Philip Hill & Partners, jointly with the merchant bankers Hambros and Erlangers, contracted with Liggett to purchase one million Boots shares at £7 each.

In January 1933 Hambros requested the Treasury for permission to issue those shares on the London market. Officials gave their agreement, but Montagu Norman, governor of the Bank of England, at once vigorously objected, as $23 million would have to be remitted to the United States: he had the power to block that transaction under exchange control measures introduced during the UK economic crisis of 1931. Neville Chamberlain, Chancellor of the Exchequer, had no alternative to overruling the Treasury's earlier agreement, a U-turn which Hill and his associates had only grudgingly accepted.

Three months later Hill, indignant at having recently had another of his projects, to buy the US-owned British United Shoe Machinery Company – which supplied virtually all shoe-making equipment in the UK – turned down, was further incensed to learn that the Tobacco Securities Trust (TST), an offshoot of the UK-based British American Tobacco, had taken steps to buy the Boots shares still on offer for £6.75 a share. The Treasury had its own reason to be vexed at the news, as it suspected that Reginald McKenna, a former Chancellor of the Exchequer and currently chairman of TST and the Midland Bank, had been at the 'centre' of that move; it deplored the fact that the dollar funds required would come from overseas holdings which, if remitted to Britain in the normal fashion, would have augmented the Bank of England's scarce currency reserves. Although not given to inflicting small pinpricks on those who had outwitted him, Hill withdrew his accounts with the Midland Bank and transferred them to Coutts' bank.[13] Boots would once again cast a shadow over Beecham during a later chairman's bid for Glaxo (see Chapter 14).

As it happened, Hill had been officially on leave from Beecham since September 1932 owing to what was minuted as a severe illness. By then he looked what he was, an ex-soldier of the ranks who had boxed in his day but had run to fat; weighing eighteen stone, he limited his exercise to occasional rounds of golf. Not returning to the Beecham board until October 1934, he did chair the company's annual general meetings of June 1933 and July 1934, where he showed off his gift of repartee. To one shareholder who wanted her dividends paid shortly after Christmas, in time for the January sales, he rejoined, 'Madam, I would like my dividends sent home every Friday night'; characteristically, he later gave way to her request.[14]

That absence coincided with significant changes in Hill's personal life.

After two failed marriages to divorcees prominent in London society, in 1930 he chanced to meet at a dinner party Phyllis Partington, daughter of a manufacturer's agent. Twenty-five years his junior, she had reportedly been a hostess in Kathleen Meyrick's notorious night-club at 43 Gerrard Street, London. Said to be 'half speak-easy [selling liquor outside permitted hours] and half brothel', it was eagerly patronized by the bright young things who featured in two of Evelyn Waugh's novels, *A Handful of Dust* and *Brideshead Revisited*, as being run by the fictional 'Ma Mayfield' of the Old Hundredth (the fictional 100 Sink Street). There Phyllis performed some kind of stage turn, the nature of which is now mercifully forgotten.[15] Because Hill's current estranged wife refused a divorce, Phyllis changed her name to his and moved in with him; they finally married in 1934. A practised golfer, she then took up horse racing, and later owned Mustang which ran, but was unplaced, in the Derby race of 1944.

Once Hill was in harness again by the autumn of 1934, Nicholas resigned as managing director and became vice-chairman. Hill, now financial adviser as well as chairman, sought two further periods of leave lasting six months apiece, in the early months of 1935 and 1937. Otherwise he holidayed from January to March in Miami, well away from the smoke pollution of London.[16] Through cable, telephone and postal communications, he kept in regular contact with his multifarious business interests in Britain.

In 1928 Hill had made clear his objective of making Beechams Pills Ltd into a truly global business, as a method of compensating for its cyclical performance at home. To test his success to date, no country-by-country figures have survived before 1940/41, when overall exports since 1922/23 had declined from 34 to 24 per cent of total sales. By 1934 he was able to report that the company and its subsidiaries were marketing their products in virtually all overseas countries, with satisfactory results everywhere except in North America (for which see below). He did point out that a medium-sized company such as his, which offered a relatively limited range of products, found it difficult to build up adequate selling organizations abroad. He therefore had to work through sales agencies, less satisfactory outlets because most of them also acted for rival manufacturers.[17]

As late as 1936, he admitted that the need to pay high dividends and interest out of profits had prevented him from allocating large enough funds to the company's development reserve, earmarked for expansion abroad as well as in Britain. The following year he sent representatives from St Helens to eleven countries, nine in the British empire plus the United States and Cuba.[18] South Africa was not visited, nor India, which became newsworthy from the medicinal viewpoint in 1930 only because a boycott virtually halted the drugs business there for several months.

The company's current trade in North America was far from healthy. Its United States branch made losses in two years between 1928/29 and 1940/41, and the other years' profits were low, in spite of its still generous advertising expenditure. Quite as disappointingly, losses by the Canadian factory occurred in no fewer than seven years between 1928/29 and 1937/38. Harold F. Ritchie of Toronto (see Chapter 10) was largely to blame, as in a fresh agreement of 1929 he extracted from Beecham a steep commission of 12½–15 per cent and also sole agency rights in Latin America, Australia and New Zealand. The company's directors tolerated that expensive arrangement until 1931, when they sacked him.

Instead, they set up two subsidiaries, Beechams Pills Inc. in the United States and Beechams Pills Canada Ltd, closing the two unprofitable factories on each side of the Niagara border. James Grayson and Walter Rigby, both Beecham employees since the 1880s (see Chapter 5), were retired, and Janvier Inc. of New York became the United States agent responsible for packing the remedies that the Arner Company manufactured in nearby Buffalo. Until wartime restrictions on exports came into force in mid-1941, the pill mass and ready-mixed powder were shipped out from St Helens. For Canada, the sole agent was Richards Glass Co. Ltd of Toronto, packaging Beecham's pills that had been exported in bulk. Given their recent dismal performances, in April 1938 the company valued its assets in the two countries at a nominal £1 each.[19]

The Australian branch was just beginning to earn good profits when the country, being dependent on exports of primary products such as wool, was hit by the world recession from 1929 onwards. To save on foreign exchange, the government in Canberra froze currency transfers abroad, so that by the end of 1930, Beecham had no less than £13,800 unremitted earnings held there. Although it spent £8,500 on local advertising in 1931, by the year's end the total outstanding had risen to £25,000. When it reached £34,000 early in 1933, the board devoted £14,000 to buying the leasehold factory in Melbourne. Not until March 1935 did the Australians officially release the accumulated sum of £45,000.[20]

Hill did not let up on his UK acquisition programme for Beecham. In 1935–36 he purchased two small firms, once again in Watford which had become a centre of medicinal activity. Ashton & Parsons Ltd manufactured the tonic Phosferine, as well as some baby powders, while Natural Chemicals Ltd imported from Switzerland Phyllosan tablets for debility, aimed chiefly at the aged. He further demonstrated his growing interest in scientific matters when in 1936 he donated on Beecham's behalf £14,200 to establish a new laboratory for pathology, bacteriology, biochemistry and pharmacy at the Royal Northern Hospital in Holloway, north London.

Hill also contributed £1,000 annually to the hospital for running expenses. Herbert Skinner, of its pharmacy department and a past president of the Pharmaceutical Society, was appointed pharmaceutical adviser to the Beecham group of companies. Skinner systematically updated the formulae of all units' proprietary medicines in line with the latest research findings, and tested whether employees making Beecham's powders were at risk of dermatitis.

Hill might have stressed that the hospital could analyse products more thoroughly than was possible in his own laboratories. Instead, he portrayed to shareholders that donation as a form of 'advertising and business propaganda', designed to 'place proprietary articles on a higher plane' than hitherto. His ill-considered remarks were picked up by the *British Medical Journal*, which retorted that Beecham's efforts to push nostrums had been consistently attacked by doctors. The medical profession, it continued, 'cannot have it both ways: it cannot decry the evils of patent medicines and self-medication and at the same time accept gifts from those who make profits out of such activities'.[21]

The initial rumpus having died down, in October 1937 Princess Alice, Duchess of Gloucester, formally opened the hospital's Beecham laboratory. That initiative must have been at the behest of his consultant, (Sir) Charles Dodds, who defied the gibes of other doctors for becoming involved in the commercial world. Dodds kept alive Hill's interest in ethical medicines: ones prescribed by doctors and not advertised to consumers, although the company was some decades away from manufacturing them.

The Select Committee on Patent Medicines (see Chapter 7) had as long before as 1914 recommended how to rid the industry of deceitful claims and other undesirable practices. Yet successive post-war governments had done little to implement those reforms. A sequence of parliamentary bills to control the industry had failed to pass into law, often for trivial reasons. As recently as March 1936, a distinctly feeble private members' bill for regulating patent medicine advertisements had been counted out for lack of support by MPs in the House of Commons. Some blamed that outcome on energetic lobbying by the industry and its supporters, who discouraged members from entering the chamber; in point of fact the whips had arranged the second reading on Grand National Day, when MPs in droves took themselves off to the races at Aintree in Lancashire. Manufacturers were also criticized for increasingly resorting to devices, such as changing brand names, to evade payment of the medicine stamp duty.[22]

In July 1938 Lord Horder, the royal physician, condemned in the House of Lords the 'quack medicines' that were bleeding the public to the tune of some £30 million a year, or nearly as much as the nation was currently spending on all its hospital services. As coy of naming names as Rosebery had been in 1894 (see Chapter 4), he cited a 'famous group of patent and proprietary medicine vendors, catering chiefly for nervous and digestive disorders' which had just put aside nearly £1 million for press advertisements during that year. Its soaring profits and share prices 'give some indication of the lucrative nature of the concern and of the great expansion of the quack medicine trade'. For good measure, he quipped about Hill's recent benefaction to the Royal Northern Hospital: 'I am unable to inform your Lordships if the donation was earmarked for the treatment of patients who had doctored themselves with the company's medicines.' On the contrary, all the Beecham money went on research.

Hill refrained from making any public comment, despite having offered Beecham an independent route into clinical pharmacology. Horder may have based his £1 million estimate on a current report in *World's Press News* that the previous year's advertising expenditure on the company's products had come to £670,000.[23]

That figure of 'something like a million pounds a year' spent on all forms of publicity had been confirmed by Holmes in an interview with *Chemist and Druggist* in September 1935.[24] However, Beecham's own advertising expenditure in the three years 1935/36 to 1937/38 averaged only £86,000 a year (see Table 12.2), which indicates the financial clout of its subsidiaries by then. The dividend on deferred shares had indeed risen from 15 per cent in 1930/31 to 85 per cent in 1937/38, when shareholders received a 100 per cent bonus in new 5 per cent preference stock after investments had been revalued. As recently as 1936/37 Hill had increased the amount of issued deferred shares from the initial £250,000, and then only by less than £50,000, although net worth – of assets less liabilities – had grown from £1.6 to £2.6 million.

Rather, Hill was preoccupied with a new set of take-overs (shortly to be discussed below) and with the Chancellor of the Exchequer's recent pledge to abolish the medicine stamp duty, together with retailers' licences, as from 2 September 1939. He commended the Chancellor's announcement as 'probably the most important event' in the history of proprietary medicines; once all shops were allowed to sell those medicines, the number of outlets for Beecham's products would be vastly extended. He disclosed that some of the largest retailers in Britain, including Woolworths, had already approached him, being at the moment prohibited from stocking patent medicines. The 2nd of September, when the country was again on the brink of war, turned out to be as ill-starred as 4 August 1914, the date of the Select Committee's report. The government postponed the abolition of the duty, and in 1941 replaced it by a 16 per cent purchase tax on all commercially prepared drugs and medicines. That tax ruled out any possibility of avoidance.[25]

In 1938–39, Hill made his three most far-reaching acquisitions for Beecham, which between them tripled the company's turnover. The first, in mid-1938, was that of Macleans Ltd, manufacturing chemists of Brentford, in west

London. Established in 1919 by the New Zealand-born (Sir) Alexander Maclean (1872–1948), it made a range of products which included a toothpaste, a stomach powder and Fynnon salt for rheumatism, all enjoying brisk sales in Britain and overseas.

Alexander Maclean had previously worked in the United States. As a representative of the Spirella corset company he must have learned the hard way about marketing. He had somehow acquired technical knowledge as well, so that by 1935 his London factory was operating on highly scientific lines, using continuous flow methods. He also had two laboratories, one for analytical work and one for original research, the latter run by Walter McGeorge, a trained scientist who was to play a key technical role in Beecham's future progress until he retired in 1967.

Maclean and his managing director, Major Henry E. Meade, jointly held the controlling shares; both faced the eventual problem of death duties, then at a maximum rate of 50 per cent, and were anxious to sell out.[26] Hill had earlier offered to buy the company, only to be rebuffed by Macleans' directors, who did not judge Beecham to be out of the top drawer. He bided his time; once when driving past Macleans on the way from London to his Berkshire home in Sunninghill Park, he observed to a passenger, 'I have heard there is a bright young man in charge of that business, and I would like to get it.' The youngster concerned was in fact a director and company secretary, Leslie Lazell, an accountant in his early thirties who had worked there since 1930.[27]

The ambitious Lazell relished Macleans' strength in both marketing and research. Being his company's delegate on several industry-wide committees, he had come to know the branch managers of American pharmaceutical corporations such as Sterling Drug and also Colgate, Macleans' chief rival in the UK toothpaste market. Those encounters convinced him that if British businesses hoped to keep ahead of the powerful competition from across the Atlantic, they would need to invest heavily in research.

As soon as Macleans came up for sale, Lazell approached Sterling Drug, as he looked forward to working under the more dynamic American style of management, and to benefiting from its generous research budgets. Sterling Drug's directors in the United States began negotiations but shortly afterwards pulled out, alarmed by the mounting threat of war in Europe. A stockbroking firm, Myers & Co., which had recently acted for Macleans, then induced its directors to arrange a meeting with Hill.

The principal, 'Mossy' Myers, had recently dissuaded Macleans from making an ordinary share issue, as Eno Proprietaries, which made the celebrated fruit salt (see Chapter 6), had depressed share prices in medicinal companies by its poor results. The resulting dip in the market gave Hill the chance to offer £2.2 million for Macleans, which was accepted.[28]

Hill in this instance paid cash for his acquisitions, which he raised by a separate share issue altogether. He placed the Macleans shares in a wholly owned subsidiary, Beecham Macleans Holdings Ltd, which raised £1.5 million in 5 per cent preference shares on the strength of Macleans' excellent profits, as high as £316,000 in 1937/38. That arrangement neatly side-stepped investors' chronic pessimism about the Beecham parent company which, so Hill boasted to shareholders, still turned out more than 570 million pills a year, but would henceforth benefit from Macleans' earning power and reputation for dynamism. City analysts noted with approval that his clever linking of Beecham and Macleans had substantially enhanced Hill's reputation as a financier, and made clear the substantial competitive advantage his company now enjoyed.

To his own shareholders, Hill stressed the potential value of the Macleans acquisition in yielding cost savings and also pooling management expertise: something he had referred to before, without doing much about it. During the negotiations, Lazell took the opportunity to buy, with Hill's agreement, a glucose drink named Lucozade from a Newcastle chemist's business, W. Owen & Son, for £90,000. No one then anticipated the crucial role that Lucozade would play in Beecham's later fortunes.[29]

A few months later, in October 1938 Hill concluded the second of his major acquisitions, that of Eno Proprietaries Ltd for £2 million. As already shown, Beecham had earlier used the Canadian firm of Harold F. Ritchie as sales agent in Canada and Australasia. Harold Ritchie, after acquiring Eno, died in 1933, and Eno Proprietaries then became a UK registered company to take over his extensive world-wide interests. The latter's results had proved to be disappointing, and the consequent collapse in its share price gave Hill the chance to offer 5 Beecham deferred shares for 8 ordinary Eno shares. That purchase, on such advantageous terms for himself, allowed him to make a £900,000 issue of Beecham deferred shares, which proved to be popular even though overshadowed by that September's Munich crisis. The Beecham board showed its gratitude to Hill by presenting him with a cowshed, costing £5,200, for his Sunninghill residence.[30]

The third acquisition, in July 1939, was of the County Perfumery Co. Ltd of north London, for £600,000, paid for by 5½ per cent preference shares in Beecham Macleans Holdings. In addition to a smokers' toothpaste and Hiltone hair bleach, County Perfumery manufactured Brylcreem. That toiletry item had started life in 1928 as a male hair preparation, which combined pure emulsified oils and hair tonic ingredients: a significant improvement on the current messy brilliantines, oils and gums. At first sold exclusively to men's hairdressers for use in their salons, since 1935 Brylcreem had been advertised to the public by the agents, Royds & Co., with the kind of flair shown for Amami shampoo. By 1938 it was the country's leading hair product for men, with annual turnover of £400,000 – compared with £20,000 in 1928 – and a healthy profit of £61,000. The chairman, Neils Fabricius, became managing director of this subsidiary, and was promoted to the Beecham board in 1941.[31]

Thanks largely to Hill's recent acquisitions, in 1939/40 Beecham's turnover, at £5.3 million, was more than five times that of 1929/30. Published earnings, which still failed to include the undistributed profits of subsidiaries, were nearly £600,000: almost a four-fold increase on those of ten years previously. As the market value of its deferred shares had risen by 76 per cent since 1931, commentators for the time being ceased to dismiss them as speculative. On the operational side, however, Stanley Holmes as managing director seems to have lost the decisive authority of his earlier years, doubtless because he now had parliamentary duties to perform. At the general election of 1935, Hill had allowed him to stand once again as an MP. Having served as a Liberal from 1918 to 1922, he was elected as a Liberal National and Conservative. Thereafter he seemed to spend an undue amount of time in parliament, for example when introducing two private members' bills, on inheritance and coastal protection, in 1937–39.

Those outside distractions may explain the shortcomings in a memorandum Holmes submitted to the Beecham board in October 1938, about structural changes considered desirable after the recent purchases of Macleans and Eno Proprietaries. He proposed three committees of directors and managers, for home trade advertising, home sales, and export sales respectively. The advertising committee would be responsible for the agencies employed, advertising copy, the prices charged, and so on. Holmes also suggested that subsidiaries not attached to another 'entity of the Group' should be amalgamated with other units.

To those not very forward-looking recommendations he tacked on, without comment, some alternative suggestions proffered by a colleague: doubtless Nicholas, with whom relations were still bad. Those advocated forming a broader marketing company, which would sell virtually all Beecham products, in addition to purchasing raw materials on behalf of the units. Likewise, an export committee could take charge of all overseas transactions. Had such radical suggestions been accepted, those bodies might soon have become the nucleus of a much-needed centralization process.

Having no time for indecisiveness, Hill within a month personally set up no fewer than six committees, on finance, sales, factory reorganization, advertising, product development, and exports. Some of the committees in due course submitted positive ideas, for example to close down inefficient factories on congested London sites and transfer their operations to St Helens or elsewhere. Only the export committee favoured the alternative plan, as a new body to manage the whole of Beecham's activities abroad. However, by the time most of the committees had reported, the threat of war diverted senior managers' attention to more pressing matters, such as having reinforced concrete air raid shelters built.[32]

Early in 1939, Sir Thomas Beecham provided some welcome light relief by asking the board to sponsor, on the pirate Radio Luxembourg, a series of Sunday evening concerts at 8–8.30 p.m., to be given by the London Philharmonic (punningly known as the 'pill-harmonic') Orchestra which he had founded in 1932. The company had earlier employed that radio channel on Sundays at 9.15 p.m., at a time when the British Broadcasting Corporation (BBC), under the Scottish-born Sir John Reith, put out 'gloomily puritanical' programmes to help round off the Sabbath. Beecham had hired some of the most popular broadcasters of the day, such as the dance band conductor, Jack Payne, the comedienne Mabel Constanduros, and Christopher Stone as compère. Now the board allotted £19,000 from the company's development fund for this latest musical venture, approving the insipid sponsorship plug, which Rowed would have derided:

> Beechams is the greatest name in home medicines, and famous for
> Beecham's pills, Beecham's powders and Beecham's lung syrup.

The radio concerts were broadcast weekly from April until hostilities began in September 1939.[33]

Shortly after the declaration of war, four senior directors met at Hill's Sunninghill home, and formed a special committee to assume all the board's powers and functions for the duration. That body, comprising Hill, Holmes, Hobrow (by then assistant managing director) and George Morrison (who in 1935 had succeeded Austin Scott as general manager) would if possible meet subsidiaries' directors every six weeks. Holmes then went off to Switzerland for an eye operation, but was back home by February 1940. Lazell, successor to Hobrow as company secretary, remained outside this circle. That June, a chance event projected him into a post that would keep him fully stretched for at least a decade.

Meade and Sir Alexander Maclean's son, Ashley, joint managing directors of Macleans, proposed to evacuate their company's offices to an undoubtedly safer venue at Reading, about 30 miles west of the Brentford site, while they expected the factory to stay put. Hill discussed this notion with Lazell, who strenuously opposed what could only set factory employees a poor example. All the irreplaceable accounting and other records, he maintained, could be securely housed on the spot in a ventilated bomb-proof shelter. Hill thereupon appointed Lazell to take charge of Macleans, unobtrusively releasing Meade and Maclean to outside jobs, although Meade stayed as a non-executive Beecham director until 1948. Lazell entirely fulfilled his chairman's confidence in him. Over the seven years spanning the war, Macleans earned the highest return on capital of all the Beecham subsidiaries.[34]

Lazell later recalled the experience of running a company of Macleans' size and complexity under wartime conditions as a kind of crash course in management, not least to do with industrial relations: as he later wrote, 'the circumstances of war applied a magnifying glass to everything and forced quick decisions.' He joined the Beecham board in June 1940, and the special committee shortly afterwards.

When the Eno factory in the east end of London was destroyed by bombing that September, he at once transferred manufacture of its fruit salt to Macleans. Walter McGeorge, the gifted scientist now running the Macleans' laboratory, soon modernized Eno's antiquated production methods, which had involved using a bicycle pump to keep the salts flowing. Once the mass bombings of London began, Beecham opened up an office at Esher in Surrey, while Hill transacted much of his business from Sunninghill Park. After that residence was requisitioned for the American Air Force in 1942, he and his wife moved to a Lutyens-designed mansion at nearby Windlesham Moor.

Meanwhile, Beecham's special committee authorized managers to build up stocks of materials and finished products, to a maximum of six months' use, as a precaution against future shortages and price rises. Even so, Lazell and McGeorge had much trouble in tracking down substitutes for scarce or unobtainable ingredients such as glycerine for toothpaste and glucose for the recently acquired Lucozade. County Perfumery likewise ran into difficulties over supplies of white base oil and beeswax for Brylcreem. Thanks to George Royds' sagacious advertising strategy, the authorities allocating materials were tolerably generous over that much sought-after hair preparation, on condition that adequate supplies went to NAAFI canteens for the services and to those of munitions workers. Royds' Brylcreem advertisements featured well-groomed male models in RAF uniforms, thereby earning aircrews the affectionate name of 'Brylcreem boys', and Beecham much helpful editorial publicity.[35]

Soon nation-wide shortages set off inflationary pressures. Holmes was determined to keep prices of all Beecham products as low as possible, painfully recalling the hostile public reactions to excessive profits during the First World War. When during a parliamentary debate in 1941 MPs accused consumer goods firms of profiteering, he pointed to the government's stringent price curbs. Indeed, toilet preparations in particular were tightly regulated; then at the end of 1942 a price standstill was imposed.

Not being a political animal, Lazell harboured none of Holmes's scruples about discipline over prices; he resolved to maintain product quality as far as shortages allowed, as well as appropriate levels of advertising. Because most of

Macleans' output was counted by officialdom as medicinal and therefore free of control, he induced a reluctant Holmes to sanction price increases. Before him was the awful warning of County Perfumery, which ended the war earning wholly inadequate profit margins, despite the huge demand for Brylcreem. Even worse, Amami shampoos were – in Lazell's words – 'ruined', never fully recovering their goodwill with consumers, who found both the ingredients and the packaging to be unacceptably poor in the interests of economy.[36] Too many people felt that there were limits to their patriotism.

The government does not seem to have arranged, as it had in the previous war, bulk purchases of Beecham's pills for the forces. Service personnel, when constipated, had to buy their own remedies or obtain 'number nine' aperient pills from medical officers or orderlies. When in 1941 a doctor MP, hostile to nostrums, asked a Treasury minister for the total value of contracts awarded to Beecham, he was told that, as far as could be ascertained, none had been signed with any government department. The minister forgot Macleans' official contract to make an anti-gas ointment, of which it was the largest provider in Britain, as Hill reminded shareholders in the *Annual Report* for 1940/41.[37] Apart from the Eno factory, Beecham's properties suffered little damage from enemy bombing. Even though most pill ingredients had to be imported, the St Helens factory seems to have had a reasonably untroubled war.

Although the wartime shortage of newsprint sharply reduced the scope for advertising, Royds did his best to keep Beecham's pills before the public. In the 1930s, the company had in the main targeted young people and those with youthful outlooks. Holmes personally vetoed the 'keep regular' slogan, fearing derision among opponents in the House of Commons. Only in 1941, when the 'radio doctor', Charles (later Lord) Hill – no relation of Philip – began to startle breakfast-time listeners to the BBC with regular talk of bowels and their movements, did Beecham dare to claim that a 'timely dose' of its pills would 'ensure a regular, gentle natural bowel action' and thereby 'ward off liverishness, stomach upsets, morning drowsiness and other signs of ill-health to which you may have become accustomed'.

At the outbreak of war, Beecham had put out reassuring if bland messages, such as 'In times like these, old friends are best'. By 1942, pithier motifs seemed more appropriate to reflect the country's more sombre but resolute mood; the advertisement earlier quoted bore the heading, 'I keep fit and so can You'! Once national newspapers were reduced to four pages, advertising agents increasingly shifted notices to the provincial press. By the war's conclusion, Royds had to admit that the authorities were preventing him from hiring enough advertising space to ensure an acceptable level of sales for Beecham's pills.[38]

The company's research activities might have been expected to languish under the stresses of war. However, from 1940 onwards Lazell purposefully extended the scope of the Macleans laboratory, recruiting scientists –mainly refugees – for more fundamental investigations than merely testing its products, most notably on the biological side. Then in 1942, Hill launched an initiative to bring about swifter progress in research, prompted by Dodds, whom he had just named Beecham's chief consultant.

Although Hill was by then known to be needing regular medical attention for cancer, he set up an *ad hoc* committee of directors, which he chaired, to draw up plans for a central research laboratory. The committee judged that the future of proprietary medicine firms lay in developing ethical products, since the rapidly maturing government plans for a comprehensive health service would require a range of more sophisticated drugs. The most promising fields of research were biology and bacteriology, and the proposed laboratory would need to receive up-to-date information about the latest scientific discoveries from all parts of the globe.[39]

Hill underlined his commitment to research that year by purchasing the associated Watford businesses of Endocrines-Spicer Ltd and Harwood's Laboratories Ltd which made the tonic Serocalcin. That acquisition brought into the Beecham company Douglas Stafford, who later became one of its senior figures in the search for penicillin. Hill's other corporate purchases included Carnegie Bros Ltd, manufacturers of surgical dressings as well as fine chemicals, and A. Rowland & Sons Ltd of London, which since 1793 had been turning out macassar oil, a hair-beautifier widely celebrated in its day but belonging to the Regency era of 1811–20 rather than to Brylcreem's, although it was still being made in 1951.

Never one to let an opportunity slip by, in May 1943 the research-minded Lazell submitted to the board a detailed memorandum on that subject. He proposed that the central laboratory should be on an entirely new site and be based on the research facilities at Macleans. The board instructed him to set up that function, as far as wartime restrictions allowed. Lazell must have consulted with both Hill and Dodds; however, in September Holmes, who had very different plans for Beecham's future, persuaded the ailing Hill to inform the board that it would do better to acquire businesses outside the proprietary medicine trade. As certain – unspecified – negotiations were in hand, £225,000 worth of Veno's shares would be sold to provide funds to purchase such businesses.

That year, as his health inexorably declined, Hill planned to retire and hand over the chairmanship to Holmes. Lazell would become managing director, and Hobrow, then assistant managing director and clearly expecting promotion, would be asked to resign. Holmes succeeded in stalling that arrangement which went against his own schemes; instead he told Hill that

Lazell could not be spared from Macleans during the war, and could then take the managing directorship.[40] Eager to live until peace returned, Hill continued as chairman, but died of prostate cancer at his home on 15 August 1944, aged 71.

As one of Beecham's most creative entrepreneurs, Hill had with characteristic flair uncoupled its pill activities from a debilitating link with the Covent Garden estate. His subsequent acquisitions, most notably of Macleans, Eno's and the makers of Brylcreem in 1938–39, had helped him to realize his ambition of establishing Beecham as the largest household product company in Britain, with turnover up ninefold to £9 million and trading profit from £150,000 to £400,000 between 1928 and 1944. He had also pointed the company towards a more scientific future by purchasing, or striving to purchase, some research-based firms and by promoting the creation of a central laboratory.

Like the founder Thomas Beecham, Hill was industrious to a fault, his motto being 'Start early and work late'. When someone suggested to him, 'There are rewards in life other than money', after a moment's thought he replied, 'What are they?' Whether or not the response was ironical, his long day very often ended in informal gatherings at which he and his cronies talked shop or played poker. Yet he enjoyed attending race meetings with his wife Phyllis, in earlier times relaxed with rounds of golf, read popular novels of the Edgar Wallace type, and watched films, a pastime to which he was addicted.

A memorable achievement of Hill's was to rescue the Royal Opera House in Covent Garden for the nation. During the war it was leased out as a dance hall; yet Hill, its owner as chairman of Covent Garden Properties, who had also served on the Royal Opera House Company board since 1933, was anxious to return it to its proper use. In April 1944, much to the anger of Mecca Cafés, the current lessees, he freed the theatre by leasing it to the music publishers, Boosey & Hawkes. Mecca unsuccessfully took him to court, and in 1946 it reopened for staging opera and ballet.

As so many of his business contacts vied with one another for his attention every minute of the working day, Hill restricted himself to the largest strategic issues, in which he revelled, leaving to subordinates the tactics which bored him. Thus he never fulfilled his promises to reorganize the multitude of Beecham subsidiaries along more rational lines, in order to save on costs and effort.

Lazell much later hazarded the guess that, had he secured good management, Hill could 'by means of further acquisitions, have quickly built a great international company'. Hill is known to have been enquiring from outside experts about the most effective means of competing against the major American manufacturers of proprietary goods. However, the war and his worsening health robbed him of the opportunity to do so.[41] In the event, it would be Lazell's task, after 1951, to follow his lead by making Beecham into a giant multinational enterprise. Chapter 12 shows how an interregnum of nearly seven years was to follow and put at risk the maintenance of Beecham's recent impressive progress.

The Beecham Group adrift, 1944–1951

W HEN Philip Hill died in August 1944, Stanley Holmes became chairman, at the age of 66, while continuing as managing director. Louis Nicholas, who still had no affection for Holmes, nevertheless stayed on as vice-chairman. The other executive directors remained in post: Bernard Hobrow as assistant managing director, George Morrison as general manager, Gordon Dunbar the export director and Lazell in charge of Macleans. Holmes assured Lazell that he would be making no senior management changes before the war ended; Lazell must have wondered if he would ever achieve the managing directorship already promised to him.

The secretary of Covent Garden Properties, Charles Heselden, was well placed to observe the antics that followed Hill's departure. 'As soon as the old man died', he stated, 'all the performing seals got down off their little stools and started fighting with one another'.[1] His sardonic remark encompassed all those involved in any part of the Philip Hill empire, from Timothy Whites and Taylors and the Scribban-Kemp cake and biscuit companies to the manifold London property interests. On the Beecham board, men of such divergent characters as Holmes, Nicholas, Hobrow and Lazell, at odds among themselves over the company's way ahead, could scarcely be expected to pull together as a united team.

Hence the Beecham enterprise appeared to have stalled between 1945 and 1951. As Holmes aged and found himself increasingly committed to his parliamentary and public duties, senior executives jockeyed for position and freely aired their personality differences. Holmes had no secure power base: as he himself had no children, he appointed two of his nephews as company secretaries, Donald Parry from 1940 until he joined the army, and E. M. Price Holmes from 1945 onwards. Holmes had persuaded Hill to earmark the assistant managing directorship for Parry after demobilization; that move was now blocked. Price Holmes became a director in July 1950, only to resign six months later. He then resumed his secretaryship, being ousted as soon as his uncle retired in 1958. As the new chairman, Holmes identified three tasks for the future. The first was to lay down a clear corporate strategy, so as to improve earnings and the market value of shares. The second entailed wresting control of the Beecham subsidiaries back to the centre, after wartime disruptions and Hill's lengthy period of illness. He now instructed all subsidiaries to hold regular board meetings, which he would attend in person.[2]

However, his memorandum of 1938 (see Chapter 11) had shown up an inability to take decisive action, and he failed to grasp the overriding problem of the hundred or so companies purchased by Hill for Beecham which had hardly at all been co-ordinated. Unit managers were often inadequately paid and lacked motivation, and the chairman's attendance each month to hear reports did little to spur them into greater efficiency.

A third, and – for Holmes – crucial, task was to reduce the company's dependence on proprietary medicines. In 1939 he had been embarrassed by the publication, in the Left Book Club series, of Simon Haxey's *Tory M.P.* The chapter on those MPs' extensive business interests, making clear the immense power they wielded over the production of everyday goods and services in Britain, contained a two-page spread on Holmes's business links with twenty Beecham subsidiaries. It quoted Lord Horder's statement of 1938 in the House of Lords that the £30 million-odd spent by the nation annually on patent medicines was almost as great as total expenditure on its hospital services.

Haxey also highlighted Beecham's and Veno's recent apparently generous dividends as 'hard to beat in any industry'.[3] By now a senior back-bench MP, knighted in the New Year's honours list of 1945, Holmes felt it unbecoming to be known as the chairman of Beechams Pills. At the next annual general meeting in July 1945, he therefore had the company's name changed to the Beecham Group Ltd. As he informed shareholders, pill sales by then represented no more than 3 per cent of group turnover.[4]

Holmes was in any case convinced that the tide of events was irreversibly moving against proprietary medicines. Once Britain's coalition government had in 1944 agreed to introduce a comprehensive post-war National Health Service (NHS), as occurred four years later, two consequences were bound to follow. First, professional organizations would intensify their anti-nostrum campaigns, as the BMA did in 1944 and the Pharmaceutical Society of Great Britain in 1947, demanding not only controls over the sales and advertising of those remedies but also officially sponsored programmes to educate the public through such bodies as the Central Council for Health Education. The declared object was to combat 'the meretricious claims of patent foods, drinks, medicines etc.'.[5]

Second, even if government failed to take any action against patent medicines, demand for them was expected to melt away once doctors were able to prescribe to patients ethical medicines free of charge. Yet the admittedly less comprehensive Lloyd George scheme since 1911 of national health insurance, providing for medical treatment by panel doctors and free prescriptions for insured people (see Chapter 7), had done little to reduce patent medicine demand. Indeed, consumers' expenditure on them, allowing for inflation, was slightly higher than it had been in 1912.[6] The Second World War had caused the public's dosing with laxatives, aspirins, tonics, cold cures and vitamin pills to soar.

Civilians on war work had higher take-home pay than before 1939 and little to spend it on, while supplies of those medicines in shops were plentiful. Official data revealed that health insurance prescriptions issued for minor ailments were fewer in number than before the war; many would-be patients just could not spare the time from their jobs or running a home to queue in overcrowded doctors' surgeries. Moreover, as late as 1943, the patent medicine industry was estimated to be spending about £2¼ million a year on advertisements in the press, out of a national figure for all products of £29 million. Whereas manufacturers of other consumer goods had reduced their advertising expenditure by 90 per cent on average, the outlay on behalf of patent medicines fell by only 28 per cent.[7]

Such a widespread habit of self-medication therefore promised to be almost impossible to eradicate, even in the forthcoming NHS era. The influential weekly journal, the *Economist*, in 1945 offered its own explanation of such dependence:

> The truth is that people do not want to be positively healthy. The
> suggestion exercised by the patent medicine advertisers falls on
> receptive ground. People take patent medicines not because they
> are fatigued, anaemic, nervous, overworked and suffering from
> sleeplessness and headaches, but because they like to think they are.
> Even when they do not positively enjoy poor health, there is still a
> superstitious belief that good can be made better by regular doses
> of medicine … There is more faith in a vitamin than in a Brussels
> sprout.[8]

As long before as 1886 (see Chapter 2) the *Chemist and Druggist* had likewise commented on the way ordinary people preferred to buy some remedy or other with allegedly definite curative powers rather than to submit to being catechized about their illnesses by the medical profession.

Since that faraway date, marketing techniques had advanced mightily. The public was now bombarded by advertisements about health problems, or the causing of offence in one or other region of personal hygiene, that only the given products could cure. Beecham's fun advertisements, which after all had taken some thought to devise, had had their day. A story-line introduced in the 1930s was as basic as that of a strip cartoon; say, of a worried young woman exclaiming, 'Oh! This cold/headache/rheumatic pain! I must take a Beecham's powder.' Further down, all smiles, she sighs with relief, 'Ah! That's better!'

Holmes believed that whereas the group would find intensive R&D and manufacture of pharmaceuticals both costly and risky, it could build on its considerable expertise in selling to grocers. His answer was to diversify into wholesale grocery firms. Once food rationing ended in due course, he argued, a massive demand would emerge for those firms' products, which the group could sell to retailers alongside its existing range of household goods.

In the autumn of 1944, Holmes visited F. James (Newport) Ltd, which made a range of Nunbetta foodstuffs. He then despatched Lazell and Dunbar to inspect that company's works and assess whether or not it was worth buying. Lazell at that time claimed to welcome the purchase, but much later recalled with a certain 'shame' his enthusiastic response as being 'a measure of our ignorance of the grocery trade at that time, or of our reluctance to cross swords with the chairman'. The Newport firm was duly acquired.[9]

In January 1945, Beecham closed its wartime offices at Esher, and returned to the London headquarters in Pall Mall. That month, Hill's seat on the company board was filled by Brian Mountain. His elderly father, Sir Edward Mountain, chairman of Eagle Star, had appointed Hill as director of that prestigious insurance company in 1929; the two men had become so close in their business outlooks that their first telephone calls of the day were invariably to each other. As a Beecham director, the son now represented the significant institutional investors Eagle Star and the Philip Hill Investment Trust (as it had become in 1942) of which his father was by then chairman, and advised the group on financial matters.[10]

That October, Louis Nicholas retired from the Beecham Group on health grounds; he was not replaced as vice-chairman. By then 70 years of age, he had succeeded Hill as chairman of Covent Garden Properties, currently said to be in a 'dreadful mess', its earnings hard hit by rent controls and depressed property values. Few could recall the services he and his accounting skills had rendered to the executors after Sir Joseph Beecham's death and to the company ever since, but of late people knew him as Hill's conscientious and loyal lieutenant. He died in 1955; the *Liverpool Echo* hailed him as 'one of Merseyside's best-known industrialists'.[11]

Holmes also tackled the urgent problem of overseas trade. In August 1944 he had set up an export committee, of Dunbar, Hobrow and Lazell, to draw up a rescue strategy. Most of the company's markets abroad were so disorganized as to need a thorough overhaul; those on the Continent of Europe had been the least affected because of the small amount of trade done there. Far more worryingly, the United States and Canadian branches were once more in trouble over manufacturing and sales alike.

Towards the end of 1945, therefore, Holmes and Dunbar arrived in New York to consult with the chief executives of Beechams Pills Inc. and of the subsidiaries in Canada and Latin America. Simultaneously, the company's agents in Australia, New Zealand, South Africa and India came to Britain for discussions. Thanks to those personal contacts, Beecham was able to take advantage of the buoyant post-war demand for its products, by increasing overseas sales from under a quarter to nearly a third of total turnover between 1945/46 and 1950/51. Even more encouraging, over that period export trading profits rose from 15 to 46 per cent of total earnings.

A problem in the Western Hemisphere was that although the United States and Latin America by 1946/47 accounted for nearly a third of Beecham's overseas sales, its pills made up only a small fraction of that total. US sales had declined steadily since 1936 to the equivalent of £6,000 ten years later, so that despite £3,000 worth of advertising there was still a loss of £700. The group's only lucrative asset there was an Eno Proprietaries factory at Bloomfield, New Jersey, which supplied seven Eno branches in Latin American countries. As that branch had a controlling interest in the Western Hemisphere business (but not elsewhere in the world) of Scott & Bowne Inc., makers of the cod liver oil-based Scott's Emulsion, the main products sold in the US were the fruit salts and emulsion, which even so contributed only 15 per cent to the group's overseas trading profits. By 1950/51 those proportions had increased slightly to 33 per cent of sales and 21 per cent of profits.[12]

Although Holmes's master plan for the Beecham Group had small room for R&D, Lazell was busy setting up the central laboratory in accordance with the board's earlier approval, to carry out research of a kind that was beyond the scope of experimental laboratories attached to busy factories. The Finance Act of 1944 had eased the problem of cost by allowing capital spending on research to be treated as an expense which was spread equally over five years; all other research outlays could be offset against the current year's profits. McGeorge and his assistant, the German Jewish refugee Ernst Koch, were already touring round country houses south of London to find suitable premises, and in January 1945 Lazell was allowed to buy Brockham Park, a currently requisitioned mansion in 150 acres (60 hectares) of land near Betchworth Park in Surrey.[13]

Two months later, the group registered a subsidiary, Beecham Research Laboratories Ltd (BRL). Its nucleus was the Macleans laboratory, which under McGeorge already had two decades of scientific expertise behind it. McGeorge, now appointed BRL's managing director, joined the main board in the following December. Even though Holmes was going after food companies, Lazell resolved to promote such R&D as he could afford, in the hope of discovering ethical, namely prescription, medicines as the money-spinners that the chairman's groceries were unlikely to be.

Lazell's prime candidate was penicillin, still at the fermentation stage of development throughout the world. However, when in 1941 a consortium of five – later seven – British pharmaceutical companies had set up the Therapeutic Research Corporation Ltd to work together in this field, Beecham had not been considered for membership. Towards the end of the war, the company had approached the Ministry of Supply for a licence to manufacture penicillin, only to be rebuffed because its unimpressive research effort at that time was not directed towards ethical products. However, in 1945 it did receive a contract from the Air Ministry to make, with penicillins bought in from outside, pastilles designed to combat infection when airmen had incurred severe facial injuries.

Also in 1945, McGeorge visited the United States to gather information about the latest penicillin production methods, which the group might be able to acquire on licence from one or other American drug companies. According to Lazell, he 'made the rounds', but no corporation was willing to help. To be sure, the Beecham Group could hardly start from scratch as long as its resources were so limited.[14] A return it submitted to the Federation of British Industries at that time showed its annual research expenditure to be £50,000 – unchanged from the sum agreed by the board in 1943 – with 28 qualified staff; 23 were chemists, two biologists, two engineers and one physicist. Post-war shortages of skilled manpower currently made it difficult to recruit the four extra chemists and four food scientists it reported as needing. In 1947, once the army had released Brockham Park from requisition, McGeorge and his team started up work there; yet R&D was in for a long haul.[15]

Meanwhile, Holmes was pressing ahead with his scheme to buy into groceries. In May 1945 he acquired two major food concerns, C. & E. Morton Ltd for £180,000 and Purnell's Food Products Ltd for £75,000. Like the original St Helens factory, Morton could be envisaged as a relic of Victorian commercial grandeur. Founded in 1850, for decades it had acted as agent for prestigious British food manufacturers, undertaking part of Huntley & Palmers' export trade in biscuits and cakes. When hit by the slump of 1929, the Reading firm had been forced to cancel that arrangement, leaving the Morton family directors to struggle on with greatly reduced business. They and their advisers had then called in John Buckley (1883–1972), an industrial consultant, to recommend changes in its organization.

Having proposed sacking a clutch of mediocre senior executives, Buckley was invited to become Morton's managing director. He had already enjoyed a model career in the army, first of all in the South African war and then being awarded the DSO and MC in the First World War, before moving into business. British industry, still in the main family-dominated, needed men of Buckley's – and Holmes's – calibre to act as consultants and then to work on modernizing weak firms.

In 1939, at the age of 56, Buckley had rejoined the army as a lieutenant-colonel. He was soon made brigadier, becoming principal priority officer in the War Office. Two years later he was appointed Controller-General of Economy there, being promoted to major-general in 1942. At the end of the war, newly made CBE, he returned to the Morton company.

Lazell never had much time for Buckley, any more than for Major Henry Meade, his own pre-war senior colleague at Macleans. As army types (in Lazell's words) they 'had no idea [of] how the masses lived and felt'. Indeed, the hothouse atmosphere of the War Office scarcely matched Lazell's experience of running an outer London factory virtually single-handed, under wartime bombing and all kinds of restriction. Buckley proved to be energetic, decisive and tough during his time with Beecham; yet many of his actions grated on Lazell's mind.[16]

Buckley was soon drawn into the Beecham hierarchy, at first as Holmes's deputy in the new Morton subsidiary. In February 1946 he travelled to the United States and organized local manufacture of Morton products for the North and Central American markets. When that March the newly formed Beecham Food Products Ltd took over all the food companies, he was made its vice-chairman; he then negotiated the purchase of R. W. Holden Ltd and North of England Lard Refineries Ltd. In October, he joined the Beecham Group board.

Acquisition of consumer product businesses proceeded apace. The soap manufacturer T. F. Bristow & Co., widely known for its lanolin shampoos sold mainly through chemists, was bought for £100,000. An attempt to enter the toilet soap business, as the junior partner of a chemical manufacturer which supplied washing materials to laundries, foundered. Meanwhile, Lazell's bid to acquire several American companies making ethical products came to nothing through the board's lack of enthusiasm.[17]

At the time when in 1947 Beecham bought two overseas food companies, in South Africa and Australia, it had 111 subsidiaries, 52 in Britain and 51 export companies. There were eight overseas branches, mainly in Australasia and North and South America. The group's current net profit was only just over 3 per cent of turnover, or a fifth of the average achieved a decade earlier. That year the board had the opportunity to purchase H. W. Carter & Co. Ltd of Bristol, makers of the blackcurrant drink Ribena, only to turn it down on what Lazell regarded as unconvincing grounds. When he at last acquired

Ribena in 1955, he had to pay an appreciably higher price; yet it turned out to be one of the group's money-spinners.[18]

Possibly Brian Mountain, as financial adviser, suggested to Holmes that it was time for him to delegate to others some of his senior executive functions. In mid-1947, therefore, Holmes announced that the group's current size did not allow him time to deal with day-to-day affairs on top of planning its future strategy. He therefore offered Lazell, together with Hobrow, the managing directorship. Lazell had no intention of accepting that post unless on his own and with full executive powers; when he refused Holmes made him, Hobrow and Dunbar joint assistant managing directors. Lazell did not move into head office when Hobrow objected to his presence there; in any case he was happy to stay with Macleans while he was so busy rebuilding markets for its products. He recognized that those new appointments were merely window-dressing, as they did nothing to make the top management impose more effective control over the dozens of subsidiaries.[19]

Since the economy-conscious Hobrow remained as Holmes's right-hand man at headquarters, Lazell correctly feared that some drastic cost-saving measures would follow. Sure enough, in December 1947 Holmes out of the blue set up a committee of directors, chaired by Hobrow, to investigate the group's research activities. Lazell, excluded from that committee, resigned his assistant managing directorship and induced Dunbar to do the same. Hardly to his surprise, the committee in due course secured few economies, and uncovered only some trivial cases of over-spending. It did, however, recommend the establishment of a standing sub-committee of the board, to which Lazell *was* nominated, for approving and overseeing R&D expenditure, authorizing projects, and determining the allocation of costs between the various units. Lazell concluded that 'research was not going very far, and too many people had a finger in the pie, some by no means friendly'.[20] Hostile colleagues on the board did not take long to show their hands.

One sign that matters were beginning to return to normal after the war, at least in one direction, was a board instruction to group branches in 1948 to destroy all stocks of ingredients, finished products and containers that had been prepared according to wartime substitute formulae. Even so, the year's early months brought the group little solace. Although turnover was up by 13 per cent on the previous year, its profit margin fell slightly. An atmosphere of inertia persisted at the top. When in February the Swiss-based pharmaceutical firm Drugs Ltd offered the group its British interests for £400,000, Holmes turned it down, blaming the country's economic problems and shortages of group funds. Yet that firm's Silvikrin and other attractive shampoos would have strengthened the Beecham lines, now that Amami had lost its shine with the public and Brylfoam shampoo had not repeated Brylcreem's runaway success.

A year later, the board changed its mind on Drugs Ltd, which it bought for County Perfumery. Less happily, much management time and effort were spent on extending the manufacture and sales of the Sherley subsidiary's dog and chicken foods, and on planning a scheme for the breeding and sale of dogs. A canine shop was opened at 96 New Bond Street, London, for shampooing and other care as well as the marketing of dog-lovers' requisites. After significant losses, late in 1950 both the shop and kennels were closed down.[21]

Undeterred by those highly peripheral activities, during September 1948 Lazell recruited as a consultant the distinguished organic chemist who had formerly been involved in penicillin research, Sir Ian Heilbron.[22] Then results for the year to March 1949 showed turnover up by no more than 1 per cent, the only improvements being overseas. Profits were lower by a fifth, so that the board cut the dividend on deferred shares from 40 to 36 per cent: a move denounced by the financial papers as it rattled the market while saving only £30,000 out of £218,000 retained profits. The price of deferred shares plunged by nearly a third, driving up the net dividend yield from 5½ to over 7 per cent. The *Investors Chronicle* unkindly mused on whether Beecham shares should 'really be put in the bargain basement category'.[23]

To the many disgruntled shareholders who wrote in, Holmes replied that branded medicines – their sales not after all much affected by the introduction of the NHS – were currently taxed at 33 per cent and were vulnerable to purchase tax changes at short notice, while their steadily mounting production costs were difficult to recoup through higher prices. However, analysts knew only too well that Beecham's shares were unique among leading industrials because those shares were so largely unbacked by tangible or realizable assets. Indeed, the group's goodwill figure, at nearly £4.6 million, exceeded the £4.2 million of fixed capital.

Some years later, such unimpressive results could have attracted a take-over bid from outside financiers, bringing with them plans for a new management team and badly needed venture capital. Even though institutional investors generally at that time hesitated to use their shareholding power to force new strategies on under-performing companies, Eagle Star and other institutions may have brought about one change, announced in March 1949. Holmes, by now over 70, handed over to Buckley the managing directorship, citing the vastly increased volume of his parliamentary duties and other outside work. Hobrow was a further beneficiary from the reshuffle, being upgraded to administrative director.[24]

Those appointments had to be sold to Lazell, who still felt that the managing directorship was his by right. In his mid-40s, he could afford to bide his time, but as a *quid pro quo* he insisted being given direct control of the Beecham Research Laboratories, which he at once brought under Macleans' wing. He could then finance running costs out of the profits of the Macleans health drink, Lucozade, which by 1951 would be earning about a half of the Beecham Group's profits.[25]

R&D activities were thus largely protected when that June the board cut the current year's central grant to the laboratories from £50,000 to £30,000. Lazell could, however, draw scientific knowledge from the Macleans laboratory, with its long tradition of research, and from Lucozade Ltd's expertise in glucose therapy. In May 1949 he bought C. L. Bencard (1934) Ltd for £30,000. That was a small manufacturer of a nationally acclaimed range of allergy preparations, then earning £12,000 a year but capable of substantial expansion. It had useful research facilities in ethical medicines and also specialist marketing skills in that field which Beecham had hitherto lacked.[26]

Once appointed managing director, Buckley convened a special directors' meeting and singled out three areas that required immediate attention: the home trade in proprietary medicines; activities overseas; and capital expenditure, which should be controlled through the introduction of budgets. His plans proved to be more innovative than Holmes's had been.

Buckley's review of the proprietary business in Britain was commendably searching. While he rated as 'excellent' the Macleans and County Perfumery companies that Lazell ran, he found a great deal wrong with the Watford group, which included the units that made Eno's fruit salt, Phosferine and Phyllosan, and also the recently acquired pharmaceutical firms of Endocrine-Spicer and Harwood's Laboratories. He sacked the Watford group's managing director and appointed the manager of Eno's in his place. He also judged that it was high time to transfer the Veno operations to St Helens. Nearly two decades had passed since the previous failed attempt to merge the two production units (see Chapter 11). George Morrison, recently down-graded from general manager to head of the pills subsidiary at St Helens, vigorously opposed the plan and was allowed to resign. With his departure, as Lazell put it, all the old managers on the two sites had gone. Gregory had died in 1943, but Lazell forgot Frank Moss, who stayed on as the wholly dependable St Helens works manager until his death, when only 56, in 1955. Once the second extension to the St Helens factory, planned as early as 1946 and costing £125,000, was completed four years later and the plant for making the cough remedy installed, the Manchester works were closed.[27]

Aware that staff incentives were morale-boosters, in 1950 Buckley launched a profit participation scheme. Twenty per cent of all profits over the current level would be shared out between permanent employees in proportion to their earnings. However, in an era of poor company results, it was badly timed, and Lazell had to scale down the scheme in 1952.[28]

Buckley was equally decisive about overseas trade. He found the Beecham Export Corporation to be out of control. Dunbar, its head since 1939, had been flouting the board's regulations by introducing unauthorized capital projects, running up substantial liabilities, and altering the formulae of products without permission. He was dismissed and the exporting functions in the main handed back to their production units. That move was calculated to revive energies and morale within subsidiaries, and thus stimulate increased efficiency and cost reductions.

The third aim, to bring capital expenditure to heel, demonstrated Buckley's understandable concern about the group's finances. Its accounting methods had in some ways improved since the Hill era: recorded profits now included all the earnings of units, rather than just their dividends sent to head office, while for the first time a consolidated balance sheet had appeared in the 1947 annual report. Yet the units' resources largely escaped direct control from headquarters. How far Buckley discussed that weakness with Brian Mountain as adviser on finance is not known. Perhaps they felt powerless to force through any kind of financial centralization as long as Holmes and Hobrow in effect ruled the group. Then in August 1949 Mountain resigned from the board after his father had died and left him with numerous business interests to administer.

Mountain's successor on the Beecham board was Kenneth Keith. A trained accountant, Keith had had a good war, being mentioned in despatches and ending as a lieutenant-colonel. He then worked for the director-general of the Foreign Office's Political Intelligence Department, before joining the Philip Hill Investment Trust. In his early 30s, as a Beecham director he was bound to be far more energetic, in representing the institutions' interests and offering trenchant financial advice. To Lazell, Keith's arrival on the scene proved to be a godsend. Allowing for inflation, the group's profit in 1948/49 was 15 per cent lower than in 1945/46; a year later there was to be a further fall in real terms of 10 per cent. In Lazell's words, Beecham was then 'going downhill rapidly', so that drastic measures were more than ever needed.[29]

As late as 1950, board members showed that they had not yet come to terms with the NHS, which in their view 'continued to operate to the detriment of [medicinal] tonic lines'. They regretted that the Germolene ointment, for example, was losing ground because penicillin medicines, prescribed cost-free by doctors, had become so popular. That year's general election returned the ruling Labour government with a majority of only five, and the Conservative opposition kept up pressure on ministers night after night in the House of Commons. As an MP in his seventies, Holmes could not have had much energy left for overseeing corporate affairs.

Beecham's managing director and administrative director were constantly bickering, and the witty company solicitor, Monty Gedge, recalled the frequent rows between the over-fussy Hobrow and the rumbustious Buckley when he quipped about 'arguing from the Particular to the [Major-]General'.[30] However, the pair were agreed among themselves over two matters. Each coveted the chairmanship, Hobrow being prepared to serve as managing director until Buckley's retirement, and both felt that the sooner Holmes went the better.

The early months of 1950 were too soon to have benefited much from Buckley's recent initiatives. As the 40 per cent dividend was restored when the the 1949/50 results appeared, the share price did not plunge as much as the disappointing 2 per cent profit margin deserved. To the ever grumpy shareholders, Holmes could only explain that, with the post-war sellers' market in foodstuffs now at an end, turnover and profits in the group's food companies had fallen sharply. In fact, proprietary medicines and toiletries between them earned three-quarters of home profits and nearly nine-tenths of earnings overseas, and were therefore rightly entitled to almost the whole of the company's £1.7 million advertising budget in Britain. Those results clearly showed up Holmes's earlier misjudgment in chasing after food companies.[31]

At some time in 1950, over lunch, Keith discreetly sounded out Lazell regarding the terms on which he might eventually accept the group managing directorship. Lazell replied that he had no particular wish to serve under Holmes, but would reluctantly do so in the interests of continuity, if he were granted a free hand in all operational matters. They did not have to wait long before matters came to a head. Buckley's contract as managing director was due for renewal early in 1951, and at nearly 68 he now had the last chance to bid for the chairman's post.[32]

Although the group's results for 1950/51 showed some improvement, with turnover up by 11 per cent and profits by nearly 14 per cent, the net dividend yield remained high, at nearly 6½ per cent. The outbreak of the Korean war, in which British troops were engaged, set off a sharp increase in many countries' defence expenditures and in world demand for raw materials generally.

Against that background of rising prices, Lazell's account of Buckley's and Hobrow's subsequent handling does not quite tally with the chronology in the board minutes, which are considered first. After an autumn visit to the United States, Buckley was prevented from attending the January 1951 board meeting by a serious illness, duly minuted. He was well enough to be at the meeting in late March, when he vigorously criticized the management and strategy of the Eno subsidiary; its managing director was eventually sacked in 1953. Yet ten days later, on 2 April, he had his appointment terminated on the grounds of continuing ill health, being paid £10,000 in lieu of notice. At the end of June, he again got into touch with Lazell, clearly to extract more money, but the earlier arrangement stood.[33]

the higher interest rate burden. The revival finally arrived with the outcome for 1953/54. For the first time, trading profits exceeded £3 million on sales that were down to £23.5 million, resulting from the disposal of wholesale groceries, completed in mid-1954.

Since Philip Hill had failed to convert the Beecham subsidiaries into an integrated company, those had long enjoyed too much financial independence. Lazell now began to rein them in, through making them submit sales and profit forecasts. However, he could not regroup them into more logical entities without having to pay the heavy stamp duties then levied on transfers of businesses from one company to another. As the Beecham Group already held their deferred shares, in 1954 he was able to buy out, at a cost of £1.1 million, the preference shares of certain units, including Veno and A. F. Sherley, which were held by outside shareholders. That move saved £91,000 a year in dividends and profits tax. Once those subsidiaries were entirely under his control, he could close them down and merge their functions in the group's larger operating companies.

Liquidating the preference shares of other subsidiaries, and of the Beecham Group itself, was a larger and more expensive task, as their current rates of interest ranged from Eno's 5–5½ per cent and C. & E. Morton's 7 per cent to Beecham's 10 per cent. Their repayment early in 1955 cost £4.2 million, largely met by an issue of £3.5 million 4¼ per cent loan stock. Lazell took the opportunity to convert the deferred into ordinary shares and to double their denomination to 5s. (25p) each. Eno and C. & E. Morton then ceased to exist as separate companies. All in all, Lazell must have hoped that the group's major travails were behind him.[5]

As Beecham's financial performance gradually improved, Lazell turned his attention to longer-term strategic questions. When addressing the board for the first time as managing director in 1951, he had revealed two overriding ambitions: to ensure that his R&D activities were 'vindicated' by the lucrative development of ethical drugs, and to establish a viable business in the United States. Beecham brands, he argued, could never succeed throughout the rest of the world until they had made good in the American market.

Lazell refused to admit that Beecham was over-diversified by having both a medicinal and a product side. Instead, he maintained that the group was 'not nearly so complex a collection [of units] as in Unilever, or in Warner Lambert or American Home Products of the USA', all highly profitable enterprises. Even so, he had a difficult balancing act to perform. Proprietary medicines may have been the largest of the group's three product categories – the other two being foods (including drinks) and toiletries – accounting for nearly two-fifths of total sales and half of those overseas. Yet household products had to be carefully nurtured because of their massive and reliable earning power. No other company in the world, he boasted, had four such distinctive brands as Brylcreem, Lucozade, Eno's fruit salt and Macleans' toothpaste.[6]

In 1951/52 those four star performers between them had accounted for 45 per cent of the group's overall sales and 54 per cent of its profits, receiving the lion's share of its £33 million advertising outlay. His acquisition, early in 1955, of H. W. Carter & Co., which made the blackcurrant drink, Ribena, and fruit squashes under the Quosh name, gave him the opportunity to assemble what he called 'the soft drink business of my dreams'. Another group product since 1952 was Coca-Cola, bottled under franchise for sale in south-east England and some northern counties.

Those brands already sold extensively through grocers, and Lazell therefore planned to set up a powerful national distribution system which would by-pass the wholesalers. He felt capable of supplying grocery outlets as efficiently and economically as did giant rivals such as Unilever and Procter & Gamble, which he disrespectfully called 'soapers'. Although beverages predominated, he chose to name his new subsidiary Beecham Foods Ltd, as C. & E. Morton's tinned foodstuffs were also included. It would be run by the efficient British arm of the Harold F. Ritchie agency.

After a Colgate vice-president was head-hunted for the unit's managing directorship and then withdrew, Lazell appointed in his place Robert Craig Wood, formerly with Procter & Gamble's British affiliate, the US-owned Thomas Hedley of soap and detergent fame. In April 1955 he brought together the sales arms of Lucozade, Ribena and the Morton foods, introducing a single punch card system for all their transactions.

His attempt to merge diverse systems on such a scale landed the entire integration project in deep trouble. Small-volume orders poured in and overloaded the system, many orders being incorrectly entered. For some weeks, no one dared to inform Lazell about the extent of what he later referred to as a 'complete shambles'. When the truth emerged, he moved out Craig Wood, who resigned. He and Rintoul then jointly spent more time and effort than they could spare on a rescue operation. In 1955/56 the group's profits earned in Britain fell by £280,000 to £2.4 million, while debts owed by grocers for its foods and soft drinks were £1 million higher than normal, thus forcing up the level of its bank borrowings.

It took longer than expected to recover from that débâcle; yet the Beecham Foods affair was significant as the first real test of Keith's earlier undertaking, on behalf of the institutional investors, to back Lazell if problems arose, as long as he could offer a workable recovery plan. In September 1955 Keith persuaded the institutions to prove their confidence in Lazell by subscribing to a £2.4 million Beecham share issue.[7] The results for 1956/57, showing sales to have risen by 6.5 per cent and trading profit by 23 per cent, furnished clear evidence of Lazell's capacity to put the entire fiasco behind him. With over £800,000 undistributed profits retained in the group. Beecham now had the funds, as well as shareholder support, to undertake a massive capital investment programme.

Even so, Lazell was not put off from adding to Beecham Foods the right kinds of food companies. In 1958 he acquired Thomas & Evans of Glamorgan, which brought with it an efficient distribution system for its Corona soft drinks, and also Pure Lemon Juice Ltd, well known for its PLJ brand. He even overstretched the group's core activities by purchasing also James Pascall Ltd, a medium-sized but highly regarded confectionery business, and amalgamating it with R. S. Murray & Co., a C. & E. Morton subsidiary which made boiled sweets known as Murraymints. Murray and Pascall, even once fully integrated, proved to be no match for their powerful national competitors in that field, and its annual losses ran at £650,000. After J. Mackintosh & Sons Ltd, the toffee-making giant, declined to purchase the business, in 1964 it went to Cadbury Fry, shortly to become Cadbury-Schweppes.

After all its trials, Beecham Foods settled down to overtake medicines as the group's largest single product category. Equipped with 1,700 delivery vehicles on the roads of Britain, it was highly lucrative at home, although enjoying only meagre sales abroad. For Lazell, the division's initial turmoil had been a close-run thing.[8]

Lazell's creation of Beecham Foods, requiring a sizeable workforce to run it and operate technical services such as a punch-card system, acted as a catalyst for a long overdue reform: providing the group with an appropriately roomy headquarters. The head office was still at 55/56 Pall Mall in central London and the secretarial function nearby at No. 68, but other departments had to be housed in Piccadilly or Bond Street. Macleans and the consumer research department were in Brentford, on the Great West Road, better known as the A4.

A suitable venue came up when the government-owned British Overseas Airways Corporation, situated close to Macleans, transferred its headquarters to London Airport, further west at Heathrow. Beecham then bought a 75-year lease of the building for £70,000 per annum and took possession of it.

Beecham House, its predictable name, was a large rectangular edifice of stone and brick, having a tower of eight storeys which dwarfed the surrounding blocks of one to three levels. Inside its entrance was a large green-carpeted reception area, and the maze of buildings to the rear were linked by what the Americans, when they arrived three decades later (see Chapter 15) saw as 'miles of bland brown rubber-tiled corridors'. To their more sophisticated eyes, 'the boardroom reflected the 1930 look: dark brown walls and camel leather chairs surrounded a huge, round, custom-built wooden table'. Units began their move in December 1955, everyone being finally settled in a year later.[9]

However preoccupied he was with Beecham Foods and with plans for a new headquarters, Lazell maintained his resolve to 'vindicate' R&D operations by developing ethical drugs.[10] Having earlier kept the group's research activities afloat by funding them from the Macleans earnings (see Chapter 12), he had in 1951 brought those activities back into head office. Their operations came under McGeorge as group technical director. Lazell maintained his close personal interest in all aspects of the scientists' work. To concentrate their minds, he limited R&D expenditure to fixed percentages of medicinal sales, namely 7½ per cent of prescription medicines and 2½ per cent of proprietary brands. He judged that those financial curbs 'sharpened our thinking, kept us on our toes, and encouraged our best men to work on our most worthwhile projects'.[11]

Hitherto the 50 research scientists, 18 being graduates (but none as yet women), had concentrated on testing and improving the quality of Beecham products, for example by investigating the effect of light on the colour of Lucozade. Many of them now moved over into basic research. Perhaps because of limited experience at that stage, their initial projects had little success. They set out to discover improved allergy remedies, to supplement those made by C. L. Bencard, and they investigated amino-acids and anti-tubercular drugs. Their work on compounds to do with the alkaloid atropine yielded the sole product to reach the market: Nacton, for treating acute dyspepsia and peptic ulcers.[12] Then in 1954, Lazell began his journey towards penicillin, although by a distinctly roundabout route.[13]

Natural penicillins were obtained by microbiological fermentation. That process began to impact directly on Beecham's research plans when the manufacture of Eno's fruit salt was found to be under threat from a likely shortage of tartaric acid, no longer so plentiful owing to new processes of wine-making. Once the group's chief consultant, Sir Charles Dodds, learned about that problem, in 1954 he contacted (Sir) Ernst Chain, an early pioneer of penicillin development and currently operating a fermentation plant at his laboratory in Rome, who agreed to help.

In April 1955 Chain travelled to see Lazell in London, where he made clear that production of tartaric acid by synthetic means would be too costly; Beecham therefore accepted the need to find secure supplies elsewhere. Chain put to him an alternative suggestion. Pharmaceutical companies throughout the world were currently using microbiological methods of screening soil samples for promising moulds, but failing to achieve a break-through to more efficacious drugs. Hence Beecham should pursue the alternative chemical route so as to see if it could lead to the evolution of semi-synthetic penicillins.

Lazell had first of all to obtain the Beecham board's agreement in principle to begin antibiotic research. Although the majority of executive directors, plus Keith, were supportive, some non-scientists on the board displayed an unjustified 'easy optimism' in expecting swift break-throughs, and failed to appreciate the hard slog ahead. Others were equally unrealistic in their reluctance to authorize further substantial outlays on research before seeing the delivery of some commercially viable drugs.

Holmes as chairman, newly ennobled as Lord Dovercourt, even went public over his opposition to the group's laying out good money on risky R&D. In the company's *Annual Report* for 1953/54 he revealed that Beecham had spent nearly £1 million on research since 1945 without – he might have added – much to show for it. Moreover, he doubted if further development expenditure on ethical medicines could be justified as long as the Ministry of Health was forcing down the prices of prescriptions supplied by drug companies to the NHS.

Lazell ignored Dovercourt's scruples. Taking his time to consider Chain's advice, in September he made the most far-reaching decision of his life, to begin research on penicillin: one which, if successful, would convert Beecham for the first time into a pharmaceutical company. The first stage was to have a new £50,000 fermentation pilot plant manufactured in Rome under Chain's direction, for shipment to Britain; he told colleagues that he was 'not now afraid of the cost of the [eventual] plant at £500,000'.[14]

Four of his scientists, including a microbiologist and a biochemist, spent some months in Rome being trained in the fermentation process. By the time of their return, the new plant was up and running at Brockham Park. There they began a sequence of assays or experiments, using both biological and chemical methods, to uncover the characteristics and curative power of the penicillins found in batches of the fermentation broth. The chemical assay revealed the amount of penicillin each sample contained, while the biological assay measured its effectiveness against harmful bacteria.

In Rome the scientists had been led to expect the two methods to yield broadly similar results, and were prepared to blame any discrepancies on random factors. At Brockham Park, however, the assays showed that the chemical method yielded greater quantities of penicillin than by biological means. Hence the observed difference appeared to be a systematic one, as a certain element in each brew belonged to the penicillin family but had no power to kill bacteria. That element was identified as the core or nucleus of penicillin, named 6-amino-penicillanic acid, or 6-APA for short, which lacked the side chain or active molecule found in ordinary penicillins. In August 1957 – only three months after making their discovery – the Beecham scientists applied for a British patent over 6-APA.

Their next hurdle was how to discover which side chains to add, by what was known as an acylation process, in order to create a biologically active penicillin. The group's results for 1956/57, mentioned above, provided the welcome assurance that Beecham would have no financial problems when moving to the next laborious stage, as trading profit was no less than £4.4 million, or £1.9 million after tax. Shareholders, whose dividend increases had not risen in line with company earnings, received only 2½ per cent extra that year, allowing £800,000 to be retained for capital purposes. To Lazell's frustration, the scientists were at first able to recover only small quantities of 6-APA. Over a year passed before they had enough to carry out a thorough search for types of antibacterial penicillins, by adding chemical side chains to modify the core. Of the 200 different side chains tried, only a few were active enough to be worth following up.[15]

During that search process, Lord Dovercourt retired in 1958 as chairman, shortly before his 80th birthday, having offered no further public comments on R&D. A former subordinate of his reminisced that 'he seemed to have the makings of a strong man, but did not achieve it'.[16]

The more single-minded Lazell, who predictably succeeded him, at once changed his second title from managing director to chief executive. He appointed Rintoul as executive vice-chairman, jointly with the non-executive Keith. The six full-time executive directors comprised the four heads of the major subsidiaries, plus McGeorge as head of research and Spry at finance. Lazell required all of them to concentrate on policy matters, allowing the brightest younger men, trained up by himself, to manage those subsidiaries. He had at last established an effective line of command; yet a reorganization along multi-divisional lines was still in the future.

Although the pilot stage of penicillin manufacture was on the way to success, the Beecham Group lacked both the hardware and the specialist knowledge to move towards full-scale production. Lazell therefore needed to call on American technology, and in December 1958 McGeorge approached Bristol-Myers of New York, a corporation already well advanced in the manufacture of natural penicillins, through its subsidiary, Bristol Laboratories Inc. After intensive bargaining, Lazell and McGeorge persuaded that corporation to undertake the necessary development work. In return, Beecham formally granted an exclusive licence to market its future penicillins in the United States, paying a 5 per cent royalty until such time as the group had set up there its own marketing organization for pharmaceuticals.

By coincidence, Professor John C. Sheehan, an organic chemist at the Massachusetts Institute of Technology (MIT), had been likewise undertaking research into methods of synthesizing 6-APA, financed by Bristol-Myers. In March 1957 he had patented his techniques, five months before the Beecham patent. Soon after Lazell and McGeorge had reached agreement for Bristol Laboratories to develop their semi-synthetic penicillin, in April 1959 Sheehan was one of the latter's team who met Lazell and his top scientists at Brockham Park.

That meeting foreshadowed a fruitful collaboration between the two companies, with Sheehan contributing expert knowledge on the next stage of progressing from semi-synthetic to even more effective synthetic drugs. However, citing legal problems about disclosure, he refused to enlighten the eager Beecham scientists on the details of his apparently further advanced process. Soon they began to doubt whether he was really capable of converting his synthetic discovery into marketable drugs, because a purely chemical compound was not known to possess the required antibacterial powers. Within months, personal disagreements led Sheehan to withdraw from the otherwise harmonious Beecham-Bristol negotiations.

For the following two decades, Sheehan with extraordinary persistence conducted a vigorous campaign to establish that his patent of March 1957 had priority over the later Beecham one. Beecham claimed that Sheehan's patent was invalid because his purely synthetic version could never work; in the event, his researches did fail to yield any drugs.

Not until 1979 did the US Board of Patent Interference conclusively uphold Sheehan's priority. However, it declined to accept his charge that Beecham had acted fraudulently in the course of the interminable experiments, designed to corroborate its claim that Sheehan had never been able to produce a commercial penicillin. Beecham must have spent millions on those experiments as well as on legal fees; it is not clear whether the $30 million, which MIT received from the now validated Sheehan patents, came from Bristol-Myers or directly from Beecham. None of the latter's *Annual Reports* nor, it seems, the British press ever discussed this long drawn-out controversy.[17]

In November 1959, Beecham was at last able to launch its first penicillin, Broxil (phenethicillin), with the aid of a phenoxymethyl penicillin bought in from Bristol-Myers. That was followed in September 1960 by Celbenin (methicillin), named after C. L. Bencard, which could destroy a range of staphylococci resistant to earlier penicillins. However, health care practitioners badly needed a broad-spectrum antibiotic that would be effective against a wider range of bacteria, most notably those causing ear, nose and throat infections, pneumonia and meningitis. Beecham met that requirement with Penbritin (ampicillin) in mid-1961, which caused fewer side-effects than existing types and could therefore be safely given in large doses. Owing to production difficulties, the drug had initially to be restricted to hospital use, and did not become available for general prescription until the second half of 1963.

Penbritin turned out to be the group's most lucrative single product to date, outstripping even Brylcreem and Lucozade. Bristol-Myers had also agreed to supply the necessary production facilities by designing a £3.5 million antibiotic manufacturing unit at Worthing in Sussex, and to train its senior staff. The factory was completed in 1960 and extended in 1965.

Lazell eloquently recalled that the beginning of 1962

> marked a time in the affairs of [the] Beecham Group when the tide
> of success, previously running strongly along the advertised proprietary
> products channel, altered course and thereafter ran with increasing
> strength along the pharmaceutical channel.[18]

Later that year, Beecham added to its penicillin range Orbenin (cloxacillin), an oral drug particularly effective against skin and respiratory infections. For dangerously ill patients, it could be injected together with Penbritin.

The final penicillin developed under Lazell's chairmanship was Pyopen (carbenicillin), in 1967. Another broad-spectrum drug which could be injected, it was found to be of use against severe and hitherto fatal infections in vulnerable patients such as the elderly and very young.

As Chain wrote in 1970 to (Sir) Robert Armstrong, principal private secretary to Edward Heath, the prime minister, when recommending Lazell for an honour (which was never given), in recognition of the outstanding services he had rendered to the economy and prestige of Britain,

> The discovery of the semi-synthetic penicillins by the Beecham
> research workers was the most important advent [event] in the field of
> bacterial chemotherapy since the discovery of the original penicillin
> and the antibiotics that followed it.[19]

For Beecham, during the 13 years since Lazell had resolved to enter the field, its sales of pharmaceutical products had risen from virtually zero in 1950/51 to nearly £33 million in 1968/69, when its trading profits exceeded £10 million, a margin of 30 per cent. That ratio was almost double the 16 per cent earned from toiletry products, which three years previously had taken over from Beecham Foods as the largest product group with £53 million sales. Food and Drink products were less profitable, with under 7 per cent earnings on sales of £35 million. For all the progress in pharmaceuticals, Beecham remained a highly diversified company.

Lazell's second priority, disclosed to the board in 1951, was to create a powerful Beecham presence in the United States.[20] Such an objective had to be fitted into the group's overseas involvement as a whole, which that year accounted for a third of total sales but earned nearly half of trading profits. As explained above, although its principal subsidiaries had previously been responsible for their own exporting, in 1953 he centralized all transactions abroad in an overseas department, later Beecham Overseas Ltd.

The ever-active Rintoul oversaw the operations of all territories outside

Britain except the Western Hemisphere. In continental Europe, he began to set up sales agencies because the group's only factory there was one in France, for Eno's. His expansion programme was held back by Lazell's unwillingness to spend adequate funds on the Continent until group ventures in the United States were fully profitable. Lazell subsequently regretted that delay, which meant that Beecham lost out to American rivals which were benefiting from that market's growth after the establishment of the European Economic Community (EEC) in 1957.

Lazell took personal control of the group's operations in the Western Hemisphere, aiming to visit the United States at least twice a year: his efforts there never entirely came up to expectations. The group's *Annual Report* for 1951/52 showed that the United States and Latin America had accounted for 30 per cent of total overseas sales, and Canada for 8 per cent. Thereafter, published results for 1953/54 covered the whole of the hemisphere, rising from 42 per cent to 50 per cent in 1959/60. Until 1951, the products sold had been mostly fruit salts and emulsions. Now he was resolved to market a few of his best-selling brands, most notably Brylcreem and Macleans' toothpaste.

To provide effective management on the spot, having a thorough knowledge of the American market, he looked for a partner in a joint venture. Plough Inc. of Memphis, Tennessee was a respected manufacturer of aspirins and other generic drugs, but the proprietor, with the unlikely name of Abe Plough, demanded too high a partnership share, and negotiations broke down. Mistakenly, Lazell chose to go it alone.

As Canadian operations were appreciably more profitable than those in the United States, he established a new company, Beecham (Canada) Ltd, with its base in H. F. Ritchie's Toronto office (see Chapter 10), to manage business for the entire hemisphere. Its president was the highly experienced Robert Alexander. Maurice Bale, a marketing specialist, remembered by Lazell as 'young, enthusiastic, and clearly a two-fisted fighter',[21] became executive vice-president for the United States. The main factory was that of Eno-Scott & Bowne at Bloomfield, New Jersey, which ran a network of branches throughout Latin America.

As early as 1953, Lazell was able to carry out the first effective launch of Brylcreem in the United States. To manufacture this and other Beecham specialities for the whole of the hemisphere, he planned a factory at Clinton, New Jersey, a few miles from the Bloomfield plant and paid for by a $1.25 million loan from the Bank of Montreal. It took six years to organize an adequate distribution system throughout the Union; advertising costs alone swallowed up no less than two-thirds of sales receipts.

Thus Brylcreem did not begin to make a profit there until 1956/57, and four further years passed before its accumulated losses were paid off. It did well until it came under intense pressure from gels and other rival brands made by

Bristol-Myers and Chesebrough-Ponds, but in 1968 had sales of nearly $13.5 million (£5.6 million). His attempt to launch the Silvikrin shampoo in 1960 had proved an expensive failure.

The introduction in the United States of Macleans' toothpaste during 1963 achieved better results, because Lazell's teams had become more 'professional' after a decade of hard slog. They were able to establish the toothpaste and making it profitable in a third of the time taken with Brylcreem; once again they came up against sustained competition, most notably from Colgate's Ultrabrite brand. In 1968, when he retired as chairman in Britain, that product and Brylcreem had almost identical sales levels at $13.4 million (£5.6 million). Those were the only items sold by his firm of Beecham Products Inc., together representing just one-tenth of the group's turnover world-wide.

For all the energy and resources he had put into marketing there, the results came as a disappointment to Lazell, who correctly guessed that his successor as chairman would not be 'so besotted with the USA as I was', and certainly 'not dreaming my old dreams of a US company bigger than the parent'.[22] His uphill struggle, promoting just two brands, would surely have had much greater impact had he bought into an existing American-owned medicinal firm so as to supply local knowledge. Rather late in the day, during 1965 he had opened talks, which proved abortive, with the chairmen of two possible corporate partners. One of those, the chairman of S. E. Massengill & Co., of Bristol, Tennessee, showed interest but decided not to sell; six years later, he did so under the subsequent Beecham regime.

Sir Joseph Beecham, also a twice-yearly visitor to the United States, had much earlier grasped the advantage of learning American business practices of value to operations in Britain (see Chapter 5). Lazell followed suit, for example in making Beecham the first British company to market its products along American lines, directing every effort towards both discovering consumers' wants and then striving to gratify them.

Lazell expected all board members, not just the designated director, to become personally involved in marketing matters. He even boasted of improving on American practice by requiring the chief executive, and later on the divisional managers, to lead their respective marketing teams. In 1960 Beecham was the second largest advertiser in Britain, after Unilever, being still fourth in 1970, utilizing consumer surveys of the US market research company, A. C. Nielsen Co.[23]

Likewise, Lazell knew well that there was a great deal to learn from American technology; yet he found it difficult to acquire know-how on an arms-length basis from corporations there. As late as 1961 he had no R&D facilities in the United States. However, soon afterwards he established Beecham Research Laboratories Inc., jointly with Ayerst Laboratories, a subsidiary of American Home Products that three decades later once again crossed the Beecham path. Then in 1966 Beecham Products Inc. set up a research laboratory for toiletry products, regularly sending information back to Britain. Lazell explained to shareholders that its overseas research laboratories, especially in the United States, were particularly useful in keeping 'our business ahead with new product development'.[24]

A year later the group completed, at its own expense, a $4.5 million (£1.6 million) antibiotics factory at Piscataway, New Jersey, designed to supply penicillins throughout the Western Hemisphere. That project was overseen by Graham Wilkins, one of the most promising of his younger executives, who had been responsible in Britain for setting up the marketing organization for the group's penicillins.[25] In 1968, Beecham Products Inc. was merged with Beecham Inc., a company newly floated on the New York Stock Exchange to raise $10.6 million; that sum was intended to pay for the Piscataway factory and the extension it already needed.

For well over a decade, the Continent of Europe had to take second place in Lazell's overseas strategy. Then in 1964/65, Beecham's operations in the United States made a $2 million (£840,000) profit, from Brylcreem alone as the Macleans campaign was still at an early stage, and he felt himself ready to act in Europe. He found the problems there differed sharply from those in America. Since 1945, British suppliers of products had earned a poor reputation among Europeans for ignoring local preferences or needs in the brands they offered and in their marketing campaigns, while deliveries often arrived late and were unreliable in quality.[26]

Lazell's solution was to do what he should have done in America, and acquire sound businesses in the heart of the Continent, using the US management consultants, Booz-Allen & Hamilton to identify French and German companies to acquire. In 1964 he began to buy into, and later secured control of, Margaret Astor AG, a leading cosmetics producer in West Germany. He was prepared to enter a specifically non-core business because that company's widely advertised products were in brisk demand over much of Western Europe. Besides, its management was both highly professional and well motivated, eager to sell Beecham products alongside its own. Hence that acquisition proved to be a turning-point in the group's conquest of the continental European market. In 1966 Lazell purchased a Monaco-based firm, called Lancaster after the wartime British bombing aircraft and a maker of beauty treatment products for wealthy French and Italian consumers. He planned to use the two businesses as the nucleus of an organization to open up markets throughout the Continent, to be discussed below.

The growing pace of overseas activity imposed a noticeable strain on Beecham's senior managers. As early as 1959, Lazell reported that he had sent abroad a larger number of executives than ever before, finding such assignments a 'good training' for young men of energy and ability. However, as he approached his sixtieth year in the new decade, he found himself under an unprecedented level of stress. 'The period of 1961–69,' he later recalled, 'was probably the most hectic in the whole history of the [Beecham] Group.' He could have delegated some of his responsibilities as chief executive; yet he felt comfortable in maintaining overall control, after having needed to step in all too often when things had gone awry.

Having from the outset endured perennial shortages of senior executives, he noted in a secret file their competence in carrying out their allotted duties. That shortage became critical when Neils Fabricius, his marketing director, died in 1960, John Rintoul – vice-chairman since 1959 – in 1963, and the financial director, Michael Spry, two years later. Those losses, in his words, 'decimated' the group's most senior cadre. Douglas Stafford succeeded Rintoul as executive vice-chairman, but never achieved Rintoul's close relationship with Lazell.[27]

Together with management of the right calibre, Beecham needed a robust organizational structure, so as to transform it from a unitary to a multi-divisional company, one containing a number of product divisions, which would undertake day-to-day operations and allow the head office to concentrate on wider policy issues. Although the group had in 1955 gained control of most subsidiaries by eliminating their preference shares, seven years passed before Lazell assembled all units in three divisions, respectively covering Food and Drink, Toiletries, and Pharmaceuticals.

The divisional chairmen were made responsible for earning minimum returns on capital employed; yet their subsidiary companies remained as separate units. Lazell's ensuing problems, most notably over the toiletries division, forced him to make a number of – not always wise – management changes, and dashed his hopes of personally concentrating on pharmaceuticals and leaving consumer products to others. By 1963, he later remembered, 'the demands of the Pharmaceutical Division on our best executive blood had resulted in damage to our proprietary business'.[28]

A more radical restructuring scheme in 1964 did little to help. Lazell retained the three existing divisions, but split toiletries between Europe (including Britain) and the North American area to which he still clung. He did, however, merge all subsidiaries into the Beecham group. Then in 1968, the prospect of Britain's eventually joining the European Economic Community led to the setting up of a European Division, responsible for pharmaceutical and consumer products there. Douglas Stafford was put in charge; his deputy was Frank Lomax, praised by Lazell as a 'tremendous worker of Spartan integrity'. Between them they set up a workable management structure in every European branch, and chose the most advantageous sites for future production units. The first, planned but not yet begun in Lazell's final year, was a pharmaceutical factory at Heppignies in Belgium, to manufacture semi-synthetic penicillins for all Western European countries. They built up marketing teams in each specialist field, and began a process of Europeanization by appointing a Dutch national as a divisional director.

All those burdens provoked Lazell into public utterances over a quite separate cause of vexation: the Ministry of Health's ever-intensifying efforts to regulate the pharmaceutical industry. The cost of drugs prescribed under the NHS had soared; because neither patients, bitterly hostile to prescription charges, nor doctors, who resisted any threat to clinical freedom, had proved to be easy targets, the ministry attempted to bear down on manufacturers' charges.

The UK Voluntary Price Regulation Scheme of 1957 had restricted drug prices paid by the NHS to the level charged for those that were exported. In 1967, Beecham of its own accord cut the price of its leading pharmaceutical brand, Penbritin, to 40 per cent of the initial selling price of six years earlier. Even so, the government's frustration over the massive drugs bill, fed by watchdog bodies such as the Public Accounts Committee, led to its setting up successive official inquiries. Those demanded unacceptably high quantities of data and other written evidence from the companies under scrutiny.[29]

Lazell was already using the chairman's statement in the group's *Annual Report* to deliver a running commentary on his fraught relations with officialdom. In the 1960s, such critiques covered roughly half the total length of his statements, denying shareholders vital information about the group's manifold activities. Interference by the state, he argued, was 'making it increasingly difficult for a company like Beecham to operate efficiently'. Stung by official charges of excessive pricing, he rejoined that, having introduced his first penicillin drug in 1959, only four years later did he recoup in profits the entire cost of R&D. Nor, he added, was he yet earning a return on the capital costs incurred in that venture.

He reserved his most vehement outburst for the Sainsbury Committee of 1965, which inquired into the relationship between the pharmaceutical industry and the NHS. He was incensed to learn that a 'socialist' government had appointed a high-profile Labour supporter as committee chairman. His written evidence has unfortunately vanished from the file in The National Archives, but the committee is known to have dismissed his arguments, as giving a 'somewhat slanted' account of what Beecham was up to; thus the group omitted to mention the substantial costs of marketing its latest penicillin, which far outstripped its outlay on R&D.

To be sure, Lazell might have tried to educate the committee about the group's need for intensive but costly marketing activity, to ensure that

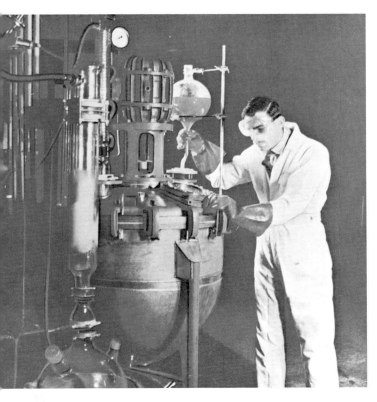

13.3 Reaction fermenting vessel, used in the manufacture of penicillin, 1959.

ANNUAL REPORT, 1959/60

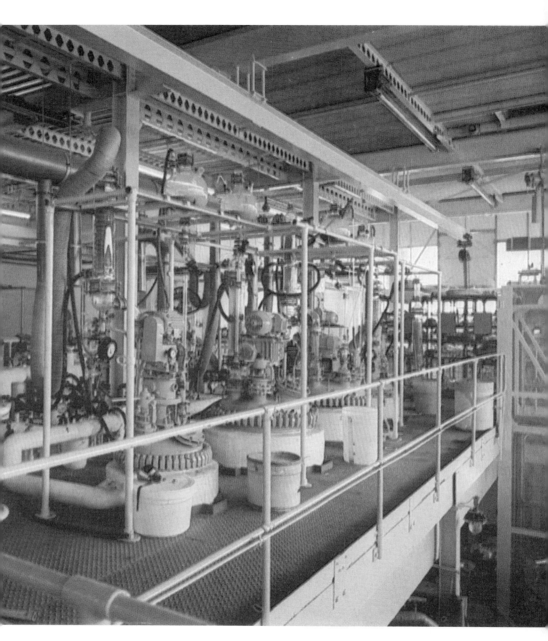

15.3 Chemical plant at Beecham Research Centre,
Harlow, Essex, 1979.

ANNUAL REPORT, 1979/80

15.4 Macleans' Aquafresh toothpaste factory, Clifton, New Jersey, 1979.

ANNUAL REPORT, 1979/80

15.5 Kenneth (Lord) Keith, a distinguished banker and non-executive Beecham director. He became interim chairman after unseating Halstead in 1985.

ANNUAL REPORT, 1985/86

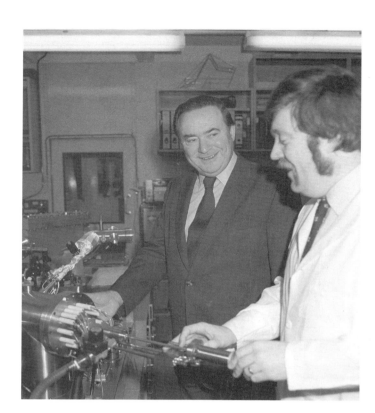

15.6 Sir Ronald Halstead a chairman, inspecting a mass spectrometer, to determine the chemical structure of ne compounds, 1985.

ANNUAL REPORT, 1984/85

15.7 Robert Bauman, US-born and a Harvard Business School-trained chairman 1986–89, with John Robb, chief executive and managing director, 1986.

ANNUAL REPORT, 1986/87

16.1 Bauman, chief executive of SmithKline Beecham, and Henry Wendt, its 'patrician' chairman, both from 1989 to 1994.

ANNUAL REPORT, 1989

16.2 Jan Leschly, SmithKline Beecham's chief executive 1994–99, energetic and impetuous. His attempt to agree a merger with Glaxo Wellcome was finally achieved by Garnier in 2000. Photographed in 1991.

ANNUAL REPORT, 1991

16.3 Jean-Pierre (J.P.) Garnier, with 'a ferocious intellect bubbling away like a pressure cooker': chief executive of SmithKline Beecham, 1999–2000, and then chief executive of GlaxoSmithKline 2000–08. Photographed in 2004.

MANAGEMENT TODAY, MARCH 2004

16.4 Sir Richard Sykes, chairman of Glaxo Wellcome and joint architect – with Garnier – of GlaxoSmithKline, and chairman 2000–02.

JAN CHLEBIK, IMPERIAL COLLEGE, LONDON

prescribers of drugs were made aware of its latest offerings, and also that those drugs had wide enough sales to recover in full the scientific and capital costs of that R&D. When published in 1967, the Sainsbury Report recommended – much to Lazell's disgust – that new drugs should no longer bear brand names, and that the length of patent protection for drugs should be reduced. As it happened, the report was almost wholly disregarded by government as being a thin and sloppy piece of work, in the Treasury's judgment 'pretty disappointing and inadequate'.[30]

The group's 1967/68 *Annual Report* noted for the first time that the company was contributing £20,000 to the opposition Conservative party. There Lazell expressed particular irritation that some top executives were being subjected to 'detailed interference [by government] with business'. Stafford as vice-chairman had for two years spent half his working hours in dealing with the Sainsbury Committee's queries, while McGeorge, technical director until he retired in 1967, was spending a quarter of his time on complying with regulations on the safety of drugs. The Medicines Act of 1968, Lazell maintained, was hobbling the industry in many respects through excessive regulation; perhaps he deliberately overlooked the need for powerful controls after the earlier tragedy of Thalidomide, a Distillers Company drug that had caused many deformities before birth.[31]

In 1968 Lazell retired at the age of 65. During his 17 years as leader, the Beecham Group's sales had increased nearly seven times and profits seven and a half times; as prices generally in Britain had almost doubled over that period, its real growth had been about three and a half times. Given the problems he had inherited, from poor financial results to an outdated corporate structure to a shortage of managerial talent, its rate of progress was highly commendable, although he readily conceded that his ambitions had always run ahead of his ability to deliver. Above all, he was gratified to have restored a sense of purpose to the group.

A contemporary study of the UK's major enterprises made clear the quality of Lazell's leadership. That concluded that Beecham was 'one of the few British companies encountered [in its survey] that seemed to set out a consistent corporate strategy and then implement it'. Indeed, the four prongs of his overall strategy, namely recasting the group's internal structure, expanding involvement abroad, introducing American-style marketing, and promoting innovative R&D, had skilfully reinforced one another. Between 1964/65 and 1968/69 the group achieved the highest return on capital of Britain's largest 300–400 companies.

In a further summary of his achievements, a newspaper columnist wrote in 1970 that 'Lazell forced Beecham deep into the drugs business and transformed it from a home-based to a world-wide enterprise'.[32] Yet he left his successor as chairman with the massive entrepreneurial task of how to maintain and broaden the global presence of a company that was only 27th in the roll-call of the world's largest pharmaceutical corporations.

Edwards and the bid for Glaxo, 1968–1975

WHEN IN 1968 Lazell announced his retirement from the Beecham Group, there was no successor-in-waiting for the chairmanship. His disappointment over Beecham Foods (see Chapter 13) had not encouraged him to recruit senior managers from outside the group, and its many acquisitions since 1945 had brought with them few executives of entrepreneurial calibre. The one internal candidate for the post was Douglas Stafford, acquired with the firm of C. L. Bencard in 1949 (see Chapter 12) and currently Lazell's right-hand man. However, at the age of 58 he made clear that he 'wished to take things more easily' and retire after two years. For continuity's sake, he was persuaded to remain as executive vice-chairman until 1972.

In the second managerial tier, Graham Wilkins and Ronald Halstead were both group board members and divisional chairmen, the one – now recalled from the United States – in charge of pharmaceuticals and the other of Beecham products. Still in their early 40s, they 'needed more time in the firing line running their Divisions' according to Lazell, who observed that it was no bad thing to have to look outside the group for a chairman. Managers who had worked under him for years would almost certainly follow his intrusive example by putting a 'finger in every pie'. The time was therefore ripe for a new kind of chairman altogether; in short, 'a member of the Establishment'.[1]

It was Kenneth Keith, the longest serving director after Lazell, and not for the first or last time Beecham's kingmaker and regicide, who suggested Sir Ronald Edwards for the post. Edwards was different enough from Lazell in temperament if not in origins. Another Certificated rather than a Chartered Accountant, he had risen from an equally unprivileged background (his father was a gas fitter), but had made good by a dissimilar route. He would be the first chairman of Beecham to have a university degree, but only after part-time study; his success in life was hailed as 'a tribute to the old-style correspondence course'.[2] In 1949 he had been appointed an economics professor, specializing in industrial organization, at the London School of Economics.

There Edwards set up a fortnightly seminar on the problems of industrial administration. Speakers were mainly prominent businessmen, whose combined expertise gave him an unrivalled knowledge of UK business practices and growth strategies, distilled by himself in three volumes on corporate organization and government involvement in industry. Lazell spoke twice at the seminar, in 1960 on Beecham's history and structure and eight years later with a typically spirited defence of 'marketing in a competitive economy'.[3]

Since 1962 Edwards had been chairman of the Electricity Council, responsible for Britain's power supplies; his term of office providentially expired in 1968. Aged 58, and unlike his contemporary, Douglas Stafford, not looking forward to a quieter life, he was well placed to bridge the gap until Wilkins, Halstead or another might be ready for the chairman's seat. Edwards later claimed to have taken on the Beecham post not for the pay – although he doubled his salary – but because it gave him an opportunity to weigh the conduct of private-sector business against that of public service.[4]

Some observers saw his genial and bespectacled countenance as that of an ineffectual academic. In fact, he suffered from hereditary glaucoma, and he could metaphorically see through people and complex issues quite as perceptively as Lazell had done. Wilkins later hailed him as the 'rare combination of a man with a very easy manner and a very formidable intellect', aided by 'a prodigious capacity for work'.[5] Others noted his 'mixture of candour, self-confidence, clear-mindedness and apparent imperviousness to stress'.[6] Having gained the respect of ministers and civil servants at the Electricity Council, he anticipated that people would listen when he stood up for the Beecham Group and the pharmaceutical industry in a less acerbic manner than that adopted by Lazell.

Thus in the group's *Annual Reports*, Edwards conveyed his equally trenchant views in more coded language. His first Chairman's statement, in the *Report* for 1968/69, observed that:

> My predecessor referred last year to the particular danger for Beecham inherent in various Government measures and policies. Since then some of these dangers may have receded but others remain. The present Board [members] rate them no less seriously and will do everything in their power to protect the Company's proper interests.

The 'dangers' highlighted by Lazell (see Chapter 13) had been, internally, hampering the group's progress by making 'unnecessary' demands for information and by enacting an inordinately large flow of laws and regulations, and externally, by 'the crushing burden of public expenditure' and hence of corporate taxation.

Edwards joined the Beecham board in May 1968 and took over as chairman that November. He was given the use of a larger chauffeur-driven car than his previous one at the Electricity Council, and also the opportunity to rent a more spacious flat in Lowndes Square, Kensington. In this central London location, he could conveniently entertain business and other visitors, with plenty of scope to take them to the theatre or elsewhere: such hospitality would have been more difficult from the head office in Brentford.

Meanwhile, Lazell became president of the group, remaining in charge of Beecham Inc. and encouraged to offer directors advice on general policy and marketing issues, especially by travelling overseas. However, in 1969 Lazell gave up that advisory role, being appointed honorary president and concentrating on Beecham Inc. He finally retired in 1972.[7]

To counter the charge that he was merely a layman who had been foisted on a science-based company, Edwards stressed that he had always been interested in pharmacy, and would have become a doctor if 'things [his family circumstances] had been different'.[8] To elicit the best results from such a varied assembly of technologists and marketers, he pictured himself as an orchestral conductor. 'If you start trying to play the instruments as well,' he maintained, 'you get some pretty rotten tunes.'[9]

Edwards therefore created his own managerial structure, headed by a chairman's committee including Stafford as vice-chairman and Wilkins and Halstead as divisional chairmen. For longer-term planning, he established a Group Research Unit to think up and assess ideas for new and original pharmaceutical products. Because 'the whole group thrives on responsibility', the man on the spot should be given as free a hand as possible.[10] Incidentally, its only woman board member to date, the personnel director Philippa Lane, had lasted only from 1961 to 1966.

To Lazell, it had been second nature to make rapid decisions, based on years of hard-won industrial experience. Edwards, by contrast, preferred to give time to studying all sides of any problem before him. He therefore recruited from the Electricity Council a personal assistant, an unprecedented step in Beecham's lean head office. Robert Stevens, officially a divisional director and later a group controller, acted as a sounding board for the ideas which Edwards was forever throwing out. Edwards then distilled into a brief memo the pros and cons of any intended action, to the bafflement of subordinates who were used to receiving crisp instructions.

If he found it difficult to decide on questions at short notice, he was better than Lazell at tackling really broad strategic issues. Once appointed chairman, he investigated why Britain's domestically owned pharmaceutical industry appeared to be so inconspicuous on the global stage. For example, Beecham's 27th place in the world pharmaceutical league was eleven points behind the

UK leader, the Glaxo Group. Neither company was a major supplier of drugs to the NHS, which relied for three-quarters of all its prescriptions on branches of foreign companies, enjoying as they did ampler R&D and marketing resources than were available to any single British producer.

Currently, the UK consumed less than 3 per cent of the drugs sold throughout the world, of which its companies produced only 6 per cent, well behind the United States, Japan and Germany. To become a significant player in the global drug scene, Beecham would need to expand on a far greater scale than hitherto. That growth could not be achieved internally, but only by acquiring other pharmaceutical businesses.

As it happened, Edwards' first purchase, early in 1969, was of the relatively small British company, Horlicks Ltd, for £9.7 million. Horlicks Malted Milk, originally an American product, had been manufactured in Slough, near London, since 1906. While sales never exceeded those of the lower-priced Ovaltine, it made its mark in 1933 with the arresting slogan, 'night starvation'.

In a burst of creative imagination which even Charles Rowed could not have surpassed, the firm asserted that everyone used up reserves of energy while asleep, without taking in any nourishment to replace it. 'Breathing alone takes twenty thousand muscular efforts every night'; hence all should prepare for the rigours of sleep with a draught of Horlicks.[11] Since 1945, however, Horlicks' sales had declined as its loyal adherents faded away and younger people had their own means of achieving sound slumber. Beecham therefore replaced the current laggard management with a more vigorous team, which doubled Horlicks' profits within two years.

In 1970, the group purchased Findlater Mackie Todd, makers of Dry Fly sherry, to operate in conjunction with the wine and spirit importing subsidiary, F. S. Matta, bought in 1967. No one seems to have asked whether diversifying into the liquor trade might serve to draw the group away from its core competences.

Although Beecham's pharmaceuticals made trading profits of £10 million in 1968/69, the group still derived over £11 million of its income from branded products. Thus Brylcreem contributed almost £3 million to earnings, and Lucozade, Macleans' toothpaste and Eno's fruit salt about £1 million each; Beecham's powders and Phensic, both sovereign headache and influenza remedies, between them made £1 million profit. Half of all group sales took place abroad, where two-thirds of its trading profits were earned.[12]

Continental Europe since 1969/70 provided more of those earnings than did the Western Hemisphere, and during 1971/72 became the largest of the group's overseas sales areas. Most notably, the Margaret Astor cosmetic business in Western Germany was making great strides; by 1970 its sales were equivalent to £5 million, earning £900,000 profits. The beauty-treatment business, Lancaster in France, too, by then earned £560,000 on a £3.4 million turnover. Beecham utilized those companies' marketing facilities to open up continental European markets to a whole range of its own products from the UK. The Belgian pharmaceutical factory at Heppignies, with a workforce of 400, came on stream in 1971, processing Penicillin G and side-chains shipped over from Britain. Within a year prescription medicines were the fastest growing items in the group's European operations.

That rate of progress on the Continent encouraged Beecham to acquire further European companies. In 1970 it bought, for nearly £13 million, Fischer & Fischer of Western Germany, makers of Badedas foam baths, after-bath toiletries and UHU all-purpose adhesives. Beecham's *Annual Report* hailed that purchase as 'one of the [group's] major events of 1970/71', bolstering its 'already considerable international strength'. It thereby gained a further market for its own toiletries throughout much of Western Europe, to be offered side by side with the Fischer brands. Preparing for his own retirement, in April 1971 Stafford handed over control of operations there to the dynamic Lomax.[13]

The group's performance in the Western Hemisphere was, however, falling badly behind that in continental Europe. American rivals' targeting of Brylcreem and Macleans' toothpaste did not let up, and the recession of 1969–70 badly affected overall sales there. Hence that area's trading profits fell year by year until 1971/72. Lazell, as the current chairman of Beecham Inc., for several years lacked an effective management team to conduct operations in the United States as briskly as Stafford and Lomax were doing in Europe. It did not help that an extension to the Piscataway factory ran into a series of technical problems.[14]

Then in 1971 William Petley was appointed Beecham Inc.'s chief executive. Formerly group financial director 'of outstanding ability and iron nerve' (to quote Lazell), he was 'an abrasive personality and could not hide his contempt for lesser intellects who were his peers or superiors'. Working closely with Lazell, whom he held in high regard, he now set up a wholly owned US Pharmaceutical Division, responsible for running Beecham Laboratories Inc., the 51 per cent-owned subsidiary. He also masterminded what was the second major stage in Beecham's penetration of the American market, the first since Lazell's relaunch of Brylcreem in 1953: its acquisition for nearly £23 million of S. E. Massengill & Co., which had eluded Lazell six years earlier (see Chapter 13). Massengill's OTC brands were mainly feminine hygiene products, then an American speciality comprising what were popularly known as 'douches, deodorants and drugs'. As it also had a pharmaceutical side, the new unit was able to strengthen the group's activities in both market sectors alike.[15]

Massengill's impressive sales force for prescription medicines tripled the number of Beecham's representatives in the United States; once integrated, that force would be capable of promoting all group brands throughout the Union. The arrival of Beecham executives in Massengill's head office at Bristol, Tennessee, brought about a cross-fertilization of ideas. Although the integration process was said to have been completed in an 'incredibly short period', it took up more of Beecham Inc.'s management time than could be comfortably spared, and Lazell subsequently admitted that he had left a 'mess' in the US Pharmaceutical Division when he fully retired in 1972. That year the Western Hemisphere's profit margin was only 17 per cent, as against Europe's 27.5 per cent.[16]

In October 1970 Wilkins, now Group Pharmaceutical Co-ordinator in Britain, had launched a new penicillin, Floxapen (flucloxacillin). Although a narrow-spectrum drug, to treat specific conditions such as skin and respiratory infections, it was a significant advance on Orbenin, being as effective on half the latter's dose. A year later the broader-spectrum Magnapen (Ampicillin plus Floxapen) appeared, as a stop-gap treatment to be administered while laboratory reports on a sick patient were awaited.[17]

Beecham, still manufacturing in Britain a high proportion of its pharmaceuticals, planned a new £11.5 million factory at Irvine New Town in Scotland. At the same time, buoyant demand throughout the Far East made essential a third overseas pharmaceutical plant, in Singapore, to join those already established in the United States and Belgium. Costing nearly £5 million, it was completed by the end of 1972. Those capital commitments were not at the expense of R&D, outlays on which in 1971/72 came to £6.9 million, well over double the £2.7 million of 1967/68. Brockham Park, still the centre of the group's chemotherapeutic research, was extended at a cost of £1.5 million, while non-antibiotic drugs would be developed in a newly built laboratory at Harlow in Essex. Although Edwards' Group Research Unit had come up with only minor novelties such as Mac-Lemon for colds and Hilltop hair shades, existing OTC medicines were selling well, most notably the Vitamin B Orovite brand, Maxolon for gastric disorders and Bencard's allergy remedies.

Three years after the group acquired Vitamins Ltd of Harmondsworth, London, in 1970 it set up Beecham Agricultural Products Ltd. Its laboratory at Walton Oaks, Surrey, carried out nutritional and animal health research. That category accounted for only 5 per cent of group sales and 1 per cent of its trading profits. Here was a further diversification into new and less familiar product lines.[18]

By far the most dramatic event in Edwards' chairmanship was his hostile bid to acquire the Glaxo Group: a move seen by *The Times* as 'one of the most ambitious plans in recent years to reorganise the British pharmaceutical industry'. Having had a restructuring project in mind for several years,

Edwards made no bones about who should initiate it. 'If I had created a strong pharmaceutical company in Britain,' he later declared with some consequence, 'I would feel I had done the country a service.'[19]

Meanwhile, Beecham had no prospect of dominating the industry by internal growth alone. Between 1968/69 and 1970/71 its sales and trading profits had increased by no more than 50 per cent in real terms, allowing for inflation. Although other company chairmen might have been more than satisfied at such progress, Edwards knew that he could achieve his reorganizing goal only through taking over one of his British-owned rivals. He ruled out any merger with an overseas competitor, as a sure way of destroying Beecham's special identity.

Among British companies, he was aware that the Wellcome Foundation, 26th in the world pharmaceutical league but at that time ring-fenced by its charitable status, and ICI – the fourth largest UK enterprise with aggregate sales over eight times his own but ranking only 37th by pharmaceutical sales – were 'not really marriageable'.[20] That left only the Glaxo Group, Britain's pharmaceutical leader and globally in 16th place.

Glaxo had over the past decade quadrupled its turnover and profits, largely through buying up some older-established British pharmaceutical companies, such as Allen & Hanburys and Evans Medical. Only the former of those two appear to have brought it any long-term financial or technical benefits. Its historian, Edgar Jones, stated that Glaxo had become 'an unwieldy and labyrinthine group without a clear operational framework', while outsiders saw it as 'a group run by boffins [back-room scientists] incapable of understanding the realities of corporate life'. Glaxo of itself therefore seemed unlikely to set off a major shake-up of the industry.[21]

For Edwards, planning a take-over of Glaxo promised to be an audacious venture. Beecham's total turnover and market capitalization exceeded those of its rival, but only a third of its own sales were of pharmaceuticals, well below the latter's two-thirds. Beecham had the advantage of being a far higher-profile company, celebrated for its skills in marketing consumer brands and equally for its record profits year after year, encouraging shareholders to expect a 15 per cent annual dividend rise. In 1970/71 its rate of return on capital was exceeded only by IBM of computer fame.

Such a merger with Glaxo would indeed create a pharmaceutical giant, ninth in the world and enjoying, as Edwards put it, 'the size, speed of impact and marketing muscle' for really effective competition against its powerful American and continental European rivals. To prepare for his swoop, he is reported – on unimpeachable evidence – to have held a private talk with Glaxo's chairman, Sir Alan Wilson, a close friend and formerly his deputy at the Electricity Council.[22]

Among the hundreds of seminar papers given at the London School of Economics by UK business magnates were many which drew Edwards' attention to the competitive advantages enjoyed by larger firms through their economies of scale. On the basis of his discussion with Wilson, he was now convinced that the latter had agreed in principle to a future amalgamation. If the sharp-minded Edwards mistook the other man's reaction, one of his advisers should have reminded him about Glaxo's *Annual Report* of 1969, where Wilson had stated that in the pharmaceutical industry 'medium-sized companies have been the only successful innovators over long periods'; instead, 'giant companies seem to lack the necessary creative atmosphere'. Once the bid was announced, *The Times* recalled that statement, and emphasized that Wilson was not given to change his mind.[23]

Apparently unaware of Wilson's strong conviction about large drug companies' lower creativity, Edwards put the scheme to his professional advisers, Hill Samuel. That merchant bank, a successor to the Philip Hill Investment Trust, had been formed in 1970 by the recently knighted Sir Kenneth Keith, acknowledged to be one of the most powerful bankers in London. Hence the financial and real costs of such a step must have been exhaustively investigated. As Keith was a Beecham director, Edwards should perhaps have spotted a conflict of interest and sought an independent adviser; Hill Samuel's enthusiastic response could hardly have been an objective one. The reaction of Lazell to the bid is not known, but he was regularly in touch with Edwards over matters of common interest Had he violently disagreed, the whole scheme would hardly have gone ahead.[24]

When Edwards consulted the Beecham directors, they did suggest a testing of the water by holding preliminary discussions with the entire Glaxo board. However, rumours about a take-over had been swirling around for too long, and any leak could well cause the Glaxo price to soar and make the whole scheme too costly. He therefore sprang the bid on that group without notice: an act which was to cost Beecham dear. His remark that 'shotgun marriages are not very satisfactory' proved to be all too correct.[25]

The shotgun was clearly in view when, on 2 December 1971, Edwards and Wilkins met Wilson at Glaxo's head office in Clarges Street, London, and offered his shareholders eleven 25p Beecham shares and £360 worth of 5 per cent loan stock for every nine Glaxo shares. The bid valued the latter's shares at 430p, well above their current market price of 366p. Edwards then moved to a press conference at Hill Samuel's office in Wood Street, near the Guildhall, and laid out his proposals for restructuring the pharmaceutical industry. Currently, he maintained, British drug companies were spending on R&D only a quarter of their major overseas competitors' expenditure, while conditions in the industry were becoming more difficult and costly now that delays in bringing new drugs to market were steadily on the increase.

Glaxo lost no time in convening an emergency board meeting, which rejected the bid outright as not being 'in the interests either of the shareholders of the Glaxo Group or the pharmaceutical industry'.[26] Paul Girolami, that group's dynamic financial director, was away overseas; as soon as he returned, his implacable opposition ensured that Glaxo would employ every device to beat off the raiders. Wilson left it to him and to (Sir) Austin Bide, the deputy chairman, to lead the defence. They at once lobbied the government to have the bid referred to the Monopolies Commission.

Conservative ministers of the day, after having abandoned the interventionist stance of their pre-1970 Labour predecessors, were loath to become entangled in industrial matters. The Secretary of State for Trade and Industry, John Davies, whom Edwards had previously informed about his plan, turned down Glaxo's demand, on the recommendation of the inter-departmental Merger Panel, charged with screening the terms of the bid.[27]

Then in mid-December Wilson, deploying his famed skill as a 'master of dialectic', entered the fray by asserting that whereas over the past decade Glaxo had three new products to its credit, namely the ointment Betnovate, as well as an antibiotic and an asthma drug, Beecham had produced only one significant drug, namely Penbritin. To achieve even that discovery, he added, the Beecham people 'have done nothing but play molecular roulette. They have been developing, not innovating.'

Wilson's remarks caused grave offence to Sir Robert Robinson, the Nobel prizewinner acknowledged to be the leading organic chemist of his generation. In a letter to Chain, Robinson repudiated Sir Alan's 'fantastic claims' as displaying 'his crass ignorance of the actual situation'. Chain in turn wrote to Edwards, from his own personal knowledge dismissing Wilson's assertion that Beecham's laboratories had made no really novel discoveries since 1957. On the contrary, he maintained, as all properly informed scientists knew, the group's designing of the broad-spectrum and bacteria-resistant semi-synthetic penicillins 'represent the biggest advance in bacterial chemotherapy in the past 20 years'.[28]

Meanwhile, Girolami and Bide were energetically hunting for a corporate 'white knight' that would enter the lists to rescue them from Beecham's clutches. The company they chose was Boots the chemists. Even though it was well down the pharmaceutical sales league table, negotiations proceeded with surprising rapidity. Within forty days of Edwards' bid, on 12 January 1972 Glaxo and Boots announced their scheme for a friendly merger, claiming that both fitted together 'in harmonious and complementary fashion', given their very similar industrial and commercial philosophies.

Glaxo emphasized the advantages it would enjoy through its support from 'one of the best known and most successful retail operators in the United Kingdom', capable of providing 'a powerful buffer against the vicissitudes of international trading'. Boots privately welcomed the scheme as a heaven-sent opportunity to join the world's pharmaceutical top table that was otherwise beyond it. Having a higher aggregate turnover than Glaxo, it announced that it would formally initiate such an amicable scheme.

Some journalists observed that the projected Boots-Glaxo combine would lack the powerful marketing strength that Beecham stood to contribute, and also turn out to be 'inherently more insular' despite publicly announcing plans for substantial expansion overseas. They doubted whether Glaxo would gain anything from the proposed integration. Apart from ownership of a wholesaling subsidiary, Vestric, Glaxo was purely a production company, whereas Boots happened to be in essence a retailer, with 2,000 chemists' stores and only a tenth of its output comprising pharmaceuticals.

On the other hand, Glaxo and Beecham together would form a horizontal merger of two powerful manufacturing companies. Thanks to Lazell's reforms, Beecham was by then an integrated company with four functional divisions, and thus organizationally stronger than Glaxo, which still resembled the old Beechams Pills firm of the Hill era as a loose confederation of unco-ordinated businesses, its profit margin being consistently below Beecham's. Amalgamation with Boots would draw Glaxo some distance away from the core pharmaceutical business it clearly aspired to become. The relatively short time it had taken to reach agreement, and the potential hazards of assembling a viable and profitable combine out of such diverse elements, pose the question of whether Glaxo's cosying up to Boots had been merely a diversionary tactic.

Genuine or not, the Boots-Glaxo merger plan raised the offer value of Glaxo's shares to 503p, well above the original figure of 430p. Beecham was therefore forced to increase its bid to 535p, which Boots trumped with a 573p counter-offer. By then the whole issue had become so complicated through the announcement of the rival Glaxo-Boots proposed link-up, that – as Girolami had no doubt anticipated – a referral was far more likely. Hence on 4 February John Davies, the secretary of state, bowed to parliamentary and media pressure and dispatched both merger proposals to the Monopolies Commission, to investigate whether or not those would be against the public interest To limit the period of uncertainty, Davies expected the commission to report its findings by July.

Taking no chances, in mid-March Girolami announced a move that would convincingly see off Beecham, or in corporate takeover jargon administer a poison pill to the aggressor. That was a 'scheme of arrangement' to form his group into a new company, Glaxo Holdings Ltd. Each 50p share of the existing Glaxo Group would be swapped for one ordinary share, together with 60p worth of unsecured loan stock. As that group's balance sheet had hitherto contained no loans, over £41 million of its reserves were to be capitalized in that new loan stock. All shareholders would thus be 18 per cent better off, giving them the same kind of advantage as Beecham had promised. Glaxo itself would not be out of pocket, because interest on the loan stock was payable out of pre-tax revenue, whereas a higher ordinary share of equivalent value would be subject to tax. Girolami had been sailing close to the wind; the Inland Revenue had to allow that ingenious scheme through, but took action to make sure that it could never be used again.[29]

The four months or so, spent by the Monopolies Commission on its deliberations, were memorable for the vehement battle of words between the two original protagonists, Boots choosing to remain on the sidelines. The Glaxo directors, building on Sir Alan Wilson's earlier assaults, claimed that Beecham had been carrying out ethical drugs research for no more than twenty years – 'on the contrary, since the 1940s', came the retort – and was temperamentally biased towards consumer products. By striving 'merely to exploit a commercial demand for medicines', it had a corporate philosophy totally at odds with Glaxo's own stance as 'predominantly an ethical pharmaceutical company'. In private conversations they hinted that 'we don't really regard Beecham as one of us', whereas they and the Boots top brass were 'the same sort of people'.[30]

For its part, Beecham played its strong suit of marketing skills. It might have quoted a recently published report by a sub-committee of the government-sponsored National Economic Development Council (NEDC), on 'International marketing in the pharmaceutical industry'. British-owned companies, the report stated, could no longer rely on Commonwealth markets and would scarcely shine in continental Europe as long as the UK remained outside the EEC; they therefore needed to deploy their marketing strengths abroad more aggressively. That committee deliberately avoided discussing the potential advantages that the British sector of the industry would enjoy from becoming less fragmented. Senior NEDC staff did apparently hold informal talks with the parties concerned, in order to suggest a merger of Glaxo, Beecham and ICI: a fruitless initiative never revealed to the Glaxo board.[31]

Beecham argued before the commission that its sizeable overseas marketing organization complemented Glaxo's set-up so neatly that their joint post-merger activities could benefit the UK balance of payments by £27.5 million over three years. That over-precise estimate inevitably aroused derision among its opponents, who rejoined that if the Beecham people were to think of employing the same promotional methods for ethical drugs as they did for consumer goods, the medical profession would only be turned off its brands. In reality, senior Beecham managers such as Wilkins had some years of experience in advanced pharmaceutical marketing.

The Glaxo people had by no means finished rubbishing Beecham. Edwards' bid, they maintained, sprang from weakness as its UK patent for Ampicillin was due to expire in 1975. They dismissed his group's R&D efforts as too ineffective and narrowly based. Beecham's answer was that it relied to a greater extent than its British competitors on the efficient multi-disciplinary project system, already employed to spectacular effect in evolving semi-synthetic penicillins.[32]

Glaxo's most devastating salvo was that a take-over would irreparably undermine its own incomparable R&D programme. Its chairman, Wilson, personally informed the commission that successful research depended not so much on the funds available as on the brainpower of individual scientists. Hence any drive to integrate the R&D activities of two such differently motivated companies was bound to sap the morale of the staffs affected and reduce the chances of generating truly innovative ideas. Beecham submitted that eliminating duplication from the two companies' research programmes would allow more therapeutic areas to be investigated, in greater depth. It did, however, promise to allow the respective laboratories to remain independent of each other, rather than being merged into one entity.

The commission, lacking any member who had first-hand experience of scientific questions, accepted Wilson's word on the paramount public interest issue at the heart of its inquiry. That was not marketing, as Beecham had anticipated, but the likely impact of its bid on the volume and quality of pharmaceutical research in general. Commission members therefore closely scrutinized the relationship between size of firm and R&D in the whole industry. On the basis of recently published studies – only one relating to Britain – they found that research intensity, or the ratio of R&D expenditure to pharmaceutical sales, tended to increase with corporate size up to a maximum of £150–180 million turnover and then decline. Two limited exercises undertaken on the commission's behalf studied the ratio of research intensity to size in 15 major British pharmaceutical companies, as well as the number of basic innovations produced by 36 of the world's largest drug multinationals. Once again they concluded that giant companies were not necessarily more successful at research than smaller ones.

All in all, Glaxo's publicity campaign against the bid was appreciably more hard-hitting than Beecham's: companies threatened by hostile bids, and fighting for their existence, are not given to pulling punches. Underlying all its submissions was a 'distaste' for a merger since Beecham's 'image as a thrusting seller of non-ethical medicines and toiletries would damage the work of Glaxo as a well-backed scientific company and seller of ethical medicines'.[33] That bargain-basement image, already held by many commentators and shareholders alike, continued to haunt Beecham for a decade or more: an unwelcome consequence of Edwards' misjudgment in having sown the wind and reaped the whirlwind.

In July 1972, the Monopolies Commission delivered its report, which ran to almost 300 paragraphs. While accepting Beecham's case about the potential benefit from a merger which could yield a higher level of overseas involvement and admitting that 'Beecham has been successful in marketing its own ethicals', it concluded that both the Beecham and the Boots merger projects were against the public interest, on R&D grounds. Beecham's success in its bid would jeopardize the discovery and development of new pharmaceutical products, and also undermine the morale of the scientists currently in Glaxo's laboratories, while a merger with Glaxo would remove any incentive for the Boots people to work hard on research.[34] The Glaxo directors were vastly relieved to be free of Beecham's aggressive intentions; at the same time, they had the opportunity to dump the not very sensible plan to link up with Boots, about which Wilson for one had been unhappy.

Edwards' disappointment at the Monopolies Commission's rebuff was intensified by the predictable loss of Wilson's personal friendship. After several months' reflection, in October 1972 he drafted a memorandum – discussed with a few confidants – to the Department of Trade and Industry. That underlined some shortcomings in the commission's procedures, such as its taking too narrow a view of the public interest, and made one or two more specific suggestions: for example, more members needed with business experience, and no lawyers as chairmen. He duly sent a revised version to the department, and held a meeting with ministers, whose reactions are not recorded.

Far more fundamental was his subsequent critique, made during a public lecture in November 1974, of the commission's findings. Those had, he claimed, overlooked the crucial fact that each year fewer and fewer therapeutically significant new pharmaceuticals were reaching the market in saleable form. One estimate had shown that between 1958 and 1970 'only about 50 single drugs ultimately reached turnovers in excess of £10 million per annum [the minimum level of sales to make a drug commercially successful] in the major markets of the world'. Indeed, most of those blockbusters had been produced by pharmaceutical giants deploying substantial R&D budgets.

To him, corporate size mattered also because of an 'insurance effect', allowing those giants to take greater investment risks than smaller firms could possibly do. Moreover, distribution and marketing organizations throughout the world had to 'depend for their continuity and development on a reasonably strong flow of new products'. Hence the Monopolies Commission had been wrong on both the research and the marketing issue.[35]

By contrast the victorious Girolami, who had led Glaxo's defence with such panache and adroitness, later dismissed Edwards' bid as a 'sterile exercise' which lacked any sound industrial logic and was designed to benefit those holding Beecham shares, at the expense of Glaxo and of the whole industry's future; in fact, Edwards had sought to ensure that both companies' shareholders would receive equal treatment. The historian of Glaxo, Edgar Jones, took the sympathetic view that Edwards was right in aiming to consolidate the fragmented pharmaceutical industry, but that he failed to see the take-over venture through to a satisfactory conclusion.[36] Yet Edwards could do little once he had been thwarted by the entrance of a white knight, in the form of Boots, and by the poison pill of a corporate restructuring that safeguarded Glaxo from further hostile bids.

Although Edwards enjoyed a reputation for being impervious to stress, he did at that time suffer occasional fibrillations, or irregular heart-beats, which he feared might further affect his glaucoma. Although Edgar Jones asserted that he retired in 1972, in reality Edwards stayed for a further three years until his 65th year. Immediately after publication of the Monopolies Commission's report, he called a meeting of senior executives to discuss the group's future. What concerned him above all was the Beecham share price, which had slumped during the months of awaiting the judgment. However, it improved when the results for 1971/72 were published, only days before the report, disclosing that the volume of sales had risen by a fifth and trading profits by one-seventh, higher than forecast. The *Investors Chronicle* for once commended the group, this time for maintaining an unblemished record, and advised readers to hold on to their Beecham shares.[37]

As to its next move ahead, a further bid at home on the Glaxo scale was clearly ruled out, as calculated to reopen old wounds. Yet the financial press kept rumours coming that the group was poised to embark on fresh ventures, for example against Fisons, Reckitt & Colman and – even more bizarrely – Scottish and Newcastle Brewery. To counter Glaxo's assertion that the expiry of the Ampicillin patent in 1975 had provoked the bid, Beecham revealed that that drug currently accounted for only 6 per cent of its profits, and that the more powerful antibacterial Amoxil (amoxycillin) had been launched that May. In any case, it added, the group was stepping up non-antibiotic research.[38]

For certain, future significant growth would have to take place abroad. Continental Europe remained the largest of its overseas areas in terms of sales, profitability and growth alike. To build on that strength, the group planned to take full advantage of Britain's entry into the EEC in January 1973, by introducing a fresh organizational structure. A separate division for Western Europe, dating from 1967, was no longer appropriate, and the new grouping thereafter comprised Beecham Pharmaceuticals under Wilkins, Beecham Products under Halstead, and Beecham Inc., directed by Edwards but with Petley as president. Thus the three brightest younger executives were now actively running the group's operations. Edwards kept the executive vice-chairmanship vacant; whoever he appointed in due course would be regarded as his heir apparent.

Group results for 1972/73 and 1973/74 seemed to be excellent, even though the pound had weakened against most of the world's major currencies, now that two-thirds of trading profits were being earned outside Britain. Edwards did boast, in the latter year's *Report*, that 'there are few other UK companies of comparable size to Beecham which can demonstrate such an international spread of interests or such a rate of overseas growth'.[39] He admitted that trading conditions in Britain remained difficult owing to inflation. Prices of imported ingredients had been steadily rising, while wages and other cost increases were squeezing home profit margins. To compound the group's troubles, government legislation restricted dividend levels, thus pressing down on its share price. The three-day week of January to March 1974, a consequence of the threat to electricity supplies during the coal miners' strike, caused unwelcome disruption to its domestic output.

That year's acquisitions were predominantly in continental Europe, where Beecham bought for £20.5 million the Lingner Group in Western Germany, which had thriving businesses in most neighbouring countries. It offered a range of OTC medicines, and its best known toiletry product was Odol, Germany's leading mouthwash. That brand, currently sold in Britain through a London subsidiary, had been extravagantly advertised there from 1906 onwards as 'the world's favourite dentifrice',[40] and had maintained its popularity ever since. Beecham with commendable despatch merged Lingner's operations with those of Fischer & Fischer. As the French market for veterinary products was the largest in the EEC, Beecham purchased for £1.7 million Laboratoires Néolait SA in Brittany. It sold the latter's animal health and nutritional brands throughout France by means of its own extensive marketing organization.[41]

A further reorganization by Beecham, in April 1974, signalled that the Western Hemisphere, by then the smallest of the group's overseas areas, should no longer be the chairman's personal fief, as it had been since Lazell's time. Instead, its two sides were integrated into Beecham Pharmaceuticals and Beecham Products respectively. According to Edwards, that new arrangement would 'help to ensure that decisions on research and development, investment, and manufacturing and marketing policy are based on a fully comprehensive view of the relevant factors'.[42] Wilkins was appointed group executive vice-chairman, clearly to impose integrated governance which had hitherto been wanting. Petley succeeded him as head of Beecham Pharmaceuticals, despite admitting that he was a 'layman in the field of chemistry'.

Now that the three highly gifted top executives, earlier brought on by Lazell, were in operational charge of the group, they did not always enjoy harmonious relationships with Edwards. His donnish methods of conducting business, holding the view that decision-making took time, and that it was worth proceeding by consensus, must have been frustrating for them. To be sure, Edwards had fostered the careers of all three, so that any one of them could have been in the running as his successor. As it happened, it was the eldest and least assertive, Wilkins, whom he chose for the key post of executive vice-chairman: clearly not the one of the trio who reminded Edwards of the young (Sir) Arnold Weinstock, the ebullient and innovative chairman of the General Electric Company.

Edwards could now permit himself more time for outside commitments. Although he continued the £20,000 annual donation to the Conservatives, he was determined to avoid direct personal links with any political party. Being already well known to every kind of politician and civil servant, he was at various times approached by prominent figures in all main UK parties. For example, in 1972 the Social Services minister, Sir Keith Joseph, a Conservative, requested his comments on a forthcoming speech – which caused a furore – about a generational 'cycle of deprivation'. Edwards did not challenge that provocative phrase, but tactfully indicated that it was not well defined.

Having already been on the board of ICI since 1969, five years later, at Keith's invitation, Edwards became a director of Hill Samuel – still Beecham's corporate financial adviser – while (Sir) Frank McFadzean, chairman of Shell, joined the Beecham board. The cosy world of interlocking directorships held by those and similar industrial and financial magnates intrigued the author, Anthony Sampson, who had earlier dissected the state of contemporary UK society in *Anatomy of Britain* (1962) and subsequent updating volumes.

Sampson probably read too much into Edwards' hobnobbing from time to time with the country's top people. According to that author, Hill Samuel exerted the most pervasive influence of all in the city of London. Impressionistically portraying the versatile Edwards as 'half-don, half-tycoon and half-bureaucrat' and the model of a new-style insider, Sampson reckoned him to be 'a master operator in the world of power'.[43] No doubt Edwards *was* a nimble player in the merry-go-round that would later project him – however reluctantly – into the chairmanship of the vehicle manufacturing company, British Leyland. Yet Keith and Hill Samuel had done him no favour by not warning him of the shoals ahead, during the discussions before he launched the Glaxo bid.

Sir Ronald Edwards retired as chairman of Beecham in May 1975 on his 65th birthday. Notwithstanding his failed bid for Glaxo, he departed with the claim that most of his other aspirations for the group had been met, total sales having more than tripled and trading profits doubled in seven years.[44] To follow in the steps of such an innovator as Lazell had not been an easy task, even for a man of his broad administrative experience. Yet he did match up to Lazell's expectations of his being an organization man by setting up, if rather late in the day, a strongly led managerial structure.

Edwards had put his considerable weight behind the group's overseas expansion. Thus realizing the strategic position of Japan as the world's second largest market for drugs, in 1973 he had established a subsidiary and built up agencies with local companies there. Now that overall sales of pharmaceuticals in Britain were no more than 6 per cent of world demand, Beecham needed to become truly international, just as the NEDC researchers had stressed.

During his first year of 1968/69, aggregate sales outside Britain had been slightly lower in value than those at home. Seven years later, two-thirds of group turnover comprised exports or sales by subsidiary companies abroad. Continental Europe's share had risen from less than one-seventh to nearly a third of the total, although that of the Western Hemisphere had halved in both sales and profit terms. It should perhaps have been more of a concern that the current acquisition programme caused lower-earning consumer products steadily to overtake pharmaceuticals in importance, thereby confirming some of the earlier gibes by Glaxo about Beecham's dependence on proprietary brands.

Following his retirement as chairman and appointment to the advisory role of group president, Edwards aimed to spend much time overseas, in his own words Beecham's 'eyes and ears' while inspecting its many installations around the world. Once he discovered that travelling for Beecham and his favourite pastime of sailing were beginning to pall, he was persuaded to take on the chairmanship of British Leyland.[45] His plans to turn round what was acknowledged to be the UK's most troubled company tragically ended when he died in the following January, struck down by jaundice on top of liver failure during a minor operation.

It is worth putting on record that, for one brief shining moment during his chairmanship, a respected British author seriously posed the question, 'Who has been running the [UK] country all this time: the Government, Beecham's Pills or Hill Samuel's bank?'[46] After the departure of such an establishment figure, the group could never again be claimed to stand anywhere near the centre of financial power in Britain.

15

From Wilkins to SmithKline Beecham, 1975–1988

I N MAY 1975 Graham Wilkins was elected chairman of the Beecham Group at the age of 51. In infancy his elder sister, unable to pronounce his first name, had called him 'the beautiful Bobby', and he remained 'Bob' for life. Lazell had looked forward to one or other of his protégés succeeding Edwards, and Wilkins was the first Beecham chairman to have risen through its ranks and also to have a university degree in science. As if to emphasize their very different backgrounds, Edwards quipped that Wilkins, unlike himself, could actually spell Ampicillin.

A group employee since 1945, Wilkins had initially worked as a research scientist in Macleans' laboratory on testing the quality of toothpaste and Lucozade. He then decided, in his own words, that he was 'better at managing people rather than molecules',[1] and proved his worth when, having been despatched at short notice, he restored to profitability a failing toothpaste plant in India. For five years in the 1950s he was vice-president of Beecham (Canada) Ltd. Stafford, then managing director of Beecham Research Laboratories, recalled him to Britain in 1959, shortly after the first penicillin, Broxil, was launched. Wilkins organized the marketing of the group's pharmaceutical products throughout the world (see Chapter 13). A year later he succeeded Stafford, and went on to create Beecham's Pharmaceutical Division; he and Halstead as his assistant set up the first group detail force in England, of medical representatives to canvass general practitioners about its prescription medicines.[2]

The previous chapter traced Wilkins' steady progression to high office under Edwards. More heavily built than his two predecessors, he was everyone's image of a reassuring country doctor (he hailed from a small Somerset village) and characterized by a colleague – not on the Beecham board – as 'enormously sound, sensible, highly experienced and of the utmost integrity', a tower of strength in tricky situations. If he appeared a little on the stodgy side, he was not loath to stir up political controversy, most vocally over what he regarded as the iniquitous treatment of the pharmaceutical industry by Labour ministers, whom he accused of being driven by 'simplistic ideas'.

Already smarting over the Labour party's threat to take one (never specified) British pharmaceutical company into public ownership, he resented the official counter-inflation measures for rigidly controlling prices and dividends. Those curbs only intensified the group's difficulties arising from the Pharmaceutical (formerly Voluntary) Price Regulation Scheme, that had so aggravated Edwards for lowering the rate of return on drug sales. At a sensitive stage in Whitehall's efforts to restrict national pay levels, he was provoked to declare in his Chairman's Statement in the 1977/78 *Annual Report*:

> We are getting dangerously close to totalitarianism when a Government which lacks the will to seek parliamentary approval for a policy [on incomes] is prepared, regardless of constitutional propriety, to use almost any other means to achieve its ends.

He therefore enthusiastically continued the group's donations, as it had done since Lazell's time, of £20,000 a year to the opposition Conservative party and £1,000 to the right-wing Centre for Policy Studies. In that same statement, his last before the general election of 1979, he urged the Conservative government-in-waiting to espouse market forces and fiscal responsibility by cutting taxes. Even so, he had 'misgivings' over its likely resolve once it regained power.[3]

Those misgivings were amply fulfilled under the incoming regime of Margaret Thatcher, moving him to lament that the level of public expenditure, and hence of taxation, remained too high. Yet in 1980 he accepted a knighthood for services to exports. Despite some highly unwelcome government initiatives towards the end of his chairmanship, three years later he raised Beecham's political donations to £30,000 for the party and £5,000 for the think-tank.

Wilkins, acting as his own chief executive, retained Keith as vice-chairman, but without executive powers. As the first non-accountant to head the group since 1944, he must have welcomed Keith's mature and expert advice, presenting as it did a different viewpoint from his own. He himself believed, as firmly as Edwards had done, that Britain's pharmaceutical industry needed a thorough overhaul. However, he was not the kind of man to leap in with a hostile bid for a sizeable company such as ICI or Fisons.

Instead, like both his predecessors Wilkins was tireless in striving to promote lucrative new drugs. He therefore increased R&D expenditure from 2.7 per cent of total turnover in 1975/76 to 3.6 per cent in 1983/84, a year when Glaxo's proportion was as high as 6.4 per cent. Despite his reputation for exerting constant pressure on his scientists to push new brands 'along the road', he was not rewarded with a blockbuster.[4] Instead, he offered to customers around the world an array of drugs, adapting them as necessary to recipient countries' special needs. It frustrated him that official regulations made the testing of new compounds into such a painstaking and long drawn-out process, averaging eight years from the development stage before a new brand could be brought to market. That left little more than a decade until the patent ran out: scarcely enough time to recoup all the preliminary costs.

Although the UK patent on Ampicillin expired in 1975, that drug continued to sell briskly in a number of markets, while the improved version of Amoxycillin did well in continental Europe. Petley, as his successor in charge of Pharmaceuticals, made some improvements that were valuable without grabbing the headlines. Thus newly developed processes helped to increase yields of the basic Penicillin G and to recover greater quantities of 6-APA than ever before from penicillin brews.

Facing severe competition from rivals, the Beecham laboratories resolutely tackled the still crucial problem of how to combat bacterial resistance to antibiotics. It helped that by 1976 Brockham Park had evolved new compounds that made its penicillin range that much more effective. The most novel was the penicillin-like clavulanic acid, which protected other antibiotics from the enzymes secreted by resistant bacteria. Augmentin, launched in Britain during 1981 and in the United States shortly afterwards, being essentially Amoxycillin plus that acid (officially co-amoxiclav) offered greater success in combating bacteria than had been achieved by any other penicillin.[5]

To guard against the group's becoming over-dependent on antibiotics, in 1972 Edwards had announced that it was increasing R&D expenditure in other therapeutic areas (see Chapter 14). A laboratory at Great Burgh in Surrey now specialized in allergies, virology and human biochemical problems. Its opening in 1976 released space at Brockham Park for concentrating on antibacterial chemotherapy, while research on animal health took place at Walton Oaks. By 1980, three-fifths of Beecham Pharmaceutical's research was into non-antibiotic medicines. Sales of anti-allergy drugs, many under the Bencard name, were progressing satisfactorily, as were those of Pollinex for asthma and hay fever and Maxolon for gastro-intestinal disorders. Beecham also planned to enter the rapidly growing market for antidepressants: four years later it launched its first tranquillizer drug, appropriately named Anxon.

However, that flurry of laboratory construction and activity did nothing to increase the relative strength of the pharmaceutical side, despite Wilkins' personal intervention as a scientist. Between 1975/76 and 1983/84 Beecham Pharmaceuticals' share of total turnover fell from 38 to nearly 28 per cent, and of trading profits from 61 to 46 per cent. In value terms, that turnover rose 2½ times and profits a trifle less. As the index of UK retail prices increased by roughly the same amount, and assuming that inflation rates were comparable overseas, the Pharmaceutical division was scarcely growing at all in real terms. By contrast, Beecham Products' sales and trading profits increased four-fold over those eight years, or by 60 per cent allowing for inflation.

Wilkins did not publicly show the concern he should have done over that growing imbalance between the two divisions. In 1979 he declared himself happy to pay as much 'attention and emphasis' to extending the consumer product business as to boosting pharmaceuticals, because the former was needed to take the strain of the uncertainties inevitable in the latter ventures. 'One of our great strengths,' he argued, 'is the flexibility and resilience which spring from a major presence in two quite separate markets.'[6]

Such a comforting view was not one that would have had any resonance with the Glaxo people. Edwards' bid had jolted its directors, headed by Girolami – like Lazell a gifted and energetic accountant – into setting up a centralized organizational structure, under a high-powered Group Management Committee. In 1980 it established a multi-divisional structure. Four years later, Girolami began to divest Glaxo of non-pharmaceutical assets, from wholesaling and foodstuffs to generic medicines and veterinary products. Although in 1985 Glaxo's total turnover, at £1.4 billion, was only just over a half of Beecham's, its trading profit at £363 million slightly exceeded the latter's £335 million. By 1988, therefore, he boasted that Glaxo's pre-tax profits and market capitalization were well over twice those of Beecham.[7]

To be sure, Beecham would at that stage have been incapable of following the Glaxo path of relying on pharmaceuticals alone. It is unclear why Wilkins did not exert pressure to tilt the group back towards higher-earning pharmaceuticals. The arrival of a blockbuster drug would have done a great deal to strengthen his hand; yet this burly and clever man was probably too much at ease with himself to act decisively enough as chairman. He would have disagreed with Edwards' statement that because the drives of individual executives needed some friction against which to pit their wits, an organization should never be allowed to run too smoothly.[8]

Wilkins' main problem was that the strong-minded Halstead, in charge of Beecham Products, had become the executive 'number two' in the group, a status confirmed by his being ranked above Petley, by then at Beecham Pharmaceuticals, in the *Annual Report's* list of directors. A Cambridge graduate in the natural sciences, Halstead had joined the group in 1954, becoming product manager at Macleans before setting up medical representative teams in Britain under Wilkins. Since then he had specialized in marketing.

Halstead recalled that as a boy, he had helped his parent, a grocer, on the family stall in Lancaster, selling geese on Christmas Eve against rival stall-holders by means of a loud voice and claims of the best quality. 'That way,' he observed, 'you get goods that don't come back and customers that do.'[9] He and old Thomas Beecham would have relished swapping yarns.

As marketing vice-president of Beecham Products Inc. from 1962 to 1964, Halstead masterminded a toothpaste campaign in the United States which, according to Lazell, 'completed his education' in promotional skills. Meanwhile he had on his own initiative studied marketing policy at New York University Graduate School. In 1964 Lazell brought him back to run Beecham Food and Drink Divison, two years later renamed Beecham Products.[10]

Observers were impressed by Halstead's being a kind of human dynamo. Ernest Saunders, of Guinness fame, who had once worked under him, remarked on his 'fearsome reputation for toughness. American techniques, he said, were what it was all about, and the soft [*laissez-faire*] English approach would not do.'[11] At Beecham Products, Halstead accepted no excuses whatever when driving his marketing teams to build up and maintain brand shares.

Halstead maintained that it was better to purchase businesses with established reputations than to spend time on developing new products. To him, an acquisition policy was the equivalent of pharmaceutical R&D, as the newcomers brought into the group not only tangible assets and brands but also technical and marketing expertise.[12] Thus in the 1960s, when mixer drinks to dilute whisky or gin were growing in popularity as supermarket shopping took off, he had purchased Hunts of Yarmouth to introduce canned and bottled tonic water. During Wilkins' chairmanship he bought no fewer than 17 consumer product companies. Since 1980 alone, he had expended no less than £250 million on corporate acquisitions.

Only two of those purchases were British, neither remotely of Glaxo's size. Scott & Bowne, celebrated for its Scott's Emulsion (see Chapter 12), was an old associate of Beecham, which as long before as 1938 had taken over its Western Hemisphere business by acquiring Eno Proprietaries. In 1978 Halstead now bought for £14 million all its interests in the rest of the world, most notably in Britain and Australia, including products such as multi-vitamins and sun creams.[13] The second British acquisition was of the Bovril Group, bought in 1980 from the provision millionaire, Sir James Goldsmith, for £42 million. Halstead judged that its celebrated brands of Bovril, Marmite and Ambrosia rice pudding could be easily fitted into the group's still very thriving food and drink operations.

Halstead's other acquisitions were intended to strengthen Beecham's presence in the United States and continental Europe. The costliest to date, at £47 million, was a purchase in 1976 from the American pharmaceutical giant, Merck, of its Calgon consumer product division, producing water and fabric softeners – already familiar in Britain – throat lozenges and a cough mixture.[14] Halstead was thus aiming to widen the group's product range and goodwill in the American consumer market and thus triple its sales there. Merck, currently second in the world pharmaceutical league, just like Glaxo was moving in the opposite direction from Beecham through disposing of its non-core units.

The American Jovan Inc., acquired in 1979 for £40 million, specialized in fragrances, or perfumes. Its sales had of late been running at the equivalent of £37 million annually, and Halstead grasped the opportunity to expand the highly lucrative fragrance market in the United States, as well as in Britain, continental Europe and elsewhere in the world. Not surprisingly, pharmaceuticals were meanwhile falling behind. In 1980 Beecham was no higher than 34th in the ranking of drug sales in the United States, ideally its most important market.

Such increasing imbalance clearly weakened the Beecham group, by helping to explain its lack-lustre performance between 1977/78 and 1979/80. Over those three years turnover went up by more than a fifth, but trading profits remained virtually static, and even fell slightly in 1979/80. Beecham ordinary share values, which had for some time hovered around 180p, in 1980 reached a low point of 120p. To be sure, earnings were depressed by currency losses owing to the strong pound, while the substantial resource cost of launching Aquafresh toothpaste in the United States affected sales of other consumer products there.[15] Yet that campaign soon proved its worth by securing a 15 per cent share of the toothpaste market.

Then, as the world economy gradually emerged from its recession, and the previously overvalued sterling currency depreciated by a quarter against the dollar, Beecham's share price rose uninterruptedly until in 1982–83 it averaged as high a level as 350p. On the back of its improved profit margins and competitiveness overseas, during the autumn of 1981 Augmentin (see above) made its appearance in Britain. The group advertised the drug as effective against more bacterial infections than any other orally taken penicillin or the fungus-derived cephalosporins, the latter being an important antibiotic range in Glaxo's armoury. However, Augmentin made a slow start and did not gain approval in the United States for another three years. By 1981/82, overseas business accounted for two-thirds of group turnover. Then a welcome growth in pharmaceutical sales led to an increase in their earnings of over a third, so that for the first time they contributed half of total trading profits.[16]

Not that Halstead let up on his acquisitions. In 1982/83 those included two American corporations, J. B. Williams, which sold toiletries and proprietary medicines in the United States and continental Europe, and DAP Inc., which held a third of the US market in sealants and other home improvement projects. Those purchases jointly cost over £100 million, paid for out of a successful £197 million rights issue. The group now had to accommodate two substantial non-core product groups, do-it-yourself as well as perfumes.

Results for 1982/83 disappointed the market. Although reported turnover and profits increased by 17–18 per cent, at least a third of that growth was due to exchange gains. Sales had been strong in continental Europe and further east, but Wilkins had to warn shareholders that the year's progress had not been achieved without pain. He undertook that everyone in the group would be made to work hard at increasing efficiency, above all in reducing costs.[17]

Beecham's share price, having recovered late in 1980, now began a lengthy downward slide. However, as the world was by then well into a mild economic recovery, hopes were high that group performance would improve in 1983/84. That year, aggregate turnover and profits turned out to be up by 13–14 per cent; yet alarmingly, while sales of consumer products increased by nearly a fifth, those of pharmaceutical sales showed a rise of less than 4 per cent and its trading profits of under 6 per cent.

The *Investors Chronicle*, never backward in pointing out that the Emperor Beecham's finery was less than met the eye, expressed the doubts of many concerned parties by enquiring whether Beecham should now be regarded as a consumer goods group with pharmaceutical interests. To be sure, some promising new drugs were taking their time to appear. Augmentin awaited official approval in the United States and Japan, but Nabumetone, for arthritis, the injectable broad-spectrum antibiotic Timentin and a drug for thrombosis could not yet be sold in Britain.[18]

In July 1983 Petley took early retirement from the group. Whether he departed for personal reasons – that he and Halstead did not get on – or over policy differences is not known, but his successor, the easygoing John Pollard, later remembered as being averse to change, could scarcely have possessed the dynamic qualities required to keep the pharmaceutical division on its toes as Halstead was doing with his consumer product people. Wilkins chose that moment to appoint Halstead as group managing director, to be combined with his divisional post. They were joined on the Executive Committee by Pollard and Edward Bond, the group financial controller; Halstead undoubtedly dominated the proceedings. Even so, Wilkins' announcement early in 1984 that he would retire that July, when only 60, came as a total surprise.

Wilkins, later said to have recently 'let things drift a bit', looked forward to more leisure time with his family and on the golf course and the waterways.[19] Besides, he had his outside directorships, of Hill Samuel since 1977 and of Thorn EMI since 1978. Although Halstead was the automatic successor at Beecham, some had reservations about him owing to his close identification with consumer products. At the age of 57, that ebullient man had the energy and stamina to make Beecham's life still more eventful than it had recently been.

Once appointed, Halstead kept up the group's practice of government-bashing. A resolute campaigner for free markets and the abolition of price curbs, he complained about the Department of Health and Social Security's measures to force drug manufacturers' rates of return on capital below the average rates in UK industry as a whole. He was further incensed in November 1984 when that department restricted the range of medicines that could be prescribed on the NHS, by striking out most laxatives, antacids, pain-killers and vitamin tablets; Beecham's multi-vitamin Orovite was one casualty. However, as a supporter of another grocer's offspring, Mrs Thatcher – who awarded him with a knighthood in 1985 – he distanced himself from the 'fashionable' criticism of government policies in general.[20]

Halstead's declared strategy was to promote Beecham's growth by 15–20 per cent annually, so as to make it one of the country's three or four largest British companies by market capitalization; that measure currently put eight blue-chip enterprises ahead of the group.[21] To that end, he raised the amount spent on acquisitions over the following year to no less than £380 million. He must have been backed by the Executive Committee, which included Pollard, in charge of Pharmaceuticals, the 49-year-old John Robb, who took over Beecham Products, Donald McClure, head of the newly established Cosmetics and Home Improvements Division, and Edward Bond at finance.

Aware that the current system of policy-making and head office internal communications were not working as they should, Halstead established a line of command that allowed for delegation. Each divisional chairman and managing director would periodically report to the board on how the Executive Committee's instructions were being carried out. To emphasize the importance of information-sharing, in June 1985 he organized a conference of senior executives in Frankfurt, Germany. He also began a drive to speed up the launch of new drugs. It really looked as if he was on the way towards establishing a corporate structure that would enable Beecham to operate as a single entity rather than as a holding company with two divisions yielding little if any synergy.[22]

Then Halstead continued to favour home improvements and cosmetics as the group's preferred growth points, in 1984/85 spending over £100 million on buying home improvement companies.[23] Those were mainly in the United States, but a fifth of that sum went on purchasing Copydex plc and Uni-Bond (Holdings) plc, British companies which specialized in adhesives and a range of do-it-yourself lines. On the toiletry side, in January 1985 he bought British American Cosmetics from BAT Industries – the former British American Tobacco – for the unprecedented sum of £125 million. Among its most prestigious subsidiaries were Yardley & Co. of London, dating back to 1770 and celebrated for its English Lavender soap and perfumes, as well as Lenthéric Ltd and Morny Ltd with their impressive range of fragrances. Halstead planned to double the group's sales of all those brands, by marketing the products of what he renamed Bond Street Cosmetics jointly with the Lancaster and Jil Sander ranges.[24]

Although outside observers had difficulty in grasping the logic of Halstead's current expansion programme, they did allow him a few months' honeymoon period. Then from October 1984 onwards the market value of Beecham ordinary shares began to slide, leading some corporate finance experts in London to speak openly of possible takeovers by American or Japanese companies, such as SmithKline Beckman of Philadelphia. However, given the Beecham group's widely recognized knack of choosing worthwhile acquisitions, by the end of the year its share price had improved to just over 350p.[25]

Halstead was gratified to learn that American investors had of late 'discovered' Beecham shares. He endlessly stressed that while the group was unique in British industry for its spread of products, 'in the US we are what is called "diversified drugs"', a 'very highly rated category, including companies like Bristol-Myers and American Home Products'.[26] Yet the first real test of his stewardship would come when the group's results to March 1985 were announced in mid-year.

Turnover for 1984/85 was then found to have risen by 18 per cent, but operating profits only by 9 per cent, allowing for exchange rate adjustments. More worryingly, the absolute level of profits earned by Consumer Products may have been higher than those of Pharmaceuticals – where no new blockbuster drug was after all in sight – but its profit margin was only half as large. A mixed picture emerged from overseas. The group's turnover and profits were lower in continental Europe than in America, where Amoxil was the most widely prescribed antibiotic, but launch costs for Augmentin and Timentin had halved earnings there.[27] All in all, Beecham was finding itself increasingly exposed to potential predators.

If a Shakespearian tragedy was about to unfold, two opening scenes were played off-stage during the summer of 1985, when poor corporate performance brought down two chairmen-cum-chief executives of British blue-chip companies. By coincidence, those entrusted with pulling those companies round were both Beecham men, namely Wilkins and Keith. Thorn EMI, the electrical giant, had suffered a 31 per cent fall in profits after its chairman, Peter Laister, had made a number of policy blunders, which reduced the share price by half. That June, Wilkins and other non-executive directors forced Laister out, in what was remembered as 'the most dramatic boardroom coup the City [of London] has witnessed for years'. Wilkins, elected in his place, rapidly restored the company's former level of profitability in a show of energy he had scarcely displayed at Beecham.[28]

Two months later Keith, a non-executive director of STC, better known as Standard Telephones and Cables, was prompted by its institutional investors to sack Sir Kenneth Corfield, its chairman, after some blunders that included the botched acquisition of ICL (International Computers Ltd). Keith was then asked to take over.[29] No one, least of all Keith, at that time anticipated that the same drastic surgery would be performed on Halstead, although in 1951 he himself had rid the group of Buckley and Hobrow when its performance was likewise unacceptably mediocre (see Chapter 12). Halstead by then exercised greater control over Beecham than either Edwards or Wilkins, having no strong deputy. Keith as sole but non-executive vice-chairman was therefore the main counterweight on the board. He had already warned Halstead that he must correct the increasing imbalance between the group's two divisions, something that was not heeded.

Halstead's response was to plan the group's largest ever single acquisition to date, for £255 million, of Norcliff Thayer Inc., which made OTC medicines such as Tums, then the second most popular antacid remedy sold in the United States, and the Oxy range of treatment for acne. That purchase was financed largely by American bank loans, thereby increasing the group's overall debt. Outsiders condemned the purchase for costing too much and for hardly at all benefiting Beecham's ethical drug side. Halstead did himself no favour when, being interviewed for a feature article in that October's *Management Today*, he let slip the injudicious remark that 'people are bored with the fact that our results are so consistently good'.[30]

Keith begged to differ. To be sure, Beecham was not facing the same kinds of financial crises as Thorn EMI and STC had done. Instead, a less immediate but deep-seated problem in the group was about to be disclosed when the half-year results to September were published. Those would show a meagre 2 per cent increase in overall trading profits, while pharmaceutical earnings had actually declined. Once exchange rate adjustments were made, Beecham had not shown any growth at all. Quite as worryingly, while pharmaceuticals had been struggling, consumer products had failed to generate enough earnings even to meet the current R&D bill, that year running at £86 million, or 3.3 per cent of turnover.

Convinced – as he put it mildly – that 'things were not quite right', Keith acted with all speed. On the morning of 11 November 1985, supported by the two other non-executive directors, Lord McFadzean the chairman of Shell and Denis Allport, chairman of Metal Box, he summoned Halstead and in a few words demanded his resignation. Unlike Buckley in 1951, Halstead went quietly, no doubt expecting that his departure would pass off without undue comment.

Unfortunately for Halstead, Keith ratcheted up the whole affair by calling a press conference that same afternoon and releasing the half-year results, with the comment that 'the group required a younger and more dynamic management, and that this dynamism should start at the top'. In contrast with 1951, the institutions had exerted no pressure, but Keith had been shaken by some earlier pointed criticisms in reports by leading stockbrokers. In his seventieth year, he proposed himself as caretaker chairman, appointing John

Robb, currently chairman of Beecham Products, as chief executive at the age of 50. Robb had the reputation of being a hard taskmaster, not over-creative but good at delivering results.[31]

Halstead's abrupt dismissal startled the market, causing Beecham's share price to plunge. Commentators predictably looked back to Edwards' bid for Glaxo 14 years earlier. Then, according to *The Times*, 'Beecham was a much-fancied glamour stock', as against the less alluring Glaxo. Currently, Beecham shares were worth only a fifth of Glaxo's, which was enjoying the runaway success of its blockbuster Zantac for duodenal ulcers. Writing about Halstead, two broadsheet newspapers – whose sub-editors should have known better – headed their pieces with the nineteenth-century threadbare phrase of a 'bitter pill'.[32]

Some articles blamed Halstead for paying too much attention to his outside interests. He responded by pointing out that those interests took up only one-tenth of his time, and that his 'Whitehall contacts were important for the company', without making clear the nature of those links. Others pointed to his failure to impose on Beecham an overall strategy and sense of purpose. They cited regular squabbles between the two divisions, even at board level. Communications with business analysts and the press were said to be poor, so that incoming telephone calls were too often not returned.[33]

As stated above, Keith had spoken to Halstead on a number of occasions about his excessive concentration on proprietaries. Halstead was not unaware that Beecham's pharmaceutical side needed to be built up, as in the long run its medicines could provide greater shareholder value. If an unnamed former senior executive was to be believed, there was indeed a great deal of work to be done on that side. The Pharmaceutical Division 'had been standing still for a while, maybe even for about twenty years'. Such a remark might well have been sour grapes.[34] Yet perhaps none of Lazell's three successors in the Beecham chair had enthused its research teams as he had done in the heady days of the 1950s and 1960s.

Keith had his battle plan ready. He at once engaged an executive-search – known as a head-hunting – company to locate a new chairman, all too conscious that a predator might at any time launch a hostile take-over bid during the current period of uncertainty. ICI and Unilever were spoken of as likely bidders, both with the intention of breaking up the group. Unilever is said to have approached the American drug corporation, SmithKline Beckman, to see if it would acquire Beecham's pharmaceutical assets, while Unilever itself would retain those lucrative food, soft drink and household brands that had for so long competed with its own products.[35]

In the event, no bids came Beecham's way, and John Robb as chief executive found himself fully stretched in the task of restructuring the group. His most urgent need was to reduce costs and also dispose of non-core activities; the first to go would be the home improvement and wine and spirit businesses, which should never have been acquired in the first place. Within a year, he had 13 disposals under way, encouragingly set to raise £237 million. With Keith's approval, he honoured Halstead's earlier commitment to purchase Norcliff Thayer Inc., the manufacturer of OTC products, as calculated to strengthen Beecham's presence in the United States. The group's long-term debt increased to more than £500 million by March 1986, and gearing – or net borrowing – was up from 14 to 33 per cent of shareholders' funds. As Lazell had found in the early 1950s under similar pressure to restore the group's fortunes, a major problem was its shortage of working capital.[36]

Keith and his recruiting team soon discovered that no entrepreneur of sufficient calibre in Britain was available or willing to take on Beecham in its current state. They therefore extended their search across the Atlantic. That move did not disappoint Keith, who rated top executives in the UK as 'sleepier, less adventurous, less mobile and less ambitious' than their American counterparts. 'Too many British chairmen,' he added from many years' experience of banking and industry, 'sit on their backsides in their offices and study figures and the bottom line.'[37]

Early in 1986 he tracked down an entrepreneur who had positive ideas about shaking up the Beecham Group from its foundations. Robert Bauman, then aged 54, had no experience in pharmaceuticals, having started his career as a coffee salesman in General Foods Inc., before becoming chairman and chief executive of a financial services and aerospace conglomerate. A recent take-over by another conglomerate had demoted him to a vice-chairman's post, and he was anxious to become his own master once again.

Bauman succeeded Keith as Beecham's chairman that September, at a £700,000 annual salary, the second highest in Britain. He insisted on having executive powers, a proviso that reduced to the rank of managing director John Robb, who in nearly a year had achieved so much on the group's behalf as chief executive. Otherwise Bauman came over as outgoing, clean-cut and youthful in looks, relaxed and unpompous. Some were put off by his Harvard MBA graduate's 'florid business school speak, as though he had memorized motivation manuals from the US marines', notorious practitioners of organizational jargon. At Harvard Business School he had learnt, by means of its case-study method, leadership skills needed to develop decision-making, and as a team leader how to manage those with conflicting views and objectives.[38]

In the event, Bauman spent his first few months in listening carefully to the views of executives and other staff, only to be dismayed at finding what he viewed as a rigid hierarchical outlook and the lack of a unified corporate ethos. Thus middle managers, first-rate in their specific jobs, were to his mind not pulling their weight in the group as a whole because they ignored the wider picture. The Beecham Pharmaceuticals people he found especially difficult to tame. While energetically chasing after a useful pipeline of drugs, they seemed weak on the marketing side; Beecham turned out to have fewer co-partnership agreements over drugs than most of its rivals.

The Consumer Product executives were appropriately 'lean and mean', holding their own over price and quality against the likes of Unilever and Procter & Gamble; yet their record on developing new products was poor. No fewer than four-fifths of all group earnings came from brands that were 60 years old. Hence, he concluded, the Beecham Group could never reach its potential until he had pressured all employees into working as a team to implement a forward-looking and coherent corporate strategy.[39]

Bauman therefore started with the board. Keith and Robb had already moved out certain directors; that gave him the opportunity to recruit outside businesspeople of mature experience, who would assist him to force through his transformation plan. Early in 1987 he appointed (Sir) Hugh Collum to be head of finance. In his mid-fifties, Collum had for some years been Cadbury Schweppes' financial director, and was now ready to take on a fresh challenge elsewhere. He arrived to discover few of the techniques currently employed in Britain's most advanced companies, such as strategic planning, a treasury function to raise capital and manage corporate funds, and internal auditing.

In July 1987, Peter Jackson of BOC (the former British Oxygen) became head of personnel, which he pointedly renamed human resources. Like Collum, he found a great deal that needed up-dating, in his case salary levels, a management development programme, and performance appraisal. The third of those who may be called Bauman's 'enforcers' joined in January 1988, six months after Keith's retirement from the board: the American-born Joanne Lawrence, an earlier subordinate at Avco Corporation of Bauman, who recruited her as head of corporate communications.[40]

Bauman's eight-member Executive Management Committee (EMC) was the first to hear his preliminary ideas on the way ahead. Most urgently, he felt he had to convince a seemingly complacent and even antagonistic management about the vital need for change, if necessary by imposing tough measures. That initiative should help Beecham to rise from 23rd in the world pharmaceutical league to global leadership within five years. To make specific recommendations on how to achieve that ambitious goal, a management consulting firm would be required. The one chosen was the US-based Booz-Allen & Hamilton. Although some managers were later claimed to have argued that Beecham had never before employed outside consultants, Lazell had in fact sought that same firm's advice on two separate occasions. Bauman insisted on Booz-Allen's staff working alongside group employees and instilling in them an appropriate degree of enthusiasm for reform.[41]

Booz-Allen first of all tackled the Pharmaceutical Division, where senior managers allegedly remained 'sceptical [over the need for change] and recalcitrant'. It found that the division badly needed greater resources, to ensure not only adequate levels of R&D expenditure, but also more effective marketing of its drugs. Booz-Allen also scrutinized the EMC's ultimate target of achieving world leadership in the industry. It found that to outperform its peer groups in both the United States and continental Europe, Beecham's profits would have to grow by 15–20 per cent a year, and earnings per share by upwards of 20 per cent annually: all virtually impossible targets to meet.

To be sure, earlier group chairmen had expressed similar aspirations, without in the event being capable of fulfilling them. Now the EMC and consultants alike came to accept, as Bauman later expressed it, that 'Beecham couldn't do it alone'. For example, its R&D expenditure in 1987/88 was £114 million, only half of Glaxo's £230 million in 1988. As it sorely needed far greater research facilities in the United States – the primary global source of pharmaceutical know-how – Beecham must seek a merger of equals with one American corporation or another which could offer appropriate marketing as well as R&D skills to carry forward its planned reconstruction programme. After 130 years of independence, Beecham was poised to encounter, through a process of amalgamation, the most momentous event in the whole of its history.[42]

Table 15.1   *Beecham's sales and net profit, 1950/51–1988*

	Home sales	Overseas sales	Total sales	Net profit
	(£000)			
1950/51	16,060	7,007	23,067	918
1951/52	16,985	8,426	25,411	887
1952/53	16,906	8,246	25,152	767
1953/54	15,265	8,246	23,511	1,061
1954/55	14,628	8,155	22,783	1,483
1955/56	17,791	9,402	27,193	1,579
1956/57	18,495	10,479	28,974	1,863
1957/58	22,924	11,228	34,152	2,511
1958/59	27,940	12,468	40,408	3,196
1959/60	34,510	15,449	49,959	3,790
	(£ million)			
1960/61	37.1	19.2	56.3	4.1
1961/62	39.0	19.6	58.6	4.0
1962/63	37.1	19.5	56.6	4.1
1963/64	39.7	21.4	61.1	4.6
1964/65	42.2	24.8	67.0	5.2

	Home sales	Overseas sales	Total sales	Net profit
1965/66	44.9	32.1	77.0	7.8
1966/67	48.3	38.2	86.5	9.4
1967/68	63.7	51.8	115.5	10.9
1968/69	68.7	65.2	133.9	12.6
1969/70	78.8	82.3	161.1	14.8
1970/71	83.0	98.9	181.9	18.1
1971/72	93.4	125.7	219.1	20.8
1972/73	109.0	150.8	259.8	24.9
1973/74	137.7	200.7	338.4	29.1
1974/75	160.0	276.4	436.4	32.8
1975/76	199.4	367.2	566.6	50.1
1976/77	232.7	488.1	720.8	68.9
1977/78	259.8	606.3	866.1	76.2
1978/79	308.9	614.2	923.1	80.4
1979/80	357.6	670.8	1,028.4	80.6
1980/81	543.8	650.9	1,194.7	88.2
1981/82	586.1	820.9	1,407.0	119.0
1982/83	633.7	1,068.7	1,702.4	151.9
1983/84	675.6	1,268.4	1,944.0	161.8
1984/85	731.2	1,557.9	2,289.1	167.3
1985/86	849.0	1,753.7	2,602.7	174.5
1986/87	857.7	1,872.4	2,730.1	200.4
1987/88	687.6	1,792.6	2,480.2	239.4
1988	674	3,628	4,302	367

Sales and net profit: 1950/51–1987/88 Beecham Group *Annual Reports*.

Note: profit figure for 1950/51 higher than that in Table 12.1, as it includes subsidiaries' retained net profits.

Towards GlaxoSmithKline,
1988–2000

I T TOOK SIX MONTHS, until May 1988, for the Beecham Group's directors to narrow down their search for a suitable partner to five American pharmaceutical corporations. When vetting those candidates, executives had in mind two criteria, or what they called 'key screeners': the need to find a shared vision of creating an integrated global company, and, more tangibly, ownership of extensive research and development, and marketing assets, in the United States.[1]

The most promising corporation to emerge was SmithKline Beckman of Philadelphia. (The phonetic similarity between Bauman, Beckman and Beecham, however distracting, was purely coincidental). That corporation already knew a great deal about Beecham, as two years earlier it had considered purchasing the group's pharmaceutical operations if Unilever's anticipated bid had gone ahead. Even longer established than Beecham, dating from 1830 and affectionately dubbed 'the fine old house',[2] in 1988 SmithKline stood 11th, to Beecham's 23rd, in the ranking of world pharmaceutical sales. Prescription drugs accounted for almost half of its turnover, as against Beecham's 28 per cent.

A merger currently seemed out of reach, as SmithKline's market capitalization was about a fifth higher than Beecham's, thanks to the immense popularity of its drug Tagamet, for combating ulcers: the first in the world to achieve blockbuster status with $1 billion annual sales, and an early example of 'discovery by design', where knowledge gained about the causes of illness and about the effects of drugs on humans allowed scientists to target a promising compound and test it in a methodical way rather than by the previous 'blind' chemical screenings, or even relying on 'serendipity'.[3] From 1985 onwards, however, Tagamet was being overtaken by Glaxo's rival product, Zantac; although having an almost identical molecular structure to Tagamet, it was marketed far more aggressively around the world.[4]

Moreover, SmithKline's purchase in 1982 of a diagnostic equipment company, Beckman Instruments, out of the Tagamet profits had done little to strengthen the corporation.[5] That entry into a new and non-core field had distracted its senior management from utilizing to the full its considerable knowledge base in biochemistry and molecular genetics. For a decade it failed to launch a new product of any importance, so that the ending of patent protection for its other successful drug, Dyazide, was a further setback.[6] In 1987–88 SmithKline's net earnings fell from $570 million to $229 million, thus reducing its capital market value to the level of Beecham's, at £3.5 billion ($5.6 billion).

Once a basis of equality had been reached, Bauman opened negotiations with its chairman, Henry Wendt. Two years his junior and employed at SmithKline since 1955, Wendt was characterized as 'patrician, very genteel and diplomatic'.[7] Their first few meetings involved sizing up each other's very differing characters, to see if they could work together in harmony. The ambitious and single-minded Bauman was clearly the dominant figure; he had impressed his shareholders and the markets alike by the progress he had made in reviving Beecham's fortunes. Wendt, on the other hand, as chief executive before becoming chairman in 1987, had presided over what some journalists had called his corporation's period of 'lost opportunity and management incompetence'.[8] Only after establishing a rapport did the two men turn to questions of organization and finance.

Both envisaged a merger of equals, to avoid giving bonuses to either group of shareholders. However, only two previous British companies had made cross-border amalgamations of that kind, both with Dutch competitors, respectively forming Royal Dutch Shell in 1907 and Unilever in 1927. A transatlantic link-up seemed more complex owing to the widely differing legal, accounting and taxation systems in their two countries. Even so, both parties overcame all hurdles, and in April 1989 they announced the creation of SmithKline Beecham (SB), capitalized at £9 billion, and the first pharmaceutical merger on that scale.[9]

The combine was registered in July as a British-owned company, its head office being in London, still a major financial centre offering significant tax advantages. However, since SmithKline had extensive if lately under-employed R&D facilities in Upper Merion, Philadelphia, SB's operational headquarters would be sited there. The issued ordinary share capital was £332 million, divided between A and B shares, plus £20 million worth of the US-based SmithKline Beecham Corporation preferred shares. Because Beecham was contributing far more in profits, a £1.3 billion loan stock was created, to be liquidated within a year. A straight exchange of shares then took place, using a financial device known as stapled stock to give comparable rights to SB investors in the two countries. Beecham shareholders were offered 87.8 Class A shares, plus £175 worth of loan stock, for every 100 existing shares.

Those in SmithKline received one preferred and five new ordinary B shares in exchange for each of their shares. That arrangement stood until 1996, when it was replaced by a single class of ordinary shares.

Wendt became chairman, regarding as 'traumatic' the prospect of moving to London, 'but I can think of worse places', he graciously admitted; it cost the company £52,000 a year to rent a house for him there.[10] Bauman would be in overall charge as chief executive. Eight board members were appointed, four from each side, a woman being made a non-executive director in 1991; eight years later there would be two women directors to eleven men. Beecham's main pharmaceutical specialities included antibiotics such as Augmentin and the cardio-vascular Eminase, while SmithKline contributed Tagamet and vaccines as well as further cardio-vascular drugs. While Beecham had its largest market in continental Europe, SmithKline was strong in Japan as well as the United States, where Beecham's 750 strong sales force would join the 1,150 of SmithKline. With a combined research staff of 5,000, R&D expenditure would be as high as £393 million, at last ahead of Glaxo's £323 million.

Wendt at once drafted 'The promise of SmithKline Beecham', setting out the merger's overall objective: namely, to form a more powerful healthcare company than either unit could have created on its own. Shortly afterwards Joanne Lawrence, the recently appointed American communications executive, invented the phrase *Simply Better* (a pun on SB, which chose to register it as a trade mark).[11] Human resources and communications were to be the crucial factors in achieving that goal; 'in a winning organization, everyone works together – heart and mind – in pursuit of a higher purpose', in SB's case to enhance its performance and thereby its competitive advantage. Senior executives, from Bauman down, would ensure that management targets were fulfilled. Bauman relentlessly kept up the pressure at every level, coercing his people into acceptance that innovation was a continuous process. As soon as they achieved any given goal, he imposed further ones so as to keep up the momentum of change.

After their retirement Bauman, jointly with the former human resources director, Peter Jackson, and Joanne Lawrence, wrote *From Promise to Performance: A Journey of Transformation at SmithKline Beecham*, published by Harvard Business School Press in 1997. Essentially a manual about how to lead a workforce to pursue radical corporate change, the book chronicles each step in SB's early progress through four phases: defining a new strategy, building a new structure, developing a new corporate culture, and designing an appropriate management system. Its version of events, valuable as a first-hand account, is presented very much from a head-office perspective.

Philip Streatfield, a manager at SmithKline who remained with SB until 2000, in his version of events provided an insight into life away from headquarters. In 1989 he greeted with 'disbelief' the news of his corporation's merger with a company 'that we knew was second-rate compared to our operation', and later with dismay evidence that the 'former Beecham people' were rapidly gaining the upper hand. Sceptical about instructions from on high that all managerial decisions must be objective and based on rational argument and not on emotion, he admitted that he and his colleagues had to gauge which of their recommendations would be acceptable to senior ranks. They reckoned that although Bauman set targets, he lacked the superior knowledge to grasp in any situation what the right answer should be.[12]

A more general narrative of events to 1994 appears in the case study published by the French business school, INSEAD, entitled 'The making of the *Simply Better* healthcare company: SmithKline Beecham'. It is based on plentiful quantitative data and informed commentaries, in the context of the industry as a whole and the market for its products. Its theme is how the merger and SB's subsequent strategic initiatives 'fundamentally transformed what industry analysts had described as two "also-rans" into a formidable player ranking fourth among the world's leading pharmaceutical firms'.[13]

Bauman would have been aware of the academic studies presenting evidence that no acquisition in the drugs industry over the previous 30 years had increased market share for the firms concerned.[14] To disprove those findings, he resolved that his merger should be far more thoroughgoing than earlier ones had been. He therefore embarked on what the *Economist* graphically termed a 'wrenching top-to-toe reorganisation designed to eliminate, once and for all, any vestiges of the two separate companies'.[15] His instrument was a seven-member and equally driven Merger Management Committee (MMC) which exercised control over no fewer than 300 multi-disciplinary teams.

Their labours were assisted by the prestigious American consultancy giant, McKinsey & Co., of New York, a familiar name in British industry for having advised many of the UK's most famous commercial names, as well as the Post Office, the British Broadcasting Corporation and British Rail. Each SB departmental manager was required to liaise with his opposite number on the other side of the Atlantic, aware that one or other of them would eventually be made redundant.

That integration programme shrank the workforce from nearly 63,000 to 57,000, mostly by redundancies in Britain and the rest of Europe, but none in the United States. Bauman insisted that administrative and production staff must be the ones to go, through the closure of no fewer than 60 manufacturing plants and 25 distribution centres; he rightly spared marketing and R&D employees, closing only seven research facilities.

All his pressures clearly had an adverse effect on employees' working and personal lives, so that a number of executives resigned. Thus Robb, who had done so much to keep Beecham afloat after the coup and was then downgraded from chief executive to general manager, left in September 1988 while the merger talks were still in progress, as did James Pollard, head of the not yet tamed Pharmaceutical Division. Others suffered health and family breakdowns. Even Wendt as chairman later commented that 'people tire of incessant change; they become anxious to return to a stable and predictable organization.' Bauman would not yield an inch, resolutely declaring that 'we cannot afford to lose momentum; our sense of urgency needs to be maintained' because 'change is a continuous journey and not a destination', so that 'no decision is perpetual and there is no "right" way of doing things that cannot be improved'.[16]

The merger inevitably pressed hard on SB's finances. Its direct costs amounted to £77 million, and the group had to make a £500 million provision for restructuring, intended to bring costs down and thus pay for itself over three years. Although in 1989 turnover rose by 14 per cent, trading profit was up by only 3 per cent. The level of group borrowings alarmed commentators by exceeding £1.75 billion, which reduced net assets to a negative figure of £275 million.

Early in 1990, Bauman and Wendt visited staff at nearly a hundred of the group's centres scattered round the world. There they outlined SB's overall strategy: to achieve at least a 15 per cent annual growth in its performance. As such a rate of growth depended largely on success in the two areas of R&D and marketing, the costs of both functions would have to be reduced, to match cut-backs in manufacturing and administration.

Top management's insistence on R&D being monitored each quarter to check costs and staff numbers came as a 'bolt of lightning' to independently minded group scientists.[17] John Chappell, head of Pharmaceuticals and tipped as Bauman's eventual successor, angrily reacted when head office took matters further by declaring that SB must increase its gross profit margin from the current 61 per cent to at least 66 per cent; trading profit per employee would therefore have to rise from £13,000 to at least £33,000. When Chappell gave notice to quit, only two years after the departure of his predecessor, James Pollard, Bauman and Wendt concluded that it was time to recruit heavyweight replacements, equipped with years of pharmaceutical experience, from outside the group, predictably from the United States.

In mid-1990 Jan Leschly, formerly president of the Squibb Corporation, of Princeton, New Jersey, joined the SB board as head of Pharmaceuticals, being assured of consideration for the chief executive's post four years hence, when Bauman planned to retire. A tall and edgy Dane with an abrasive manner, Leschly brought with him the reputation of a hard task-master. The press endlessly recycled his previous sporting record as the world's tenth-best tennis player, a one-time quarter-finalist at Wimbledon. Quick-thinking and a rapid talker, he was credited with making up his mind on all issues in five minutes; unsurprisingly, his decisions did not always turn out to be sound ones.[18]

Hugh Collum at finance prophesied that the recalcitrant Pharmaceutical Division would 'have a grenade thrown into it' by the new man.[19] Sure enough, Leschly speedily cleared out the division's entire senior management, and then overhauled the group's R&D programme, claiming that the two former companies' research operations had not yet been adequately integrated. He set a target that within five years one quarter of all SB drugs should be new ones. As the patent for Tagamet would be expiring in 1994, as early as 1991 he launched in the British market Seroxat, an anti-depressant which two years later reached the United States as Paxil. That was joined by Relafen for arthritis, Kytril for nausea, to be introduced in the continental European and Japanese markets, and Havrix, a hepatitis A vaccine for Europe.[20]

Leschly intended to meet his target partly through collaborative agreements with rival companies, by co-marketing and licensing SB's products and also buying in new drugs. Smaller biotechnology firms, mainly in the United States and Britain, were already evolving potentially useful compounds that they themselves could not afford to develop and market. Thus he arranged to join with Genelabs Technology Inc. to develop a vaccine for hepatitis E and C. By 1994 SB had over 130 agreements of that kind, having created what was hailed as one of the best networks of external alliances in the industry.[21]

Also in 1990, Jean-Pierre Garnier (known as JP) was head-hunted from Schering-Plough of Madison, New Jersey, to become SB's president for North America. His appointment, at the early age of 43 – Leschly being 50 – confirmed the key role that the United States was now playing in SB's grand strategy, both as a source of technical knowledge and as a market for its production. French-born but a naturalized American, he had gained a Ph.D. in pharmacology; as an entrepreneur he was very much in the hyperactive Bauman and Leschly mould. 'His intensity, compared with most bosses, is extraordinary, such is the aggressive drive and speed with which he discourses in his French-inflected American', a journalist wrote much later. 'All the time you get the impression of a ferocious intellect bubbling away like a pressure cooker fit to burst.'[22]

Garnier continued to reside in the United States, where £2 billion worth of SB's total £4.5 billion sales took place in 1990, earning 46 per cent of group trading profits. The company's research centre in Philadelphia, which Garnier ran, contained 267 laboratories employing 2,000 research staff, or one-fifth of its world-wide total.[23] In Britain, SB was able to sell off the Ambrosia, Bovril and Marmite assets, together with the fragrance businesses of Yardley/Lenthéric and Astor/Lancaster, for a net total of £330 million. Those divestments and the initial benefits from restructuring increased the year's trading profits, chiefly from pharmaceuticals, by 30 per cent, although turnover had risen by only 5 per cent. Group borrowings were reduced to £680 million, while the general improvement in performance helped the share price to rise by a third, outperforming the market by one-tenth.

Leschly was later to admit that 'it took two to three years before we had one company', at the stage when the merger had been consolidated throughout all its installations. On top of all the ambitious targets already set for the group, Leschly and Garnier proposed an even steeper one: to turn SB into the world's largest healthcare enterprise within five years. In the autumn of 1991, with Bauman's enthusiastic approval, they planned even bolder measures based on radical new ideas. Since 1989, as trading profits passed the £1 billion level, its market capitalization had increased from £7 billion to £12 billion; yet that still left an estimated £3 billion gap between itself and the industry leader, Merck. Without powerful initiatives, SB could well descend into the lower half of the world's top 20 pharmaceutical companies.

Early in 1992, the group therefore unveiled a master plan for the next two to five years. Leschly would consolidate the R&D operations into four therapeutic categories, basically covering the nerves, inflammation, infections, and the heart and lungs. Those categories were to be split up between group research units throughout the world. On the consumer products side, demand for OTC medicines should be increased to replace prescription drugs as they came off patent. In August, SB therefore concluded a $660 million (£426 million) agreement with Marion Merrell Dow of Missouri to pool OTC sales in the United States – the world's leading market in self-medication – making SB the fifth largest OTC provider there.[24] Yet that year's results proved to be disappointing, with turnover up by only 11 per cent and trading profit by 8 per cent. Even so, earnings per share had increased by a half since 1989, while its ordinary share price was at its highest for some years at 550p, up from 250p at the date of the merger. SB had come a long way, but much remained to do.

In two important respects, 1993 proved to be a turning point in the group's fortunes. SB entered the crucial field of genetics, and it astutely healed the rift between the pharmaceutical and the consumer brands sectors.

The genetic revolution, elsewhere lately under way, had the potential to double and redouble the pace of biological discovery over a decade. In February SB's head of research, George Poste, explained to senior managers how current work in genetics would make it possible to identify the structure and function of genes, the hereditary chromosomes transmitted down the generations. An individual's complete set of those genes was known as a genome, strikingly portrayed in SB's *Annual Report* for 1994 as 'the body's complete instruction book written on skeins of DNA tightly coiled in the chromosomes at the heart of the cell'. Knowledge obtained from mapping the genomes should enable scientists to grasp the underlying mechanism of disease, rather than having all too often to treat the symptoms alone. Once they understood individual susceptibilities to illness, they would be given greater opportunities to deal with prevention as well as cure.

On Poste's recommendation, in May 1993 SB bought a 7 per cent share in Human Genome Science Inc. (HGS) of Maryland, which held the world's largest genetic database on people. At a cost of $125 million (£81 million), that stake gave SB access to information which, its R&D team anticipated, would in time assist the discovery of far more sophisticated drugs and vaccines. SB was the first major pharmaceutical company to invest in gene sequencing, and its scientists throughout the world had the opportunity to access HGS's database as needed. High-speed computers, pioneered by SB's collaborators, generated sequences for as many as 20,000 genes a year. The group installed those computers at its eight research establishments in five continents, to store the data and link them with already known sequences.[25]

From a scientific point of view the share purchase, creating the largest biotechnical corporate partnership until then, has been described as 'the genomics era's big bang', propelling forward that area of research. Financially, too, in the longer term SB stood to achieve substantial benefits, as HGS went on to uncover far more significant genes than either could possibly utilize on its own. The two partners were therefore able to lease the spare ones to other pharmaceutical corporations. As Poste later maintained, while many outside observers had criticized SB for the high cost of the original purchase, 'history has shown [that] we got the bargain of the century'.[26]

Also in May 1993, Leschly completed yet another radical review of the group's corporate strategy. That involved integrating the healthcare potential of the four sectors of Pharmaceuticals, Consumer Brands, Clinical Laboratories and Animal Health. The most problematical sector was Consumer Brands, where SB badly needed to dispel the commercial image that had dogged Beecham for too long. He therefore renamed it Consumer Healthcare, to include OTC medicines, oral care (for example, Macleans toothpaste and mouthwashes) and nutritional drinks such as Lucozade, Ribena and Horlicks. All personal care products, including Amami and Silvikrin shampoos and Brylcreem, had to be sold off, together with the last surviving toiletry brands, mainly those manufactured in continental Europe.[27]

Leschly's reforms boosted the level of turnover by nearly a fifth in 1993 to £6.2 billion and trading profit by 12 per cent to £1.2 billion. As earnings per share were continuing their rise from 18p in 1989 to no less than 30p that year, SB found itself one of Europe's top 25 enterprises in terms of market capitalization. The board felt confident enough about the group's overall progress to announce in April at the Annual General Meeting that both Wendt and Bauman would be retiring in a year's time, as agreed at the time of the merger.[28]

By coincidence, that announcement came shortly after Glaxo's deputy chairman and chief executive, Ernest Mario, had been sacked by Girolami, chairman since 1985, whose dismissal four years earlier of Mario's predecessor, Bernard Taylor, had not yet been forgotten. Mario, an American unschooled in British ways, had reportedly made some tactical misjudgments, falling out with the US Food and Drug Administration over some regulatory issue and being worsted in a dispute with SB over a patent.[29]

There was no love lost between Leschly and Mario: a handicap for both companies in an era of gradually increasing mutual co-operation. However, although Glaxo's total turnover fell a little short of SB's, its trading profits were nearly 50 per cent higher, with earnings per share at 43p to SB's 30p. It also had the ulcer drug Zantac as its blockbuster at a time when SB's far less popular Tagamet was only a year away from losing its patent protection. Mario's successor was the microbiologist (Sir) Richard Sykes, whose actions would increasingly impact on SB's strategy over the next few years.

In April 1994 Leschly succeeded Bauman as chief executive, while Wendt handed over the chairmanship to Sir Peter Walters, former chairman of British Petroleum and the Midland Bank and an SB non-executive director since 1989. Walters' solidly British background would, it was hoped, quell fears that the group was becoming too Americanized.[30] At once Leschly tackled the second major event of the decade, the managed care revolution.

Partly because of more stringent official regulations after the sedative Thalidomide was found to cause birth defects, drug prices generally had been soaring. National providers of drugs, whether governments in Britain and Japan or medical insurers in the United States, therefore put pressure on supply firms to keep down costs. On the distribution side, American pharmaceutical benefit management companies had emerged to secure the most advantageous wholesale prices through large-scale purchasing and to achieve economies by modernizing delivery systems.

Just when President Bill Clinton was planning his (ultimately abortive) Health Reform Programme, aimed at accelerating the United States' trend towards managed pharmaceutical care and the containment of drug costs, within a month of becoming chief executive Leschly acquired for $2.3 billion (£1.6 billion) Diversified Pharmaceutical Services Inc. (DPS), one of America's three leading benefit management companies. His intention was to market SB's branded products alongside American-made drugs through DPS; to that end he contracted with its former management company, United Healthcare, to gain access to data on the 6 million US members of the health maintenance organization system. The Federal Trade Commission thereupon opened an investigation, after which it banned exclusive sales arrangements of that nature on competition grounds: a move that destroyed SB's chances of ever making DPS profitable.[31]

In October 1994 Leschly went on to buy from Eastman Kodak the consumer health business of Sterling Winthrop Inc. for £1.9 billion ($2.9 billion), later selling off its North American operations to Bayer AG of Germany for $1 billion. At a time when SB was supplementing its OTC range with non-prescription versions of drugs such as Tagamet HB for heartburn, that purchase made it the largest seller of OTC products throughout continental Europe – on top of its impressive record in the United States – and hence the third largest in the world. One noteworthy product acquired was Panadol, the top-selling painkiller that contained no aspirin.[32]

Leschly's ambitious purchases of DPS and Sterling Winthrop's assets, both for cash, forced up the group's gearing ratio – of net borrowings to shareholders' funds – to 205 per cent, thereby increasing the burden of interest payments. To meet the costs of integrating those purchases, restructuring charges came to £580 million. Although trading profit in 1994 increased by 15 per cent to £1.24 billion, net earnings fell below £700 million. For once the group's share price held, as SB had shown itself able to offset that year's expiry of the Tagamet patent by successfully marketing alternative drugs such as Seroxat/Paxil and Engerix B; not yet blockbusters, but reasonable earners.

There was a small but telling sign that relations with the UK government were on the mend. To bolster the anti-Labour campaign by earlier chairmen from Lazell to Halstead, the Beecham Group had since 1967 been making annual donations to the Conservative party (see Chapter 13). Unexpectedly, in 1991 SB increased that sum from £30,000 to £50,000 a year and doubled to £10,000 the regular contribution to the Centre for Policy Studies. Then in 1992 and 1993 its only payments were £5,000 to the latter, no donations being made from 1994 onwards: a move towards political neutrality that Glaxo followed a year later.[33]

Leschly, while chief executive designate, had in mid-1993 formed a 'Vision 2000' team, later renamed 'SB: Beyond 2000', to draw up the group's longer-term strategy. Animal Health was vulnerable as the smallest of SB's four divisions, with steadily shrinking profit margins. Late in 1994, therefore, he sold that division to Pfizer for $1.45 billion (£920 million). Thus SB would from then on concern itself exclusively with human healthcare. He took the opportunity of that and recent acquisitions to integrate the group's supply arrangements in markets outside continental Europe and North America.[34]

Then in January 1995 Leschly found himself confronted with the totally unexpected news that Glaxo had launched a bid for its smaller British-owned rival, Wellcome: the largest hostile take-over in UK corporate history. Girolami while chairman had ruled out any acquisitions, but his successor, now

Sir Richard Sykes, reversed that policy. Wellcome, ranking only 25th in the pharmaceutical league, currently had a shortage of drugs in its pipeline, while its most lucrative product, Zovirax for herpes, was due to come off patent in 1997. It was also at odds with the regulator over some newer drugs such as Retrovir for Aids. Sykes persuaded the vendors' principal shareholders, the Wellcome Trust, a medical charity, to sell its 40 per cent stake. Glaxo then made a £9.3 billion cash offer, partly financed out of the £2 billion liquid resources that Girolami had built up.[35]

The Glaxo Wellcome combine became the dominant British-owned player in the industry, and thus presented a potential challenge to SB. Small, wiry, lean and dapper, Sykes at 53 was credited with possessing 'a formidably sharp mind, a rare (for a scientist) gift for communication and a terrier-like enthusiasm'. Leschly and Garnier might well match his restless energy; yet Sykes had an additional drive not fully appreciated by SB's non-British duo. His father, when working for the UK machine tool makers, Alfred Herbert Ltd of Coventry, had watched helplessly as foreign operators came to dominate that industry in Britain. Sykes was resolved that the British-owned sector of the pharmaceuticals business should not suffer the same fate.[36]

The *Economist*, always with an eye for a good pun, characterized his bid for Wellcome as 'waging Sykological warfare' in a move 'to wrest market power back from the administrators and distributors who now hold the health-care purse-strings'.[37] Sykes himself, being equally concerned at the unduly high level of Glaxo's current overheads, aimed to spread its substantial R&D and marketing expenditures over the two former companies' annual revenue, up from £5.7 billion to £7.9 billion. Only two years remained before the patent on its blockbuster drug Zantac, together with that on Wellcome's Zovirax, expired.

Meanwhile, Leschly could draw comfort from SB's own success in having evolved further drugs to replace Tagamet, such as the antibiotic Augmentin and Havrix, the world's first vaccine for hepatitis A, now universally on sale. The SB results for 1995 showed turnover up by 8 per cent and for the first time exceeding £7 billion, while trading profits, at £1.6 billion, yielded a handsome 23 per cent margin, pharmaceutical profits being up by nearly 13 per cent. OTC sales were already benefiting from the inclusion of Sterling Health's medicines.

Then Sykes's bid for Wellcome set off a rash of mergers in 1995–96 among competitors, such as the Swiss Ciba-Geigy with Sandoz to create Novartis, and the Swedish Pharmacia with Upjohn of Michigan. SB's share price had been rising ever since early 1994, but stalled as investors realized that the group was up against the same problem as the former Beecham had encountered in the late 1980s. However optimistic the forecasts it issued about its future performance – of 15 per cent compound increases in annual earnings to 2000 and beyond – it had no prospect of becoming a world pharmaceutical leader without entering into a fresh merger.

Even so, Leschly chose to concentrate on forming SB into a truly globalized company. In 1995 he set up the Worldwide Supply Operations (WSO), which linked up its supply chain right through from purchasing to the manufacture, packaging and distribution of final products. His Facilities Integration Programme reduced the number of manufacturing sites from 79 to 61. WSO's logistical counterpart, Project Enterprise, was founded three years later, with supporting software, to standardize the transaction systems between plants and markets, thereby improving lead times in manufacturing, levels of consumer service, and the use of working capital.[38]

In January 1996 Leschly planned to integrate – under J. P. Garnier, newly promoted from head of Pharmaceuticals to the group's chief operating officer – the management of Pharmaceuticals, Consumer Healthcare, and also a newly formed Healthcare Services Unit to include both DPS and Clinical Laboratories, both admittedly in poor shape. He also brought together into a brand-new research centre, at New Frontiers Science Park in Harlow, Essex, the group's R&D scientists from four existing sites. He claimed that such a move ended the 'old identities' of Beecham and SmithKline in this field.[39] With some panache, he announced his determination to transform SB into a 'world-class, customer-driven company' as 'one of the global mega-players in the healthcare industry beyond the year 2000', categorically dismissing any merger talk.[40]

By August 1996 Leschly had changed his mind, when he commissioned SB's financial adviser, the investment banking firm Morgan Stanley, to draw up a list of potential partners in the industry for a merger of equals. That top secret exercise bore the code name of Project Hoops, after the metal ring used in basketball. The companies being investigated were disguised by the names of well-known American basketball teams.[41]

Predictably, the first company on that merger list was Glaxo Wellcome. In March 1997, therefore, Leschly held exploratory talks with Sykes. Having recently completed a massive integration programme with Wellcome, Sykes, now chairman, laid down stringent conditions. SB would have to sell off its consumer healthcare assets, and thereby reduce its potential merger stake to one-third. Sykes also expected his own new chief operating officer, Sean Lance, to be executive head of any combine: a post that Leschly yearned to hold himself. Indeed, at that time Sykes may have lacked interest in SB as he was busily chasing a more attractive partner elsewhere.

A recent case study of Glaxo has suggested that the acquisition of Wellcome had 'bought time but did not solve any of [Glaxo's] fundamental problems', of finding new drugs that were not coming forward from its own pipeline. 'This left Glaxo almost immediately searching for a second, bigger deal.'[42] Sykes is known to have proposed that year, and again in mid-1998, a merger with the Swiss firm, Roche, itself only two-thirds the size of Glaxo Wellcome but with a seasoned marketing force of 750 that had spectacularly assisted Glaxo in the US to make Zantac into a blockbuster there. As it happened, Roche turned down both of his overtures.[43]

Leschly likewise rejected Sykes's terms, and looked to the next name on Morgan Stanley's list.[44] As no other British-owned company happened to be 'marriageable' – the word used by Edwards in 1971 – the only alternative was a further transatlantic merger.

In November Leschly therefore made contact with John R. Stafford, chief executive of American Home Products (AHP) of New York, a diversified-drugs corporation that stood eighth in the global pharmaceutical league table, SB being ninth; conveniently, it had extensive R&D operations in Philadelphia close to SB's. Such a merger deal would create the world's leading drugs company, with a record market capitalization of £75 billion.

A twopence-coloured piece in the *Sunday Times* pictured Leschly as the 'ferociously driven Dane', in a 'dark and heavy' frame of mind,

> brooding over a move that would catapult him into the top tier of the world's industrialists. Within his grasp lay the biggest deal [of any industry] in corporate history, one that, after a career in which the biggest prizes always seemed to elude him, would take him into the same league as Microsoft's Bill Gates, Intel's Andy Grove and General Electric's Jack Welch.[45]

AHP could boast a higher turnover, equivalent to £9 billion as against SB's £7.8 billion, although its trading profit was slightly lower. The range of both companies' products appeared to be close enough for an integration programme to yield estimated annual savings of £1.5 billion. Yet many commentators were frankly astounded at Leschly's choice of corporate partner. To them AHP was pedestrian in its strategy and performance, financially conservative and lacking both glamour and vision.

Relying heavily on its OTC medicines, most notably oral contraceptives, AHP undertook very little in-house research. SB, on the other hand, was an R&D- and marketing-intensive enterprise through and through, being dubbed 'touchy-feely' or emotionally driven in a way that the colourless AHP was not. On top of everything, AHP faced massive penalties in the American courts as its appetite suppressants, Redux and Pondimin, were under investigation for causing heart problems.

Senior AHP executives on their part had understandable reservations over their opposite numbers' dynamism, as calculated to clash with their own more measured ethos. A financial analyst portrayed the SB people, strung up to breaking point after a decade of relentless conditioning from Bauman onwards, as follows: 'They're an egotistical bunch. I think they want to conquer the world.'[46] Mutually wary or not, SB and AHP went ahead with negotiations.

As soon as news of the talks became public, on 20 January 1998 SB's share price soared, only to fall back when investors grasped that any merger would be of equals and yield them no rewards. Worse still, the combined company would inevitably fall into American ownership; hence its listing on Wall Street in New York would curb British fund managers' rights to hold its shares. Then more political worries began to be raised.

According to industry reports, never denied by Glaxo Wellcome, Tony Blair as British prime minister feared that the UK economy would lose control of SB's substantial assets in what was acknowledged to be one – the other being oil – of the country's most successful and lucrative industries. Blair is therefore said to have contacted Sykes, a familiar face on educational and scientific committees, and requested him to take action to keep SB in British hands. On 24 January, Sykes accordingly interrupted the negotiations with AHP, by telephoning Leschly and asking, 'Jan, is it too late?'[47] Already struggling with AHP over financial issues, Leschly at once broke off those talks, and agreed that he and Garnier should meet Sykes, together with Glaxo Wellcome's new chief executive, Robert Ingram, and its finance director, John Coombe.

Arriving in New York on Monday, 26 January, the parties remained in virtually continuous session, allowing themselves very little sleep in an effort to reach consensus before any leaks occurred and caused turmoil in London and elsewhere. Their common view of an advanced healthcare product and service company appeared to be not so different from the meeting of minds between Beecham and SmithKline in 1989. However, the resulting pressure of time made the memorandum of agreement, arrived at on Wednesday the 28th, less watertight than it should have been.

The two companies' relative share valuations fixed the equity division at 59.5 per cent for Glaxo Wellcome to 40.5 per cent for SB. Sykes would be executive chairman and Leschly chief executive of a future Glaxo-SmithKline combine, Sykes's previous candidate, Sean Lance, having been of late eased out as allegedly not up to it. Although having two designated executive posts, and joint chairmanship of the Merger Integrating Committee, seemed like a recipe for trouble, on Thursday 29 January the SB board agreed to these terms, set out in a document that Sykes was having printed. Only then did Leschly inform the jilted AHP directors that negotiations with them would not be resumed. Next day, after Glaxo Wellcome's board had likewise given its approval, news of the merger was officially released.

That news lifted SB share values by 65 per cent and Glaxo Wellcome's by a fifth, and reverberated around the world's pharmaceutical community.

Cynical observers muttered that Leschly had taken up with AHP 'simply to flush out Sir Richard'. Even they could not have envisaged the next startling twist in this convoluted saga.[48]

Only three weeks later, Sykes delivered yet another of his psychological bombshells. On 20 February he abruptly summoned the other four negotiators to meet him in New York. There he stated that the memorandum, as drawn up, would just not work; in particular, a radical change would be needed in the allocation of the proposed top posts. At the ensuing lunch, tempers allegedly became so frayed that not a single mouthful was eaten, and both sides' delegates returned to Britain in a rancorous mood.[49]

Back in London, a mini-summit attempted to resolve the impasse. Sir Peter Walters, SB's chairman, and Leschly called a meeting with Sykes and his deputy chairman, Sir Roger Hurn. That broke up when the SB people twigged that they were being manoeuvred into what Leschly later called 'a takeover without approval [consent]'. On the 23rd, therefore, he publicly announced that the negotiations were at an end, accusing Glaxo Wellcome of breaking a solemn compact – which the signed memorandum was not – and not at all logically maintaining that the two sides had come up against 'insurmountable differences'.[50]

On the London Stock Exchange, reaction to the news was dramatic, setting off a fall of £13.5 billion in the joint value of the two companies' shares, much to the disgust of investors who had bought them on the unwarranted expectation of making a profit from the merger. While Glaxo Wellcome merely informed the Stock Exchange that the merger discussions had terminated, Sykes was reported to be active behind the scenes, urging SB's major institutional investors to pressure Walters and the other non-executive directors into firing Leschly.[51] However, the notion of a third boardroom coup, after those of 1951 and 1985, found little favour among the institutions.

Tony Blair's reaction to news of the débâcle is not known, but the House of Commons Science and Technology Committee, meeting in April, expressed serious alarm at the consequent risk to the national interest, as Glaxo Wellcome and SB between them accounted for a fifth of the UK's total private-sector expenditure on scientific research. Having looked forward to the merger as being what they called 'an opportunity to create a national champion with R&D at its heart', that month committee members interviewed Sykes and Leschly to ferret out what had gone wrong.

The two men's evidence to the committee left those members none the wiser. Its report concluded that the merger talks must have been poorly researched; if not, both sides could only have entered those talks 'in denial of their [companies'] mutual incompatibility'. Hence, it went on, 'they had

readily embarked on an adventure [or gamble] with major assets', and should be
held to account for such headstrong behaviour. The two principals were never
censured, and the last word went to Sean Lance, who as Glaxo Wellcome's
passed-over chief executive was convinced that he could have done a better
job had he still been in post: 'They've made a right real cock-up of the
negotiations', he stated. 'Egos took precedence over future strategies.'[52]

In fact, between 1998 and 2000 far more was at stake between the companies
than merely a clash of personalities. For instance, their organizations and
strategic outlooks, having developed along entirely separate paths, differed
in many respects, and would have to be brought into some kind of harmony
before any future merger could be made to work. Thus SB appeared to be more
globalized than Glaxo Wellcome, thanks to the WSO. One analyst partly
hit on the truth by saying in 1998 that both companies supported 'as large
an R&D spend and marketing infrastructure on as slim an administrative
production and distribution base as possible'.[53] That was broadly correct for
SB; Glaxo Wellcome's failure to pursue a comparable slimming exercise would
markedly reduce its bargaining power over the next two years.

The anxiety felt by the European Commission and the US Federal Trade
Commission that the Glaxo-Wellcome merger would deter innovation in
that new combine – admittedly to do with the specific area of anti-migraine
drugs – were allayed by Sykes's almost obsessive determination to achieve a
'critical mass' or optimum size for his R&D expenditure, as the sole means
of ensuring a healthy pipeline of drugs. However, he neglected the problem of
overheads, alarmingly high even before his acquisition of Wellcome. Between
1998 and 1999 he even allowed employee numbers to rise by 14 per cent.

The strategy adopted by Leschly, on the other hand, involved seeking to
make his group's R&D effort more productive by giving research scientists
greater personal initiatives. He continued to limit research to the four
therapeutic areas he had laid down in 1992, as furnishing the most appropriate
mix of drugs for the American market, which by then accounted for 51 per
cent of SB's total sales, compared with Glaxo Wellcome's 42 per cent. As to
its organization, he introduced a so-called hollowing-out process. In 1998–99,
so far from increasing his workforce, he reduced it by 8.5 per cent overall,
mainly in production and administration, while allowing numbers to rise in
R&D, sales and marketing.

Leschly duly slimmed down the group's production side, through fresh
agreements with biotechnology and other companies to develop drugs on
behalf of SB, which would be responsible for the costly downstream processes
of clinical trials and beyond. He closed many of his group's 67 plants around
the world and formed the remainder into 'centres of excellence'. Sales and
marketing, in which SB currently enjoyed a competitive advantage, were

likewise strengthened. Between 1995 and 1999, SB's turnover therefore rose by nearly 20 per cent to £8.4 billion and trading profit by almost 40 per cent to £1.7 billion, whereas Glaxo Wellcome achieved increases no higher than 11 per cent and 2 per cent respectively.[54]

To be sure, Sykes's scientists had failed to discover replacement drugs for Zantac and Zovirax, since 1997 no longer shielded by patents. Those in the pipeline, optimistically earmarked to take over, all failed tests with the US Food and Drug Administration or proved to be ineffective on other grounds. Now that SB's performance was catching up with that of Glaxo Wellcome, Sykes's relations with Leschly improved beyond recognition. In spite of their earlier disagreements, the two were soon collaborating to harmonize their structures and adopt each other's most appropriate business practices.

In February 1999, Leschly announced a Global Supply Initiative, to make therapeutically active compounds in Britain and Ireland, and then have them processed in five sites world-wide, including the United States, Puerto Rico and continental Europe. SB would be the first company in the world to link primary production with a secondary packaging system. That October, Sykes launched his Strategic Master Plan, which basically aligned Glaxo Wellcome's manufacturing supply chain to that of SB, ensuring uninterrupted provision of drugs to the public. As Garnier later recalled, 'by observing best practice on each side we ended up [in] transforming our companies'.[55]

Leschly in turn followed Glaxo Wellcome's lead in concentrating more exclusively on pharmaceuticals and healthcare. In April 1999 he sold to an American competitor the loss-making Diversified Pharmaceutical Services for $700 million (£403 million), less than one-third of its original price. The *Sunday Times* had earlier characterized its acquisition in 1994 as 'arguably one of the worst purchases by a big British company in recent years' because Leschly had too late found himself barred from exclusive dealing.[56] For SB a happier outcome was its disposal in August of Clinical Laboratories for $1 billion (£633 million) plus a 29 per cent stake in the acquiring firm, Quest Diagnostics.

By September 1999, much of the pharmaceutical industry was in the throes of a merger mania, infectious enough for half its major units throughout the world that year to plan – without necessarily completing – amalgamations of one kind or another. The American giant, Warner-Lambert, opened negotiations with AHP, only to precipitate a counter-bid from Pfizer. A resulting Pfizer-Warner Lambert combine, which once again left the luckless AHP out in the cold, promised to be the undisputed global leader.

The overheated atmosphere throughout the industry appears to have moved institutional investors in Britain to give Leschly a 'bad beating' for allegedly holding up a merger, and put pressure him on him to resign: a step they had hitherto avoided. Early in November, Leschly gave Sykes a lift in SB's corporate jet to a pharmaceutical industry conference in Switzerland. Perhaps he took the opportunity to inform Sykes in advance of his announcement, to be made in a month's time, that he would be retiring as SB's chief executive in the following April, eight months early, and handing over to Garnier.[57]

Once Leschly made his retirement public in December, an immediate jump in the SB share price reflected investors' conviction that their months of waiting for a merger were as good as over. Sykes had already focused on Garnier as 'one of the best guys in the business', and with almost indecent haste he now proposed secret face-to-face talks with SB. Early in the new year, so as to evade the curious, negotiating teams from the two companies met in France. Given that the recent alignment of their structures had made both sides familiar with one another's workings, the deliberations proceeded without a hitch. On 17 January 2000 the two parties jointly announced the long awaited merger of equals.

The new GlaxoSmithKline (minus a hyphen, and GSK for short) would be British-owned, 75 per cent of its shareholders being UK residents, with its head office at Greenford, to the west of London.[58] However, SB's pressure ensured that the operational headquarters were to be in Philadelphia, rather than at Glaxo Wellcome's Research Triangle Park in North Carolina. Sykes became the non-executive chairman, having been tipped for a prestigious academic job as rector of Imperial College of Science, Technology and Medicine in London. SB also won the chief executive's slot for Garnier, who would continue to be based in Philadelphia. His opposite number in Glaxo Wellcome, the American-born Robert Ingram, would be serving under him as chief operating officer.

Likewise, an SB executive, Tachi Yamada, was made chairman of R&D, in preference to the Glaxo Wellcome candidate, James Niedel, whose colleague, John Coombe, became chief financial officer. SB's shareholding stake in the new combine rose almost imperceptibly from 40.5 per cent to 41.25 per cent. Some analysts felt that SB should have held out for 45 per cent; others, including the *Financial Times*, judged that it had 'certainly done better [than previously] in terms of the management carve-up – not a bad result for the smaller company'.[59]

By securing the key strategic positions on GSK's future board, Garnier and his colleagues were ideally placed to implement the hollowing-out policy that had served their former group so well in recent years. Few would by then have remembered that three decades earlier, Sir Ronald Edwards had striven to create a British pharmaceutical giant by means of a hostile bid for Glaxo. That bid had come to nothing; yet it now looked as if SB, rather than Glaxo Wellcome, would largely control the future running of GSK. Edwards might have appreciated the irony of that unexpected reversal of fortune.

Table 16.1   *SmithKline Beecham's sales and net profit 1989–2000 (£ million)*

	Home sales	Overseas sales	Total sales	Net profit
1989	728	4,169	4,897	130
1990	801	3,963	4,764	847
1991	562	4,123	4,685	638
1992	456	4,763	5,219	711
1993	483	5,681	6,164	813
1994	498	5,994	6,492	72
1995	560	6,451	7,011	970
1996	580	7,345	7,925	999
1997	607	7,188	7,795	978
1998	624	7,458	8,082	1,118
1999	671	7,710	8,381	1,276
2000	–	–	8,612	1,508

Sales 1989/99. SmithKline Beecham *Annual Report*. 2000 GlaxoSmithKline *Annual Report*.

Net profit 1989/99. 'Profit attributable to shareholders'.

Epilogue

ALTHOUGH Glaxo Wellcome and SB reached an agreement on a merger as early as January 2000, two moves by the American competition regulator, the Federal Trade Commission (FTC), delayed its introduction until the following December. First, the FTC ruled that the new combine would illegally dominate the market in the areas of herpes and nausea suffered by cancer patients undergoing chemotherapy. It therefore required SB to sell off Vectavir for herpes to the Swiss Novartis and Kytril for nausea to another Swiss company, Roche. Likewise, Glaxo Wellcome was made to discontinue work on a further herpes drug, and to compensate the biotechnology firm, Cantab, for assistance already given.

The second delay arose when in September the FTC objected that the company would have the power to dominate the market for anti-smoking drugs if Glaxo Wellcome's Zyban were to be on sale concurrently with SB's Nicorette gum and Nicoderm patches. The two companies' lawyers denied that any overlap existed, as the former was a prescription-only medicine while the latter pair fell into the OTC category. The FTC accepted that argument, and the merger went ahead on 27 December.[1]

GlaxoSmithKline (GSK) now became the second largest pharmaceutical enterprise in the world, behind the recently merged giant, Pfizer-Warner Lambert. Its market capitalization exceeded £110 billion ($165 billion), while annual turnover came to £15 billion ($22.5 billion), or 7.4 per cent of the still fragmented global drugs market. It claimed industry leadership in a number of therapeutic categories, ranging from anti-infectives and the central nervous system to respiratory, digestive and metabolic areas. It also held a dominant position in vaccines and a strong showing in consumer health care and OTC medicines. Only in the treatment of heart diseases and cancer did it admit to falling short of leadership.

Spending £2.5 billion on R&D in 2000, it employed no fewer than 16,500 research staff, nearly 50 per cent in the United States. It had 7,500 marketing representatives to cover the whole of that nation, which in 2000 accounted for nearly 47 per cent of GSK's sales and 48 per cent of its trading profit. A quarter of its operating assets were in America, compared with 56 per cent in the European region, where 15 sites in nine countries manufactured nearly all of GSK's major pharmaceutical products.

GSK planned to achieve £1 million savings over three years, 75 per cent in administration, in addition to £750,000 in R&D, a sum which Sykes undertook to reinvest in research. He further promised that, as long as the UK government maintained its relatively benign stance towards the country's pharmaceutical industry, he would maintain roughly half of its R&D expenditure in Britain. The new group's first *Annual Report*, covering the year 2000, did not disclose the percentages of research activity taking place in each part of the world. However, GSK is known to have divided work geographically between three therapeutic areas, namely anti-infectives and cardiovascular diseases in the United States, neurology and respiratory diseases in Britain, and psychiatry in Italy.[2]

As to the ungainly name of GlaxoSmithKline, Glaxo had pride of place as the combine's senior partner, while the inclusion of SmithKline acknowledged that here was in every sense an Anglo-American company. Its head office remained in London (see Chapter 16), but its operational headquarters were in Philadelphia, that function later shared with Research Triangle Park, North Carolina. The *Financial Times* was one of the very few media outlets to note the passing of both Beecham and Wellcome from among Britain's most historic corporate names.[3] So ended the history of Beecham as a separate company, leaving one question for the historian to address.

Although its name survived until 2000, had the Beecham spirit gradually eroded through its various reorganizations and changes of ownership, however essential those had been for long-term survival? A distinctive Beecham ethos had in fact sprung up from an early date. Nineteenth-century employees spoke about proper working methods as 'Beecham' and deviations as 'not Beecham'. Such a feeling for correct conduct may have encouraged many operatives to stay on despite low wages and long hours (see Chapter 6). Somehow that ethos persisted despite the unprogressive and mindless routine at St Helens during the first quarter of the twentieth century, which so appalled Philip Hill on his initial visit to the factory in 1924 (see Chapter 10).

Then from 1951 onwards Lazell as a hands-on innovator nurtured, and transmitted to the whole of his staff, a feeling of unswerving loyalty to the company as it responded to his strong leadership. In his reminiscences, he wrote

We were intensely proud of Beechams and of what we had made of it. We believed in its destiny and were dedicated to building a great international company capable of competing with the powerful US corporations which dominated so many of the markets in which we were involved.

Beecham, he added, 'has always made efforts to make employees feel that they belong', while conceding that in his time the group did not go as far as it might have done to achieve that goal.[4]

Just as fundamentally, an independent study of 1953 characterized the group as 'one of the strongest and most successful of Britain's industrial and commercial giants', thanks to enjoying a 'sense of continuity, coupled with the dynamic of expansion'.[5] Then twice in subsequent decades, Beecham staff found themselves under outsiders – those unfamiliar with their traditions – as chairmen, who introduced routines at variance with their well-tried working methods.

Sir Ronald Edwards, from 1968 onwards, made a point of tolerating any friction among his top managers, which he caused by such habits as composing memos that, so far from giving clear instructions, debated different sides of a given problem (see Chapter 14). By contrast, Robert Bauman and Jan Leschly as his successor took drastic action to stamp out resistance within the group to their American innovations in both structure and methods of implementing reforms. Bauman's scheme of amalgamation with SmithKline in 1989 was intended to be so all-encompassing as to obliterate every trace of the two merged companies (see Chapter 16).

The Beecham of old had, it seemed, gone for ever. Yet in 1998, Leschly informed the Science and Technology Committee's inquiry that his current array of pharmaceuticals, by that time the 'driving force' behind SB, had to a considerable degree sprung from 'excellent science' carried out in the UK. 'We are very proud of that,' he added, 'and that was certainly the Beecham heritage.'[6] Instead, what had already started to disappear one by one were the surviving visible symbols of that heritage. On the proprietary side, when in 1993 Consumer Brands became Consumer Healthcare, the still very lucrative Brylcreem – a star acquisition by Philip Hill – Silvikrin and other products had to be sold off, because they fell outside the healthcare category.

A year later the factory at St Helens, meticulously planned by Joseph Beecham over a century before and twice extended between 1934 and 1956, was closed down and handed over to the town's education authority. Its future had been under threat even before the merger of 1989, but once the toiletries and other OTC medicines, comprising the majority of its output, were sold off, it had to go. That break with Beecham's geographical roots made 500 local employees redundant.[7] At the end of 1996 Brockham Park, its central laboratory for the past fifty years and the spot where Beecham's scientists had evolved the first semi-synthetic penicillins, also went. Most of its research activities, together with those of SB's three other sites, moved to Harlow in Essex (see Chapter 16), and Brockham Park was turned over to the housing developers.[8]

Beecham's pills could still be bought, from the late 1950s onwards in tubular containers that replaced the boxes. By 1986, when nearly 50 million were sold that year – almost entirely in Britain – they had been converted to tablet form. Then in 1998 SB unobtrusively announced that, owing to a steady fall in demand, 'as part of an ongoing rationalization process' it was discontinuing manufacture of the pills:[9] by coincidence, just 150 years after Thomas Beecham had set up his pill firm.

Over that century and a half, Beecham's total output of pills can be estimated as upwards of 40 billion, or 40,000 million. The powders and a range of its cold and influenza remedies, by 1999 worth £24 million in sales,[10] kept before the public its brand name, prominently displayed on hoardings, on the sides of buses and in television advertisements during the annual cold and cough season.

In the intervening years of ever more rapid change, Thomas Beecham's tiny barque (see Chapter 1), which he had launched 'on the ever-shifting sea of commercial uncertainty' had, by combining a drive to innovate with fostering a powerful ethos of corporate loyalty, grown into one of the world's most prestigious supertankers. Perhaps embedded in its double bottom have been at least a selection of Beecham mementos.

Sir Thomas Beecham's ancestry

WHILE THIS BOOK WAS BEING COMPLETED in 2007, the BBC broadcast several television series, entitled '*Who do you think you are?*', which gave celebrities of the day an opportunity to trace their family history. Not surprisingly, some programmes included dramatic moments, showing men as well as women in tears when presented with evidence of the shocking deprivation or (under the Nazi regime) brutality suffered by some of their ancestors. Other celebrities remained philosophical in spite of discovering that family legends that they came of grand forebears, such as Irish aristocrats, were demolished by the facts.

As Sir Thomas Beecham was of greater cultural consequence than many who appeared in these BBC programmes, an investigation of his genealogical background is appropriate. Here two questions can be posed. First, where did his basic characteristics come from? Second, has the present investigation revealed any surprises?

Basic characteristics

The distinguished musical critic, Frank Howes, described Sir Thomas as 'the greatest, perhaps the only, executant genius ever thrown up by music in Britain'. Thomas's 'unmistakable stamp of genius', Howes explained, sprang from 'an ear finely sensitive to blend, gradation and balance of tone … combined with fire in the belly, fire in the eyes and rhythm in the blood'.[1] However, like most individuals with such prodigious gifts, Thomas had marked character limitations. His biographer, Charles Reid, who knew him well, portrayed him as 'a philosophical "dead-ender". His writing, conversation, speeches, tantrums and genial hedonism denoted that, in his mind, the arts, with music in the van, and all other joys and elegances of Western civilization, were life's purpose – and end; in the sense that a brick wall is an end.'[2] Neville Cardus, another long-standing observer and friend, agreed that Thomas 'didn't seek beyond the notes and form of music for some inner meaning'. Hence, for example, he never discussed religion, except to ridicule the devotional works of even the most eminent composers, from the *Missa Solemnis* ('third-rate Beethoven') to Elgar's *Dream of Gerontius* ('holy water in a German beer barrel').[3] Once he mischievously followed a performance of *Gerontius* with an encore (to use his word, a lollipop), of Johann Strauss' *Blue Danube*.[4]

Cardus also highlighted Thomas's 'Lancastrian gusto, even some hints of provincial arrogance', and yet balanced by a secretiveness in personal matters.[5] Cyril Meir Scott and Cardus refer as early as 1905 to his shyness, which he seems to have retained throughout his life.[6] The scholar and music broadcaster, Bernard Keefe, on the basis of acquaintance with him in his riper years, concluded that 'the public bravado and wit were defence mechanisms – he was a rather shy and vulnerable, childlike personality.'[7] The whole man was reflected also in his physical make-up. He had 'a back like a bull', so that 'to the very end he presented an impressive pair of shoulders to orchestras the world over'. Yet his legs were surprisingly short, and his hands and feet resembled those of a child.[8]

Possible genetic influences

Some facets of Sir Thomas's many-sided character can be traced back to his ancestry. Thomas Beecham, his grandfather and founder of the pill firm, was rumbustious and lacking in self-awareness, but totally unmusical. It was the elder Thomas's first wife Jane, born in Bangor, who had inherited a Welsh love of music and ability to sing well, and she managed to pay for Joseph Beecham – our Thomas's father – to be given music lessons. Despite a crippling shyness, Joseph had a passion for music, which he was unable to gratify by performing with any great skill on the piano, organ or violin. All these forebears were of short stature; unlike Thomas, all had religious beliefs, mainly as Congregationalists.

Joseph came to know his future wife, Josephine, through their shared musical tastes; she also sang well and maintained her piano playing into a lonely old age.[9] Her preoccupation with the births of ten children up to 1894, a determination to run their Huyton residence without a housekeeper, plus her husband's later acts of ill-treatment, left her with few opportunities to encourage Thomas's musical development. Once he began to give performances, she did subsidize some of his early concerts, but his memoir, *A Mingled Chime* (1944), significantly recalls her almost as a stranger. Joseph 'never seems to have consulted his wife over the children's welfare or upbringing'. Instead, for advice on major family matters he relied on his solicitor and the local Congregational minister, whose conservative ideas seldom accorded with young Thomas's lofty aspirations.[10]

Some surprises

Oddly enough, Josephine Beecham's genetic origins turn out to be far from conventional, with no known musical connections. As explained in Chapter 3, her family was said to be of Spanish extraction, and to have migrated to England from Lille in northern France, the alleged location of Josephine's birth. Her father, William Burnett, a silk dealer and barber, was remembered in the family as having occupied a small house at the corner of Liverpool Road and Sandfield Crescent in St Helens, and as being known in the town for displaying eccentric habits.[11] However, no independent proof of his existence or of his residence in the town has been traced in the Census records or local directories of the period.

In reality, Josephine had been born in Everton, Liverpool on 28 May 1850, no father being entered on her birth certificate, or on the baptismal register (as Josephine Burnett Dickens) of Manchester Cathedral, a few months later on 8 August.[12] Even so, on her certificate of marriage in 1873, she attested that she was the daughter of William Burnett, silk dealer.

Josephine's mother, Martha, went under the successive surnames of Dickens, Burnett and Bowen. As the main events of her life – in so far as they can be unearthed – are given in Chapters 3 and 7, they are briefly listed here:

1819   Born at St John, New Brunswick (now Canada), to John Dickens, sergeant in 40th Regiment of Foot, and his wife, Mary McGrath.[13]

1841   Dressmaker, in lodgings at Hulme, Lancashire.[14]

1844   Liaison begins with Henry Burnett (no marriage in UK discovered), producing three children:
Henry Burnett Dickens, b.1845, Hulme.
George William Burnett Dickens, b.1847, Manchester.
Josephine Burnett Dickens, b. 1850, Everton, Liverpool.[15]

1851   Census: If, as seems likely, Martha and her family were resident in Manchester that April, their names and particulars might have been in the volumes of the Census that were discarded as having been damaged by water. Of those, some 82 per cent have more recently been decyphered, her name not being included.
See www.1851–unfilmed.org.uk.

1851–60 liaison with Charles Bowen, warehouseman (no marriage), producing five children:

Alfred Bowen Dickens, b. 1851, Manchester
Adelaide Mary Bowen Dickens. b. 1852, Liverpool
Eugene Bowen Dickens, b. 1854, Liscard, nr Birkenhead
Charles Bowen Dickens, b. 1856, Liverpool
Jane Jessie Martha Dickens, b. 1859, Wallasey, Cheshire.[16]

1861   Census, Martha (and family), 'widow, milliner', at Kennet
            Cottages, Liscard.[17]

1871   Martha (and family), 'widow, no occupation', at Croppers Hill,
            St Helens.[18]

1873   Josephine marries Joseph Beecham at St Helens parish church.

1879   July: Martha Bowen, George Burnett, Eugene Bowen and
            an infant Bowen embark on the *Greta* sailing vessel for
            Melbourne, Australia; October, Martha and party arrive at
            Melbourne.[19]

1895   February: Martha Bowen, 'relict of Charles Bowen', dies
            (cancer of the rectum, 2 years), in Geelong, near Melbourne;
            buried there. Not known which relatives are with her.[20]

Conclusion

Most ordinary people from the past survive only as names in official records. Those records tell us nothing about what they were like as individuals, unless – as is unlikely in Martha's case – they appeared before a court of law. Hers therefore remains one of the great untold stories, of a clearly resourceful female, whose destiny took her in the course of an eventful life across three-quarters of the globe, from North America to Britain and then to the antipodes.

Like Sir Thomas Beecham, the eldest grandchild whom she saw for only a few short months before her departure for Melbourne, she was a survivor. As a lone young woman, she supported herself as a dressmaker; she later brought up her numerous progeny to respectable trades, and then in her fifties endured a three-month voyage under sail to Australia. There she managed her affairs successfully enough to be buried in some style.

Thomas, on the other hand, enjoyed the high life to a degree that Martha could never have dreamt of. With his grandfather's unselfconsciousness and no notion of prudence, he indulged in escapades that for the most part involved money; he must have been one of the few individuals outside the criminal classes who perfected the art of evading the kind of financial disaster that could have finished him. Whether Martha ever went in for moonlight flits to escape creditors, or, as he did, walked away from debts that could not be proved, is not known, but Thomas's friend, the composer Ethel Smyth, put it well:

> Rumours of bailiffs, of hairbreadth escapes, of desperate expedients, were for ever circling round the name of this brilliant portent in the musical firmament, to ascertain whose [current] address was a problem not even his own business manager ... was always able to solve.[21]

Thomas had the knack of 'disappearing almost before people's eyes'.[22] At the same time, to compound the anarchic side of his nature, he fought running battles with officialdom, and especially with the legal profession.

In person, by correspondence and in the press, he railed against individuals and bodies that, had he welcomed them, could doubtless have supported him in his costly ventures. When a group of well-wishers set up a limited company to assist him with his debts (see Chapter 9), he omitted to pay their dividends or debenture interest, forcing that company into liquidation and causing much unnecessary animosity.

At the end of his life, he scored what he would have regarded as his most striking triumph against the UK's revenue authorities. As a tax exile, he was allowed to spend only a limited number of days a year in Britain, a land where – he asserted – 'it is impossible to live [because of the climate] and nobody can afford to die'.[23] In 1961, having outstayed in London his legal allowance of time, he was nowhere to be found. In fact, he died of a coronary thrombosis in his wife's flat in central London.[24] Some day an inventive novelist will weave together the contrasting but interlocked tales of Martha Bowen and Sir Thomas Beecham.

The Beecham family tree

James Beecham = Charlotte Lowry
[1792]

Joseph (1799–1839) = Sarah Hunt (1801–87)
[1820]

Thomas (1820–1907) = (1) [1847] Jane Evans (1813–72)
= (2) [1873] Sarah Pemberton (1844–77)
[no issue]
= (3) [1879] Mary Sawell (1851–1937)
[no issue]

Joseph (1848–1916) = Josephine Burnett (1850–1934)
[1873]

Emily (1874–1965)
= Utica Welles (1881–1977)
[1903]

Thomas (1879–1961)

Josephine (1881–1959)

Edith (b.1884)

Henry (1888–1947)

Elsie (1889–1984)

Amy (b.1894)

Thomas (1909–88)

Adrian (1904–82)

he was only ten years old. No Beecham's annual of Christmas carols was ever published, and the *Musical Portfolios* contain no such parody. Even so, his invention of this absurdity was given fresh life when the rhyme appeared under his name in three British dictionaries of quotations.[7] Thus the story is likely to do the rounds for as long as the Beecham name is remembered.

Notes and references

Introduction

1 The author's article, 'Twentieth-century American contributions to the growth of the Beecham enterprise' in J. Slinn and V. Quirke (eds), *Perspectives on Twentieth-Century Pharmaceuticals* (Oxford and Berne: Peter Lang, 2010, pp. 217–40), further reveals the extent of the tangible and intangible assistance obtained during that century by the Beecham Group, and later by SmithKline Beecham, from sources in the United States.

Chapter 1: Not quite a Smilesian hero, 1820–1865

1 For information in this, and in subsequent chapters, I am greatly indebted to Anne Francis (see Acknowledgements), for her pioneering and indispensable biography of Thomas Beecham, *A Guinea A Box* (London: Hale, 1968).

2 S. Smiles, *Self-Help* (London: John Murray, 1859), p. 317.

3 T. A. B. Corley, 'Thomas Beecham, 1820–1907', in D. J. Jeremy (ed.), *Dictionary of Business Biography* [*DBB*] (London: Butterworth, 1984), 1, pp. 246–8, and in H. C. G. Matthew and B. Harrison (eds), *Oxford Dictionary of National Biography* [*ODNB*] (Oxford: Oxford University Press, 2004), 4, pp. 798–9.

4 E. H. Hunt, *Regional Wage Variations in Britain, 1850–1914* (Oxford: Clarendon Press, 1973), pp. 18–19.

5 *St Helens Reporter*, 30 May 1890, letter by Thomas Beecham to refute statements in *Tit-Bits*, 17 May, p. 95, that he had lived in Granborough. Owing to the variety of sources (especially press cuttings on microfiche) used over several decades to obtain references, it has sometimes been impossible to note exact page numbers of all newspapers cited.

6 H. J. C. Grierson (ed.), *Letters of Sir Walter Scott* 11, 1828–31 (London: Constable, 1936), p. 365, 16 June 1830.

7 Francis, *A Guinea A Box*, p. 28.

8 Ibid., pp. 30–4.

9 A. Arber, 'Herbal', *Chambers's Encyclopaedia* (London: Newnes, 1959), 7, p. 52.

10 Francis, *A Guinea A Box*, p. 34.

11 *Chemist and Druggist* [*CD*] 10 October 1942, 'Centenary of A Notable Business', reprint pp. 3–9.; Francis, *A Guinea A Box*, pp. 34–5. The pill machine is now in the St Helens Museum.

12 Ibid., pp. 32, 54; Beecham Archives [BA], St Helens Local History and Archives Library, Thomas Beecham's Bible (with poem), 1837, BP 2/2/4.

13 *St Helens Reporter*, 30 May 1890; T. C. Barker and J. R. Harris, *A Merseyside Town in the*

Industrial Revolution: St Helens, 1750–1900 (Liverpool: Liverpool University Press, 1954), p. 378; the reference on that page to the *St Helens Newsletter*, 31 May 1890, is incorrect.

14 Francis, *A Guinea A Box*, p. 39; R. Mullen, *Anthony Trollope: A Victorian in his World* (London: Duckworth, 1990), pp. 226, 240.

15 C. Reid, *Thomas Beecham, An Independent Biography* (London: Gollancz, 1962), p. 30.

16 Francis, *A Guinea A Box*, p. 48.

17 Written by Thomas Beecham in his copy of Edward Young, *Night Thoughts on Life, Death and Immortality* (Halifax: William Milner, 1841), inscribed 'Thomas Beecham His Book, 1843', and quoted by kind permission of Mr E. Moss.

18 Hunt, *Regional Wage Variations*, pp. 37–42.

19 S. Dowell, *A History of Taxation and Taxes in England to 1885*, 2nd edn (London: Longmans Green, 1888), 4, pp. 352–60.

20 W. E. D. Allen, *David Allens: The History of A Family Firm, 1857–1957* (London: John Murray, 1957), p. 82, quoting from S. Marriner, 'History of Liverpool, 1700–1900', in W. Smith (ed.), *A Scientific Survey of Merseyside* (Liverpool: Liverpool University Press, 1953), pp. 115–16.

21 Smiles, *Self-Help*, pp. 8, 12.

22 A. Marshall, *Industry and Trade* (London: Macmillan, 1921), p. 358.

23 F. Crouzet, *The First Industrialists* (Cambridge: Cambridge University Press, 1985), pp. 146–52.

24 BA, Statutory Declaration by Thomas Beecham, 10 September 1906, BP 1/3/12.

25 Marriage certificate of Thomas and Jane Beecham, 26 May 1847; D. Vincent, *Literacy and Popular Culture in England, 1750–1914* (Cambridge: Cambridge University Press, 1989), pp. 22, 29.

26 Francis, *A Guinea A Box*, p. 49.

27 For Kershaw see *CD* 13 April 1907, p. 545 and *Pharmaceutical Journal* [*PJ*] 14 August 1886, p. 139.

28 BA, Thomas Beecham's pocket book extracts, 1856–57, BP 1/4/1.

29 T. A. B. Corley, 'Sir Joseph Beecham, 1848–1916', *DBB* 1, pp. 243–6 and *ODNB* 4, pp. 797–8.

30 BA, Thomas Beecham's pocket book extracts, 1856–57, BP 1/4/1.

31 R. Mathew(s), *The Unlearned Alchymist* (1662), BA, BP 1/1/1; F. Mohr and T. Redwood, *Practical Pharmacy: The Arrangements, Apparatus, and Manipulations of the Pharmaceutical Shop and Laboratory* (London: Taylor, Walton and Maberly, 1849), pp. 347 ff.

32 *Post Office Directory of Lancashire* (1858), p. 449; Poll Books, Wigan, 28 March 1857 and 30 April 1859, kindly supplied by Christine Watts, on behalf of Wigan Heritage Services Manager.

33 *PJ* 18, 1858–59, p. 198.

34 BA, Poster of Sale, November 1858, BP 1/6/3; Francis, *A Guinea A Box*, p. 66.

35 Francis, *A Guinea A Box*, p. 66.

36 *Victoria History of the Counties of England [VCH]: Lancashire* 3 (London: Constable, 1907), p. 375.

37 Francis, *A Guinea A Box*, p. 68; *St Helens Intelligencer*, 6 August 1859; J. Brockbank, *History of St Helens, with Local Landmarks* (St Helens, 1896), pp. 42–3, 'Beecham's Pill Palace', being illustrated on p. 43; *Answers*, 22 October 1898; Barker and Harris, *A Merseyside Town*, p. 378; *CD* 24 April 1897, p. 656.

38 1861 Census, Hindley, S. Lancashire: housekeeper to David Lloyd, a textile merchant, RG 9/2778/24. Born at Wigan in November 1838, she had been a member of the Beecham household in the 1851 Census, HO 107/2199. Either through marriage or death, her name does not appear in the Census for 1871.

39 *St Helens Weekly Press*, 14 September 1861; Francis, *A Guinea A Box*, p. 86. For Bible entry see BA, BP 2/2/4.

40 Francis, *A Guinea A Box*, pp. 75–6; *CD* 10 October 1942, centenary reprint, photograph on p. 4.

41 'Medical Act', 21 and 22 Victoria, 1858, in G. K. Rickards (ed.), *Statutes of United Kingdom* (London: Eyre & Spottiswood, 1858), C. 90, pp. 299–312. Penalties in Clause 40.

42 *Progressive Advertising*, 25 July 1902, p. 451.

43 British Medical Association, *Secret Remedies: What they Cost and What they Contain* (London: British Medical Association, 1909), p. 175.

Chapter 2: Britain's patent medicine industry in the nineteenth century

1 This chapter is partly based on T. A. B. Corley, 'Nostrums and nostrum-mongers: the growth of the UK patent medicine industry, 1635–1914', unpublished paper, 2002. See also R. Porter, *Health for Sale: Quackery in England, 1660–1850* (Manchester: Manchester University Press, 1989), esp. pp. 222–36. This erudite and entertaining book does not consider the patent medicine industry as such nor its growth. It was reprinted, with illustrations, as *Quacks: Fakers and Charlatans in Medicine* (Stroud: Tempus Publishing Ltd, 2003), pp. 305–24. See also P. S. Brown, 'Social context and medical theory: the demarcation of nineteenth-century boundaries', in W. F. Bynum and R. Porter (eds), *Medical Fringe and Medical Orthodoxy, 1750–1850* (London: Croom Helm, 1977), pp. 216–19.

2 315 brands had disappeared by 1893: *CD* 2 November 1893.

3 For multiplier of 6 for turnover see *CD* 29 August 1896, p. 347; for consumers' expenditure, duty of 'one-ninth of what is charged for the medicine' of James Morison, *Trial of Joseph Webb for Manslaughter at York, Summer Assizes, 1834* (London: G. Taylor, 1834), p. 4; multiplier of 'nearly 10 times', *CD* 15 November 1872, p. 362; 7.83 in *Lancet*, 15 December 1888, p. 1193. As the multipliers for 1907 and 1913 in A. Prest and A. Adams, *Consumers' Expenditure in the United Kingdom, 1900–1919* (Cambridge: Cambridge University Press, 1954), p. 157, were 8.72 and 9.9 respectively, that of 7.25 in British Medical Association, *Secret Remedies*, p. 184, making a deduction of 25 per cent from its original estimate of 9.7 to meet certain sources of error, seems too low. Hence one of 9 is taken here.

4 *Parliamentary Debates, Hansard*, House of Commons, 286 Col. 807, 26 March 1884; there were then an estimated 800–1,000 owners of proprietary medicines.

5 *CD* 26 June 1886, p. 630.

6 F. B. Smith, *The People's Health, 1830–1910* (London: Croom Helm, 1979), p. 257; see also 'Patent medicines' in ibid., pp. 343–5.

7 R. Boyson, *The Ashworth Cotton Enterprise* (Oxford: Oxford University Press, 1970), p. 255.

8 J. R. McCulloch, *A Descriptive and Statistical Account of the British Empire: Vital Statistics* 2, 3rd edn (London: Longmans, 1846), pp. 542–3, in W. Farr, *Vital Statistics: A Memorial Volume of Selections from [his] Reports and Writings* (London, Edward Stanford, 1885), p. 498; *Registrar General's 35th Annual Report* (London: HM Stationery Office, 1875), Supplement, pp. xxvii–viii, ibid., p. 513: an estimate for the early 1870s.

9 L. Davidoff and C. Hall, *Family Fortunes: Men and Women of the English Middle Class, 1780–1850* (London: Hutchinson, 1987), p. 307; J. Burnby, 'Pharmaceutical advertisement in the 17th and 18th centuries', *European Journal of Marketing* 22, No. 4, 1988, p. 37; Porter, *Health for Sale*, p. 239; Porter, *Quacks*, p. 328.

10 J. Liebenau, 'The rise of the British pharmaceutical industry', *British Medical Journal* 3 October 1990, pp. 724–8, 733; T. A. B. Corley, 'The British pharmaceutical industry since 1851', in L. Richmond, J. Stevenson and A. Turton (eds), *The Pharmacy Industry: A Guide to Historical Records* (Aldershot: Ashgate, 2003), pp. 14–32; G. Tweedale, *At the Sign of the Plough: 275 years of Allen & Hanburys and the British Pharmaceutical Industry, 1715–1990* (London: John Murray, 1990), pp. 11–12; for the Evans firm see A. E. Smeeton, *The Story of Evans Medical, 1809–1959* (Liverpool: Evans Medical Supplies Ltd, 1959) and *CD* 15 July

1884, pp. 326–7, 31 January 1891, pp. 148–51, 14 January 1905, pp. 46–7 and 30 December 1916, p. 1291.

11 *The Town*, 19 May 1838, p. 408; Francis, *A Guinea A Box*, p. 159.

12 T. A. B. Corley, 'James Morison, 1770–1840', *ODNB* 39, pp. 183–4; W. Helfand, 'James Morison and his Pills', *Transactions of the British Society for the History of Pharmacy* 1, 1974, pp. 101–35; *Medical Circular* 11, 5 January 1853, pp. 9–10, 12 January 1853, pp. 25–7.

13 *Lancet*, 28 August 1858, p. 237; *Medical Times and Gazette*, 11 September 1858, p. 284.

14 *Law Journal Reports* 1851 n.s. 20, Part 1, Chancery and Bankruptcy (London: Ince, 1851), Morison v. Moat, pp. 513–29.

15 *Morisoniana: The Abridged Family Adviser of the British College of Health, 110ᵗʰ thousand [sic]* (London: College of Health, 1868).

16 *Report of a Trial in the Supreme Court of the State of New York: Morison & Moat v. Moses Jacques & J. B. Marsh* (New York: W. Mitchell, 1834), kindly supplied by Harvard Law Library.

17 *Lancet*, 20 July 1839, p. 635; Will, The National Archives [TNA], PROB/1/1931/516, 4 July 1840; IR 26/1555/474, September 1845.

18 *The Town*, 12 August 1837, p. 88.

19 G. Storey et al., *The Letters of Charles Dickens*, 7, 1853–1855, p. 629; 8, 1856–1858, p. 162 (Oxford: Oxford University Press, 1993 and 1995).

20 For Cockle and Scott see I. Loudon, 'The vile race of quacks with which the country is infested', in Bynum and Porter, *Medical Fringe*, p. 113; T. A. B. Corley, 'James Cockle, 1782–1854', *ODNB* 12, pp. 370–2; *Monthly Gazette of Health* 7, 1822, p. 119; *The Satirist*, 7 January 1838, p. 8; 'The Advertising System', *Edinburgh Review*, February 1843, p, 6; *The Satirist*, 28 April 1839, p. 130.

21 British Medical Association, *More Secret Remedies* (London: British Medical Association, 1912), p. 100.

22 Will TNA, PROB 11/2166/805; IR 26/2024/97, 5 March 1855.

23 T. A. B. Corley, 'Thomas Holloway, 1800–1883', *ODNB* 27, pp. 763–5.

24 C. Bingham, *The History of Royal Holloway College, 1886–1986* (London: Constable, 1987), p. 16; A. Harrison-Barbet, *Thomas Holloway: Victorian Philanthropist* (London: Royal Holloway, 1994), p. 19; *The Times*, 2 December 1862, p. 10.

25 *Medical Circular*, 19 January 1853, p. 45, 26 January 1853, pp. 67–8, 2 February 1853, pp. 86–7.

26 'A Sketch of the Commencement and Progress of Holloway's Pills and Ointment, January 1863'; 'Mr. Holloway's Letter to Mr. Driver, 14 October 1877, the 40th Anniversary of the Commencement of the Business', Surrey Record Office, THPP.

27 *The Town*, 14 July 1838, p. 466, 21 July 1838, p. 471, 28 July 1838, p. 485, 11 August 1838, p. 501. For two advertisements on same page, see *The Satirist*, 22 April 1838, p. 128.

28 Death certificate, 21 December 1872: 'Felix Albinolo, Agent, aged 87, at Poland Street, Westminster, Union Workhouse: senility, certified'.

29 G. C. Boase, 'Thomas Holloway: Pill Maker and Philanthropist', *Western Antiquary* 4, 1884–85, pp. 183–7.

30 *Medical Times*, 5 January 1884.

31 *CD* 15 January 1884, p. 10.

32 *Lancet*, 10 October 1840, p. 288, 17 October 1840, p. 131, 24 October 1840, p. 164.

33 *Lancet*, 30 May 1846, p. 606.

34 *Punch*, No. 70, 12 November 1842, p. 200; *Edinburgh Review* 77, February-April 1843, pp. 5, 42.

35 *English Reports* 51, Rolls Court 4 (London: Stevens & Sons, 1905), pp. 81–5: Holloway v. Holloway, 9 November 1850.

36 M. Lutyens, *Effie in Venice* (London: John Murray, 1965), p. 59; *CD* 15 January 1884, p. 31.

37 A 400-page bound heavy leather 'Thomas Holloway Ledger: Analysis of Sales, 1860–1899',

19 Registrar-General's Office, New Zealand, Death Certificate of Helen McKey Bennett, widow of the late John Bennett, Napier, New Zealand, 7 July 1920; *Napier Daily Telegraph*, 8 July 1920. Principal Registry of Family Division, London, Will of Helen McKey Taylor [*sic*], proved 12 January 1921. My thanks are due to Miss K. Israelson, Reference Librarian, Napier Public Library, for providing information (including cemetery records) about Helen Taylor's death and burial.

20 TNA, J4 8966/119, 22 January 1918.

21 London Metropolitan Archives, E/BER/CG/E/12/003, 7 September, 12 November 1917.

22 Company registered 13 January 1918. TNA, J4 8974/1641, 31 October 1918; 9167/321, 10 March 1920.

23 TNA, J15 3467/1968, 21 June 1918; J4 8974/1641, 31 October 1918.

24 TNA, J15 3467/1968, 21 June 1918; J4 8968/425, 13 March 1918.

25 TNA, J4 9400/693, 29 March 1922; 9402/1025, 23 May 1922; 9509/335, 28 February 1923.

26 Reid, *Thomas Beecham*, p. 181; TNA, B9 869, 10 October 1919.

27 Ibid.

28 TNA, B9 870, 27 April 1922; J4 9400/683, 30 March 1922; B9 869, 12 October 1921; *The Times*, 23 March 1921, p. 4.

29 TNA, B9 869, 16 May 1919; J4 9509/335–6, 27–8 February 1923.

30 Beecham, *A Mingled Chime*, pp. 258–9; Jefferson, *Sir Thomas Beecham*, pp. 90, 156; R. Capell, Obituary, *Musical Times* 102, 1961, pp. 283–6; Reid, *Thomas Beecham*, p. 90; cf. BA, Garland Wells & Co. (o/a Emily Beecham, re Thomas's annuity to her which remained unpaid) to H. Beecham, 7 April 1925, BP 1/3/16.

31 London Metropolitan Archives, E/BER/CG/E/12/003, 28 October 1919; Keyworth, *Cabbages and Things*, p. 53; K. Clark, *The Other Half* (London; John Murray, 1977), p. 29.

32 T. Mann, *Buddenbrooks* (1901, Harmondsworth: Penguin Books, 1971); M. B. Rose, 'The family firm and the management of succession', in J. Brown and M. B. Rose (eds), *Entrepreneurship, Networks and Modern Business* (Manchester: Manchester University Press, 1993), pp. 127–33; D. S. Landes, 'Technological change and development in Western Europe, 1750–1914', in H. J. Habakkuk and M. Postan (eds), *Cambridge Economic History of Europe*, Part 1 (Cambridge: Cambridge University Press, 1966), 6, pp. 563–4.

33 *Law Reports: King's Bench Division, 1921*, The King v. Henry Beecham, 18 July 1921, pp. 464–72.

34 BA, H. Beecham to Executors, 20 July 1922; H. Beecham to C. Rowed, 3 August 1922, BP 1/3/16; private information.

35 TNA, J4 9399/497, 8 March 1922; 9400/627, 27 March 1922.

36 T. A. B. Corley, 'Philip Ernest Hill, 1873–1944', *DBB* 3, pp. 235–9 and *ODNB* 27, pp. 169–71; Keyworth, *Cabbages and Things*, p. 117–48; Beecham, *A Mingled Chime*, pp. 197, 263.

37 For acquisition of option see BA, Cox and Cardale (o/a Hill and Wheeler) to Bremner Sons and Corlett (o/a executors), 22 November 1923, BP 1/3/16; S. D. Chapman, 'Sir Arthur Wheeler, 1860–1943', *ODNB* 58, pp. 427–8; L. Dennett, *The Charterhouse Group, 1925–1979: A History* (London: Gentry Books, 1979), pp. 15–17; Y. Cassis, 'The emergence of a new financial institution: investment banks in Britain, 1870–1939' in J. J. Van Helten and Y. Cassis (eds), *Capitalism in a Mature Economy: Financial Institutions, Capital Exports and British Industry, 1870–1939* (Aldershot: Edward Elgar, 1990), pp. 139–58.

38 TNA, J4 9621/685, April 1924; J15 3691/1271, 15 April 1924.

Chapter 10: Beecham Estates and Pills Ltd, 1924–1928

1 Prospectus of Beecham Estates and Pills Ltd, *The Times*, 26 May 1924, p. 22; *Economist*, 24 May 1924, p. 1065.

2 Beecham Estates and Pills Ltd, Board Minutes, 'List of cheques requested by Sir Thomas

Beecham', 21 May 1924; ibid., 5 June 1924 'repayment forthwith'; A good account of the period from 1924 to 1928 is in Keyworth, *Cabbages and Things*, pp. 75–97.

3 Prospectus, *The Times*, 26 May 1924, p. 22.

4 Board Minutes, 10 July 1924.

5 Information from J. M. Keyworth.

6 Ibid.

7 Board Minutes, 26 June, 10 July 1924.

8 E. Waugh, *Brideshead Revisited* (London: Chapman & Hall, 1945), p. 49.

9 BA, C. Rowed, W. Moss and C. J. Scrymgeour, 'Rise and fall of various patent medicines', April 1924, BP 1/9/6, pp. 1–4.

10 Board Minutes, 2, 9 October 1924.

11 Ibid., 11 December 1924, 8 January, 12 February, 14 May 1925.

12 Ibid., 9 October 1924, 11 June 1925.

13 T. A. B. Corley, 'Sir William Veno, 1866–1933', *ODNB* online edition http://www.oxforddnb.com/view/article/93363, May 2005.

14 G. Jones, 'The multinational expansion of Dunlop, 1890–1939', in G. Jones (ed.), *British Multinationals: Origins, Management and Performance* (Aldershot: Gower, 1986), pp. 29–30.

15 Board Minutes, 9 January, 12 February, 12 March, 2 April 1925.

16 Ibid., 11 June 1925; H. G. Lazell, *From Pills to Penicillin: The Beecham Story* (London: Heinemann, 1975), pp. 78–9.

17 Board Minutes, 20 January, 18 March, 15 April, 9 September 1926.

18 Ibid., 13 October 1926.

19 Ibid., 10 September 1925; R. H. Nichols and F. A. Wray, *The History of the Foundling Hospital* (London: Oxford University Press, 1935), pp. 272, 323.

20 *The Times*, 20 August 1925, p. 16 ('laughter'); Keyworth, *Cabbages and Things*, p. 81.

21 *The Times*, 17 February 1927, p. 20.

22 Board Minutes, 10 June 1926, 12 May 1927, 18 January 1928.

23 Board Minutes, 26 June, 17 July 1924, 8 January, 12 February 1925.

24 Lazell, *From Pills to Penicillin*, p. 114; Board Minutes, 13 November, 11 December 1924, 8 January, 2 April, 14 May, 11 June, 9 July 1925.

25 Board Minutes, 26 June, 18 September, 13 November 1924, 10 June, 8 December 1926, 12 May 1927.

26 C. Rowed, *The Rowed Name*, privately published, Lancashire, 1921 [BL Catalogue 1860 d. 1(58)]; Board Minutes, 9 June, 11 July 1927.

27 Board Minutes, 10 September 1925; information from Mrs Frank Moss.

28 *Statist*, 24 September 1927, pp. 495–6; Dennett, *The Charterhouse Group*, p. 17.

29 Board Minutes, 9 November 1927; *Investors Chronicle*, 24 December 1927, p. 1433; Keyworth, *Cabbages and Things*, p. 93.

30 Ibid., pp. 98–9.

Chapter 11: The Beechams Pills company, 1928–1944

1 Beechams Pills Ltd, Prospectus, *The Times*, 27 January 1928, p. 20. For a well-informed summary of events in the Hill era and later, see 'In Beecham's box', *Cartel* (Journal of International Co-operative Alliance) 3, No. 5, July 1953, pp. 192–5.

2 Board Minutes, 15 February 1928; Lazell, *From Pills to Penicillin*, p. 29; Keyworth, *Cabbages and Things*, p. 130; Board Minutes, 12 July, 27 September 1928.

3 F. Dickens, 'Edward Charles Dodds, 1899–1973', *Biographical Memoirs of Fellows of the Royal Society* 21, 1975, pp. 253–4; J. Slinn, *A History of May & Baker, 1834–1984* (Cambridge: Hobsons Ltd, 1984), p. 99.

4 *Investors Chronicle*, 11 June 1932, p. 1180; *Economist*, 24 June 1933, p. 1376.

5 H. G. Lazell, 'The Years with Beechams', *Management Today*, November 1968, p. 69.

6 Lazell, *From Pills to Penicillin*, pp. 23–4, 27; Keyworth, *Cabbages and Things*, p. 135.

7 *Beecham Group Journal* 1, No. 3, Summer 1961, p. 10; *The Times*, 24 April 1961, p. 19, 26 April 1961, p. 19; Board Minutes, 11, 23 December 1930.

8 Dennett, *The Charterhouse Group*, p. 28.

9 Board Minutes, 11 June 1931; Lazell, *From Pills to Penicillin*, pp. 78–9.

10 *CD* 27 June 1931, pp. 754, 758, 8 July 1933, pp. 38–9, 4 November 1933, pp. 552–3.

11 *CD* 30 May 1936, pp. 629–32; *Industrial Chemist*, June 1937, pp. 234–7, with thanks to Sally Horrocks for the reference.

12 Huntley & Palmers Ltd, Executive Committee Minutes, 22 December 1931, Charles Palmer to Philip Hill, 16 February 1932, Hill to Palmer, 27 December 1934, Palmer to Hill 9 January 1935, Executive Committee Minutes 1 and 15 January 1935, 'no action'; Hill to Palmer, 2 May 1938, Executive Committee Minutes 31 May 1938, 'not to be entertained'.

13 H. Cox, 'Antagonising the Treasury: TST and the repatriation of Boots the Chemists', in 'Business on trial: the Tobacco Securities Trust and the 1935 Pepper Debacle', *Business History* 49, No. 6, November 2007, pp. 771–3. I am very grateful to Howard Cox for a copy of this paper, for his full notes from TNA, T 160/530, 13071/01, 'Boots Share Deal, 1933–1934', and for much helpful advice on this episode; J. E. Greenwood, *A Cap for Boots: An Autobiography* (London: Hutchinson Benham, 1977), pp. 33–52, cf. Hill's doubtless exaggerated remark to Greenwood, 'he had not the faintest interest in the drug business' as 'the property market and finance was [*sic*] all that really interested him', ibid., p. 43; Keyworth, *Cabbages and Things*, p. 201. For Montagu Norman's hostility towards Hill see D. Kynaston, *The City of London: Illusions of Gold, 1914–1945* (London: Chatto & Windus, 1999), 3, pp. 394–5.

14 Keyworth, *Cabbages and Things*, p. 147.

15 A. Waugh, *The Fatal Gift* (London: W. H. Allen, 1973), p. 16; E. Waugh, *A Handful of Dust* ([1934] Harmondsworth: Penguin Books, 1951), p. 70; *idem*, *Brideshead Revisited*, pp. 101–3; re Phyllis's stage turn, information from Sir Harry Moore, formerly of Hill Samuel.

16 Keyworth, *Cabbages and Things*, p. 203.

17 Beechams Pills Ltd, 1st AGM, *Economist*, 13 July 1929, pp. 7–8; 6th AGM, *Economist*, 14 July 1934, p. 88.

18 Ibid., 8th AGM, *Economist*, 30 May 1936, p. 523; 9th AGM, *Economist* 15 May 1937, p. 422.

19 BA, USA, Beechams Pills Inc., Report, 1934–47, April 1947 and Canada, Beechams Pills (Canada) Ltd, Report, 1934–47, April 1947; Board Minutes, 28 April 1938.

20 Ibid., 16 July 1931, 13 July 1933, 14 March 1935.

21 Ibid., 15 October 1936; 9th AGM, *Economist*, 15 May 1937, p. 422; full-page advertisement in *The Times*, 30 May 1938, p. 9; comment in *British Medical Journal*, 4 June 1938, p. 1214.

22 T. A. B. Corley, 'UK government regulation of medicinal drugs, 1890–2000', *Business History* 47, No. 3, July 2005, pp. 337–51, esp. 340–1.

23 *Hansard*, House of Lords, 5th series, 110, cols 1176–86, 26 July 1938; *World's Press News*, 14 July 1938.

24 *CD* 7 September 1935; Board Minutes, 16 June 1937 for current year's advertising allocation.

25 10th AGM, *Economist*, 10 June 1939, p. 629; Corley, 'UK government regulation', pp. 341–2.

26 Lazell, *From Pills to Penicillin*, pp. 7–21; 'Modern methods in pharmaceutical manufacture', *Industrial Chemist: Pharmaceutical and Cosmetic Supplement*, October 1935, pp. 118–23, November 1935, pp. 133–9.

27 T. A. B. Corley, 'Henry George Leslie Lazell, 1903–1982', *DBB* 3, pp. 690–4 and *ODNB* 32, pp. 940–1.

28 Keyworth, *Cabbages and Things*, pp. 131–2; Lazell, *From Pills to Penicillin*, pp. 20, 23, 115.

29 *Investors Chronicle*, 17 September 1938, pp. 573–4; *Economist*, 10 September 1938, p. 522;

Lazell, *From Pills to Penicillin*, pp. 25–6.

30 For Eno see *CD* Special Issue, 27 June 1936, pp. 738–40; *Investors Chronicle*, 8 October 1938, p. 714; Lazell, *From Pills to Penicillin*, p. 28; Board Minutes, 20 October 1938.

31 Lazell, *From Pills to Penicillin*, pp. 28–9; *Annual Report 1956/7*, pp. 13–17.

32 Lazell, *From Pills to Penicillin*, pp. 30–5; Board Minutes, 10 November 1938, 9 February 1939.

33 *CD* 26 September 1936; Board Minutes, 12 January 1939.

34 Board Minutes, 7 September 1939; Lazell, *From Pills to Penicillin*, pp. 36–7.

35 Ibid., pp. 37, 92; Board Minutes, 1 February 1940.

36 E. L. Hargreaves and M. M. Gowing, *Civil Industry and Trade (Civil History of Second World War)* (London: HM Stationery Office, 1952), pp. 83, 531–6, 560–2; Lazell, *From Pills to Penicillin*, pp. 40–1.

37 *Hansard*, House of Commons, 1940–41, 373, Col. 669, 16 July 1941, 374, Col. 500, 30 September 1941; *Annual Report 1940/1*, p. 3; Lazell, *From Pills to Penicillin*, p. 37.

38 BA, 'G. S. Royds Ltd, Beecham's Pills Advertising, 1939–48', BP 3/3/2; typical wartime advertisement, *Investors Chronicle*, 23 August 1941, p. 237.

39 Lazell, *From Pills to Penicillin*, pp. 46–58; Board Minutes, 15 September 1943.

40 Lazell, 'The Years with Beechams', pp. 68–9.

41 Lazell, *From Pills to Penicillin*, p. 29; Keyworth, *Cabbages and Things*, p. 202.

Chapter 12: The Beecham Group adrift, 1944–1951

1 Lazell, *From Pills to Penicillin*, p. 59; *idem*, 'The Years with Beechams', pp. 68–9.

2 Board Minutes, 22 August 1944.

3 S. Haxey, *Tory M.P.* (London: Gollancz, 1939), pp. 80–1, 84, 112.

4 *Annual Report 1944/5*, p. 4.

5 *Lancet*, 24 May 1947, p. 717.

6 *Investors Chronicle*, 4 May 1940, p. 681.

7 R. M. Titmuss, *Problems of Social Policy (Civil History of Second World War)* (London: HM Stationery Office, 1950), pp. 528–30.

8 *Economist*, 6 January 1945, pp. 4–5.

9 Lazell, *From Pills to Penicillin*, pp. 59–60; Board Minutes, 1 November 1944.

10 Keyworth, *Cabbages and Things*, p. 157.

11 Ibid., pp. 51, 215; *Liverpool Echo*, 5 and 6 June 1955.

12 Board Minutes, 22 August 1944, 27 February 1946; Lazell, *From Pills to Penicillin*, pp. 114–16.

13 Ibid., p. 50.

14 E. Jones, *The Business of Medicine: The Extraordinary History of Glaxo* (London:Profile Books, 2001), pp. 65–6; Lazell, *From Pills to Penicillin*, pp. 51–2.

15 *Idem*, p. 72; R&D data from unpublished FBI sources, kindly supplied by Sally Horrocks.

16 T. A. B. Corley, *Quaker Enterprise in Biscuits: Huntley & Palmers of Reading, 1822–1972* (London: Hutchinson, 1972), p. 217; Buckley's obituary, *The Times*, 28 October 1972, p. 16; Lazell, *From Pills to Penicillin*, pp. 9, 60.

17 Ibid., p. 61.

18 Ibid., pp. 98–100.

19 Board Minutes, 19 June, 23 July 1947; Lazell, *From Pills to Penicillin*, p. 61.

20 Ibid., p. 63.

21 Board Minutes, 25 February 1948; *Annual Report 1949/50*, p. 15; Board Minutes, 25 October 1950.

22 Ibid., 1 September 1948.

23 *Investors Chronicle*, 20 August 1949, p. 445.

24 Lazell, 'The Years with Beechams', pp. 69–70; W. P. Kennedy and P. L. Payne, 'Directions

for future research', in L. Hannah (ed.), *Management Strategy and Business Development* (London: Macmillan, 1976), p. 250; Board Minutes, 9 March 1949.

25 Lazell, *From Pills to Penicillin*, p. 63; *idem*, 'The Years with Beechams', p. 142; Board Minutes, 27 April 1949.

26 H. G. Lazell, 'Development and organisation of Beecham Group Ltd', London School of Economics: Seminar on Problems in Industrial Administration 1959/60 252, 23 February 1960, p. 3; G. J. Wilkins, 'A Record of Innovation and Exports', in G. Teeling-Smith, *Innovation and the Balance of Payments* (London: Office of Health Economics, 1967), p. 15.

27 Board Minutes, 27 April, 29 June 1949; Lazell, *From Pills to Penicillin*, p. 79.

28 Ibid., p. 69.

29 Board Minutes, 12 September 1949; Lazell, *From Pills to Penicillin*, p. 64; For Keith see obituary, *The Times*, 6 September 2004, p. 25, and R. Roberts, 'Kenneth Alexander Keith, Baron Keith of Castleacre (1916–2004), in L. Goldman (ed.), *Oxford Dictionary of National Biography, 2000–2004* (Oxford: Oxford University Press, 2009), pp. 599–602.

30 Evidence of J. M. Keyworth.

31 *Investors Chronicle*, 9 September 1950, p. 482.

32 Lazell, *From Pills to Penicillin*, p. 64.

33 Board Minutes, 31 January, 21 March, 2 April, 27 June 1951.

34 Ibid., 2 April, 18 July, 19 September 1951.

35 Lazell, *From Pills to Penicillin*, pp. 64–5, *The Times*, 29 August 1951, p. 9.

36 Lazell, *From Pills to Penicillin*, p. 65–6.

Chapter 13: Lazell: Creator of a pharmaceutical company, 1951–1968

1 Essential, if understandably one-sided, sources are the three writings by Lazell, *From Pills to Penicillin*, 'The years with Beechams' and 'Development and organisation of Beecham Group Ltd'.

2 Lazell, *From Pills to Penicillin*, pp. 2, 200.

3 *Investors Chronicle*, 1 September 1951, p. 561; *Statist*, 1 September 1951, pp. 281–2.

4 *Statist*, 5 September 1953.

5 Lazell, 'Development and organisation of Beecham Group Ltd', p. 8; *Investors Chronicle*, 6 November 1954, pp. 1375–6.

6 Lazell, 'The Years with Beechams', p. 73; *idem, From Pills to Penicillin*, pp. 188, 200, 96.

7 Ibid., pp. 98–100; R. Heller, *The Naked Manager* (London: Barrie & Jenkins, 1972), p. 194; Lazell, 'The Years with Beechams', p. 72; *Investors Chronicle*, 8 September 1956, p. 815.

8 Lazell, *From Pills to Penicillin*, pp. 58, 156–60; *Investors Chronicle*, 27 September 1957, p. 1007.

9 Lazell, *From Pills to Penicillin*, pp. 102–3; R. P. Bauman, P. Jackson and J. T. Lawrence, *From Promise to Performance: A Journey of Transformation at SmithKline Beecham* (Boston MA: Harvard Business School Press, 1997), p. 51.

10 A brief account of Beecham's work on developing semi-synthetic penicillins is in R. Bud, *Penicillin: Triumph and Tragedy* (Oxford: Oxford University Press, 2007), pp. 124–8; relevant correspondence and reports are in Wellcome Library, [Sir Ernst] Chain Papers, esp. Dodds to Chain, 27 April 1955, PP/EBC, F 44, and Doyle's report of a visit to the United States, 22 April 1959, F66.

11 Lazell, *From Pills to Penicillin*, pp. 73, 76.

12 Wilkins, 'A Record', p. 15; E. M. Tansey and L. A. Reynolds (eds), 'Post Penicillin Antibiotics', *Wellcome Witness to Twentieth Century Medicine* (London: Wellcome Trust, 2000), 6, pp. 25–39; G. T. Stewart, *The Penicillin Group of Drugs* (Amsterdam: Elsevier, 1965), pp. 20–8; R. W. Clark, *The Life of Ernst Chain: Penicillin and Beyond* (London: Weidenfeld & Nicolson, 1985), pp. 132–9. Beecham's and others' penicillins are fully documented, from the

technical viewpoint, in S. Selwyn, *The Beta-Lactam Antibiotics: Penicillins and Cephalosporins in Perspective* (London: Hodder & Stoughton, 1980), esp. pp. 34–7, and by G. N. Rolinson, 'Forty years of β-lactam research', *Journal of Antimicrobial Chemotherapy* 41, pp. 587–607, a personal account by Beecham's senior microbiologist, closely involved in the project.

13 T. A. B. Corley, 'Beecham and the development of semi-synthetic penicillins, 1951–1970', Centre for Institutional Performance, University of Reading, Discussion Paper 2003–1 (2003), pp. 1–26; Sir E. Chain, 'Thirty years of penicillin therapy', *Proceedings of Royal Society of London*, Series B 179, 1971, pp. 293–319; Lazell, *From Pills to Penicillin*, Chapter 12, 'The Discovery', pp. 135–50; Wellcome Library, Chain Papers, first meeting in Brussels, summer 1954, PP/EBC, F 172.

14 Ibid., Chain to McGeorge, 26 September 1955, F 49; *Annual Report 1953/4*, p. 8; Lazell, *From Pills to Penicillin*, p. 142; D. Wilson, *Penicillin in Perspective* (London: Faber & Faber, 1976), pp. 257–69.

15 Lazell, *From Pills to Penicillin*, p. 166; Wilkins, 'A Record', p. 18.

16 Keyworth, *Cabbages and Things*, p. 129.

17 J. C. Sheehan, *The Enchanted Ring: The Untold Story of Penicillin* (Cambridge MA: The MIT Press, 1982), pp. 126–71, esp. pp. 160, 173, 177; Bud, *Penicillin*, pp. 126–7; Tansey and Reynolds, 'Post Penicillin Antibiotics', p. 32.

18 Lazell, *From Pills to Penicillin*, p. 151.

19 Wellcome Library, Chain Papers PP/EBC, Chain to (Sir) Robert Armstrong (Principal Private Secretary to Prime Minister), 13 November 1970; Armstrong to Chain, 'will be fully considered [but in the end rejected]', 19 November 1970, F 171.

20 Lazell, *From Pills to Penicillin*, pp. 96, Chapter 11, pp. 114–34, Chapter 16, pp. 180–8. J. H. Dunning, 'Revisiting UK FDI in US manufacturing and extractive industries in 1960', in G. Jones and L. Gálvez-Muñoz (eds), *Foreign Multinationals in the United States: Management and Performance* (London: Routledge, 2002), pp. 50–69, esp. p. 56, discusses Beecham's production in the United States from 1954 onwards. John Dunning kindly gave me access to the very informative questionnaires on which his article was based.

21 Lazell, *From Pills to Penicillin*, p. 119.

22 Ibid., p. 187.

23 Ibid., p. 194–9; T. A. B. Corley, 'Best-practice marketing of food and health drinks in Britain, 1930–70', in G. Jones and N. J. Morgan (eds), *Adding Value: Brands and Marketing in Food and Drink* (London: Routledge, 1994), pp. 215–36. Lazell aired his trenchant views on this topic in 'Marketing in a competitive economy', London School of Economics: Seminar on Problems in Industrial Administration 1968/9 394, 3 December 1968, pp. 1–12, and in *The Labour Party: Report of a Commission of Enquiry into Advertising* (London: Labour Party, 1966), pp. 8, 10, 152: 'When you are selling a [patent] medicine, there is always an invisible ingredient: I call it faith', because 'with a great many minor ailments you can achieve a cure or a relief much more effectively if the consumer has infinite faith in it'.

24 *Annual Report 1966/7*, p. 9; Dunning, 'Revisiting UK FDI', esp. p. 56.

25 T. A. B. Corley, 'Sir Graham John [Bob] Wilkins, 1924–2003', *ODNB, 2000–2004*, pp. 1187–8.

26 For Europe see Lazell, *From Pills to Penicillin*, Chapter 15, pp. 171–9; J. M. Stopford and L. Turner, *Britain and the Multinationals* (Chichester: John Wiley, 1985), pp. 75–6, 79.

27 Lazell, *From Pills to Penicillin*, pp. 151, 169.

28 Ibid., pp. 128, 155, 176; *Annual Report 1967/8*, p. 8.

29 J. Slinn, 'Price Controls or Control through Prices? Regulating the Cost and Consumption of Prescription Pharmaceuticals in the UK, 1948–67', *Business History* 47, No. 3, July 2005, pp. 352–66; Wilkins, 'A Record', p. 20.

30 C. Webster, *The Health Service since the War* (London: HM Stationery Office, 1996), 2, pp. 215–24; TNA, MH 104/32, Sainsbury Committee, impolite comments on Beecham's written evidence (latter now missing from file); Treasury's negative view on Committee

Report, Webster, op. cit., p. 220.

31 Esp. *Annual Report 1967/8*, pp. 9–11.

32 Lazell, *From Pills to Penicillin*, p. 191; D. F. Channon, *The Strategy and Structure of British Enterprise* (London: Macmillan, 1973), pp. 147–8; *Observer*, 24 May 1970. For general assessment, see Corley, 'H. G. L. Lazell', *ODNB* 32, pp. 940–1.

Chapter 14: Edwards and the bid for Glaxo, 1968–1975

1 Lazell, *From Pills to Penicillin*, p. 190.

2 M. Ackrill, 'Sir Ronald Stanley Edwards, 1910–1976', *DBB* 2, pp. 237–44 and *ODNB* 17, pp. 962–3. She has very kindly allowed me to quote from her MS, 'Enterprise in Theory and Practice: A Biography of Sir Ronald Edwards', now held in the London School of Economics Archives, Coll Misc 1189, Chapter 7, 'Beecham Group, 1968–75', pp. 247–310.

3 R. S. Edwards and H. Townsend, *Business Enterprise: Its Growth and Organisation* (London: Macmillan, 1958); *idem*, *Studies in Business Organisation* (London: Macmillan, 1961). The third, *Business Growth* (London: Macmillan, 1966) contains an article by A. E. V. Houchen, then chairman of Beecham Food and Drink Division, on 'The marketing of branded consumer goods', pp. 55–76. See also Edwards' lecture, 'The case for competition', *Journal of the Royal Society of Arts* March 1971 (pre-Glaxo bid), when he declared that 'there is a long way to go before this country [the UK] has to content itself with only one major pharmaceutical firm', p. 214. It is not known what made him change his mind by the end of the year.

4 *Evening Standard*, 6 October 1970.

5 *Annual Report 1974/5*, p. 12.

6 *Financial Times*, 3 December 1971.

7 *Annual Report 1968/9*, pp. 11–12, *1969/70*, p. 10.

8 *Evening Standard*, 6 October 1970.

9 *Observer*, 24 May 1970.

10 *Observer*, 10 October 1971.

11 T. A. B. Corley, 'Sir Joseph Horlick, 1846–1921', *ODNB* 28, pp. 112–13; *idem*, 'Best-practice marketing', pp. 224, 263ff.; Turner, *The Shocking History*, p. 198. Beecham had in 1904 employed a comparable phrase, 'that tired feeling' (see Chapter 7). The company's scientists devoted much time to research into whether Horlicks did genuinely cure 'night starvation': evidence of H. Townsend.

12 Lazell, *From Pills to Penicillin*, p. 193.

13 *Annual Report 1970/1*, pp. 1, 7; Lazell, *From Pills to Penicillin*, p. 176.

14 *Financial Times*, 23 February 1971; Lazell, *From Pills to Penicillin*, pp. 186–7.

15 Ibid., p. 187; *Annual Report 1970/1*, p. 7; *Sunday Times*, 28 February 1971.

16 *Financial Times*, 6 July 1971; Lazell, *From Pills to Penicillin*, p. 187.

17 *Annual Report 1970/1*, pp. 7, 10, *1971/2*, p. 8.

18 *Annual Report 1969/70*, p. 13, *1970/1*, p. 11, *1971/2*, p. 8. T. A. B. Corley and Andrew Godley, 'The veterinary medicine industry in Britain during the twentieth century', *Economic History Review* (forthcoming, 2011).

19 *The Times*, 27 March 1975, pp. 21, 25.

20 *Financial Times*, 3 December 1971.

21 Sir P. Girolami, 'The Development of Glaxo', unpublished paper, 1985 (updated to 1989), p. 3; Jones, *The Business of Medicine*, p. 150; *The Times*, 12 November 1985.

22 *The Times*, 3 December 1971, pp. 12, 20; Jones, *The Business of Medicine*, p. 182, evidence of Sir Arthur Knight.

23 *Economist*, 15 November 1969, p. 84; *The Times*, 16 December 1971, p. 23.

24 Evidence of Paul Lazell, on his father's likely response. My thanks are due to Mr Lazell

for some helpful discussions on his father's career.

25 *Financial Times*, 3 December 1971.

26 The following paragraphs owe much to the well-documented account in Jones, *The Business of Medicine*, pp. 181ff.

27 J. Fairburn, 'The evolution of merger policy in Britain', in J. Fairburn and J. Kay (eds), *Merger and Merger Policy* (Oxford: Oxford University Press, 1989), pp. 193–230, esp. pp. 196, 199.

28 *The Times*, 16 December 1971, p. 23; Wellcome Library, Chain papers PP/EBC, Sir R. Robinson to Chain, 22 December 1971, K 201, Chain to Edwards, 4 February 1972, F 173.

29 Jones, *The Business of Medicine*, pp. 187–9; PP 1971–2, 72, 'Monopolies Commission: Beecham Group Ltd and Glaxo Group Ltd: Report on Proposed Mergers [also Boots and Glaxo]'. HC 341, July 1972, p. 14.

30 *The Times*, 14 January 1972, p. 17.

31 Centre for the Study of Industrial Innovation (National Economic Development Council), *Reaching World Markets: A Report on International Marketing in the Pharmaceutical Industry*, November 1971, pp. 1–48, esp. p. 8; Jones, *The Business of Medicine*, p. 175.

32 Monopolies Commission, *Report*, para. 190, p. 36; Wellcome Library, Chain papers, PP/EBC, Chain to Edwards, 4 February 1972, F 173.

33 Monopolies Commission, *Report*, para. 197, p. 38.

34 Ibid., para. 264, p. 53, para. 294, p. 59.

35 Sir R. Edwards, *The Multinational Pharmaceutical Industry: A Commentary*, The 1974 Mercantile Credit Lecture, given at Reading University, 19 November 1974 (Reading: University of Reading, 1974), pp. 7–8, 17.

36 Girolami, 'Development of Glaxo', p. 6; Jones, *The Business of Medicine*, p. 194.

37 *Investors Chronicle*, 7 July 1972, p. 16.

38 Ibid., 27 July 1972, p. 193.

39 *Annual Report 1972/3*, pp. 8–9, *1973/4*, p. 5.

40 Richards, *Commodity Culture*, p. 172.

41 Corley and Godley, 'Veterinary medicine industry'.

42 *Annual Report 1973/4*, p. 6.

43 A. Sampson, *The Changing Anatomy of Britain* (London: Hodder & Stoughton, 1982), p. 360.

44 *Financial Times*, 27 March 1975.

45 Ackrill, MS, Chapter 8, deals with Edwards' brief chairmanship of British Leyland from 1974 to 1975.

46 A. Sampson, 'Musical chairs for Beecham brigade', *Observer*, 18 November 1979.

Chapter 15: From Wilkins to SmithKline Beecham, 1975–1988

1 *Observer*, 7 July 1985, p. 30; *The Times*, 27 March 1975, pp. 21, 25.

2 Lazell, *From Pills to Penicillin*, p. 127.

3 *Observer*, 7 July 1985, p. 30; *Annual Report 1977/8*, pp. 3–4.

4 *Wellcome Witness Seminar 6*, 2000, p. 36.

5 *Annual Report 1975/6*, p. 5, *1976/7*, p. 5.

6 Ibid., *1978/9*, p. 3.

7 Girolami, 'Development of Glaxo', p. 6.

8 *Financial Times*, 27 March 1975.

9 *Sunday Times*, 2 December 1984.

10 Lazell, *From Pills to Penicillin*, pp. 130, 135.

11 J. Saunders, *Nightmare: Ernest Saunders and the Guinness Affair* (London: Arrow Books, 1990), p. 21.

12 *Marketing*, 14 February 1985.

13 *Financial Times*, 11 July 1978; *Investors Chronicle*, 14 July 1978.

14 *Annual Report 1976/7*, pp. 4, 9.

15 *Financial Times*, 29 August, 23 November 1979.

16 *Observer*, 23 December 1984; *Marketing*, 14 February 1985; *Investors Chronicle*, 16 July 1982, p. 158.

17 *Annual Report 1982/3*, p. 3.

18 *Investors Chronicle*, 22 June 1984, p. 64, 19 July 1985, p. 57, 27 September 1985, p. 26.

19 *Financial Times*, 2 July 1985.

20 Ibid., 29 March 1984.

21 *Observer*, 23 December 1984.

22 *Director*, January 1986, p. 40.

23 *Observer*, 23 December 1984.

24 *Annual Report 1984/5*, p. 8; G. Foster, 'Beecham takes its medicine', *Management Today*, October 1985, p. 55; *The Times*, 17 January 1985, p. 16.

25 *Investors Chronicle*, 29 March 1985, p. 12.

26 *Observer*, 23 December 1984; *Marketing*, 14 February 1985.

27 *Annual Report 1984/5*, p. 8; *Investors Chronicle*, 14 June 1985, p. 90, 19 July 1985, p. 57.

28 *Observer*, 7 July 1985; *Business Week*, 2 September 1985; *Daily Telegraph*, 4 July 2003.

29 *The Times*, 3 August 1985, p. 21.

30 G. Foster, 'Beecham takes its medicine', *Management Today*, October 1985, p. 52; his claim to have been misreported was denied by the journalist concerned: *Financial Times*, 16 November 1985.

31 Ibid., 12 November 1985; *Daily Telegraph*, 12 November 1985; for Robb see *Observer*, 15 June 1986.

32 *The Times*, 12 November 1985, pp. 1, 23, 25; *Sunday Times*, 17 November 1985, pp. 58, 63.

33 *Financial Times*, 16 November 1985; *Investors Chronicle*, 18 March 1988, p. 25; Bauman, Jackson and Lawrence, *From Promise to Performance*, pp. 25–6.

34 Ibid., p. 26; D. G. Hyde and P. Haspeslagh, 'The making of the *Simply Better* healthcare company: SmithKline Beecham' (Fontainebleau, INSEAD, 1994) (A), p. 9.

35 *Observer*, 8 December, 29 December 1985.

36 *Investors Chronicle*, 20 June 1986, p. 70.

37 Ibid., 22 January 1988, p. 11.

38 Ibid., 18 March 1988; Hyde and Haspeslagh, 'The making of … SmithKline Beecham', pp. 9–10; Bauman, Jackson and Lawrence, *From Promise to Performance*, pp. 26ff.; for Harvard Business School techniques see www.hbs.edu/case/case-print.html. This author had the privilege of participating in the first Harvard Advanced Management Program held in Britain, at Durham, in 1964, which showed up clearly the superiority of American business thinking, compared with that in British industry at the time, e.g. UK executive, 'Marketing is a load of bullshit'; Harvard professor, with great forbearance, 'That's very, very interesting': T. A. B. Corley, 'Consumer Marketing in Britain, 1914–60', *Business History* 39, No. 4, October 1987, pp. 65–83, esp. p. 80.

39 Bauman, Jackson and Lawrence, *From Promise to Performance*, pp. 29–31.

40 Ibid., pp. 32–4, 45–6.

41 Ibid., p. 36, but see Lazell, *From Pills to Penicillin*, p. 173; Saunders, *Nightmare*, p. 24.

42 Bauman, Jackson and Lawrence, *From Promise to Performance*, pp. 47, 38–9; Hyde and Haspeslagh, 'The making of … SmithKline Beecham', pp. 10–12.

Chapter 16: Towards GlaxoSmithKline, 1988–2000

1 Hyde and Haspeslagh, 'The making of … SmithKline Beecham', 1, p. 12.

2 J. F. Marion, *The Fine Old House* (Philadelphia PA: SmithKline Corporation, 1980), p. 120; A. D. Chandler, *Shaping the Industrial Century: The Remarkable Story of the Evolution of the*

Modern Chemical and Pharmaceutical Industries (Cambridge MA: Harvard University Press, 2005), pp. 202–3; A. Gambardella, *Science and Innovation: the US Pharmaceutical Industry during the 1980s* (Cambridge: Cambridge University Press, 1995), pp. 95–8; G. E. Ullyot, B. H. Ullyot, and L. B. Slater, "The Metamorphosis of Smith-Kline & French Laboratories to Smith Kline Beecham [*sic*]: 1925–1998", *Bulletin of the History of Chemistry* 25, No. 1, 2000, pp. 16–20.

3 Chandler, *Shaping the Industrial Century*, p. 202; Gambardella, *Science and Innovation*, pp. 23–41; for 'serendipity' see PP, House of Commons, Session, 1999–2000, Science and Technology Committee, Fourth Report, 'Glaxo Wellcome and SmithKline Beecham', 21 February 2000, p. 6, Q. 16; p. 14, Q. 69.

4 J. Froud, S. Johal, A. Leaver and K. Williams, *Financialization and Strategy: Narrative and Numbers* (Abingdon: Routledge, 2006), p. 183. Its chapter, 'GlaxoSmithKline: keeping it going' has some excellent time series for Glaxo and Glaxo Wellcome, but the narrative of events from 1995 to 1999 deals exclusively with financial questions, and not with the co-ordinated measures to promote globalization in that company as well as in SB.

5 Bauman, Jackson and Lawrence, *From Promise to Performance*, p. 63.

6 Chandler, *Shaping the Industrial Century*, pp. 204–5.

7 Hyde and Haspeslagh, 'The making of ... SmithKline Beecham', 1, p. 7.

8 P. J. Streatfield, *The Paradox of Control in Organizations* (London: Routledge, 2001), p. 31.

9 Bauman, Jackson and Lawrence, *From Promise to Performance*, p. 83. For a view of SB's situation and prospects in the early 1990s see J. Taggart, *The World Pharmaceutical Industry* (London: Routledge, 1993), pp. 178, 441–2.

10 H. Syedain, 'SmithKline Beecham's early trials', *Management Today*, November 1989, pp. 99–104; SB's *Annual Report, 1989*, p. 90.

11 Bauman, Jackson and Lawrence, *From Promise to Performance*, p. 169.

12 Streatfield, *The Paradox of Control*, Chapters 3–4, pp. 26–75, esp. pp. 12, 5, 86, 88 for respective quotations given above.

13 Hyde and Haspeslagh, 'The making of ... SmithKline Beecham', 1, p. 1.

14 *Economist*, 24 January 1998, p. 79, quoting B. G. James, author of *The Future of the Multinational Pharmaceutical Industry to 1990* (London: Associated Business Programmes, 1977).

15 Ibid., 4 November 1989, p. 169.

16 H. Wendt, *Global Embrace* (New York: Harper Collins, 1993), pp. 165–6; Bauman, Jackson and Lawrence, *From Promise to Performance*, p. 58; Hyde and Haspeslagh, 'The making of ... SmithKline Beecham', 1, p. 20.

17 Ibid., 1, p. 18.

18 *Sunday Times*, 2 May 1993, p. 3/8, 25 January 1998, pp. 3/2, 3/3.

19 Hyde and Haspeslagh, 'The making of ... SmithKline Beecham', 1, p. 19.

20 PP, House of Commons, Session 1997–98, Science and Technology Committee, Third Report, 'Glaxo Wellcome and SmithKline Beecham: The merger proposals', 2 April 1998, p. 19, Q. 62.

21 Ibid., p. 23, Q. 89; SmithKline Beecham, *Annual Report 1994*, p. 19.

22 A. Davidson, 'J. P. Garnier', *Management Today*, March 2004, p. 38.

23 *Euromonitor*, 'SmithKline Beecham plc, 23.5.2, "Research and Development/Production"', June 2000, p. 9.

24 SmithKline Beecham, *Annual Report 1992*, p. 15; Bauman, Jackson and Lawrence, *From Promise to Performance*, p. 227.

25 Ibid., pp. 241–2; SmithKline Beecham, *Annual Report 1994*, p. 8; Bauman, Jackson and Lawrence, *From Promise to Performance*, pp. 241–2; Hyde and Haspeslagh, 'The making of ... SmithKline Beecham', 2, p. 14.

26 D. Stipp, 'Bill Haseltine [of Human Genome Sciences]', *Fortune* 143, 25 June 2001, pp. 49–55.

27 Hyde and Haspeslagh, 'The making of ... SmithKline Beecham', 2, p. 18.

28 Bauman, Jackson and Lawrence, *From Promise to Performance*, pp. 231–3; *Sunday Times*, 2 May 1993, p. 3/8.

29 *The Times*, 12 March 1993, p. 29; *Sunday Times*, 14 March 1993, p. 3/1, 2 May 1993, p. 3/8.

30 Bauman, Jackson and Lawrence, *From Promise to Performance*, p. 254.

31 Ibid., p. 273; *Investors Chronicle*, 6 May 1994, p. 8. For the Federal Trade Commission's subsequent investigation see *The Times*, 15 November 1994, p. 24.

32 Ibid., 2 September 1994, p. 9.

33 SmithKline Beecham, *Annual Reports, 1991–94*; Jones, *The Business of Medicine*, p. 241.

34 Bauman, Jackson and Lawrence, *From Promise to Performance*, p. 273; *Investors Chronicle*, 10 March 1995, p. 48; Corley and Godley, 'Veterinary medicine industry'.

35 PP, Science and Technology Committee, Session 1994–95, Second Report, 'The Glaxo Bid for Wellcome plc', *passim*; E. J. Morgan, 'Innovation and merger decisions in the pharmaceutical industry', *Review of Industrial Organization*, 19, 2001, pp. 184–6.

36 *Management Today*, December 1995, p. 56; *Sunday Times*, 16 January 2000, pp. 3/1, 3/9.

37 *Economist*, 28 January 1995, pp. 73–4.

38 SB *Annual Report, 1995*, p. 8, *1998*, p. 12, *1999*, pp. 30, 35; for Streatfield's involvement in WSO planning, see Streatfield, *The Paradox of Control*, pp. 92–5.

39 SB *Annual Report*, 1996, p. 18.

40 SB, *Annual Report 1995*, pp. 5, 8.

41 *The Times*, 2 February 1998, p. 48.

42 Froud et al., *Financialization and Strategy*, p. 188.

43 *Scrip: World Pharmaceutical News, 1998* (Richmond, Surrey: PJB Publications, 1998), p. 116.

44 Ibid.; *Fortune* 137, 30 March 1998, p. 19.

45 *Sunday Times*, 25 January 1998, p. 3/3.

46 Gambardella, *Science and Innovation*, pp. 101–2; *Economist*, 24 January 1998, pp. 78–9; *The Times*, 21 January 1998, p. 25.

47 *Sunday Times*, 1 March 1998, pp. 3/2, 3/3; PP, Science and Technology Committee Session 1997–98, Third Report, 'Glaxo Wellcome and SmithKline Beecham: The merger proposals', p. 23–4, Q. 95.

48 *Investors Chronicle*, 6 February 1998, p. 14.

49 *Financial Times*, 17 January 2000, p. 18.

50 PP, Science and Technology Committee, Session 1997–98, Third Report, p. 26, Q. 110; *The Times*, 28 February 1998, pp. 28–9.

51 *Sunday Times*, 1 March 1998, pp. 3/2, 3/3.

52 PP, Science and Technology Committee, Session 1997–98, Third Report, pp. iv–vi, esp. para. 11; *Fortune*, 30 March 1998, p. 19.

53 *Investors Chronicle*, 6 February 1998, p. 14.

54 S. Randles, 'Complex systems applied? The merger that made Glaxo SmithKline [*sic*]', *Technology Analysis and Strategic Management* 14, No. 3, 2002, pp. 346–9; B. Bátiz-Lazo, 'GSK – a merger too far?', *ICFAI Journal of Mergers and Acquisitions*, 1, No. 4 (2004), pp. 74–89.

55 GlaxoSmithKline, *Annual Report 2000*, pp. 5, 20; PP, Science and Technology Committee, Session 1999–2000, Fourth Report, 2, p. 5, Q. 8.

56 *Economist*, 13 February 1999, p. 92; *Sunday Times*, 25 January 1998, p. 3/3.

57 *Financial Times*, 17 January 2000, p. 18; *The Times*, 10 February 1999, p. 21, 12 October 1999, pp. 31, 33; *Sunday Times*, 16 January 2000, pp. 3/1, 3/9.

58 Ibid., 21 February 2000, p. 7.

59 *Financial Times*, 18 January 2000, pp. 19, 20.

Epilogue

1 Randles, 'Complex systems applied?', pp. 342–3.
2 PP, Science and Technology Committee, Session 1999–2000, Fourth Report, p. 7, Q. 17; GlaxoSmithKline, *Annual Report 2000*, p. 20.
3 *Financial Times*, 18 January 2000, p. 19.
4 Lazell, *From Pills to Penicillin*, pp. 191, 201.
5 'In Beecham's box', *Cartel* 3, No. 5, July 1953, pp. 192–5.
6 PP, Science and Technology Committee, Session 1997–98, Third Report, p. 19, Q. 62.
7 *The Times*, 3 March 1994, p. 5; for SB middle-management discussions in the early 1990s about possible factory closures, including that of the St Helens unit, see Streatfield, *The Paradox of Control*, pp. 64–6.
8 Evidence of Dr M. Cole, Head of the Biochemical Services Department and Beecham's Research co-ordinator until 1990. See his contributions to Tansey and Reynolds' edited work, 'Post Penicillin Antibiotics', pp. 34, 50–2.
9 'The Beecham's pill machine', *CD* 4 April 1987 for figure of 50 million pills; S. Anderson, '"Best for me, best for you" – a history of Beecham's Pills, 1842–1998', *PJ* 269, 21/28 December 2002, pp. 921–4, quoting 'End of an era. Beecham's pills discontinued', *PJ* 260, 1998, p. 774.
10 SmithKline Beecham, *Annual Report 1999*, p. 39.

Appendix 1: Sir Thomas Beecham's ancestry, with Beecham family tree

1 F. Howes, 'Music', in S. Nowell-Smith (ed.), *Edwardian England, 1901–1914* (Oxford: Oxford University Press, 1964), p. 439.
2 C. Reid, *Malcolm Sargent* (London: Hamish Hamilton, 1968), p. xi.
3 Cardus, *Sir Thomas Beecham*, pp. 58–9, 28–9, who states that Thomas borrowed the *Gerontius* quotation from George Moore: undoubtedly, not the philosopher, George Edward, but the lively Irish novelist, George Augustus, a friend of Beecham's mistress, Nancy Cunard.
4 J. Lucas, *Thomas Beecham: An Obsession with Music* (Woodbridge: Boydell Press), pp. 85–6.
5 Cardus, *Sir Thomas Beecham*, p. 22.
6 Scott, *My Years*, p. 162; Cardus, *Sir Thomas Beecham*, p. 23.
7 A. Blackwood, *Sir Thomas Beecham: The Man and the Music* (London: Ebury Press, 1994), p. 204.
8 G. Brooke, in H. Procter-Gregg, *Beecham Remembered* (London: Duckworth, 1976), p. 42; J. Brymer, 'Sir Thomas Beecham, 1879–1961', *DNB, 1961–70* (1981), pp. 87–90. Photographs of him, especially when at the piano, do not confirm the smallness of his hands.
9 Francis, *A Guinea A Box*, p. 166.
10 Beecham, *A Mingled Chime*, pp. 25, 41; Jefferson, *Sir Thomas Beecham*, pp. 18–19.
11 Francis, *A Guinea A Box*, p. 89; *idem, Letter to the Past*, p. 3; *Burke's Peerage, Baronetage and Knightage* (Wilmington, DE: Burke's Peerage and Gentry UK Ltd, 2003) 107th edn, 1, pp. 332–3, states in the Beecham entry – presumably derived from the family – that William Burnett was from London.
12 TNA, Birth certificate; Manchester Cathedral, baptismal register.
13 TNA, Birth certificate of Martha Dickens, 11 April 1819, Army Register Book of Births, Baptisms and marriages, no. 269.
14 TNA, Census 1841, Hulme, Manchester, HO 107/583/11.
15 TNA, Birth certificates; Manchester Cathedral, baptismal register. 'Husbands' specified in Martha Bowen's death certificate, Geelong, Victoria, Australia, 7 February 1895.
16 Ibid.
17 TNA, 1861 Census, Liscard, New Brighton, Cheshire, RG 9/2648/17.
18 TNA, 1871 Census, Croppers Hill, St Helens, RG 3865/47/6.

19 Chapter 3, note 14 gives particulars of Lloyds Lists of shipping and the relevant passenger names.
20 Reid, *Thomas Beecham*, p. 31.
21 R. Crichton (ed.), *The Memoirs of Ethel Smyth* (London: Viking, 1987), p. 286.
22 Jefferson, *Sir Thomas Beecham*, p. 24.
23 Reid, *Thomas Beecham*, p. 243.
24 Jefferson, *Sir Thomas Beecham*, pp. 242–3. In the end, substantial fines were avoided through the good offices of Sir Edward Playfair, secretary of the department of Defence, who successfully petitioned the tax authorities to lengthen his stay in Britain. See Lucas, *Thomas Beecham*, p. 339.

Appendix 2: Thomas Beecham and the hymn books

1 *CD* 12 June 1886, p. 561, 15 July 1893, p. 87 (death of Glanville).
2 *Hull Examiner*, 1, No. 1, 14 December 1889, p. 9, No.3, 28 December 1889, p. 9. The number for a child was (illogically) *three* in that source, but *one* in Francis, *A Guinea A Box*, p. 124 and in Cardus's version (see note 6 below).
3 *New York Evening News*, c. March 1893.
4 *Hansard*, House of Commons, 5th series, 52, Col. 275, 11 June 1952.
5 I. and P. Opie, *The Language and Lore of Schoolchildren* (Oxford: Clarendon Press, 1959), p. 89.
6 Cardus, *Sir Thomas Beecham*, p. 23.
7 T. Augarde (ed.), *Oxford Dictionary of Modern Quotations* (Oxford: Oxford University Press, 1991), p. 22; J. Wintle and R. Kevin, *Dictionary of Biographical Quotation of British and American Subjects* (London: Routledge, 1978), p. 60; N. Sherrin, *Oxford Dictionary of Humorous Quotations* (Oxford: Oxford University Press, 3rd edn, 2008), p. 204.

Bibliography

Books and articles

Ackrill, M., 'Sir Ronald Stanley Edwards, 1910–1976', *DBB* 2, pp. 237–44 and *ODNB* 17, pp. 962–3.

Ackrill, M., *Enterprise in Theory and Practice: A Biography of Sir Ronald Edwards*, unpublished: London School of Economics Archives, Coll Misc 1189.

Aldcroft, D. H., 'The Entrepreneur and the British economy, 1875–1914', in D. H. Aldcroft and H. W. Richardson (eds), *The British Economy, 1870–1939* (London: Macmillan, 1969), pp. 141–67.

Allen, W. E. D., *David Allens: The History of A Family Firm, 1857–1957* (London: John Murray, 1957).

Anderson, S., '"Best for me, best for you" – a history of Beecham's Pills, 1842–1998', *PJ* 269, 21/28 December 2002, pp. 921–4.

Arber, A., 'Herbal', *Chambers's Encyclopaedia* 7 (London: Newnes, 1959), p. 52.

Augarde, T. (ed.), *Oxford Dictionary of Modern Quotations* (Oxford: Oxford University Press, 1991).

Barker, T. C. and J. R. Harris, *A Merseyside Town in the Industrial Revolution: St Helens, 1750–1900* (Liverpool: Liverpool University Press, 1954).

Bátiz-Lazo, B., 'GSK – a merger too far?', *ICFAI Journal of Mergers and Acquisitions* 1, No. 4 (2004), pp. 75–89.

Bauman, R. P., P. Jackson and J. T. Lawrence, *From Promise to Performance: A Journey of Transformation at SmithKline Beecham* (Boston, MA: Harvard Business School Press, 1997).

Beecham, T., *A Mingled Chime* ([1944] London: Hutchinson, 1979).

Beecham [firm], 'A Familiar Name' (St Helens: [the] Thomas Beecham [firm], 1891).

Beecham Estates and Pills Ltd, *Annual Reports* 1924/5–1927/8.

Beecham Group Ltd, *Annual Reports* 1945/6–1987/8.

Beecham Group, 'Thanks to Beecham's pills', *Beecham Group Journal* 1, No. 3, 1961.

Beecham Pharmaceuticals Ltd, 'The growth of a famous pharmaceutical organisation' (*c.* 1960), pp. 1–9.

Beechams Pills Ltd, *Annual Reports* 1928/9–1944/5.

Belloc, H., *The Bad Child's Book of Beasts and Cautionary Tales* (London: Duckworth, 1923).

Bienefeld, M. A., *Working Hours in British Industry: An Economic History* (London: Weidenfeld & Nicolson, 1972).

Bingham, C., *The History of Royal Holloway College, 1886–1986* (London: Constable, 1987).

Blackwood, A., *Sir Thomas Beecham: The Man and the Music* (London: Ebury Press, 1994).

Boase, G. C., 'Thomas Holloway: Pill Maker and Philanthropist', *Western Antiquary* 4, 1884–85, pp. 183–7.

Boyson, R., *The Ashworth Cotton Enterprise* (Oxford: Oxford University Press, 1970).

Briggs, A., *Friends of the People: The Centenary History of Lewis's* (London: Batsford, 1956).

Briggs, P. S., *The SmithKline-Beecham Merger* (Richmond, Surrey: PJB Publications, July 1990).

British Medical Association, *Secret Remedies: What they Cost and What they Contain* (London: British Medical Association, 1909).

British Medical Association, *More Secret Remedies* (London: British Medical Association, 1912).

Brockbank, J., *History of St Helens, with Local Landmarks* (St Helens, 1896).

Brockman, H. A. N., *The British Architect in Industry, 1841–1940* (London: Allen & Unwin, 1974).

Brymer, J., 'Sir Thomas Beecham, 1879–1961', *DNB 1961–70* (1981), pp. 87–90.

Buckle, G. E. (ed.), *Letters of Queen Victoria, 3rd Series, 1886–1901* (London: John Murray, 1931).

Bud, R., *Penicillin: Triumph and Tragedy* (Oxford: Oxford University Press, 2007).

Burke's Peerage, Baronetage and Knightage, 107th edn, vol. 1 (Wilmington, DE: Burke's Peerage and Gentry UK Ltd, 2003).

Burnby, J., 'Pharmaceutical advertisement in the 17th and 18th centuries', *European Journal of Marketing* 22, No. 4, 1988, pp. 24–40.

Bynum, W. F. and R. Porter (eds), *Medical Fringe and Medical Orthodoxy, 1750–1850* (London: Croom Helm, 1977).

Cardus, N., *Sir Thomas Beecham: A Memoir* (London: Collins, 1961).

Carley L. (ed.), *Delius: A Life in Letters* 2, 1909–1934 (London: Scolar Press, 1988).

Carter, A. C. R., *Let Me Tell You* (London: Hutchinson, 1940).

Cassis, Y., 'The emergence of a new financial institution: investment banks in Britain, 1870–1939' in J. J. Van Helten and Y. Cassis (eds), *Capitalism in a Mature Economy: Financial Institutions, Capital Exports and British Industry, 1870–1939* (Aldershot: Edward Elgar, 1990), pp. 139–58.

Cassis, Y., *Big Business: The European Experience in the Twentieth Century* (Oxford: Oxford University Press, 1997).

Catholic Who's Who (London: Burns Oates, 1952).

Centre for the Study of Industrial Innovation, *Reaching World Markets: A Report on International Marketing in the Pharmaceutical Industry* (London: National Economic Development Council, 1971).

Chain, E., 'Thirty years of penicillin therapy', *Proceedings of Royal Society of London*, Series B 179, 1971, pp. 293–319.

Chandler, A. D., *Scale and Scope: The Dynamics of Industrial Capitalism* (Cambridge MA: Harvard University Press, 1990).

Chandler, A. D., *Shaping the Industrial Century: The Remarkable Story of the Evolution of the Modern Chemical and Pharmaceutical Industries* (Cambridge MA: Harvard University Press, 2005).

Channon, D. F., *The Strategy and Structure of British Enterprise* (London: Macmillan, 1973).

Chapman, S., *Jesse Boot of Boots the Chemists* (London: Hodder & Stoughton, 1974).

Chapman, S. D., 'Sir Arthur Wheeler, 1860–1943', *ODNB* 58, pp. 427–8.

Church, R., and E. M. Tansey, *Burroughs Wellcome & Co.: Knowledge, Trust, Profit and the Transformation of the British Pharmaceutical Industry, 1880–1940* (Lancaster: Crucible Books, 2007).

Churchill, W. S., *Lord Randolph Churchill* (London: Macmillan, 1906).

Clark, K., *The Other Half* (London; John Murray, 1977).

Clark, R. W., *The Life of Ernst Chain: Penicillin and Beyond* (London: Weidenfeld & Nicolson, 1985).

Corley, T. A. B., 'Sir Joseph Beecham, 1848–1916', *DBB* 1, pp. 243–6 and *ODNB* 4, pp. 797–8.

Corley, T. A. B., 'Thomas Beecham, 1820–1907', *DBB* 1, pp. 246–8 and *ODNB* 4, pp. 798–9.

Corley, T. A. B., 'James Cockle, 1782–1854', *ODNB* 12, pp. 370–2.

Corley, T. A. B., 'James Crossley Eno, 1827–1915', *ODNB* 18, pp. 462–3.

Corley, T. A. B., 'Philip Ernest Hill, 1873–1944', *DBB* 3, pp. 235–9 and *ODNB* 27, pp. 169–71.

Corley, T. A. B., 'Thomas Holloway, 1800–1883', *ODNB* 27, pp. 763–5.

Corley, T. A. B., 'Sir Joseph Horlick, 1846–1921', *ODNB* 28, pp. 112–13.

Corley, T. A. B., 'Henry George Leslie Lazell, 1903–1982', *DBB* 3, pp. 690–4 and *ODNB* 32, pp. 940–1.

Corley, T. A. B., 'James Morison, 1770–1840', *ODNB* 39, pp. 183–4.

Corley, T. A. B., 'Sir William Veno, 1866–1933', *ODNB* online edition http://www.oxforddnb.com/view/article/93363, May 2005.

Corley, T. A. B., 'James White, 1877–1927', *DBB* 5, pp. 784–90 and *ODNB* 58, pp. 588–9.

Corley, T. A. B., 'Sir Graham John [Bob] Wilkins, 1924–2003', *ODNB, 2000–2004*, pp. 1187–8.

Corley, T. A. B., 'Beecham and the development of semi-synthetic penicillins, 1951–1970', Centre for Institutional Performance, University of Reading, Discussion Paper 2003–1 (2003), pp. 1–26.

Corley, T. A. B., 'Best-practice marketing of food and health drinks in Britain, 1930–70', in G. Jones and N. J. Morgan (eds), *Adding Value: Brands and Marketing in Food and Drink* (London: Routledge, 1994), pp. 215–36.

Corley, T. A. B., 'Consumer Marketing in Britain, 1914–60', *Business History* 29, No. 4, October 1987, pp. 65–83.

Corley, T. A. B., 'Interactions between the British and American Patent Medicine Industries, 1708–1914', *Business and Economic History*, 2nd series, 16, 1987, pp. 111–29.

Corley, T. A. B., 'Nostrums and nostrum-mongers: the growth of the UK patent medicine industry, 1635–1914', unpublished paper, 2002.

Corley, T. A. B., *Quaker Enterprise in Biscuits: Huntley & Palmers of Reading, 1822–1972* (London: Hutchinson, 1972).

Corley, T. A. B., 'The Beecham Group in the world's pharmaceutical industry, 1914–1970' *Zeitschrift für Unternehmensgeschichte* 39 Heft 1, 1994, pp. 18–30.

Corley, T. A. B., 'The British Pharmaceutical industry since 1851', in L. Richmond, J. Stevenson and A. Turton (eds), *The Pharmaceutical Industry. A Guide to Historical Records* (Aldershot: Ashgate, 2003).

Corley, T. A. B., 'The use of pharmaceutical products in UK veterinary medicine', conference paper, British Society for the History of Medicine, September 2003.

Corley, T. A. B., 'Twentieth-century American Contributions to the Growth of the Beecham Enterprise', in J. Slinn and V. Quirke (eds), *Perspectives on Twentieth-Century Pharmaceuticals* (Witney, Oxfordshire: Peter Lang, 2010), pp. 217–40.

Corley, T. A. B., 'UK government regulation of medicinal drugs, 1890–2000', *Business History* 47, No. 3, July 2005, pp. 337–51.

Corley, T. A. B. and Godley, A., 'The veterinary medicine industry in Britain during the twentieth century', *Economic History Review* (forthcoming, 2011).

Cox, H., 'Antagonising the Treasury: TST and the repatriation of Boots the Chemists', in 'Business on trial: the Tobacco Securities Trust and the 1935 Pepper Debacle', *Business History* 49, No. 6, November 2007, pp. 771–3.

Crichton, R. (ed.), *The Memoirs of Ethel Smyth* (London: Viking, 1987).

Crichton, R. and J. Lucas, 'Sir Thomas Beecham, 1879–1961', in S. Sadie (ed.), *The New Grove Dictionary of Music and Musicians*, 2nd edn (London: Macmillan, 2001), pp. 66–7.

Crook, J. Mordaunt, *The Dilemma of Style: Architectural Ideas from the Picturesque to the Post Modern* (London: John Murray, 1987).

Crouzet, F., *The First Industrialists* (Cambridge: Cambridge University Press, 1985).

Davenport-Hines, R. P. T., 'Glaxo as a multinational before 1963', in G. Jones (ed.), *British Multinationals: Origins, Management and Performance* (Aldershot: Gower, 1986), pp. 137–63.

Davenport-Hines, R. P. T., 'Sir Harry C. Mallaby-Deeley, 1863–1937', *DBB* 4, pp. 84–7.

Davenport-Hines, R. P. T., and J. Slinn, *Glaxo: A History to 1962* (Cambridge: Cambridge University Press, 1992).

Davidoff, L. and C. Hall, *Family Fortunes: Men and Women of the English Middle Class, 1780–1850* (London: Hutchinson, 1987).

Davidson, A., 'J. P. Garnier', *Management Today*, March 2004, p. 38.

Decle, L., *Three Years in Savage Africa* (London: Methuen, 1898).

Deeson, T. *Parke Davis in Britain: The First Hundred Years* (Eastleigh: Parke Davis & Co. Ltd, 1995).

Dell, E., *Political Responsibility and Industry* (London: Allen & Unwin, 1973).

Dennett, L., *The Charterhouse Group, 1925–1979: A History* (London: Gentry Books, 1979).

Dickens, F., 'Edward Charles Dodds, 1899–1973', *Biographical Memoirs of Fellows of the Royal Society* 21, 1975, pp. 227–67.

Dowell, S., *A History of Taxation and Taxes in England to 1885*, 2nd edn, 4 (London: Longmans Green, 1888).

Dunning, J. H., 'Revisiting UK FDI in US manufacturing and extractive industries in 1960', in G. Jones and L. Gálvez-Muñoz (eds), *Foreign Multinationals in the United States: Management and Performance* (London: Routledge, 2002), pp. 50–69.

Edwards, R., *The Multinational Pharmaceutical Industry: A Commentary*, The 1974 Mercantile Credit Lecture, given at Reading University, 19 November 1974.

Edwards, R. S., 'The case for competition', *Journal of the Royal Society of Arts*, March 1971, pp. 209–21.

Edwards, R. S. and H. Townsend, *Business Enterprise: Its Growth and Organisation* (London: Macmillan, 1958).

Edwards, R. S. and H. Townsend, *Studies in Business Organisation* (London: Macmillan, 1961).

Edwards R. S. and H. Townsend, *Business Growth* (London: Macmillan, 1966).

Ensor, R. C. K., *England, 1870–1914* (Oxford: Oxford University Press, 1936).

Evans, R., *An Account of the Scapa Society* (London: Constable, 1926).

Evans, R., *The Age of Disfigurement* (London: Remington, 1893).

Fairburn, J. and J. Kay (eds), *Mergers and Merger Policy* (Oxford: Oxford University Press, 1989)

Farr, W., *Vital Statistics: A Memorial Volume of Selections from [his] Reports and Writings* (London, Edward Stanford, 1885).

Fears, R. and G. Poste, 'SmithKline Beecham and the future direction of medical research', *Science in Parliament* 36, No. 3, Summer 1999, pp. 10–11.

Foster, G., 'Beecham takes its medicine', *Management Today*, October 1985, pp. 51–9.

Francis, A., *A Guinea A Box* (London: Hale, 1968).

Francis, A., *Letter to the Past* (London: Dukeswood, 1994).

Froud, J., S. Johal, A. Leaver and K. Williams, *Financialization and Strategy: Narrative and Numbers* (Abingdon: Routledge, 2006).

Gambardella, A., *Science and Innovation: the US Pharmaceutical Industry during the 1980s* (Cambridge: Cambridge University Press, 1995).

Garafola, L., *Diaghilev's Ballet Russes* (New York: Oxford University Press, 1989).

Gilbert, B. B., *David Lloyd George: The Architect of Change, 1863–1912* (London: Batsford, 1987).

Gilley, S., *Newman and his Age* (London: Darton Longman & Todd, 1990).

Gilmour, J. D., *Sir Thomas Beecham: Fifty Years in the 'New York Times'* (London: Thames Publishing, 1988).

Girolami, P., 'The Development of Glaxo', unpublished paper, 1985 (revised, 1989).

GlaxoSmithKline plc, *Annual Report* 2000.

Godley, A. C., 'Pioneering Foreign Direct Investment in British Manufacturing', *Business History Review* 73, No. 3, Autumn 1999, pp. 394–429.

Gold, A., and R. Fizdale, *Misia: The Life of Misia Sert* (London: Macmillan, 1980).

Goldman, L. (ed.), *Oxford Dictionary of National Biography, 2000–2004* (Oxford: Oxford University Press, 2009).

Graham, K., 'Thomas James Barratt, 1841–1914', *ODNB* 4, pp. 32–3.

Greenwood, J. E., *A Cap for Boots: An Autobiography* (London: Hutchinson Benham, 1977).

Grierson, H. J. C. (ed.), *Letters of Sir Walter Scott* 11, 1828–31 (London: Constable, 1936).

Griffenhagen, G. B. and J. H. Young, 'Old English Patent Medicines in America', *Pharmacy in History* 34, No. 4, 1992, pp. 200–28.

Grigoriev, S. L., *The Diaghilev Ballet, 1909–1929* (Harmondsworth: Penguin Books, 1960).

Grundy, C. R., 'Sir Joseph Beecham's collection at Hampstead', *The Connoisseur* 35, February 1913, pp. 69–78, 101–8; 38, April 1914, pp. 223–34; 39, June 1914, pp. 75–84.

Habakkuk, H. J. and M. Postan (eds), *Cambridge Economic History of Europe*, Part 1, 6 (Cambridge: Cambridge University Press, 1966).

Habgood, W. (ed.), *Chartered Accountants in England and Wales: A Guide to Historical Records* (Manchester: Manchester University Press, 1994).

Haining, P. (ed.), *The Final Adventures of Sherlock Holmes* (Secaucus, NJ: Castle Books, 1981).

Hannah, L. (ed.), *Management Strategy and Business Development* (London: Macmillan, 1976).

Hargreaves, E. L., and M. M. Gowing, *Civil Industry and Trade (Civil History of Second World War)* (London: HM Stationery Office, 1952).

Harrison-Barbet, A., *Thomas Holloway: Victorian Philanthropist* (London: Royal Holloway, 1994).

Haxey, S., *Tory M.P.* (London: Gollancz, 1939).

Heindel, R. H., *The American Impact on Great Britain, 1898–1914: A Study of the United States in World History* (Philadelphia, PA: University of Pennsylvania Press, 1940).

Helfand, W., 'James Morison and his Pills', *Transactions of the British Society for the History of Pharmacy* 1, 1974, pp. 101–35.

Heller, R., *The Naked Manager* (London: Barrie & Jenkins, 1972).

Hindley, D. and G., *Advertising in Victorian England, 1837–1901* (London: Wayland Publishing Ltd, 1972).

Holcombe, H. W., *Patent Medicine Tax Stamps* (Lawrence, MA: Quartermain Publications Inc., 1979).

Holland, K., 'Beecham Group plc', *Pharmaceutical Journal* 30 May 1987, pp. 675–8.

Holloway, T., 'A Sketch of the Commencement and Progress of Holloway's Pills and Ointment', January 1863, Surrey Record Office, THPP.

Houchen, A. E. V., 'The marketing of branded consumer goods', in R. S. Edwards and H. Townsend (eds), *Business Growth* (London: Macmillan, 1966), pp. 55–76.

Housman, A. E., *Collected Poems and Selected Prose*, ed. C. Ricks (London: Allen Lane, The Penguin Press, 1988).

Howes, F., 'Music', in S. Nowell-Smith (ed.), *Edwardian England, 1901–1914* (Oxford: Oxford University Press, 1964).

Hunt, E. H., *Regional Wage Variations in Britain, 1850–1914* (Oxford: Clarendon Press, 1973).

Hyde, D. G., and P. Haspeslagh, 'The making of the *Simply Better* healthcare company: SmithKline Beecham' (A) and (B) (Fontainebleau: INSEAD, 1994).

Jackson, C. H. W., 'The great persuader', *Blackwoods Magazine*, 1975, pp. 204–19.

James, B. G., *The Future of the Multinational Pharmaceutical Industry to 1990* (London: Associated Business Programmes, 1977).

Jefferson, A., *Sir Thomas Beecham: A Centenary Tribute* (London: Macdonald & Jane's Publishers, 1979).

Jefferson, A., 'Sir Thomas Beecham, 1879–1961' *ODNB* 4, pp. 799–802.

Jeremy, D. J. (ed.), *Dictionary of Business Biography* [*DBB*] 1–5 (London: Butterworths, 1984–86).

Jerome, J. K., *Three Men in a Boat* ([1889] Harmondsworth: Penguin Books, 1994).

Johnstone, H., *The Royal Holloway College, 1887–1937* (Egham: Royal Holloway, 1937).

Jones, E., *The Business of Medicine: The Extraordinary History of Glaxo* (London: Profile Books,

2001).

Jones, G. and N. J. Morgan (eds), *Adding Value: Brands and Marketing in Food and Drink* (London: Routledge, 1994).

Jones, G., 'The multinational expansion of Dunlop, 1890–1939', in G. Jones (ed.), *British Multinationals: Origins, Management and Performance* (Aldershot: Gower, 1986), pp. 24–42.

Jubb, M., *Cocoa and Corsets* (London: HM Stationery Office, 1984).

Kennedy, W. P. and P. L. Payne, 'Directions for future research', in L. Hannah (ed.), *Management Strategy and Business Development* (London: Macmillan, 1976), pp. 237–58.

Keyworth, J. M., *Cabbages and Things* (privately published, 1990).

Kobrak, C., *National Cultures and International Competition: The Experience of Schering AG, 1851–1950* (Cambridge: Cambridge University Press, 2002).

Kynaston, D., *The City of London: Illusions of Gold, 1914–1945* 3 (London: Chatto and Windus, 1999).

The Labour Party: Report of a Commission of Enquiry into Advertising (London: Labour Party, 1966).

Landes, D. S., 'Technological change and development in Western Europe, 1750–1914', in H. J. Habakkuk and M. Postan (eds), *Cambridge Economic History of Europe*, Part 1, 6 (Cambridge: Cambridge University Press, 1966), pp. 563–4.

Law, J., *Big Pharma* (London: Constable, 2006).

Lazell, H. G., 'Development and organisation of Beecham Group Ltd', London School of Economics: Seminar on Problems in Industrial Administration 1959/60 252, 23 February 1960.

Lazell, H. G., *From Pills to Penicillin: The Beecham Story* (London: Heinemann, 1975).

Lazell, H. G., 'Marketing in a competitive economy', London School of Economics: Seminar on Problems in Industrial Administration 1968/9 394, 3 December 1968.

Lazell, H. G., 'The Years with Beechams', *Management Today*, November 1968, p. 69.

Lees-Milne, J., *The Enigmatic Edwardian: The Life of Reginald, 2nd Viscount Esher* (London: Sidgwick & Jackson, 1986).

Liebenau, J., *Medical Science and the Medical Industry: The Formation of the American Pharmaceutical Industry* (Basingstoke: Macmillan, 1987).

Liebenau, J., 'The rise of the British pharmaceutical industry', *British Medical Journal* 3, October 1990, pp. 724–33.

Longford, E., *Victoria R.I.* (London: Weidenfeld & Nicolson, 1964).

Lucas, J., *Thomas Beecham: An Obsession with Music* (Woodbridge, Boydell Press, 2008).

Lutyens, M., *Effie in Venice* (London: John Murray, 1965).

M-n [*sic*], C., 'Thomas Beecham, 1820–1907', *DNB* Supplement, 1901–11 (London: Smith Elder & Co., 1912), 1, pp. 125–6.

McCulloch, J. R., *A Descriptive and Statistical Account of the British Empire: Vital Statistics* 2, 3rd edn (London: Longmans, 1846).

McKenzie, F. A., *The American Invaders* (London: H. W. Bell, 1902).

McMullan, J., *The Way we Were, 1900–1914* (London: William Kimber, 1978).

Mann, T., *Buddenbrooks* ([1901], Harmondsworth: Penguin Books, 1971).

Marion, J. F., *The Fine Old House* (Philadelphia PA: SmithKline Corporation, 1980).

Marriner, S., 'History of Liverpool, 1700–1900', in W. Smith (ed.), *A Scientific Survey of Merseyside* (Liverpool: Liverpool University Press, 1953), pp. 107–19.

Marshall, A., *Industry and Trade* (London: Macmillan, 1921).

Marshall, A., *Principles of Economics* 8th edn (London: Macmillan, 1920).

Mathew(s), R., *The Unlearned Alchymist* (London: J. Leigh, 1662).

Matthew, H. C. G. (ed.), *The Gladstone Diaries* (Oxford: Clarendon Press, 1982).

Matthew, H. C. G., and B. Harrison (eds), *Oxford Dictionary of National Biography* [*ODNB*] 1–60 (Oxford: Oxford University Press, 2004).

Maugham, W. S., *Cakes and Ale* (London: Heinemann, 1930).

Miller, G., 'Hu[l]bert Harrington Warner, the patent medicine "king"', *Pharmacy History Australia* 4, January 1998, pp. 3–6.

Miller, G., 'Pills for pale people: the George Fulford story', *Pharmacy History Australia* 13, March 2001, pp. 3–5.

Mitchell, B. R., *British Historical Statistics* (Cambridge: Cambridge University Press, 1988).

'Modern methods in pharmaceutical manufacture', *Industrial Chemist: Pharmaceutical and Cosmetic Supplement*, October 1935, pp. 118–23; November 1935, pp. 133–9.

Mohr, F. and T. Redwood, *Practical Pharmacy: The Arrangements, Apparatus, and Manipulations of the Pharmaceutical Shop and Laboratory* (London: Taylor, Walton and Maberly, 1849).

Morgan, E. J., 'Innovation and merger decisions in the pharmaceutical industry', *Review of Industrial Organization* 19, 2001, pp. 184–6.

Morisoniana: The Abridged Family Adviser of the British College of Health, 110th thousand [sic] (London: College of Health, 1868).

Morris, E., 'Advertising and the acquisition of contemporary art', *Journal of the History of Collections* 4, No. 2, 1992, p. 195.

Mullen, R., *Anthony Trollope: A Victorian in his World* (London: Duckworth, 1990).

Murray, J., *Covent Garden: An Historical Survey from 1670 to 1914* (London, privately published, 1914).

Nevett, T., 'Thomas James Barratt, 1841–1914', *DBB* 1, pp. 189–91.

Nevett, T., 'Advertising and editorial integrity in the nineteenth century', in M. Harris and A. Lee, *The Press in English Society from the Seventeenth to Nineteenth Centuries* (London: Associated University Presses, 1986), pp. 149–67.

Nichols, R. H. and F. A. Wray, *The History of the Foundling Hospital* (London: Oxford University Press, 1935).

Norris, S., *Two Men of Manxland: Hall Caine, Novelist, T. E. Brown, Poet* (Douglas, Isle of Man: Norris Modern Press, 1947).

Nowell-Smith, S., *Edwardian England, 1901–1914* (Oxford: Oxford University Press, 1964).

Opie, I. and P., *The Language and Lore of Schoolchildren* (Oxford: Clarendon Press, 1959).

Opie, R. (compiler), *Colgate Palmolive in the UK: 75 Years of Care* (Guildford: Colgate Palmolive UK Ltd, 1997).

Porteous, C., *Pill Boxes and Bandages: Robinsons of Chesterfield, 1839–1916* (Chesterfield: Robinson & Sons Ltd, 1960).

Porter, R., *Health for Sale: Quackery in England, 1660–1850* (Manchester: Manchester University Press, 1989).

Porter, R., *Quacks: Fakers and Charlatans in Medicine* (Stroud: Tempus Publishing, 2003).

Prest, A. and A. Adams, *Consumers' Expenditure in the United Kingdom, 1900–1919* (Cambridge: Cambridge University Press, 1954).

Procter-Gregg, H., *Beecham Remembered* (London: Duckworth, 1976).

Quirke, V., 'Anglo-American relations and the co-production of American "hegemony" in pharmaceuticals', in H. Bonin and P. de Goey (eds), *American Firms in Europe, 1880–1980: Strategy, Identity, Perception and Performance* (Geneva: Droz, 2008).

Randles, S., 'Complex systems applied? The merger that made Glaxo SmithKline [sic]', *Technology Analysis and Strategic Management* 14, No. 3, 2002, pp. 331–54.

Rastrick, A. (intro.), *The Century's Progress: Yorkshire Industry and Commerce, 1893* (Settle: Brenton Publishing, 1971).

Reid, C., *Thomas Beecham, An Independent Biography* (London: Gollancz, 1962).

Reid, C., *Malcolm Sargent* (London: Hamish Hamilton, 1968).

Reid, M., *Ask Sir James* (London: Hodder & Stoughton, 1987).

Richards, J. M., *With John Bull and Jonathan* (London: T. Werner Laurie, 1905).

Richards, T., *The Commodity Culture of Victorian England* (London: Verso, 1991).

Richmond, L., J. Stevenson and A. Turton, *The Pharmaceutical Industry: A Guide to Historical Records* (Aldershot: Ashgate, 2003).

Rickards, G. K. (ed.), *Statutes of the United Kingdom* (London: Eyre & Spottiswood, 1858).

Roberts, R. 'Kenneth Alexander Keith, Baron Keith of Castleacre (1916–2004), in L. Goldman (ed.), *Oxford Dictionary of National Biography, 2000–2004* (Oxford: Oxford University Press, 2009), pp. 599–602.

Rose, M. B., 'The family firm and the management of succession', in J. Brown and M. B. Rose (eds), *Entrepreneurship, Networks and Modern Business* (Manchester: Manchester University Press, 1993), pp. 127–33.

Rowed, C., *Collecting as a Pastime* (London: Cassell, 1920).

Rowed, C., *The Rowed Name* (Lancashire, privately published, 1921). BL Catalogue 1860 d.1(58).

Sampson, A., *The Changing Anatomy of Britain* (London: Hodder & Stoughton, 1982).

Sampson, A., 'Musical chairs for Beecham brigade', *Observer*, 18 November 1979.

Saunders, J., *Nightmare: Ernest Saunders and the Guinness Affair* (London: Arrow Books, 1990).

Schupbach, W., 'Sequah: An English "American Medicine"-Man in 1890', *Medical History* 29, 1985, pp. 272–317.

Scott, C. M., *My Years of Indiscretion* (London: Mills & Boon, 1924).

Selwyn, S., *The Beta-Lactam Antibiotics: Penicillins and Cephalosporins in Perspective* (London: Hodder & Stoughton, 1980).

Sharpe, P. and T. Keelin, 'How SmithKline Beecham makes better resource allocation decisions', *Harvard Business Review* March-April 1998, pp. 45–57.

Sheehan, J. C., *The Enchanted Ring: The Untold Story of Penicillin* (Cambridge, MA: The MIT Press, 1982).

Sheppard, F. H. W. (ed.), *Survey of London* 36 (London: Athlone Press for GLC, 1970).

Sherrin, N., *Oxford Dictionary of Humorous Quotations* 3rd edn (Oxford: Oxford University Press, 2008).

Simmons, D. A., *Schweppes: The First 200 Years* (London: Springwood Books, 1983).

Slinn, J., *A History of May & Baker, 1834–1984* (Cambridge: Hobsons, 1984).

Slinn, J., 'Price Controls or Control through Prices? Regulating the Cost and Consumption of Prescription Pharmaceuticals in the UK, 1948–67', *Business History* 47, No. 3, July 2005, pp. 352–66.

Smeeton, A. E., *The Story of Evans Medical, 1809–1959* (Liverpool: Evans Medical Supplies Ltd, 1959).

Smiles, S., *Self-Help* (London: John Murray, 1859).

Smith, F. B., *The People's Health, 1830–1910* (London: Croom Helm, 1979).

Smith, M., *A Physician at the Court of Siam* (London: Country Life, 1946).

SmithKline Beecham plc, *Annual Reports*, 1989–1999.

Smyth, E., *Beecham and Pharaoh* (London: Chapman & Hall, 1975).

Smyth, E., *Memoirs* (London: Viking, 1987).

Stephenson, W. H., *Albert Frederick Stephenson* (Manchester: Sharratt & Hughes, 1937).

Stewart, G. T., *The Penicillin Group of Drugs* (Amsterdam: Elsevier, 1965).

Stopford, J. M. and L. Turner, *Britain and the Multinationals* (Chichester: John Wiley, 1985).

Storey, G., K. Tillotson and A. Easson (eds), *The Letters of Charles Dickens* 7, 1853–1855 (Oxford: Clarendon Press, 1993).

Storey, G. and K. Tillotson (eds), *The Letters of Charles Dickens* 8, 1856–1858 (Oxford: Oxford University Press, 1995).

Strachey, L., *Eminent Victorians* ([1918] London: Chatto & Windus, 1928).

Streatfield, P. J., *The Paradox of Control in Organizations* (London: Routledge, 2001).

Syedain, H., 'SmithKline Beecham's early trials', *Management Today* November 1989, pp. 99–104.

Taggart, J., *The World Pharmaceutical Industry* (London: Routledge, 1993).

Tansey, E. M. and L. A. Reynolds (eds), 'Post Penicillin Antibiotics', *Wellcome Witness to Twentieth Century Medicine* 6 (London: Wellcome Trust, 2000), pp. 25–39.

Titmuss, R. M., *Problems of Social Policy (Civil History of Second World War)* (London: HM Stationery Office, 1950).

Tomalin, C., *The Invisible Woman: The Story of Nelly Ternan and Charles Dickens* (London: Penguin Books, 1991).

Turner, E. S., *The Shocking History of Advertising!* (London: Michael Joseph, 1952).

Tweedale, G., *At the Sign of the Plough: 275 years of Allen & Hanburys and the British Pharmaceutical Industry, 1715–1990* (London: John Murray, 1990).

'Twice upon a time: the story of A. J. White Ltd and Menley & James Ltd' (Welwyn Garden City: Smith-Kline & French Laboratories, undated).

Ullyot, G. E., B. H. Ullyot, and L. B. Slater, 'The Metamorphosis of Smith-Kline & French Laboratories to Smith Kline Beecham: 1925–1998', *Bulletin of the History of Chemistry* 25, No. 1, 2000, pp. 16–20.

Van Helten, J. J., and Y. Cassis (eds), *Capitalism in a Mature Economy: Financial Institutions, Capital Exports and British Industry, 1870–1939* (Aldershot: Edward Elgar, 1990).

Victoria History of the Counties of England (VCH): Lancashire 3 (London: Constable, 1907).

Victoria History of the Counties of England (VCH): Staffordshire 8 (Oxford: Oxford University Press, 1963).

Vincent, D., *Literacy and Popular Culture in England, 1750–1914* (Cambridge: Cambridge University Press, 1989).

Waller, P., *Writers, Readers and Reputations: Literary Life in Britain, 1870–1918* (Oxford: Oxford University Press, 2006).

Waugh, A., *The Fatal Gift* (London: W. H. Allen, 1973).

Waugh, E., *Brideshead Revisited* (London: Chapman & Hall, 1945).

Waugh, E., *A Handful of Dust* ([1934] Harmondsworth: Penguin Books, 1951).

Webster, C., *The Health Service since the War 2* (London: HM Stationery Office, 1996).

Wendt, H., *Global Embrace* (New York: Harper Collins, 1993).

Wilkins, G. J., 'A Record of Innovation and Exports', in G. Teeling-Smith, *Innovation and the Balance of Payments: The Experience of the Pharmaceutical Industry* (London: Office of Health Economics, 1967), pp. 14–21.

Wilkins, M., *The History of Foreign Investment in the United States to 1914* (Cambridge MA: Harvard University Press, 1989).

Wilkins, M., *The History of Foreign Investment in the United States, 1914–1945* (Cambridge MA: Harvard University Press, 2004).

Wilson, C., *The History of Unilever* (London: Cassell, 1954).

Wilson, C., 'Economy and Society in Late Victorian Britain', *Economic History Review*, 2nd series 18, 1965, pp. 183–98.

Wilson, D., *Penicillin in Perspective* (London: Faber & Faber, 1976).

Wintle, J., and R. Kevin, *Dictionary of Biographical Quotation of British and American Subjects* (London: Routledge, 1978).

Worling, P. M., 'Proprietary Articles Trade Association', *Pharmaceutical Historian* 26, No. 4, December 1996, pp. 37–8.

Yamey, B. S., 'The origins of resale price maintenance: a study of three branches of retail trade', *Economic Journal* 62, 1952, pp. 522–45.

Young, E., *Night Thoughts on Life, Death and Immortality* (Halifax: William Milner, 1841).

Young, J. H., *The Toadstool Millionaires* (Princeton NJ: Princeton University Press, 1972).

Ziegler, P., *Diana Cooper* (London: Hamish Hamilton, 1981).

Newspapers and trade journals

Advertisers Weekly; *Advertising*; *Advertising World*; *Answers*; *Bolton Evening News*; *British Medical Journal [BMJ]*; *Business Week*; *Chemist and Druggist [CD]*; *City Press*; *Daily Telegraph*; *Director*; *Economist*; *Edinburgh Review*; *The Engineer*; *Euromonitor*; *Evening Standard*; *Fashions for*

Children; *Federal Reporter*; *Financial Times*; *Fortune*; *Gazette of Health*; *Gentlewoman*; *The Graphic*; *Health*; *Hull Examiner*; *Illustrated London News[ILN]*; *Industrial Chemist*; *Investors Chronicle*; *Lady's Companion*; *Lancet*; *Liverpool Courier*; *Liverpool Echo*; *Liverpool Post*; *Liverpool Weekly Post*; *London Miscellany*; *Management Today*; *Manchester Guardian*; *Marketing*; *Medical Circular*; *Medical Times*; *Medical Times and Gazette*; *Musical Times*; *Napier Daily Telegraph [New Zealand]*; *New York Evening News*; *Observer*; *Ohio Journal of Dental Science*; *Pall Mall Gazette*; *Pharmaceutical Journal [PJ]*; *Prescot Reporter*; *Progressive Advertising*; *Public Opinion*; *Punch*; *Quarterly Review*; *Queen*; *St Helens Intelligencer*; *St Helens Lantern*; *St Helens News*; *St Helens Newsletter*; *St Helens Newspaper and Advertiser*; *St Helens Reporter*; *St Helens Weekly Press*; *The Satirist*; *Society*; *The Star*; *Statist*; *Sunday Times*; *The Tablet*; *The Times*; *Tit-Bits*; *The Town*; *World's Press News*.

Archives

Beecham Archive (BA), St Helens Local History and Archives Library, St Helens, Lancashire.
Beecham Group corporate archives, formerly at Brentford, Hounslow, London.
Companies House, formerly London EC2 [now in Cardiff, Wales].
Corporation of London Joint Archive Service [London Metropolitan Archives], London EC1.
Family Records Centre, formerly London EC1 [now incorporated into The National Archives at Kew, Richmond, Surrey].
Guildhall Library, London EC2.
History of Advertising Trust, Raveningham, Norfolk.
Lloyds Register Information Services Library, London EC3.
London School of Economics, London WC2.
National Museum of American History, Washington, DC, USA.
Public Record Office, formerly London WC2 [now The National Archives at Kew, Richmond, Surrey].
Public Record Office Victoria (PROV), Melbourne, Australia.
Royal Holloway College, Egham, Surrey.
Surrey History Centre, Woking, Surrey.
The National Archives (TNA), Kew, Richmond, Surrey.
Wellcome Library for the History and Understanding of Medicine, Archives and Manuscripts, London NW1.

Official publications

Cases Decided in the Court of Session (Scotland) 1905–6, 5th series 8 (Edinburgh: T. & T. Clark, 1906)
English [Law]Reports (London: Stevens, 1914).
First Report of Commissioners of Inland Revenue (London: HM Stationery Office, 1857).
Law Journal Reports 1851 n.s. 20, Part 1, Chancery and Bankruptcy (London: Ince, 1851).
Law Reports: King's Bench Division, 1921.
Lloyds List [of Shipping Movements], 1879 [microfilm, Guildhall Library, London].
Lloyds Register of British and Foreign Shipping, 1879–80 [Lloyds Register Information Services Library, London].
Monopolies Commission, *Beecham Group Ltd and Glaxo Group Ltd: Report on Proposed Mergers* (London: HM Stationery Office, 1972).
Parliamentary Debates [Hansard], House of Commons, London.
Parliamentary Debates [Hansard], House of Lords, London.
Poll Books, Wigan, Lancashire, 1857 and 1859.
Post Office Directory of Lancashire (1858).
Registrar General's 35th Annual Report (London: HM Stationery Office, 1875).

Report of an Enquiry by the Board of Trade into the Cost of Living of the Working Classes, Cd. 3864 (London: HM Stationery Office, 1908); Cd. 6955 (London: HM Stationery Office, 1913).

Report of the Select Committee on Patent Medicines (London: HM Stationery Office, 1914).

Report of a Trial in the Supreme Court of the State of New York: Morison & Moat v. Moses Jacques & J. B. Marsh (New York: W. Mitchell, 1834).

Science and Technology Committee, House of Commons, Second Report, Session 1994–95, *The Glaxo Bid for Wellcome plc* (London: HM Stationery Office, 1995).

Science and Technology Committee, House of Commons, Third Report, Session 1997–98, *Glaxo Wellcome and SmithKline Beecham: The merger proposals* (London: HM Stationery Office, 1998).

Science and Technology Committee, House of Commons, Fourth Report, Session 1999–2000, *Glaxo Wellcome and SmithKline Beecham* (London: HM Stationery Office, 2000).

Trial of Joseph Webb for Manslaughter at York, Summer Assizes, 1834 (London: G. Taylor, 1834).

United States Bureau of the Census, *Fifteenth Census of the United States, 1919* (Washington DC: Government Printing Office, 1921).

United States Reports, 221: Supreme Court Cases, October Term 1910 (New York: Banks Law Publishing Co., 1911).

Index